# Samuel Hopkins Adams

## AND THE BUSINESS OF WRITING

# *Samuel Hopkins Adams*

## AND THE BUSINESS OF WRITING

*Samuel V. Kennedy III*

Syracuse University Press

*Frontispiece:* Samuel Hopkins Adams, 1936. Courtesy of Hamilton College.

This book is published with the assistance
of a grant from the John Ben Snow Foundation.

Library of Congress Cataloging-in-Publication Data

Kennedy, Samuel V.

Samuel Hopkins Adams and the business of writing /
Samuel V. Kennedy, III. — 1st ed.

p.    cm.

Includes bibliographical references and index.

ISBN 0-8156-2799-8 (cloth: alk. paper)

1. Adams, Samuel Hopkins, 1871–1958.   2. Authors, American—20th century
—Biography.   3. Journalists—United States—Biography.

I. Title

PS3501.D317Z73 1999

813'.52—dc21

[B]

98-32137

Samuel V. Kennedy III is associate professor of journalism
at the S. I. Newhouse School of Public Communications,
Syracuse University, and was editor–managing editor
of the *Citizen-Advertiser*, Auburn, New York.

# CONTENTS

# CONTENTS

# CONTENTS

# ILLUSTRATIONS

# PREFACE

O
N A SUNNY Saturday, June 20, 1959, one hundred invited guests assembled at the Wide Waters home of Samuel Hopkins Adams in central
New York. The group gathered in the garden behind the main house for a
memorial service honoring the author who had died the previous November
at his winter home in Beaufort, South Carolina, where a funeral service had
packed St. Helena's Episcopal Church.

Now it was Cayuga County's turn to remember Mr. Adams. I was invited as
a tag-along to my parents, Sam and Marion Kennedy, who had been long-time
friends from Ensenore, across Owasco Lake from Wide Waters. Although I
could remember meeting Mr. Adams only a handful of times, he was much
within my thoughts.

His beloved Hamilton College was well represented by officials such as his
old friends, secretary Wallace Johnson, librarian Walter Pilkington, and president Robert McEwen, who led the service. Mr. Adams had lobbied for me go
to the nearby Clinton campus, but my choice had been the larger Cornell
University. My new alma mater was represented at the memorial service by the
*New Yorker* poet Morris Bishop, whose booming voice had participated in my
graduation a few days before in Ithaca.

At noon McEwen began the memorial service with "It is not easy to plan
these few minutes. Ritual from the prayer book is hardly appropriate for a man
who habitually cut through form and ceremony, with their common accom-
paniment of platitude, to the heart of the matter. A few minutes of silence is
hardly appropriate in this house, which for many years was rocked with laugh-
ter and sparkled with real conversation. Eulogy would bore Sam, and we are
here in his memory."

I looked toward his home, recalling Mr. Adams's warm and bountiful hos-
pitality in a house that had a large living room packed with antiques. I remembered my one dinner party had been a treat because he always had time

for the young, probably because of his definition of old age: "Someone who is twenty years older."

As McEwen, quoting actress Peggy Wood's assessment of Mr. Adams as one who saw things plain, elaborated "that seeing things plain meant seeing them straight, for Sam, that he detested sham and hypocrisy and hedging, that he had an unswerving integrity in his writing and his life," I smiled. My last meeting with Mr. Adams had been prompted when somehow he learned of my interest in writing and had asked to read something. After sending him a manuscript of a short story, I rowed across Owasco Lake several days later to get his reaction. He minced no words in saying the short story was lousy because it failed to tell its story in narrative form. I tried to explain about my use of psychological development to the frail, hunched man, but there was nothing frail about his mind or his words as he carefully explained that a writer's first duty was to be a storyteller. I thanked him and rowed back across the lake while muttering curses.

The earlier meeting had softened by that Saturday, however, and I was impressed with McEwen's call, noting Jane Addams's words about "The Excellent Becomes Permanent," for us "to remember with gratitude an excellent man, to affirm and admit to each other that our devotion to excellence is greater because we knew him." I scanned the crowd to see those who had received the call.

Many were neighbors: the Charles, Lithgow, and Frederik R-L. Osbornes, the Legare and Robert Holes, and the George Metcalfs. Others were strangers to me: author Carl and Betty Carmer, Rochester columnist Henry Clune, Irita Van Doren and Lewis Gannett of the New York *Herald Tribune*, the Frank Taylors, and William Walling, the husband of Peggy Wood, who herself had been so exhausted by a theater tour that she could not come. Special were the Adams relatives: his daughters, Katherine Adams Adell and Hester Adams, his late wife's daughter, Mildred Harlan, and his granddaughter, Elizabeth Buckley. Standing on the second-floor balcony outside his study were his loyal handyman, Preston Huff, and his wife, Mae, set apart by their choice but as much a part of Mr. Adams's life as any of us. We all heard McEwen thank God "for the memory of our friend. For his love of his homeland, for his impatience with cant and hypocrisy, for his concern for justice, for the warmth of his friendship and tolerance."

The short service concluded with the singing by some Hamiltonians of "Carissma," and then the group adjourned to the porch of the old house where martinis were served from Mr. Adams's special mixer with its plunger. I re-marked about the absence of Admiral Cecil C. Adell and his next-door neigh-bor Jeff Kilborne, who had moved from Ensenore to Wrongside, adjacent to Wide Waters. They were on a special mission that I learned later was to spread Mr. Adams's ashes in the lake. Still later I learned that Frank Taylor, who had named his son, Adams Taylor, for the author, had spirited himself away to visit the author's study to get something to remember him by, an old newspaper spike from his desk.

I had much to remember that day, including McEwen's comment, again quoted from Peggy Wood: "We turn to him as a link with our American heritage to tell us in this darkening world what we should remember, how to be diligent, how to value the fellowship of mankind." It would be many years before those words had the meaning that I hope this biography shows.

Samuel V. Kennedy III
Ensenore, New York
March 1999

# ACKNOWLEDGMENTS

SAMUEL HOPKINS ADAMS remained resolute throughout his life that the one story he did not wish to tell was his own. He told the many who urged him to write his autobiography that he had other topics he felt were more important. From time to time other writers and a few scholars contemplated a chronicle of Adams's life, but none came to fruition.

The genesis of this work came in 1985 when I wrote an essay on Adams's muckraking of patent medicines. In early research his daughter Hester Adams offered encouragement. The essay was presented as a paper at the annual convention of the American Journalism Historians Association in Las Vegas, Nevada, and received favorable comment. The research had revealed that although Adams's patent medicine work had received the most public attention, other aspects of his life were also intriguing.

In 1989 I began a more comprehensive study of Adams as the subject of a dissertation. The reconstruction of the author's life presented challenges. Although he was a historian, Adams left few personal records. With rare exceptions he put letters he received into the wastebasket after answering them. At one point he chided himself to Marion Kennedy for throwing away his minister father's sermons. In a like manner he dismissed his own past. He kept little of his published work. Most of his drafts were discarded. His carefully maintained account books and ledgers of novel characters were not saved.

Although he was gregarious, Adams usually turned the conversation from himself to the extent that historian Louis Jones said he believed no one knew him. Even his relatives commented on the awe he engendered through his desire for personal privacy. He shunned interviews except when they would further the sales of his work. But as Adams marched through the late nineteenth century and the early twentieth, his path was commented on by contemporary writers and historians.

Moreover, Adams did leave more than ten million published words in his books, magazine pieces, and newspaper writing. Although he did not keep copies of his articles, short stories, and serials, most could be tracked down. An initial bibliography, compiled by Harold Thompson to accompany a 1937 sketch of Adams for the *Hamilton Alumni Review*, offered a starting point. Other documents in a principal Adams collection at Syracuse University added to the original list, as did records from magazines and references in his letters. His published, and sometimes unpublished, work offered a framework for a mosaic.

Because he wrote from experiences he had had, people he had known, and locales he had visited, Adams provided a rich paper trail to follow. Being both parsimonious and prolific, he left a bountiful correspondence. His friends said he disliked paying for long-distance telephone calls, so he communicated by letter to business associates and to relatives and friends. Many were willing to share the letters they had saved, along with clippings, memorabilia, and, most importantly, their memories.

Providing countless pieces of the mosaic was Adams's immediate family. The remembrances of his daughter Hester Adams were augmented by the detailed accounts of his other daughter Katherine Adams Adell. They provided many hours of conversation concerning the author during a series of interviews. It can only be regretted that neither Hester Adams, who died in 1991, nor Katherine Adams Adell, who died in 1992, lived to see the final work. George Harlan, the son of Mildred Harlan, who died in 1966, was located in Toronto through a *New York Times* "Author's Query" and shared his memories of his grandfather. A cousin, Alice Eyerman, added her memories during an interview in Wilkes Barre, Pennsylvania.

Nonfamily friends also provided assistance. Rochester columnist Henry Clune was near his hundredth birthday when he discussed his friendship with Adams. Others providing material were William Scherman, who shared his remembrances and Adams's letters; Lang Hatcher, who furnished copies of Adams's letters to his aunt, author Constance Noyes Robertson; Beatrice Champany, who shared her girlhood memories of the Adamses; and Elizabeth Richardson Steele, who provided letters, clippings, and recollections. Other persons contacted were equally willing to share memories.

These insights into Adams, the man, were augmented by the collections of Adams's letters contained in libraries. Of special significance is the rare look at the author-agent-publisher relationship that the various collections offer. Beginning with the Bobbs-Merrill collection at Lilly Library at the University of Indiana in Bloomington, his business correspondence was covered in the

Houghton Mifflin collection at Houghton Library at Harvard University, the Liveright collection at the University of Pennsylvania, and the Random House collection in the Adams papers at the Arents Research Library at Syracuse University, which also contains thousands of letters between Adams and his agents, Brandt & Brandt of New York.

Carl Brandt was helpful at the offices of Brandt & Brandt in New York City by providing Adams's financial records and insights into the author. Martha Kaplan at the *New Yorker* also provided assistance with the magazine's records. Barbara Sherlock at the *Chicago Tribune*, A. James Memmott at the Rochester newspapers, and Laura L. Sabo at the *Ford Times* spent hours finding Adams's materials.

The Brandt & Brandt business correspondence continued past Adams's death and is housed at Burke Library at his alma mater Hamilton College. Even more importantly, Burke Library, which has records on the Adams undergraduate years, acted as a repository for material he felt worth saving, including one of the most complete collections of his books. The assistance of Frank Lorenz, curator of special collections, in providing background and perspective was supplemented by the help of Waltraut Wuensch in locating materials.

Background information came also from historical societies. Peter Osborne of the Minisink Valley Historical Society furnished details on the lynching in Port Jervis, New York, that Adams covered for the *Sun*. Michelle Henry of the Chatauqua County Historical Society and John W. Nowak of the Historical Society of Dunkirk, New York, offered assistance in Adams's early days in Dunkirk. Mabel Crosby of the Cayuga-Owasco Lakes Historical Society, former Niles historian, offered her insights. Eileen O'Brien at the New York State Historical Association in Cooperstown opened its Carl Carmer collection that included letters from Adams's close friend, Charles Kilborne. The Ohio State Historical Association also assisted, as did the West Virginia and Wisconsin historical societies.

The two libraries in Auburn offered invaluable help. Bound copies of Auburn newspapers from 1900 through 1959 were read at Seymour Library. Librarian Stephen Erskine and Mary Gilmore offered help and assistance. At Cayuga Community College library director Douglas Michael provided additional aid with microfilm of early Auburn newspapers and the Earl Conrad collection. A file on Adams was made available by Pamela Scheffel of Rochester Public Library.

Of special help was Patricia Willis of Beinecke Library at Yale University whose suggestions on the Will and Inez Irwin collections provided a rich resource. At Harvard University librarians at the Houghton Library offered their time and patience.

Many colleagues at Syracuse University's S. I. Newhouse School of Public Communications were most supportive as were Bird Library and its George Arents Research Library for Special Collections of which Carolyn Davis and Mark Weimer gave expert counsel. Nearly every Bird Library department, ranging from fine arts to interlibrary loan, offered expertise and encouragement to the project.

At Syracuse University historian David H. Bennett of the Maxwell School was adviser for the dissertation, and his help and support from the beginning were invaluable. His comments and those of historian William Stinchcombe shaped the dissertation, which was ably critiqued by the dissertation committee headed by Syracuse University librarian David H. Stam. Offering helpful comments were James Roger Sharp, John Scott Stickland, and Robert Thompson.

Assistance also came from other colleagues. James Stanford Bradshaw gave early encouragement. James Boylan sent clippings of Adams columns that appeared in the New York *Tribune*. Ron Marmarelli provided information on *Ridgway's* magazine. Cecelia Friend and Frank Bergmann, both at Utica College, assisted with research.

Finally, this project is indebted to Marion Blanchard Kennedy, whose love of history and faith never wavered.

# Samuel Hopkins Adams

## AND THE BUSINESS OF WRITING

# 1

# BOYHOOD
## 1871–1887

SAMUEL HOPKINS ADAMS spent more than six decades in America's cultural life as a journalist, muckraker, novelist, biographer, and historian. Between his start as a newspaperman in 1891 and his last novel published posthumously in 1959 he averaged almost one book a year, and during many of those years his byline appeared monthly on some 450 articles and short stories in the nation's leading magazines.

Yet despite his publishing success to passing generations he became as unknown as Rex Beach, Richard Harding Davis, Rupert Hughes, Will Irwin, Anne Parrish, Alfred Payson Terhune, Stewart Edward White, and other popular authors of the early twentieth century. Why, then, is Adams important to bring out of the shroud of obscurity?

Ultimately who he was may not be as important as what he was. Becoming a free-lance writer in 1904, he spent the next half-century seeking good stories to sell and ignoring the large visionary view and rarefied style of the "serious" authors. His commitment as a yeoman wordsmith rejected the mystic nature of writing to produce a secularized, liberating, and salable product.

Adams was able through his hard work to support himself with his pen. He achieved this goal of many writers but accomplished by only a few through an appreciation for news value, detail, and facts. He used his sense of news to find topics and themes that made him a prolific magazine writer. His novels featured his attention to details that made his characterizations and dialogue popular. His meticulous adherence to, and passion for, the facts marked his nonfiction work. But the same things that earned him a living also limited his success. Quick to use contemporary themes, he was occasionally attacked for writing too close to events. His copious detail made some of his novels long and laborious. His use of facts enhanced his nonfiction but inhibited the literary quality of his fiction.

Nonetheless, success for Adams was survival. The price of survival did not mean avoiding risks. Because he had to generate income anew each year, he sought many venues for his work and used many devices. Adams was able, like Proteus, to change as the situation demanded. He wrote short stories, serials, editorials, articles, adaptations, columns, advertising copy, detective stories, novels, a game book, biographies, a western, historical biography, regional history, juveniles, science fiction, essays, movie scripts, collaborative works, ghost-written novels, and a little poetry. His work ranged from breezy romances to serious nonfiction, from sensational exposé to sensitive explanation, and from naughty novels to charming reminiscence.

His accomplishments during his life were manifold—often pioneering, seldom flashy, and never abasing. Whether battling his physical infirmities or dealing with the daunting work of writing, he asked no quarter and gave none. Ever willing to help his colleagues, he maintained his integrity based on his beliefs. He toiled at his craft as a man of his times and showed that writing was a mental and physical effort, not a spiritual activity produced with the help of a muse.

A member of the post–Civil War generation, he received a classical education at Hamilton College from which he drew not only on Latin and Greek but also on science and its Social Darwinism. After college, he went to New York and reported as a journalist on the emerging challenges of immigration, industrialization, and urbanization during the Gilded Age.

When populism led to progressivism, some gentle prodding pushed him into muckraking. A pioneer medical writer, he employed his health knowledge to attack the quacks and the patent medicines they peddled. His personal efforts helped gain passage of the Pure Food and Drug Law, one of the few concrete measures produced by muckraking. His writing on public health, cancer treatment, and drug addiction was personal and sociological. In all, he displayed an idealism that Americans would right the wrongs if they knew the truth.

Even as muckraking and progressivism dissolved into World War I, he continued to urge responsibility in medicine, business, and government. When the United States entered the Great War, he became a dollar-a-year volunteer, writing propaganda, using his fiction to support the home-front effort and joining the executive committee of the Four Minute Men speakers' bureau.

As the twenties unfolded, Adams, like many of his fellow citizens, sought new definitions in the age of jazz and the flapper. He chronicled the changing mores in a series of lurid novels under the pseudonym of Warner Fabian, beginning with *Flaming Youth*, a title that became synonymous with the decade. He used the novel *Revelry* to expose the scandals of the Warren G. Harding administration. As the motion picture became popular, he flirted with the new medium. If he could not write good scenarios or tolerate Hollywood, he could write good stories that others could adapt into some twenty films, including the classic *It Happened One Night*.

When the Great Depression changed the mood of America, he turned to more serious topics by writing history, but with a popular touch—not especially good history, but good reading. His earlier novel of the Teapot Dome scandals led to books on Daniel Webster and Peggy Eaton and a more scholarly look at Harding.

As the early events of World War II occurred, his concern over war commitments took him to the national board of America First and led him to question the motives of Democrat Franklin Delano Roosevelt, whose New Deal he had supported. Once America was in the war, however, the seventy-year-old volunteered for rationing boards. And his pen recounted traditional values as he told the story of early America in regional histories.

The fifties brought new affluence with the consumer culture as Americans sought their piece of the American dream. Adams joined the search for values with juvenile histories and reminiscing about his youth in *Grandfather Stories* and his newspaper days in *Tenderloin*.

Throughout, his lifestyle belied his demanding work or mandated it. Rising before dawn, he worked until noon. Then he played physically and socially. An athlete in college, he was a tennis addict until a bad hip forced him to concentrate on golf. He had constant summer houseguests at Wide Waters on Owasco Lake near Auburn, New York. During the winter he lived in rented quarters at Beaufort, South Carolina, where he joined the plantation society. He was at home in New York City, Santa Barbara, or the many communities he visited.

Whether at home or away, Adams attracted beautiful women as a flower draws butterflies. Women adored his courtly manners and his treatment of them as equals. His marriage to his first wife, a flighty Southern belle from West Virginia, did not last, but he and his second wife, actress Jane Peyton Adams, were devoted to each other. The women, including his domineering mother and his forceful second wife led to strong characterizations of women

1. Samuel Hopkins Adams as a young man. Courtesy of Hamilton College.

in his work. However, Adams's fascination for his women was not shared by literary critics, who often targeted them, failing to see the changing woman as dominant, erotic, and independent.

He had a special concern for privacy. He relied on it for creative isolation at the remote Wide Waters and the small town of Beaufort. His need for privacy did not disturb his friends, who enjoyed his companionship, especially the boyish enthusiasm that he refreshed with new generations of friends. Some were fellow authors, his publishers, and literary agents, but others were in business, politics, and entertainment. His attraction to the power of success offset an insecurity that caused him to adopt a defensive gruffness not unlike the irascibility of a spoiled child. Used to having his own way, he became involved in every aspect of the publishing of his work.

One constant in much of his work was a spirit of muckraking. For a relatively short period, from 1904 to 1907, he had fit the classic definition of the exposure journalist as he tackled the patent medicine industry and trusts. Afterward, he used muckraking in novels to expose the dangers of business interests corrupting newspapers. Muckraking techniques were used by Adams during World War I to expose what he believed to be the anti-Americanism of pro-German sympathy. The muckraking spirit underlay the social commentaries of the Fabian novels and Adams's initial look at the corruption of the Harding presidency. Time after time the spirit resurfaced in attempts to warn the public of the dangers of organized crime before World War II and of government by contract afterward. Even in his last novel he could not resist exposing the police practices and political corruption of the 1890s as subthemes.

Despite his idealism the landscape of Adams's life was littered with lost causes. His exposés of patent medicines did not stop their makers. His attacks on trusts were futile because simple exposure was not enough. His Washington novels did not clean up government. Lost causes did not deter Adams, however, nor dampen his optimism.

One area that showed the Adams brand of optimism was politics. Although he was a lifelong Democrat, he was not wedded to the party or to its leaders. To Adams the administration of government was more important than individuals, and he was constantly enmeshed in political issues ranging from Prohibition to world affairs, from censorship to women's rights, and from government intervention to freedom for the oppressed.

The literary critics saw Adams for what he was, a journeyman writer, who spent his working life as a reporter, creating his stories for money. He never attained the best-selling status of Harold Bell Wright nor the literary accomplishment of William Faulkner. He was a populist writer, producing readable prose. Much of it was light fiction upon which critics, using their traditional criterion of moral seriousness, were quick to pounce. Adams offered no excuses for his romances and whimsy, despite the negativism of the critics and his friends, who found them delightful but unworthy.

For most of his writing life he was an opportunist who was willing to make the most of what he had and to ignore what he did not. Although he sought an elusive "big" book, he had few pretensions about being a great writer producing great works. From the beginning he saw as the essence of his writing the telling of the story. Plot and characterization concerned him more than literary devices as he concentrated on the tale. His constant reading helped his critical acumen but did not influence his style of writing, which did not change appreciably from "Blinky" in 1897 to *Tenderloin* in 1959. He was slavish to dialogue, to description, and, of course, to telling the story.

After his death in 1958, Adams was soon forgotten, except in the memories of his friends and relatives. They recalled how he had spent his life fighting against the sham and hypocrisy that his strong sense of morality told him were wrong. His father's and grandfathers' strong feelings about the worth of the individual drove him to show how persons could triumph by determining their own destinies.

His life began during a harsh winter in Dunkirk where lake-effect snow coming across Lake Erie was measured in feet, not inches. On 26 January 1871 he became the only child of the Reverend Myron Adams, Jr., and Hester Rose Hopkins Adams. Life was relatively stable in Dunkirk where his father had come in 1869—as stable, that is, as life could be with the First Presbyterian Church minister, an independent thinker with a dislike for ecclesiasticism and rigid orthodoxy.

The independence and liberalism would have a profound influence on the boy who bore the name of two of the oldest families in America, Adams and Hopkins. Concerning his Adams ancestry, which his family has traced back to Henry Adams of Braintree, Massachusetts, Adams said in *Grandfather Stories* of his grandfather Myron Adams: "Privately, he considered the Boston Adamses rather an effete and unenterprising lot. They clung to an easeful existence in Massachusetts while the hardier pioneers of the breed were risking the perils and hardships of the wilderness that made up Western New York in 1791."[1]

One pioneer was his great-great grandfather, Captain John Adams of the Continental army, who after the Revolution settled in East Bloomfield near

Rochester in 1785. A son, Abner Adams, became a contractor on the Erie Canal. His work on the waterway connecting Albany and Buffalo resulted in the naming of a canal port near Rochester, Adams Basin. In 1799 the Abner Adamses had their first son, Myron Adams, who later became a farmer after attending Hamilton College.

Myron and Sarah Taylor Adams had five sons, the last of whom was Myron Adams, Jr. The younger Myron went to Hamilton, fought in the Civil War, and then went to Auburn Theological Seminary. There he met Hester Rose Hopkins, daughter of Professor Samuel Miles Hopkins, who was a descendant of Stephen Hopkins, a Declaration of Independence signer. His marriage not only linked two old American families but also brought together two young (he was twenty-seven and she twenty-two when they went to Dunkirk), intelligent, and vigorous individuals.

His Civil War experiences at Harper's Ferry and the Battle of Mobile Bay left the young minister emotionally scarred. Upset by the carnage, he rejected a brevet promotion to major and even refused a pension. What was more important, he renounced the Presbyterian tenet of eternal damnation for his comrades who had died in the war. His theological views attracted attention and some alarm. His position, however, was accepted by his Dunkirk congregation that, when a larger church in Jamestown made the minister an offer, raised his salary. "But he felt more and more hampered as a Presbyterian; and it was with a feeling of relief that he received and accepted a call from the Plymouth Congregational Church of Rochester," his father-in-law wrote.[2]

Western New York had been the focus of an evangelical tug of war between the Congregationalists and the Presbyterians. The Presbyterians with the Old Light traditions had dominated the New Theology of the Congregationalists, who after the Civil War tried to reassert themselves. Plymouth Church became a target. Built by Presbyterians with antislavery sentiments in 1855, the church was coveted by Congregationalists because of its location in Rochester's third ward with its well-to-do gentry, the business, professional, and political leaders of the "ruffled shirt" district.[3]

Myron Adams had been called to the church in 1876. Leaving the village of 6,917 inhabitants where Samuel Hopkins Adams would remember cheering as "the fast train went through Dunkirk," the boy welcomed the move to Rochester with a population of 62,386. "Rochester to me has always been something more than a mecca — it's been a sort of heavenly mirage in the sky," he extolled later. "The one regret of my life was that I was not born here." The move also brought him into closer contact with his grandfather Adams.[4]

The senior Myron Adams had sold his farm and moved to a cottage across the Genesee River from Plymouth Church. Living in an unfashionable section of town on insufficient income, the seventy-seven-year-old man remained active and had remarried. The boy, joined by four cousins, Jenny, Sireno, John, and Charlie Adams, had weekly visits with his grandfather Adams. They listened as the tall, bewhiskered man spun his tales of early Rochester and the Erie Canal. The canal itself, a few blocks from the parsonage, provided the boy with a place to swim, fish, and skate, especially at Wide Waters, a spot where the canal widened. He felt a special affinity with the canal, which his grandfather's tales as a builder and road trader made come alive.

During the summers Adams went east to Auburn, an industrial city of about thirty thousand. Textiles, shoes, and farm implements were manufactured in mills governed by owner families who oversaw the plants and the immigrants in them. The families formed a "South Street aristocracy" so inbred that a journalist said, "Prick South Street at one end, and it bleeds at the other."[5]

In the city also was his grandfather Hopkins. "The Hopkins house, of mid–Currier and Ives architecture, stood at the top of the Grant Avenue rise overlooking the city. Twenty or more members of the family might be guests there at one time," Adams recalled. Whereas grandfather Adams was homespun, grandfather Hopkins was erudite. Coming to the Auburn Theological Seminary in 1847, he taught church history and ecclesiastical polity. He advocated Christian liberty as opposed to religious absolutism, which must have pleased the younger Myron Adams. Known for lectures of "charming rhetoric and diction," grandfather Hopkins often read to the young "to our delight."[6]

To Auburnians, Hopkins was considered democratic in his friendships, one of which was with Harriet Tubman. She told her tales as the "Moses of her People" on her visits to the Hopkins home. "Harriet's historical importance did not impress our youthful minds. To us, she was merely a tribal teller of tales, a never failing source of adventure and romance," Adams recalled, noting, "While other youngsters of the late 1870's played Scouts and Indians, our standard make-believe was Slaves and Overseers, with Harriet as heroine."[7]

His uncle, Woolsey Rogers Hopkins, a graduate of Hamilton College and Albany Law School, also was in Auburn. His sense of humor, stories of two years abroad, and strong opinions based on wide reading made him popular. He wrote in magazines and newspapers, and these endeavors coupled with the articles by both Myron Adamses and grandfather Hopkins, who published epigrams, poems, and essays, created a writing tradition. Adding to that tradition was his great-aunt Sarah Hopkins Bradford, an accomplished writer, who regaled the young with her stories of early New York State with its circuses, canal towns, and residents. She also wrote a biography of Tubman, *Harriet, The Moses of her People,* that Adams said popularized the appellation and contained information he would draw on later.

One year before the death of his wife, Mary Jane Heacock Hopkins, in 1885, Hopkins sold the Grant Avenue house and moved to Seminary Street near where he taught. City life, however, was not enough for the man who enjoyed nature. Like many Auburnians, the educator escaped to the Finger Lakes during the summers, choosing Owasco Lake. Ten miles long and about one mile wide, the lake south of Auburn was framed by hills to the east and west. Above its treed shoreline, farmers blocked out their fields to form a patchwork quilt of different crops at various seasons of the year. Development along the lake had been faster on the west shore, spurred by access by the railroad, but Hopkins liked the east side.

The family took the South Central Railroad down the west side to the fashionable Ensenore Glen House and a boat across to the east shore for "a month of wild life." Adams's first memories of the lake were that "living standards were simplified to the verge of hardship." He explained: "No servants were taken along. All the work of a decidedly primitive camp devolved upon the family, with us children, as it seemed to me, bearing the brunt of the most distasteful chores. Grandfather said that it built character."[8]

Life at the lake was made more tolerable by the building of a cottage. In 1886 Hopkins paid $250 for an acre at Second Peacock's Point on Owasco's east side.[9] Fortunately, Myron Adams, Jr., was handy with tools and design, having planned the church in Dunkirk. He helped erect a cottage that he christened Quisisana after a hotel between Capri and Anacapri he and Hester had visited in Italy. On the lake the boy fished and sailed. On the hillside he collected puffballs and joined his Uncle Woolsey in archery and riding. The sandy-haired boy acquired the nickname of "Huck," presumably based on Huckleberry Finn. The summer location had a special meaning for the rest of his life.

In his *Grandfather Stories* Adams would call his grandfather Hopkins "more companionable," but the advantage grandfather Adams held "in appeal to youthful imagination needs no emphasizing."[10] Whether it was the story of George Eastman or of supernatural creatures or of local folklore, the youngsters were enthralled by grandfather Adams's tales. The elderly man's feelings about the evils of drinking despite his patent medicine Hop Bitters with its 40 percent alcoholic content, about the laxity of public morals, and about the causes of cancer would be themes for his grandson decades later.

Reality presented another dimension during these young years. His father's liberalism pushed the pastor of Plymouth Church to urge the adoption of a new text for the confession of faith that stressed the love of God rather than "endless punishment." Fearing for the fate of its largest church, the conservative Ontario Association of Congregational Ministers on December 27, 1880, charged him with heresy. Adams had noted in a journal written before 1873: "Speaking of political heresy, it is only another term for political independence. It is the recognition of no party obligations. The political heretic, like the heretic in religion, assumes to take what is good in all shades of political opinion and practice and eschew the rest."[11] Thus, the charges of religious heresy that might have cowed a lesser man offered the minister liberation and independence. Standing confessed, Adams did not waver, and the ministers "disfellowshipped" him, in effect ostracizing him. For him, the action simply meant he was free to develop his theological ideas.

The Rochester congregation continued to support the minister, and the effect that this public condemnation had on the young Adams, who was nearing his tenth birthday at Rochester Grammar School No. 3, appeared more attitudinal than anything else. Later he said in a biographical sketch, "Presbyterianism of a liberal, even heretical, brand enveloped my childhood." The immediate impact probably was mirrored in what he would tell a newspaper: "I guess I sort of inherited a disposition to take the unpopular attitude."[12]

Acknowledging in a 1955 interview that he looked back on boyhood with a "fine glow," he said: "I had an awfully good time when I was a boy. We got a lot out of life: simple things." Saying his pastimes "were not designed to encourage the devil," he earlier said: "We played croquet, shot at birds that we never hit, collected butterflies, indulged in whist or cribbage, sang the newest college songs, read aloud or went in a group to the church entertainment. In those days most of our entertainments were in the home."[13]

Not all the activities were in the home. Near the end of his life he recalled one of his earliest memories some eighty years earlier of being dressed in a starchy white gown with a broad scarlet sash tied in a bow and his hair curled. On a platform he recited a favorite of the day: "You scarcely expect one of my age to speak in public on the stage." In his eighties Adams noted, "That noble sentiment I still cherish."[14]

Rochester also provided Adams with contacts other than his relatives. Like many boys, he staged bullfights and buffalo hunts and disliked being told what to do and having to learn multiplication tables. His displeasure with mathematics did not stop his advancement to the Free Academy in Rochester where he developed socially, attending Miss Quinby's Dancing Class and joining Pi Phi (Perfect Friendship) fraternity. Asked about his favorite sport as a boy, Adams said: "Anything that came along." One he pursued. When he was fifteen he worked in a tree nursery in Rochester to earn money to buy a tennis racket.[15]

At home he developed an appreciation for music from his mother, whose alto voice was so beautiful that he called her "Bird," and for entomology from his father who was a naturalist, collecting butterflies and beetles. The hobby was passed on to the son. When later Adams was visiting his first wife's home in Charleston, West Virginia, he took his net out after a noon dinner. "The neighbors thought he was nuts," his daughter reminisced. Nevertheless, his interest would surface repeatedly in his writing, and in 1901 he would give the Smithsonian Institution a collection of butterflies from the Philippines.[16]

His father also was president of the Rochester Academy of Science for several years and was a member of the Spencer Club, which espoused the evolutionary theories of Herbert Spencer. The minister's support of Spencer's belief in the survival of the fittest must have pleased the Rochester businessmen of the Third Ward. And the evolutionary theories of Charles Darwin and his books *Origin of the Species* and *The Descent of Man* fueled the minister's challenge to "Old Time Religion." The intellectual ferment extended beyond religion. His inquiring mind showed in the subjects on which he spoke to the Fortnightly Club: Henry Grady, Samuel Coleridge, Quakers, Socrates, and insects. One topic not in the minister's thoughts much was politics.

Myron Adams, Jr., was not political, unlike his father, who made public speeches denouncing the Democrats, and his father-in-law, who had been involved in the early Republican party before becoming an independent. By contrast, Woolsey Hopkins, actively involved in Democratic politics, seemed to have the most influence on young Adams, who became a lifelong Democrat.

The independence of his father, the humanness of his grandfather Hopkins who scorned pretension, the love of life of his grandfather Adams, the forcefulness of his mother, and the appreciation for a good story, well told, all left their marks. In 1887 he completed his senior year at the Free Academy and headed east for Clinton, New York, and Hamilton College.

# 2

# COLLEGIAN
## 1887–1891

ADAMS ENTERED Hamilton College in September 1887, eight months after his sixteenth birthday. He followed his grandfather Adams, his father, five uncles, including Hamilton College professor Abel Grosvenor Hopkins, and Adams, Hopkins, Grosvenor, and Heacock cousins. As early as the boy's pre-teens, his grandfather Adams had assumed he would go to Hamilton from which the older man had not graduated because of "some breach in the then rigid tenets of academic discipline."[1]

Adams's father had also left before commencement. Departing after his junior year for the Civil War, he received his degree ex gratia by the board of trustees in July 1863. Although his grandfather and father had shortened tenure at Hamilton, they felt tied to the small liberal arts college ten miles west of Utica. His grandfather groused about fund-raising efforts but sent two sons to Hamilton, and his father was a resource person for the college. It seemed natural that young Adams would seek the classical education at Hamilton.

What Adams found on College Hill were eight buildings in various stages of disrepair. The college, like the country, was in the doldrums. Hamilton was led by an embattled president, Dr. Henry Darling, who tried to bring the college and the Presbyterian Church closer. Despite initial fund-raising success the president was beset by poor relations with the faculty. The students were unruly, resisting Darling's attempts at stricter discipline.

Nevertheless, Adams was one of the thirty-five freshmen, and he paid seven dollars and signed a note for thirty-one dollars covering his twenty-five-dollar tuition, five-dollar fees, and eight-dollar rent for the term. His actual yearly cost, he revealed later, was between five hundred and six hundred dollars for everything from meals to heating coal. This sum for a minister's son, who said he never had much spending money, made him "pretty hard up." Fortunately, for him, the college was noted for laxity in keeping its accounts and in collecting overdue notes.[2]

He roomed with a junior, Schuyler Brandt. If this placement of a freshman with an upperclassman was meant to provide an inspiring model for good conduct, it failed. About the only inspiration came from Brandt's habitual sleep-walking, a topic that would recur in Adams's later writings. Describing his room, he wrote: "We had no lighting but lamps, no heat but stoves, no water but what we carried, no sanitary convenience whatsoever. Our plumbing was primitive, not to say punitive." The rest was not much better. Noting that chapel was compulsory, he complained it was "very, very chilly several months of the year." Classrooms did not offer refuge: "Recitation rooms depended upon stoves which alternately burned with all the ardors of the Inferno, or subsided to a pale flicker around which, if the Prof. was compassionate, we miserably pressed."[3]

That first year he took three terms of the Gospels, English composition and declamation, an introduction to oratory that Hamilton stressed. Other courses during the first year included geometry, Homer's *Odyssey*, elocution, algebra, and Latin. Academically, Adams and the rest of the Class of 1891 did not take long to undistinguish themselves. "From the first we evinced a certain disinterest in, not to say dissociation from, the consumption of midnight oil," he wrote in a class history. His grades reflected the disinterest. He finished twenty-one of the thirty completing the freshman year.[4]

If Adams lacked academic prowess, however, he had energy. He joined Alpha Delta Phi fraternity, the banjo and guitar club, the freshman baseball nine, the freshman roster of the Foot-Ball Association, the chess club, and the Lawn Tennis Association. The listings were deceptive. He said later, "most of the extracurricular activities existed on paper only, in the pages of college publications." He noted the banjo club never plucked a string, the chess club never played a game, and the class football team never saw a pigskin.[5]

Adopting the old Greek motto, "Be bold, but be not too bold," the class, Adams said, emphasized the first half. It "developed a turbulent and unruly spirit" and "acquired a deserved reputation as a public nuisance, until the renaissance of athletics channeled our excess energies into reputable endeavor."[6] The freshman athletes were the first at Hamilton to win the interclass pennant.

The upstate intercollegiate meet was revived and won by Hamilton three of the next four years. In the spring tennis tourney Adams beat sophomore Walstein Root for the college's singles title.

If his participation in sports was off to an auspicious start, the "unruly spirit" was beginning to endanger his college future. Some of the activities were college pranks, such as raiding a cider mill and the "horning of the sems," a tradition of stripping feminine undergarments from faculty clotheslines and using them as drapes in the chapel. Others were more serious, such as Adams's proclivity for cutting classes.

On 25 April 1888 the faculty was told by his uncle, Professor Hopkins, that Adams had a second warning for too many unexcused absences from his classes. Further trouble developed in May when "the absence of S. H. Adams was referred to the Excuse Committee" and the excuse was refused. On 9 June he also was admonished for taking part in a disturbance at Saturday morning prayers. Nonetheless, he weathered his freshman year.[7]

In his sophomore year, 1888–89, he had major problems. Adams reported that members of the Class of 1891 "began to find ourselves and grow up" when classes resumed. College records indicate the faculty was not as optimistic. At the first faculty meeting President Darling was instructed "to meet the Sophomores and speak to them forbidding disturbances in connection with class exercises and intimidation of Freshmen."[8]

The first term, Adams accepted secretary-treasurer positions in the chess and banjo and guitar clubs, joined the dramatic and operatic clubs, and was listed as shortstop on the sophomore baseball team and rusher in the Foot-Ball Association. He also discovered a downtown Clinton girls' school, Houghton. Later Adams noted: "Three Ladies' Seminaries in town disseminated sweetness if not light. There we were privileged to call, upon stated evenings and within decorous hours." The visits may have prompted the minister's son to spend five dollars for an "elegant" patterned white waistcoat, which he later said had been an ambition of his since boyhood. The money came from an unexpected source.[9]

In his sophomore year Adams found a new outlet for his energy and creativity. It was writing. Although his Hamilton years reportedly included correspondence for the New York *Tribune* and a stint on the Auburn *Bulletin*, no newspaper work has been identifiable. His college poems, essays, and a short story, however, were in campus publications. Later Adams would write that while in college he had visions of himself as a writer. "In that bright dream, I strode up and down a spacious and orderly library, rustling richly in a silken robe, whilst dictating, without pause or check, page upon page of fluent romance to a fair, scholarly, and awed private secretary."[10]

His first identified published work was a poem, "The Wager," signed by S. H. A., in the January 1889 *Hamilton Literary Monthly*. The romantic ditty may have produced his first writing for money. He explained, "As a sophomore at Hamilton College I had contributed various fugitive verse to the *Lit*" and an unnamed colleague offered him three dollars for a "Poem of Passion" to give to a girl in Utica. Composing "a poem to some young siren's dark eyes," Adams gave it to his friend. He also entered another verse in a Prize Poem Contest and won a five dollar award offered by teacher Clinton Scollard for the second-place poem. His friend also entered the poem Adams had written for him and won the first prize of ten dollars, more than Adams's total of eight dollars. Adams noted the two dollar loss later: "Throughout my subsequent literary career I have been striving to catch up with that heart-breaking deficit. I have never quite succeeded."[11]

But Adams had his waistcoat and continued writing. In March 1889 the *Hamilton Literary Monthly* ran a short story by "Barclay," his college pseudonym. "The Pool in the Grounds," a fantasy told in the first person, featured early Adams's use of the supernatural, a curse, and death. Besides writing, he was also beginning to read fiction. Asked in 1955 "What book (or books) was the decisive influence in your life?" Adams said he had found Charles Kingsley the most "influential" when he began reading novels in the late 1880s. He said the "muscular Christian" Kingsley "was a lively springboard for the young mind."[12]

Academically in his sophomore year, his grades again reflected his priorities. He finished eighteen among the twenty-six remaining members of the Class of 1891. Part of the reason for his weak academic performance may have been that his winter term got off to a shaky start with the mumps. Evidently it cost him enough classroom time to warrant the faculty granting him an extra week for examinations, but it did not mitigate a first warning concerning unexcused absences. Adams's academic situation became more serious in the spring when the faculty warned him "of continued irregularity."

Various explanations have been offered of what happened next. His daughter Katherine Adell said: "He had stayed out of classes because he had a cold and then went to a party that night. They found him out and cashiered him." Fellow Hamiltonian John Hutchens, in the New York *Herald Tribune*, noted the class cutting but added that he already was on probation for using a bean shooter in Professor John Edward Hamilton's class, an action unreported in the faculty minutes.[13]

Adams late in his life blamed "a slight difference of opinion with the faculty on a matter of discipline," but earlier he wrote, "My first literary effort was a critique upon the faculty of Hamilton College, so brilliant in manner that it got me fired."[14] Faculty minutes in September 1889 merely stated, "A letter of dismission was granted to S. H. Adams to Union College."

On 17 September 1889 Adams, eighteen, registered at Union College in Schenectady, paid thirty dollars, and took courses in Latin, Greek, chemistry, German, essays, and physics. He also joined the glee club and, more significantly, was a member of the varsity football team. Concerning the latter, he wrote he was a member "of the worst Union eleven—perhaps the all-time, all-American feeblest aggregation of ground-losers—that ever hung around idly watching opponents pile up 100-0 scores against them, a result to which I contributed my due share as right halfback."[15] After one term, he returned to Hamilton.

During the winter term, beginning in January 1890, his attendance at classes improved and his writing continued. The December 1889 *Hamilton Literary Monthly*, while he was still in Schenectady, inadvertently contained Adams's sophomore essay on "Daniel Defoe and Robert Louis Stevenson." This fortunate mistake offered a look at what the young Adams valued in writing. He began by expressing his lifelong Anglophilia in saying that no one had a "keener appreciation of fiction than the English." He criticized Defoe's mechanical writing as "the work of man who has outlived enthusiasm." He praised Stevenson for using "events as expositions of character," adding that he handled humor and pathos well whereas Defoe's writing lacked these elements. He complained of the treatment of women by both writers: ignored by Defoe and subordinated by Stevenson.

The mistake over the essay appeared to be remedied when the February 1890 *Hamilton Literary Monthly* carried the poem "A Legend of the Rhine" with Adams's name and the announcement that it was the successful prize poem established by the magazine and funded by Professor Scollard. Adams said later the poem that won the prize was not his but had been written by Scollard, who had put Adams's name on it and put it in a book, *College Verses*.[16]

Back in Clinton, he rejoined the dramatic club, participated in the chess club, and became leader of the banjo and guitar club, in which he played banjo in a quartet. He survived the two terms with one warning for cutting, in part because the college had adopted new rules. The term at Union, however, did not affect his anointed place in the bottom third of the class.

His baggage from Union contained a football, and he joined some students, including George Weaver and Tom Coventry, in kicking the ball around. "I remember our surprise when we discovered the ball was oval rather than round," George Budd recalled. Student opinion had been growing for the college to help start an organization to play football. Lobbying was intense led by Duncan Lee, the college's star sprinter, Adams, and Coventry. A motion to organize won by three votes.[17]

Coventry was elected president, Lee secretary, and Adams a director. The new group joined Rochester, Syracuse, and Union in organizing the Intercollegiate Football Association of New York State. The actions were optimistic for a college that had not played a game of modern football, but Hamilton men were well versed in what Budd called "personal encounter." After exiting from chapel or the Wednesday and Saturday rhetoricals, students participated in "rows," good-natured mass scrimmages in which dive tackling was the practice.[18]

Adams returned to the campus for his senior year ten days before the term began. To cut expenses he moved out of Alpha Delta Phi and took a room at the home of a friend, senior James Robert Benton. In a letter to his grandfather Hopkins he wrote that the house was at the foot of the hill and he had use of the Bentons' library of more than three thousand volumes.[19]

The stay at the Bentons was eventful. Almost fifty years later Adams revealed to a Hamilton friend that while at his friend's home, he saw an apparition. When he was home for Christmas, Adams casually mentioned seeing a woman dressed in a nurse's uniform when he was in the library late one night. His father said when he was at the college, the house was inhabited by a girl who became an Episcopal nurse but died young and was buried on the property. Benton said he and his family had also seen the apparition, and Adams's fascination with the unexplained remained the rest of his life.[20]

In his studies he took natural religion, logic in philosophy, constitutional law, and debate and orations, and, as electives during the fall, German and English literature. Adams was feeling that his formal education was lacking, however, and in that only surviving letter from college he thanked his grandfather Hopkins for help in preparing an outline for a winter term oration, "The Duty of Educated Men to Political Parties." He admitted his knowledge of political economy and social questions was lacking. After asking for suggestions for reading and noting that he had begun *The State*, by Woodrow Wilson, he noted the college work that term was easy and that political science with Professor Hamilton was nothing more than a farce.

The criticism of Professor Hamilton was serious. The faculty minutes showed that in September 1890 a warning was given to Adams and Coventry for disorder in Hamilton's recitation class and that it was "to be accompanied with a reminder that a second warning separates them from the college." Adams had his warning (this could have been the bean shooter incident Hutchens mentioned), and he again was on the brink, a fact he did not mention in his letter to his grandfather Hopkins.

The warning not only put Adams in academic jeopardy but threatened the fledgling football team of which both Adams and Coventry were members. The reason he had reported early to campus was to practice football. "For a small college," Adams wrote, "we were a heavy and powerful team . . . we had weight, strength, speed, and spirit; everything but the experience."[21]

A football game in 1890 was one and one-half hours long with one intermission. The uniforms were thin canvas jackets latched up the front, moleskin pants, woolen stockings, and cleated shoes, all paid for by the players. The game itself consisted of flying wedges and running plays during which the halfback ran until he yelled that he was down. Adams played right tackle, switching to right halfback on a muddy field.

The first game, or practice scrimmage, was with the Syracuse Athletic Club in Utica on 15 October. If the Hamilton eleven was inexperienced, the Syracuse team knew "absolutely nothing about football." The score was a lopsided 56-0 win for Hamilton. A sparse crowd did not deter the team's newfound confidence. Nor did a broken nose chill Adams's enthusiasm. On 25 October Hamilton played its first league game with rival Union, Adams's old team, at Clinton. "They emerged from their carriages that day, grim, long-haired, formidable, with jackets coated with mud of many gridirons," Budd said.[22]

Adams, who assessed himself as "rather slow" on his feet but "a reliable tackler with a knack of being on the spot to recover a loose ball," remembered one big play. Faking an end sweep, the Union halfback plunged through the center of the line. "Just about an eighth of a second too late I recognized the play from having seen it the year before," Adams wrote, noting he helped catch the runner on the two-yard line. "I seem to recall, without shame or regret, that in my annoyance, at the moment, I tried to secure one of his ears for myself, probably as a souvenir." The ear belonged to George Daley, later sports edi-

2. The first Hamilton College football team, on which Samuel Hopkins Adams, second from right on top row, played. Courtesy of Hamilton College.

tor of the New York *World*, who scored on the next play and in 1932 recalled: "Well do I remember Sam Adams. When he made a tackle, bones rattled and the arnica bottle was needed."[23]

Union dominated the second half and won 26-10. The next games at Rochester and Syracuse universities were close but defeats. Although the team won 10-0 against Rochester on 5 November, the eleven reorganized the next day with Adams switching to right end. The team then beat Colgate University. It was Adams's last game.

As the fortunes in football turned more favorable, Adams's class cutting caught up with him. On 7 November 1890 the faculty minutes reported that an excuse of Adams for 17–20 October was refused. Adams's absence from Friday, 17 October, to Monday, 20 October, came two days after he had broken his nose. On 14 November he appeared before the faculty to state why he had been absent. The unimpressed faculty ordered that "he be separated from College for the rest of the term."

Adams returned to campus on 8 January and had his law and metaphysics examinations deferred to 17 January. He must not have been too concerned because the night before he went to a reception attended by faculty and guests from the girls' schools. Darling toasted the college; Lee recognized athletics, and Adams saluted "the Ladies." His suggestion that the scope of the Young Men's Christian Association, active on campus, "be broadened so as to embrace the young ladies" received "vociferous applause." The reception ended soon after 10:00 P.M. and Adams passed his examinations the next day.[24]

During the winter term Adams stayed out of trouble with the faculty. Classes for the second term ended early when Professor Ambrose Kelsey died in March. The third term that began 9 April under the pallor of Kelsey's death was cast into further gloom by the death of President Darling on 20 April. As the faculty was preoccupied by the loss of two colleagues, Adams avoided the faculty minutes until 1 May. On that day the Committee on Orations nominated seniors for the prestigious Clark Prize, and Adams was a candidate on "The Conception of Human Progress in Tennyson." Coventry, Lee, Weaver were other nominees as was Bayard Livingston Peck, who had the same topic as Adams.

On 3 June Adams spoke first, and he extolled Alfred Lord Tennyson's evolutionary contribution. The future progressive noted that given progress and law, "we have progress according to law, and that defines evolution" and lauded Tennyson's "faith in an ordered progress." Adams was good, but Peck was judged better by the faculty, who gave him the Clark Prize.

In an interview late in life Adams summed up his college career with "I was average—and I mean average. I won no prizes and no glory." Certainly his grades brought no glory as his four-year class rank was eighteenth of twenty-three. Nonetheless, as he prepared to graduate in June 1891, he had an optimistic assessment of the future: "The world had an appetite for work and a welcome for workers. There was a place waiting for any competent or even incompetent applicant, provided he were willing. Diplomas in hand, we of '91 marched down the Hill straight into the waiting portals of opportunity. We did not even have to knock. The door was open in advance."[25]

Five months after his twentieth birthday, he graduated from Hamilton. His body was muscular with 167 pounds on his five-foot-ten-and-one-quarter-inch frame, only one pound over his football playing weight. He stated he was a Democrat in politics and undecided in religion. But he knew where he wanted to go, New York, and what he wanted his occupation to be, journalism.[26]

# 3

# REPORTER
## 1891–1899

AFTER GRADUATING from Hamilton College, Adams moved to New York where, by August 1891, he had followed the not "uncommon path for Hill graduates" and joined the New York *Sun* of Charles A. Dana, the last of the great nineteenth century newspaper editors. At the *Sun* a Hamilton clique was led by managing editor Chester S. Lord, who had quit college at twenty, with four others including Adams's friend Walstein Root. They were part of the "bright young men" assembled by Dana, who sought to create an interesting newspaper by hiring college graduates as reporters, a new practice.

In 1891 the *Sun* was slipping in circulation under pressure from Joseph Pulitzer's *World*. The *Sun* had fallen from 150,000 to 80,000 while the *World* bounded from 20,000 to 200,000 by using Pulitzer's maxim that a newspaper should be written for the reader, not the editor. Yet the *Sun* remained a major newspaper by using the literary form in the presentation of the news. The staff was headed by Dana, Lord, and Selah M. "Boss" Clarke, the night city editor, whom Adams called the best newspaperman he knew. The trio reigned over what the twenty-year-old Adams found to be "the sternest training school of ambitious young journalists."[1]

Just being a *Sun* man did not guarantee success. Adams warned the seniors of 1910 at Hamilton, "Newspaper journalism is a trade, and not many who enter it survive." Newspaper work also offered opportunity. Journalism was changing in the last two decades of the nineteenth century when the era of the great editors became the age of the great reporters. To be a reporter in the 1890s meant status as readers were entranced by exploits of Elizabeth Cochrane as Nellie Bly and Henry Morton Stanley finding David Livingston in Africa.

Looking at the 1890s in *Tenderloin*, Adams said, "Two young godlings of Newspaper Row, Arthur Brisbane and Richard Harding Davis, outglamored the stage idols."[2]

As Adams climbed the metal spiral stairs at 170 Nassau Street, he joined two dozen staffers and became a *Sun* man like Brisbane, David Graham Phillips, Wilbur J. "Jersey" Chamberlin, Frank Ward O'Malley, and Jesse Lynch

3. Samuel Hopkins Adams, probably when he was a young reporter in New York City. Courtesy of Hamilton College.

Williams. In the same Park Row building was the *Evening Sun* with the dashing reporter Davis and reformer Jacob Riis. As impressive as these colleagues were, the *Sun* was the product of Dana, Lord, and Clarke.

At the top was the ever-formidable presence of Dana. Trained by Horace Greeley, Dana had two edicts: Be interesting, and never be in a hurry. A perfectionist in language usage, Dana said the first qualification of the reporter was to recognize the truth and then to tell it with vividness and animation. Equally imposing was the presence of Lord, who dominated the newsroom from his roll-top desk with the room's only telephone. He had taken over the hiring from Dana, and Adams said his first steps led him to Lord, whose news philosophy was mirrored in "Whatever is nearest the heart, whatever is uppermost in the mind—that is what we want to read about." He stressed the importance of the contest, saying that news came from conflict. Lord was assisted by Clarke, a stickler for well-written copy. Of Clarke, who had the most contact with the reporters of the morning paper, Lord wrote, "He had acute news sense, an inspired appreciation of news values, a genius for knowing what to print."[3]

In the *Sun's* cavernous city room Adams sat at a table desk and wrote out his first stories, mostly small items assigned from the futures book by the city editor who taught him *Sun* style, of which Will Irwin said, "One must write lucidly and with an effect of ease, and avoid stock phrases."[4] Although Adams covered an occasional big story such as the collapse of a Park Place building in late August 1891, most of his stories lacked such drama. The writers were expected to handle the routine with flair while they awaited meatier assignments.

One such story came to Adams in early June 1892. In Port Jervis, northwest of New York City, two thousand people on Thursday evening, 2 June, lynched a black named Bob Lewis for beating a twenty-one-year-old woman, Lena McMahon. Like other *Sun* reporters, Adams found no story too big for one staffer to handle, and he filed a six thousand word article on Saturday from Port Jervis. In the Sunday edition he wrote, "The townspeople are coming to the realization to-day of what the lynching will mean to the town, and hardly any one can be found who justifies the action." But he saw little chance that the leaders of the mob would be brought to justice.

Nevertheless, the Port Jervis datelines continued. Adams gave the testimony of witnesses at the coroner's inquest that began on Monday, 6 June. On 8 June his story reported, "Curiously nearly all the witnesses on the stand to-day recognized only those men in the crowd who were trying to prevent the lynching." While the inquest tried unsuccessfully to identify the lynchers, he interviewed the beaten woman and a man who reportedly had incited Lewis to assault her. When the jury's verdict of "being hanged by the neck by a person or persons unknown to the jury" came in Friday, 10 June, it merited only two paragraphs in the Saturday paper.

Back in New York Adams often handled a "beat," writing articles based on information gathered from the Jefferson Market Court or the Tombs Police Court, part of which was "the Long Walk" that covered seven police stations. His work was not limited to police news, and he became a prolific writer. Later he commented, "Back in those days, it was worth your life to get enough copy paper." Hired at the *Sun* standard, but high, fifteen dollars a week, he rose rapidly until he got a guarantee of seventy-five dollars a week, a princely sum matched only by Chamberlin. Reporters were paid space rates based on the columns produced and, in his semiautobiographical *Success* written in 1921, Adams explained a productive reporter could earn five or six thousand dollars a year.[5] At the time the salary for a congressman was five thousand dollars.

Adams found newspaper work demanding and fun. Working a day that began at 1:00 P.M. and more often than not stretched to fifteen hours, he might be done by the midnight deadline for the first edition and still be writing at 2:00 A.M. for a subsequent one. Then he would join the continuous office poker game. If Adams took to reporting, he embraced New York City like a wrestler.

In the city of immigrants and rampant government corruption Adams had fodder for countless stories. The city's population ballooned to one and one-half million. As older families moved uptown, family neighborhoods dotted Manhattan. Park Row thrived on the crime from the nearby Bowery. Next to the Bowery was the lower East side with its slums with their dumbbell tenements. Stretching from Fourteenth Street to Forty-Second Street and from Fourth Avenue to North River was the district of sin and sex called the Tenderloin. "It was the area of froth and glitter; of night life, and lawlessness. According to the point of view, it was the very essence of New York, or its enduring shame," Adams later wrote in his novel on the district.[6]

The Tenderloin survived because police practices were riddled with corruption as were politics and government. One reason for the respect that the *Sun* engendered was, as Dana's biographer and friend James Wilson said, the newspaper being "the fearless leader of popular opinion against bribery, peculation, and wastefulness in public office, and as the outspoken advocate of personal and official virtue." These lofty goals were joined with what Irwin would see as "puncturing windbags and showing up fakes." Adams himself was credited with saying, "A newspaperman without enemies has no friends."[7]

But life in New York City produced friends. Being a *Sun* man gave Adams a camaraderie that would stretch well into the twentieth century. Within months of going to the newspaper he put up ten dollars to join the Tenderloin Club. The collegiality developed informally at dinners and over after-work drinks with colleagues at "Doc" Perry's Park Row pharmacy where reporters criticized each other's work or at the New York Press Club, which Adams joined in 1892.

Clean-shaven in the days of mustaches and beards, he had a boyish look with sparking blue eyes, round face with big ears, and muscular body, kept trim by tennis. His most pronounced feature was the Adams nose. His grandson, George Harlan, recalled Adams saying he was asked at a New York bar by a man who spied his somewhat bulbous nose if he were W. C. Fields.[8]

The life and work in New York were consuming but Adams, as in the case of the Port Jervis lynching, was most challenged when he went outside New York City. Such an assignment was his coverage of a railroad switchmen's strike in Buffalo during August 1892. He filed his first story on 14 August and told of a union meeting presided over by Grand Master Switchman Sweeney, a meeting that he later discussed in an article entitled "Spotters" in a 1901 *Ainslee's Magazine.* The article on company agents told how Adams had been approached in a secluded corner of the hall "where I had hoped to remain unnoticed" by a red-bearded man who cursed him in Polish and then under his breath whispered in English: "They're onto you. Your life isn't safe here."[9]

The threat of violence expanded in the next day's report in which he described the burning of twenty railroad cars and two buildings. The next day hundreds of cars burned, and the New York militia was called to Buffalo. Although he covered the official position of the union with an interview with its leader, Sweeney, he also reported, "All day the strikers have been pouring down beer and whiskey in the saloons around the Lehigh yards, and serious times are expected to-morrow." The next day he reported troops and strikers had clashed on three occasions, with the militia stabbing the legs of the men, some of whom carried revolvers and clubs.

Another week of violence produced an average of six stories a day and ended when other union leaders came to Buffalo and told Sweeney to end the strike. Although most stories dealt with news developments, the impending end of the strike prompted Adams to write a sociological sketch of East Buffalo in an attempt to show the frustration of the strikers: "Considering all things, population, situation, and environments, there is probably no place east of Chicago less desirable to live in than the east side of Buffalo," he wrote in a page two article on 23 August 1892.

Assignments such as the Buffalo strike came from the city editor, but Adams and other *Sun* reporters had freedom to develop their own stories. He later held the title of special writer, but "he was not a specialist," Jesse Lynch Williams wrote, "he was a 'good all around reporter,' especially good at humorous and descriptive stories." Whether a story on an Irish wake that Irwin called a *Sun* classic or covering a criminal case, he was labeled by many the best reporter in New York, a title he passed on, when asked, to Frank Ward O'Malley.[10]

Unfortunately, *Sun* stories had no bylines, so knowing exactly what Adams wrote has been limited to stories identified as his. For instance, *Sun* historian Frank M. O'Brien reported that on 1 February 1893 Adams was assigned to the Jefferson Market Court, one of the most sleazy places, but *Sun* policy was that all beats and all reporters were equal. Although the assignment might be considered ordinary, Lord warned that the "deadly, dull routine writing of routine news" produced "our poorest and most slovenly newspaper results."[11] On 2 February 1893 the newspaper had three stories on the Jefferson Market Court.

In one, a twist at the end was used in a page five story of a woman, who having left home, was befriended by a couple named Steinmetz. The husband suggested she give him her jewelry for safekeeping, promising to find a secure place in which to store it. "He found a number of secure places in the shape of pawn shops." He then lost the money at the races. Any sympathy was lost when in the last paragraph the woman was identified as a co-respondent in a divorce suit and a pawned bracelet had been given to her by her paramour.

The stories showed an Adams's skill at finding the "news around the news" that the *Sun* prized and his emerging style that featured irony and an ear for dialect. He also had an awakening social consciousness that may have come from his association while covering the police headquarters at Mulberry Square with Jacob Riis and Lincoln Steffens of the *Commercial Advertiser*.

In his last novel Adams described Riis in terms of the reporters of his day: "A soberer journalist, the beloved 'Jake' Riis, told the public about the reeking, airless and lightless, dumbbell tenements of the deep East Side. Everyone read [Riis's] *How the Other Half Lives*, but nothing much was done about it because those overcrowded ant-heaps paid fat returns to some of the most distinguished families on Manhattan Island."[12] Although Steffens was "a trifle self-[c]entered, he was one of the most vital men I ever met," Adams said. "He was a political anarchist, and thought government was run by the few to suppress the many." The three men worked in a building across from the police station. As they waited for news, they played penny poker, shared their impressions of individuals such as the police board president, Theodore Roosevelt, whom Riis revered and Adams did not, and discussed their changing world.[13]

Many years later Adams received a citation that said, in part, "As a reporter for the New York *Sun*, Mr. Adams helped the world of journalism define its function as an instrument of constructive social change, through the force of his writing and through his humane understanding of a free democratic society." The stirring of the Progressive tendency joined with two trends in journalists of this era: an appreciation for science and for realism. Williams in 1915 offered a look at Adams's devotion to facts and science:

> I always feel that I must be clear sure of my facts when I venture an opinion in his presence. He owns so many facts; in so many fields, from butterflies to newspapers and including "National Health," tennis rackets and eugenics. He is as acquisitive in his way as the late J. P. Morgan was in another way.
>
> And yet he always wants more! That is why he takes the attitude of "show me — prove it." He is not really desirous of knocking you down; he merely wants to know what you've got. So many people argue to bring out their superiority; he argues to bring out the facts. . . . It is the scientific spirit.[14]

Adams later said: "Newspaper work taught me how to get at facts" and that he learned "facility, to think with pen in hand, that's the best thing a newspaper can teach a writer. That, and structure." Although he told Franklin Pierce Adams in 1926 that "he thought there was a vast amount of twaddle talked about the old days of reporting" and called his own stories "mediocre," he liked newspaper work and his young life. In 1957 he looked back at his early twenties as when he was too young to have serious responsibilities but had outgrown the constant discipline by his elders.[15]

The news of those elders in Rochester was not good. Grandfather Myron Adams died at ninety-four on 8 November 1893, two years after his second wife. Although Adams's father had published *The Continuous Creation* in 1889 and *The Creation of the Bible* in 1892, progressive heart disease sapped the minister's strength. Several leaves of absence did not restore his health, and the church in late 1895 granted him a pension. On 29 December 1895 Myron Adams, Jr., died, leaving Hester Adams alone.

While his mother was adrift, Adams was achieving growing success. *Bookman* in a 1905 profile reported: "He was assigned to cover for his paper all the big sensational murders and robberies. He had all the elements of what is known as the '*Sun* style' at its best; in particular the ability to seize upon some little, out-of-the-way incident of the life of the metropolis, and through sheer cleverness to elevate it to the dignity of a column story."[16]

His work at the *Sun* was supplemented in 1896 by a foray into magazines, following a common practice of reporters to moonlight. He had begun work on an arranged story for *Scribner's Magazine,* but before he could complete a rewrite on it, he was assigned the trial of Mrs. Mary Alice Almont Fleming. Mrs. Fleming was charged with murdering her mother by giving her a pitcher of chowder laced with arsenic and antimony.

The trial that began 11 May and stretched to late June was identified by Adams as work he did for the *Sun.* When testimony began 26 May, the Adams stories were on the front page with a runover of two or more columns on page two. In the accounts he used a narrative style and often employed a dramatic technique in reporting expunged love letters or the testimony of a friend of the defendant's daughter, who said her mother told them, "I hope you didn't eat any" of the chowder. Finally in the seventh week of the trial, the jury brought a "not guilty" verdict to the cheers of the crowd. The story ran two columns the next morning even though the verdict came in at 12:50 A.M. The trial had cost thirty thousand dollars, he reported, but what he did not say was it almost cost him his first major outside assignment.

The demands of the Fleming trial kept Adams so busy that on 20 June 1896 he wrote an apologetic letter to W. R. Burlingame at *Scribner's* about a delay in the contracted article, "The Conduct of Great Business." In its published form, "Department Store" was nine thousand words as Adams's first effort in magazines. Adams had rewritten it, a practice he would follow in the future, but he said the magazine could change it or ask him to rewrite it again.[17]

Whether *Scribner's* or Adams made any changes is unknown, but the article appeared in the January 1897 edition. The rambling article covered the economics, staffing, layout, and management of department stores, with Adams using information from Brooklyn, New York City, and Paris stores. He must have been pleased when his story was the lead article of the issue, especially because it preceded the first installment of "Soldiers of Fortune" by his idol, Richard Harding Davis.

This nonfiction venture was followed later in the year with a fiction story. Adams made the transition from nonfiction to fiction with ease. Concerning story writing, he later said, "If you have a vital interest in life, and a consuming desire to express yourself, you have a good chance to succeed as an author."[18]

The story, "Blinky," was part of a fund-raising pamphlet by the New York Association for Improving the Condition of the Poor. A proponent of the Fresh Air programs on Coney Island for convalescent children and overworked mothers, the association solicited a short story from Adams through its agent, William H. Tolman. The melodramatic plot with a sociological theme featured a young newsboy, Blinky, and a girl, Mamie Dooley, from the tenements. She had tuberculosis, and the girl and boy were sent by the association to the country, where they collected butterflies and learned about nature. The girl was cured by a month of fresh air, and the association found employment for the boy in a broker's office. Using the dialect of the Irish and some French, Adams told a story of indignation over the conditions of New York slums and optimism for those caught in them. Underlying this first published fiction was an idealism that would dominate his writing.

Not all was idealism. More than fifty years later Tolman sent Adams a copy of the pamphlet, which the author relayed to Hamilton College with a letter, noting the six top-flight illustrators including Charles Dana Gibson worked for free but that he was paid twenty-five dollars.[19]

The year 1897 was important for Adams in other ways, too. At the *Sun* Charles A. Dana died on 17 October, and the paper went into the hands of William Laffan, who had been the driving force behind the syndicate service that fed *Sun* feature stories to other newspapers. In the changeover Adams assumed some duties with the syndicate.

He also moved to Brooklyn where his mother, after going to Auburn following the death of Adams's father, came and took over the running of his home. At that time Brooklyn, which was about to give up its status as a city to become a borough, was the burgeoning bedroom of New York where many middle-class families settled in brick and wood-frame homes. Adams left the Central Park apartment life for a neat three-story row house at 219 Cambridge Place. Mrs. Adams took her duties seriously. Contacting her brother-in-law,

Abner Adams of Rochester, she had hardwood "Adams Floors" installed in the parlor, hall, and dining room in late 1897. Soon after, she became interested in joining the business.

What prompted his mother to seek a new career was not an interest in becoming a businesswoman but a new addition into the Brooklyn household, Elizabeth Ruffner Noyes. Adams had met the Charleston, West Virginia, belle at an Elmira College house party. She was a special student in music at the women's college in 1892–93 but left as a nonmatriculated student during the year. Outgoing and with a zest for life, she had a strong face with dark violet eyes and chestnut hair. In 1898 Adams went to Charleston to marry her.[20]

The wedding in the evening of 19 October 1898 was in the First Presbyterian Church and befitted "one of Charleston's leading society girls." With twelve ushers and bridesmaids the wedding was called "one of the most fashionable" in the history of the church. The bride wore a satin gown adorned only with a diamond crescent given to her by Adams. His best man was his colleague on the *Sun*, Walstein Root, who sandwiched the wedding in between covering the Spanish-American War and reconstruction in Cuba.[21] After a brief western trip, the newlyweds were in Brooklyn by 1 November. In less than one month the new Mrs. Adams's father, Philip H. Noyes, was dead. His death, coupled with the recent deaths of Adams's grandfather and father, left him in a female-dominated homelife, whatever homelife there was.

Working the fifteen-hour days, six days a week, had to produce an immediate strain on the marriage. As Lord commented, "If the young journalist chances to marry it imposes pitiful hardships on the young wife." How the strong-willed Hester Adams, suffering that first winter from a rheumatic condition, got along with the flighty Beth Adams with her Southern accent and her use of the appellation "Honey" may be guessed by his mother's proposal within one year to set up an Adams Floor franchise in Auburn.[22]

Adams, too, was getting itchy. Nearing thirty, he realized that newspaper reporting was a young man's game. And newspapers also had changed. Although *Sun* writers might resort to sensationalism to get more of that precious space, the fabrication employed by Yellow Journalism during the Spanish-American War in 1898 and afterward was not allowed. He had no love for its main exponents, Joseph Pulitzer of the *World* and William Randolph Hearst of the *Journal*. "How much the atmosphere of the *World* office was a reflection of Pulitzer's own lack of decency in his relations with underlings, I do not know. I should think there was some relationship. He was notoriously ill-tempered and abusive," Adams said. He had more disdain for Hearst, "a gay-spirited, cold-hearted, young hedonist of no principle, whatsoever." Later Adams did spot work for Pulitzer, whom he felt Hearst had forced to debase his standards. Often Hearst was a target for Adams's pen.[23]

Thus, with little future in newspapers, his mother's departure delayed only temporarily by Beth Adams being pregnant with their first child, and new vistas opening in magazine work, Adams prepared to leave the *Sun*. Although he would always think of himself as a *Sun* man — "I shall never get over my newspaper training. Nor do I want to" — he would later admit that his nine-year service was too long. "Newspaper reporting is a good job for five years, but after that a man should move along."[24]

# 4

# MAGAZINE WRITER
## 1900–1904

I N 1900 Adams's world was changing. A daughter, Hester Hopkins Adams, was born on 3 January. His mother was preparing to move to Auburn. As the *Sun* lost its shine, he looked for opportunities. One was a magazine that ran articles using factual reporting, stressing good writing and being "free from bias, just the same as a news article or newspaper." It was *McClure's*.[1]

A trafficker in ideas, Samuel Sidney McClure had been building his publishing empire. He and John Sanford Phillips had started *McClure's* magazine in 1893, using stories and money from a successful syndicate service. The magazine had catered to women, workers, and children, but the Spanish-American War in 1898 swung the magazine toward current events.

S. S. McClure's main topics of interest became articles on scientific discoveries, locomotives and trains, wild animals and exploration, and personalities. To write the articles McClure chose professional writers rather than experts, and he assembled a staff including free-lance writer Ida Tarbell in 1894 and newspaperman Ray Stannard Baker in 1898. McClure's formula worked because by 1899 circulation had risen to 360,000 and the amount of advertising topped all other magazines.

That year he had organized a publishing house. Still not content, he planned an encyclopedia, a new monthly magazine, and the S. S. McClure Lecture Bureau. Most projects of the mercurial McClure never got off the drawing board, but he was ever seeking talent. Adams's skill in writing with clarity and aggressiveness and his experience with the *Sun* syndicate made him attractive.

During 1900 Adams left the *Sun*. In July he was on Owasco Lake, and in late August he did a color story on the prize fight between Jim Corbett and Kid McCoy for the New York *World*.[2] He also showed his magazine acumen by preparing an article on one of McClure's favorite topics. Published in September, the "Training of Lions, Tigers, and Other Great Cats" was based on "interviews with leading trainers of the world." The article caught the attention of McClure in Paris. He said it was the only readable feature in the issue and ordered Adams be hired. Adams said, "I jumped at the chance to leave Park Row and join the staff of *McClure's Magazine*."[3]

Adams's transition to full-time magazine work was helped by the McClure philosophy of preoccupation with facts, of letting events and documents speak for themselves, and of a high standard of writing. Although McClure liked Adams's writing, he ordered Adams to become managing editor of McClure's Syndicate, which not only ran previously published work but also sought the stories of known and new authors. The position included talent scout work as a "literary drummer" for McClure, Phillips, and Company, the book publishing enterprise.

Although Adams said he was "a rotten editor," letters to Henry W. Boynton in 1901 showed Adams doing his best. After buying one story for syndication at thirty dollars, Adams urged the author to develop more stories involving his main character, Hackett, and suggested an eventual book, especially by placing another story with a new planned service of McClure. After another McClure plan fizzled, however, Adams returned a new Hackett story with an apology. When Boynton suggested holding the story for the contemplated fiction series of short stories, Adams urged him to sell it elsewhere, noting that it did not matter where it was published as long as the story had the author's copyright.[4]

In the late fall of 1901 McClure, who had added journalist Lincoln Steffens to the magazine, proposed one of his frequent reorganizations of the staff. He first had suggested Adams as managing editor. Then in November 1901, dissatisfied with the newspaper advertisements for the Christmas book list, McClure put him in charge of all future book advertising with McClure, Phillips, and Company. While Adams continued working with authors, he also wrote advertising copy. *Bookman* offered an assessment of his book promotion: "Readers may remember a series of 'Doyley Dialogues,' designed to exploit Conan Doyle's *The Hound of the Baskervilles*. . . . The extraordinary cleverness with which they were done, caused them to be quoted far and wide. . . . An astonishing tribute to a mere 'ad' and one of which Mr. Adams may long be proud."[5]

Adams, like other members of the McClure operation, also had the freedom to place his own stories in other publications. He took advantage of the latitude by publishing the article "Spotters" in *Ainslee's*. In the article he detailed how businesses employed confidential men to police their operations, labeling the agent as "an outcast in the business world." Adams's sympathetic treatment of the outsider in society would become a predominate theme in his writing.

He also dabbled in fiction. In September 1901 his adventure story, "Little Black Satchel," was in *Munsey's Magazine*. Appearing in "Storiettes," the fast-paced five-hundred-word yarn told of a man and woman meeting on a train and her concern over his satchel. After a train wreck, a kidnapping of the couple by five robbers, and the detonation of sales samples of high explosives in the satchel, killing the kidnappers, she told the narrator-hero to give up selling dynamite. He commented, "That strikes me as the depths of ingratitude."

Finally, almost two years after the animal trainer article appeared, *McClure's* carried another piece by Adams, this time a short story. The August 1902 "Such as Walk in Darkness" was about a blind man and his dog, which the man got rid of after an operation restored his sight and he no longer needed the "bossy" canine. The story, for which Adams received sixty dollars, was in anthologies later and was translated into several languages. It was so successful that Adams recalled "a demand for a whole series of 'em. I didn't know enough animals to make a series, but I went on writing."[6]

That writing produced in *McClure's* in January and February 1903 a two-part mystery serial, "The Flying Death." Placed on the eastern end of Long Island, at Montauk Point, which was remote when Adams had spent a month there as a young reporter, the story involved a prehistoric flying reptile and a series of murders. The publication seemed to support the *Hamilton Literary Magazine* boast in December 1902 that Adams "appears to be rushing to the front in the literary world," but for the ambitious Adams, the pace may have seemed more like a crawl; his output in magazine journalism was five pieces in the first three years of the century.

Besides his advertising work and personal writing, Adams also remained a literary talent scout, and on a western trip in 1903 he met a San Francisco journalist, Will Irwin. Born in Oneida, New York, in 1873, Irwin had moved to Colorado as a child and had attended Stanford University where he played football under Walter Camp until he broke an ankle. He had coauthored two books with Gelett Burgess and was working for the *San Francisco Chronicle* when discovered by Adams. Adams and Irwin struck up a friendship immediately despite an Irwin practical joke of having Adams wear formal attire to a party where everyone else wore cowboy garb. Before he left for the East, Adams offered to get Irwin a job on the *Sun*, which hired him in 1904. Later Irwin followed Adams to *McClure's*, and their career paths were remarkably close. Their personal relationship remained strong as Irwin explained, "The basis of our friendship, which has lasted through the years, was the fact that we could differ amicably—could even quarrel genially."[7]

Other changes were occurring in Adams's life. By the end of 1900 his mother had left Brooklyn and was living in Auburn with her father, who had retired from the seminary. Adams's last grandparent, Samuel Miles Hopkins, died on 29 October 1901. After his death, Hester Adams moved several times before settling on Chedell Place, a newly developed section. She had started an Adams wood-flooring business in early 1901 and had moderate success.

Back in Brooklyn Sam and Beth Adams, after his mother left, moved in 1900 to a five-story brick building at 1244 Pacific Street. After the birth of their second daughter, Katherine Noyes Adams, on 26 September 1901, they moved again in 1903 back across the East River to the West Central Park area, an apartment house at 2131 Broadway between 74th and 75th streets, but cockroaches drove them farther uptown to an apartment over a store in a seven-story building at 2647 Broadway between 100th and 101st streets.[8]

His moving around did not reflect his seemingly static position as advertising manager. To make matters even more frustrating for the reporter in Adams *McClure's* had taken the lead in a new type of exposure reporting. Begun in 1902 with articles by Josiah Flynt (Josiah Frank Willard), exposure writing had been catapulted into the public arena with the January 1903 issue in which the staff writers wrote articles claiming that big business and corrupt politics had blighted the American dream. Adams's "The Flying Death" light mystery was sandwiched in among Tarbell's third chapter of her history of Standard Oil, Steffens's "The Shame of Minneapolis" in his cities series, and Baker's "Right to Work" on labor, plus a McClure editorial decrying American contempt for the law.

For much of 1903 Adams must have suffered as Tarbell wound through her nine-part series and then announced a second series, Steffens hopscotched from St. Louis to Pittsburgh to Philadelphia to Chicago to New York, and

Baker focused on labor abuses in Chicago and San Francisco. Finally, Adams made his move, resigning as advertising manager in October 1903 so he could expand his efforts as a free-lance writer. In an arrangement that characterized McClure, he continued the salary of Adams, whose loyalty remained with *McClure's* where the staff provided friendships and advice.

Some advice came from Baker, who urged him to go into exposure reporting. Adams's first piece of investigative writing was "State of Kentucky vs. Caleb Powers" in March 1904. The article championed Powers, convicted as the assassin of a Kentucky candidate for governor, claiming a miscarriage of justice. Adams was credited by his woman friend, author George Madden Martin of Louisville, with saving Powers.[9]

In June he followed with an account of "Dan Cunningham: A Huntsman of the Law," detailing how a United States marshal had battled clan vengeance in the West Virginia moonshine wars. Both articles used Steffens's theme of a lone fighter involved in a personalized battle against criminality, but McClure biographer Harold Wilson noted that Adams used the technique "less speciously" in showing the breakdown of the legal process in the Appalachian region.[10]

While his published nonfiction writing progressed, Adams was demonstrating his versatility with fiction, publishing four short stories in *McClure's* during 1904. The successes with short stories did not lessen his nonfiction writing, but a new venue opened. *Collier's Weekly*, a magazine published by P. F. Collier, was placed under the charge of his son, Robert J. Collier, in 1898 after his graduation from Georgetown University and one year at Oxford. He wanted his magazine to be a leader in thought. To accomplish this objective he hired a former lawyer and drama critic, the scholarly Norman Hapgood. Writing barbed and incisive editorials, Hapgood within one year made the editorial pages dominant, but "success" still eluded *Collier's Weekly*.

The two men were shifting the magazine's fiction orientation to an increasingly political slant, seeking social change. The Powers story must have impressed Collier, who was seeking a reporter to cover politics. Collier and McClure were friends because *Collier's* was a weekly and *McClure's* a monthly. McClure biographer Peter Lyon, who interviewed Adams during his research, offered a plausible example of cooperation between the men. Collier had put two illustrators—Jessie Willcox Smith and Maxfield Parrish— under exclusive contracts. McClure, who yearned for good artists, wanted to use them. McClure, however, had a stable of skilled reporters, and Collier needed one. Lyon wrote: "As it might be between the New York Yankees and the Los Angeles Dodgers, a trade was arranged. All at once drawings by Smith and Parrish began appearing in *McClure's*. And Samuel Hopkins Adams went on Collier's payroll."[11]

For *Collier's Weekly* Adams's first byline was on a June 1904 article, "Despotism versus Anarchy in Colorado," which called for public intervention in a strike between the Western Federation of Miners and the Mine Owners Association. In late July another labor article, "Meat: A Problem for the Public," told how labor unrest between the meat cutters and the Beef Trust was causing higher prices and again urged the public to take action. The two articles, given the honored first position in the magazine, may have been a tryout for a series of Adams articles, a survey of 1904 state political campaigns. The survey also marked the initial *Collier's Weekly* use of a running series.

The seven-part series, "Doubtful States and the Silent Vote," sent Adams through the Midwest and East in September and October. Most articles focused on state issues such as corruption and referred only in passing to President Theodore Roosevelt, but 1904 was also a presidential year. The major controversy in the series came not from what was printed but from what was not.

When Adams was preparing a Missouri article, he received help from fellow *McClure's* contributor William Allen White, who told him the Republican Roosevelt, running for his first full term, was an admirer of the Democratic candidate for governor, Joseph W. Folk. Adams skirted the issue, mentioning Roosevelt only in the last paragraph as being genuinely popular in the state, but told Hapgood of a letter being circulated in Missouri in which President Roosevelt said the Republican candidate for governor was "a better man than Folk." Hapgood, a Folk backer, was incensed by Roosevelt endorsing the Republican over the reformer, but Collier told his editor to wait until he challenged Roosevelt to confirm or deny. Roosevelt stalled while he tried to contact Albert Shaw, editor of *Review of Reviews* and author of the letter, on whether Shaw had made such an assertion. Adams beat him to Shaw, who in a telephone conversation admitted a 1904 smoking gun. Confronted, Roosevelt took firm charge, passing the blame to Shaw, who wrote a new letter that contained as much praise for Folk as for the Republican candidate. "As for what Mr. Adams may say," Roosevelt wrote Robert Collier, who had revealed Adams as the author not only of the nonbylined series but also of a letter to Folk, "I care not a rap." Several days later, on another point, the president said of Adams: "I do not regard him as a truthful man."[12]

Collier backed off his support of Adams as the election neared, saying a number of times Adams was a free agent to use the information as he saw fit. Adams was aware of the Collier-Roosevelt letters but gave no hint of knowing about the president's charges against him, nor did he offer criticism of Roosevelt personally. Considering the matter closed, he went to Auburn.[13]

Although the Adamses were part of the New York scene as their circle of friends widened to include the magazine and literary crowds, his resignation from the advertising position in 1903 gave him new freedom to relocate. "As a young man," he recalled later, "my one ambition was to get out of New York City and to come back to Wide Waters. And as soon as I could, I did."[14]

In Samuel Miles Hopkins's will he had directed that the lake property, Quisisana, be sold and the proceeds distributed in six equal shares to his four sons and Hester Adams, who received two shares, hers and one for the contributions of the late Myron Adams, Jr. The buyer was Samuel Hopkins Adams. Later he renamed the property Wide Waters after that section of the Erie Canal where he had played as a youth, but in 1904 the acquisition of the primitive lake property opened the way for establishing a home outside New York.

Adams returned to Auburn in late October 1904. In early November he settled the family with his mother in her half of the double house at 40 Chedell Place. However, Beth Adams missed the glitter of New York, did not enjoy living with Mrs. Adams, and made more and more frequent trips to New York City. Nevertheless, from November 1904 Adams was a central New Yorker.

If central New York was the place of his heart, New York was the place of his profession. As his *Collier's Weekly* assignment ended, he shifted toward longer fiction. In 1911 Adams said his start in novels began with meeting Stewart Edward White. White, a Californian known for his adventure stories, was a frequent contributor to *McClure's*. Two years younger than Adams, White had been born in Grand Rapids, Michigan, but had spent his early years traveling with his lumberman father through upper Michigan and in California. After going broke in the gold rush in the Black Hills of South Dakota, he entered Columbia Law School in 1896 but was encouraged to pursue writing. His early novels reflected his interest in the outdoors and adventure: *The Westerners* and *The Claim Jumpers*, both in 1901, and *The Blazed Trail* in 1902. In 1903 he published two more books, *The Mountain* and *Conjuror's House*, about trapping in Hudson Bay where he had gone after Columbia.

In 1904 the cosmopolitan Adams and the adventurous White met in New York City. The differences in their backgrounds and temperaments were mirrored in their literary styles: White, of the red-blooded school of writing, reported that Adams, who used the sociological approach, had "more indignation." Irwin, a friend to both, described White as "a small, bald, pale youth—pallor under a tanned skin" and "one of the sweetest and kindest men I have met of late." At this time, no one would have used the adjectives for Adams. Yet Adams and White shared common interests and both saw a literature of life rather than art. They had senses of humor that they often directed at each other. By 1906 Irwin called them inseparable, adding "I think there is some kind of plan for them to live together in California when Sam retires to write those great works of which every literary person dreams."[15]

At a 1904 meeting Adams and White discussed a current tale of a merchant ship that discovered a vessel with sails set but no visible signs of life. A crew was placed aboard the stranger, but the two ships were separated in the night. The next day the ship was found, again deserted. A third crew placed aboard her also disappeared. Taking the story of the *Mary Celeste*, the two men used their fertile imaginations. Adams had an interest in the unexplained for which he sought scientific explanations. White preferred the supernatural, an indication of the spiritualism that would dominate his later life. They went their own ways but agreed each would work on his part and meet later in the year at the "Jumping-Off Place," Stewart and Betty Whites' Santa Barbara home in California.

Despite his success with short fiction and his interest in novel writing, Adams yearned for greater success in reporting and turned to public health investigations. Baker had urged him to study various preventable diseases that were killing people because of public ignorance. McClure, interested in health matters, encouraged him to make a countrywide study of tuberculosis, typhoid, and yellow fever.

By October he had finished the first article on tuberculosis. He obtained the best facts he could about the disease that was still what he called the scourge of the world. Although he noted the disease was "often curable, almost invariably susceptible of alleviation, and always preventable," tuberculosis in 1904 was the third most frequent cause of death in America. His solution—disinfection—reflected the best thinking at the time. In writing on tuberculosis Adams developed a recurring theme of the interrelationship between depressed social conditions, science, and public health. Although he said later he had become interested in medical science first, he reported, "I made public health my specialty," adding that he believed he was one of the first American writers to popularize it.[16]

Besides reporting on medical diseases and their social implications, he was heeding the further advice of Baker, who urged him to concentrate on a key ingredient of a major exposure essay—the human evildoer.[17] In the Caleb Powers and tuberculosis articles he had shot glancing blows at the Kentucky judge and the Trinity Church Corporation, which fostered the tenements that he saw as the breeding grounds for the disease. But he needed clear-cut villains.

In the first decade of the twentieth century a new type of journalism was emerging from the demands for political, economic, and social reforms urged by the populists in the late nineteenth century. This new journalism had as its goal the searching out and public exposure of real or apparent misconduct, vice, or corruption by prominent individuals—Baker's evildoers. It was called muckraking.

The articles and their writers became a force in a new progressive impulse. The exposure journalists were credited by historian Richard Hofstadter with providing the underpinnings of progressivism. "To an extraordinary degree the work of the Progressive movement rested upon its journalism," he said, adding "the Progressive mind was characteristically a journalistic mind."[18] Adams fit the mold of the muckraker as an exposure writer and progressive. Brought up in a religious household, he was college educated and his provincial beginnings had been tempered by his experiences in New York. He was young, urbane, and successful. A member of the middle class that he sought to influence, he believed in morality and Puritan righteousness. His Protestant Christianity was modified by Social Darwinism that promised a new evolutionary social order. What Adams lacked was a subject.

One topic for the muckrakers was the pure food and drug legislation that had been languishing in Congress for more than twenty-five years. Louis Filler, who has written the best history of muckraking, assessed the climate for reform: "The agitation for the Pure Food and Drug Act was a microcosm of the entire period. It showed how dependent upon each other were politics, science, and literature. Not only that: it also made clear just what the old economic life had involved, and how different the new was destined to be."[19]

In the tuberculosis article Adams had decried the use of patent medicines to try to cure the deadly disease. At Baker's further suggestion he began thinking about patent medicines, perhaps spurred on by recollections of medical huckster Asa T. Soule, whom he had known in Rochester as the manufacturer of Hop Bitters, his grandfather Adams's favorite tonic.

Patent medicines were not new.[20] And Adams was certain that some proprietary medicines in 1904 had dangerous additives and chemicals. Most ingredients were kept secret by makers refusing to disclose them either on the labels or through the patenting process, and the task of revealing the contents and their effects seemed enormous. The federal government was more concerned with pure food than drugs, restricting its laboratories to products referred by other agencies.

The patent medicine business in a nation of almost eighty-four million was estimated variously at between fifty-nine and ninety million dollars. The sales came from heavy advertising in newspapers and magazines that derived substantial income from the manufacturers. Millions bought the nostrums that were for the most part ineffectual; some of the syrups contained as much as 80 percent alcohol, and many of the tonics used cocaine and morphine.

The use of dangerous drugs in patent medicines has been explained by medical historian David F. Musto in his *The American Disease; Origins of Narcotic Control:*

> The characteristics of opium and its derivatives were ideal for patent medicine manufacturers. . . . Many proprietary medicines that could be bought in any store or by mail order contained morphine, cocaine, laudanum, or (after 1898) heroin. . . . Even "cures" for the opium habit contained large amounts of opiates. Hay fever remedies frequently contained cocaine as their active ingredient. Coca-Cola, until 1903, contained cocaine (and since then caffeine). Opiates and cocaine became popular—if unrecognized—items in the everyday life of Americans.[21]

An early leader in the battle against nostrums was editor Edward Bok, who banned patent medicine advertisements from his *Ladies' Home Journal.* Bok, eager to protect his women readers, used chemical analyses to warn of the dangers of patent medicines. In 1904, after being stung by a lawsuit, Bok launched a full-scale attack on nostrums. He hired attorney Mark Sullivan, but when Sullivan produced a lengthy article, "The Patent Medicine Conspiracy against Freedom of the Press," Bok rejected it as either too legalistic, with its discussion of newspaper contracts and its survey of state actions, or too long at seven thousand words, or both.

Bok, wishing to see the article published, then offered it to publisher Collier and editor Hapgood at *Collier's Weekly.* They had mentioned patent medicines in an editorial on pure food, but their concern was heightened by an argument with William Jennings Bryan over his *Commoner* carrying a full-page advertisement for the patent medicine Liquozone. Hapgood admitted that the reactions of Bryan and of a Liquozone lawyer to what was meant to be a humorous editorial launched him and Collier into patent medicine muck-raking. Although they bought Sullivan's article, the *Collier's* executives still needed a reporter to do a full-scale exposé.[22]

While Adams mulled a patent medicine exposure for *McClure's*, he kept to his medical writing. He wrote a positive article on modern surgery, tracing developments in operations on various organs and saying that American surgeons felt that it was "a craft perfected" although he acknowledged that there might be later advances after developments in chemistry and bacteriology. He also gathered information for a typhoid article and planned another on yellow fever.

In the November 1904 *McClure's* a promotional article described Tarbell, Steffens, and Baker, with portraits, and added a fourth member, without portrait, Adams. It quoted the *New York American*: "One of the newer writers on the staff of *McClure's* whose work is attracting attention, is S. H. Adams, a gifted writer of fiction as well as a capable contributor to 'national journalism.' He thinks and writes clearly. He has many interests and does excellent work in many lines."[23]

Adams's gamble in becoming a free-lance writer, with financial support from McClure, seemed to be paying off. He had new freedom and responsibilities. Commenting in 1920 on writing as a profession, Adams said his choice was based on a "suddenly aroused conviction that if I did not support S. H. A. nobody else would."[24]

Throughout the fall he worked on his and White's mystery story. After he finished his section of the novel, he set off on 5 December 1904 for California, Beth Adams on one arm and a manuscript tucked under the other. At the same time he was establishing himself as a medical specialist by studying the treatment of disease and public health topics. Within six months from the *Mc-Clure's* glowing endorsement in November, however, he would rejoin *Collier's* for a great crusade.

# 5

# MUCKRAKER
## 1905–1906

Adams returned from California in early 1905 after working with Stewart Edward White on their novel. He stopped in New Orleans to do yellow fever research in late January and attended a Hamilton College alumni dinner the next month in Washington where he also began his research on patent medicines for *McClure's*.

The year 1905 had begun gloriously for Adams and *McClure's*. His first medical article, "Tuberculosis: The Real Race Suicide," ran in January followed by a romantic short story, "A Man and a Brother," in February and "Modern Surgery" in March. He finished "Typhoid: An Unnecessary Evil," but then other events intervened.

The paths of publisher Collier, editor Hapgood, and reporter Adams crossed again professionally in March 1905. Adams was back in *Collier's* on 1 April with "Studies of a Strike," about a New York transportation strike, and on 22 April with a critical Adirondacks profile on "William Rockefeller: Maker of Wilderness." The pieces may have been intended to reassure Collier of Adams's reliability after Roosevelt's criticism or to establish the Adams byline for a patent medicine series.[1]

Adams went with *Collier's* in part because S. S. McClure was unexcited about his patent medicine investigation. Hapgood, however, was enthusiastic, later commenting, "Thanks to the knowledge of Samuel Hopkins Adams, his force and wit, many fires were started before that tale was ended." The series allowed Adams to couple his medical writing with the opportunity to muckrake patent medicines. His indignation over nostrums became almost a religious fervor that characterized much work of the muckrakers. "Sam Adams we considered a born muckraker. A character inherited from a line of insurgent theologians gave him firm conviction in his beliefs," Irwin wrote.[2]

Adams's February stop in Washington had been at the Bureau of Chemistry to see Dr. Harvey Washington Wiley, the chief of chemistry for the Department of Agriculture in Washington. He had begun to crusade against adulteration of food when the Senate tried in 1889 to counter the lack of control by the food industry while it was centralizing distribution. Wiley was a strong speaker and writer who created controversy in the 1890s but was unable to get national legislation.

In late May 1905 Adams wrote Wiley on *Collier's* stationery, saying that an article for *McClure's* was now scheduled as a series of six articles for *Collier's*.[3] In June he and Beth Adams went to Washington so that he could meet with Wiley, who offered advice and clippings. Wiley was mostly interested in pure foods, however, leaving the attack on patent medicines in Adams's hands.

Adams's grasp was firm. He adopted the advice he later gave to the medical profession: "Find out where the foe is before you strike. Don't hit out with your eyes shut." The reporter bought samples of the suspect medicines, had the contents analyzed, and gathered their accompanying literature. He consulted with state agricultural chemists, editors of pharmaceutical journals, and medical research experts to assess how successful these "cures" were. Then the thirty-four-year-old Adams, whose round face, large nose, slightly cauliflower ears, and long hair parted just to the right of the middle made him look ten years younger, went around the country to seek the individuals who had signed the testimonials used in advertisements and to interview nostrum sellers. He found many evildoers.[4]

They reacted in different ways. Samuel B. Hartman, a German physician whose patent medicine Peruna was so popular babies were named for it, welcomed Adams in Columbus, Ohio, with "I will tell you anything; you can't do us any harm." Hartman spoke openly although he was warned that the article might be critical. Others put detectives on Adams's trail, and at one point when he was seen on a train with a friend's wife, he was told his trip would be made public unless he dropped his investigation.[5] Adams was undaunted.

Before his legwork began, he enlisted a chemistry professor at Hamilton College, Arthur Percy Saunders, to analyze patent medicines. In an early report "Stinky" Saunders said his analysis showed the patent medicine Peruna contained alcohol of more than 22 percent by weight and 28 percent by volume. Adams said that the Peruna-makers admitted they used Cologne spirits, 90 proof after he quoted Saunders's findings.[6]

The investigation, using sleuthing techniques he had learned as a crime reporter, took Adams five months. Meanwhile, *Collier's* was whipping the public into a frenzy with its demands for reform and promises of a major exposé. In a July 8 article, "Criminal Newspaper Alliances with Fraud and Poison," Hapgood said that a series of articles was being prepared by an unnamed "prominent journalist" and singled out the patent medicines Peruna and Liquozone as targets. In the same issue an editorial quoted extensively from the typhoid article in the June *McClure's*, mentioning Adams as the author and perhaps intending to establish his credentials as knowledgeable in medicine.[7]

On 23 September an editorial item said the series by Adams, "who is already known to our readers as a careful and thorough investigator," would start 7 October. Quoting from his initial article, the item noted that although warned not to lump all patent medicines together, Adams had found an "honest attempt to separate the sheep from the goats develops a lamentable lack of qualified candidates for the sheepfold."

By the time the series began the battle lines were drawn. The patent medicine makers, seeing a plot against them, put their faith in their Proprietary Association of America to deflect criticism. Although physicians came to the fight late, a newly formed Council on Pharmacy and Chemistry had been established by the American Medical Association in February 1905 and offered promise but little hope of legislation.

On 7 October 1905 Adams delivered with the first of a six-part series, called "The Great American Fraud," a name that became the rallying cry for the campaign. In the article he outlined the problem of the public's use of patent medicines, beginning with a much-quoted warning: "Gullible America will spend this year some seventy-five millions of dollars in the purchase of patent medicines. In consideration of this sum it will swallow huge quantities of alcohol, an appalling amount of opiates and narcotics, a wide assortment of varied drugs ranging from powerful and dangerous heart depressants to insidious liver stimulants, and, far in excess of all other ingredients, undiluted fraud."

He criticized patent medicines for making outrageous claims in times of public fear like yellow fever in New Orleans. Then he warned about the use of headache powders containing acetanilid that was "prone to remove the cause of the symptoms permanently by putting a complete stop to heart action." He said the use of unspecified amounts of cocaine and opium in soothing syrups stopped pain but created drug addicts. He also blasted the press for contracts with nostrum advertisers, citing the "Red Clause" of Frank J. Cheney, maker of Hall's Catarrh Cure. The clause voided the contract if labeling legislation passed, and *Collier's* reproduced a facsimile of Cheney's contract.[8]

Naming eight patent medicines and five purveyors in the initial article, Adams also attacked the use of phony testimonials and the post office for allowing the mailing of patent medicine circulars. As a remedy, he called for legislation "pending the enlightenment of the general public or awakening of the journalistic conscience" but warned that the patent medicine dealers with $250 million at stake would oppose the "most obvious remedy." Throughout this first article he set the stage for what was to come, but he used concrete examples to support his charges of conspiracy, graft, influence peddling, and antitrust violations.

Reaction was swift. The New York State Medical Association invited Adams to its annual dinner 18 October and although he was not listed as a speaker, he was asked to talk on the "promiscuous publication of patent medicine advertisement." Response also came in *Collier's* with letters and newspaper comment in the 28 October issue under "Brickbats and Bouquets." Editors pledged to police their advertisements. The Press Committee of the Proprietary Association, firing the first salvo of a bombardment at Adams and *Collier's*, sent information to defend patent medicines.[9]

The next article, "Peruna and the 'Bracers,'" also appeared on 28 October. Adams attacked stimulant patent medicines, focusing on Hartman's Peruna but hitting Duffy's Malt Whiskey among others. He scored a major coup by revealing the Office of Indian Affairs of the Department of Interior had banned Peruna on reservations because of its alcoholic content. In a graphic Peruna was compared with bottles of other alcoholic drinks. Using Saunders's 28 percent volume figure for Peruna, plus 21 percent for Paine's Celery Compound and 44.3 for Hostetter's Stomach Bitters, the bottles were contrasted with 50 percent for bottled-in-bond whiskey, 9 percent for champagne, 8 for claret, and 5 for beer.

Adams suggested that people who wanted to make their own Peruna could do so "by mixing half a pint of cologne spirits, 90 proof, with a pint and a half of water, adding thereto a little cubeb for flavor and a little burned sugar for color." He said the cost was between seven and eight cents as compared with the dollar for a bottle of Peruna.

He noted that Peruna was supposed to cure catarrh (the common cold), but its literature suggested that it cured "whatever ails you," defining pneumonia and tuberculosis as catarrh of the lungs, dyspepsia as catarrh of the stomach, and heart disease as catarrh of the heart. Although he said the nostrum claims were exaggerated to the point of absurdity, he warned about more dangerous effects, ones such as lowering resistance to tuberculosis and masking the severity of typhoid.

He was also concerned about the hypocrites such as a Women's Christian Temperance Union leader and a clergyman, who preached abstinence while guzzling Peruna. Adams said three wineglassesful in forty-five minutes "might temporarily alter a prohibitionist's outlook on life." Citing a doctor's comment about a "Peruna drunk," he was angered by Hartman's claim that the patent medicine was not habit forming.[10] He complained that the bracers did not tell the public about their contents, so unsuspecting users became hopeless alcoholics. In the last paragraph Adams demanded that the government tax such bracers as alcoholic drinks and, further, require that each bottle be labeled with the percentage of alcohol it contained. Such calls for government action were rare in muckraking journalism.

The Mark Sullivan article that *Collier's* had purchased from Bok ran without a byline on 4 November. In the same issue *Collier's* said that it was tightening its own advertising practices. Initially Hapgood, in response to Bryan's criticism that the magazine's hands were not clean, pulled offensive ads. Now he issued a statement that said, in part: "COLLIER'S will accept no advertisements of beer, whiskey, or alcoholic liquors; no advertisements of patent medicines; no medical advertisements or advertisements making claim to medicinal effect." Assessing the cost of the crusade one year later, *Collier's* wrote, "We spoke out about patent medicines, and dropped $80,000 in a year."

Adams returned on 18 November with an attack on Liquozone, the product that had started *Collier's* on the trail of patent medicines. Noting that Liquozone was a descendant of "Radam's Microbe Killer," Adams said the mixture consisted of sulfuric and sulfurous acids diluted by almost 99 percent water and claimed to cure thirty-seven maladies ranging from asthma and dandruff to tuberculosis and cancer by killing germs and bacteria. "Just as to Peruna all ills are catarrh, so to Liquozone every disease is a germ disease," he wrote.

He visited a Liquozone factory where he saw the huge wooden vats and heard that "nothing enters into the production of Liquozone but gases, water, and a little coloring matter" over an eight- to fourteen-day process. He estimated it would take about fourteen seconds to mix the ingredients. He reported the manufacturers said they were not patent medicine men because "Liquozone is too important a product for quackery." He disclosed that the formula for the product was bought from a piano dealer in Canada and that the president of the company said, "Liquozone is liquid oxygen—that is all."

Adams noted liquid oxygen "doesn't exist above a temperature of 229 degrees below zero" and a spoonful would freeze a man's tongue, teeth, and throat solid.

A Chicago chemistry company, Dickman, Mackenzie, and Potter, told Adams that the product contained no substance deleterious to health, but he was far from convinced. To back his suspicions he hired Lederle Laboratories in New York to conduct experiments with guinea pigs infected with diseases and treated with Liquozone. The laboratory reported: "The Liquozone had absolutely no curative effect, but did, when given in pure form, lower the resistance of the animals, so that they died a little earlier than those not treated." Adams wrote that despite its claims as a germicide, "Liquozone may decrease the chances of a patient's recovery with every dose that is swallowed."

The 18 November issue showed some of the public results of the campaign. "Editorial Bulletin" cited nine endorsements of the articles by medical societies and said the supportive letters "are too numerous for us even to attempt to reply to them" but quoted one reader: "You have promised a series of articles. In God's name, what is there yet left of that slew-hole to be shown up?" *Collier's* replied, "A great deal is left."

On 25 November *Collier's* tried to prepare its readers for the next article on the dangers of headache cures that contained acetanilid, "a poison derived from coal-tar," but the warning did not mirror the ferocity of Adams's attack. On 2 December his fourth article, "The Subtle Poisons," was headed by a list of twenty-two deaths attributed to acetanilid. Saying intelligent people could avoid nostrums like Peruna and Liquozone, he warned that users were often enslaved and killed by subtle poisons concealed under a trademark name.

He singled out Orangeine, a headache powder in which the use of acetanilid was stated but unrecognized by the public because of what Adams called dangerous distortion. He said the "wickedness of the fraud" was that while "the nostrum, by virtue of its acetanilid content, thins the blood, depresses the heart, and finally undermines the whole system, it claims to strengthen the heart and produce better blood. Thus far in the patent medicine field I have not encountered so direct and specific an inversion of the true facts."

He carefully laid out his indictment by quoting a doctor who said that one of his patients, a physically fit young woman, died after taking Orangeine powders for insomnia. Adams quoted a coroner's verdict on an eighteen-year-old Philadelphia girl, "Mary A. Bispels came to her death from kidney and heart disease, aggravated by poisoning by acetanilid taken in Orangeine headache powders." Adams urged a skull and crossbones be placed on every package.

His wrath increased when he discussed the "soothing syrups" containing opium and cocaine. The intensity may have been spurred by his realization that a patent medicine had come into his own home. Historian James Young recounted from a 1955 interview: "Although not revealing the fact in his article, Adams knew first-hand about such nostrums' hazardous potential. Returning home from one of his trips, he found it touch and go as to whether his own mother had become addicted to a patent medicine containing an unlabeled narcotic."[11]

In his article Adams charged that mothers used opium- and cocaine-laced preparations to keep their children quiet or docile and that the young became enslaved by the nostrums. He urged that the government forbid the sale of the syrups to end "the shameful trade that stupefies helpless babies, and makes criminals of our young men and harlots of our young women."

The fifth article was scheduled for 23 December. Originally called "The Consumption Cure," the final title, "Preying on the Incurables," might explain why *Collier's* delayed publication until after the holiday season. At the same time the magazine corrected a misleading item in the 4 November "Editorial Bulletin," not written by Adams, that lumped Peruna and Liquozone together as using the "Red Clause." *Collier's*, vowing that it was "emphatically our duty to see that slips in detail are eliminated," absolved Liquozone.

The slips were few. In his first series on patent medicines and in a second four-part continuation on quacks and quackery he cited more than 250 nostrums, concerns, and individuals by name. "There was no sparing of feelings, there was no concealing of names, there was no hiding of institutional secrets," Montrose Moses wrote in 1915.[12] By naming many products and makers of nostrums Adams opened himself and *Collier's* to the greatest threat for muckrakers, libel.

Although Irwin said most muckrakers "shrank from libel suits," he claimed Adams "gloried in the combat." Adams's research was meticulous as he used laboratory reports, quoted from patent medicine literature, cited interviews and letters, described effects from use of the nostrums, and attacked advertisements. He also used court and doctors' records, industry literature, bankruptcy cases, advertising contracts, letters to newspapers and to himself, and transcripts of patent medicine lobbyists' statements to build his cases. Although his material was often sensational in nature, Adams tended to underplay it, holding back information, as did Steffens, who said, "Don't shoot all your am-munition at the first attack." Nonetheless, suits were threatened. Stewart Hol-brook, who consulted with Adams for his *Golden Age of Quackery*, commented that a number of firms instructed lawyers to sue Adams and *Collier's*. "The fa-vorite sum was $300,000," Holbrook wrote. Most threats dissolved. Historian Cornelius Regier said neither Adams nor *Collier's* lost a cent in libel suits, al-though Adams in "Aftermath" said two personal protests were filed with the magazine and two libel suits initiated.[13]

Not only was Adams accurate, he was persistent. He continued his push for federal legislation throughout the series. Adams argued for regulation on the suppliers rather than, as some other reformers urged, laws aimed at the user. As 1905 entered its final month, the government in Washington was now stirring. "Policies change and broaden under pressure of conditions," Adams had written in his first article, referring to federal government foot-dragging. Industry promises of self-regulation did not impress him. He continued advo-cacy, practicing an activism that called for government action.

The growing public opinion on patent medicines and the pure food sup-porters forced President Roosevelt out of a noncommittal position that, Adams said, was because pure food "wasn't political enough to interest him, at least he thought it wasn't." Pressure, however, caused Roosevelt in his 5 Decem-ber 1905 message to Congress to offer a paragraph: "I recommend that a law be enacted to regulate interstate commerce in misbranded and adulterated foods, drinks, and drugs. Such law would protect legitimate manufacture and commerce, and would tend to secure the health and welfare of the consum-ing public. Traffic in foodstuffs which have been debased or adulterated so as to injure the health or to deceive purchasers should be forbidden."[14]

Although the president did not mention patent medicines by name, label-ing of nostrums was encompassed in a pure food bill reintroduced by Sena-tor Weldon B. Heyburn of Idaho the next day. Opposed by the powerful Senator Nelson W. Aldrich of Rhode Island, who had been a wholesale gro-cer, the pure food bill appeared headed for the same suffocating fate that forty-two similar bills had in the Senate and House the previous seventeen years. Patent medicine makers also went on the offensive, joining forces with other groups, including whiskey makers, "to prevent the national government from interfering with what they considered their private property."[15]

In the 13 January 1906 article, "Preying on the Incurables," Adams switched from using one nostrum as a focus to attacking bogus remedies for tubercu-losis, a disease about which he was knowledgeable because of his *McClure's* article. He paraded various patent medicines before the public. He again showed his ability to get inside the industry, as he had with the congenial Hartman and the Liquozone factory, by meeting with nostrum makers, by visiting their places of manufacture, and by finding the "secrets" of their trade.

Adams reported that various nostrums contained morphine, chloroform, hashish, and even prussic acid, ingredients that not only did not cure but might hasten death. The shocker in the article was a coroner's report that had ruled the death of two-year-old Hilda Kreck was caused "by the poisonous effects of opium, the result of drinking the contents of a bottle of Dr. Bull's Cough Syrup." The chemistry professor Saunders had been unable to identify opium in the patent medicine but said it might be masked by other substances, so Adams used a photostatic reproduction of "Verdict in Inquest No. 821" signed by the Cincinnati coroner.

He and the coroner argued the patent medicine should have had a label with a caution or a list of ingredients so the child's mother would have known it was a poison. He attacked the Cincinnati newspapers for not reporting the name of the nostrum and extended his criticism of the press to "A Fraud's Gallery" of fifteen advertisements clipped from two New York newspapers. The article concluded with: "Every man who trades in this market, whether he pockets the profits of the maker, the purveyor, or the advertiser, takes toll of blood. He may not deceive himself here, for here the patent medicine business is the nakedest, most cold-hearted. Relentless greed sets the trap, and death is partner in the enterprise."

In his sixth and intended-as-last patent medicine article, "The Fundamental Fakes," Adams attacked advertisements, testimonials, and the publications that printed them. He hammered at the press by asserting that "printer's ink is the very life-blood of the noxious trade." He criticized the newspaper owners, the religious press, and the purveyors like Hartman of Peruna, the Lydia Pinkham company, and Dr. S. Andrai Kilmer and his Swamp Root. All proprietors promised personal attention for their clients but, Adams noted, all were uninvolved in the operations, or dead. He still challenged the nostrum claims but also featured the victims, using literary devices of the muckrakers.

Adams employed colorful descriptions, anecdotes, and dialogue. Like other muckrakers who used literary style to attract readers to their crusades, he blended facts with images. One Adams scene featured a Chicago physician dining with his family and a newspaper publisher in a western city. The publisher maintained nothing was in his paper "that I couldn't read at the table before my wife, son, and daughter." The physician then began reading the advertisements. One by one the daughter, the son, and their mother left the table.[16]

Adams believed that the correct labeling of patent medicines would bring their downfall. He took his crusade beyond *Collier's* to the medical journals. In an article in the February 1906 *Maryland Medical Journal* he broadened his attack to physicians, saying: "Since entering upon this field of work I have received from physicians enough fundamental misinformation to keep me in jail for the rest of my natural life on libel charges had I accepted one-tenth of it."

The tardiness of physicians, the American Medical Association, and medical journals to protest false advertising and unhealthy preparations had annoyed Adams at the beginning, but the medical profession played a significant role. The doctors responded to the initial articles by providing evidence and support through state medical societies. So did the AMA, which eliminated patent medicine advertising from its *Journal*. In conjunction with P. F. Collier publishing, the AMA then put Adams's initial six articles and Sullivan's "Conspiracy" article into a booklet under the title of *The Great American Fraud* with a 1905 copyright. A revised edition, adding Adams's articles on quacks, came out in 1906 and was priced below cost at a dime for a single copy and thirty-five dollars per thousand. One man bought forty-five thousand that he distributed free. A third edition came out the same year to meet the heavy demand. Two other editions in 1907 and 1912 added other articles, and *The Great American Fraud* sold a combined 150,000 copies by its final printing in 1912. Years later Adams said more than 400,000 copies were circulated.[17]

With the initial series apparently over Adams went south in February to update his information on yellow fever for *McClure's*, investigating the quarantines that had been used in New Orleans since he had visited in 1905. Meanwhile, *Collier's* said the patent medicine makers were lying low until the campaign was over. It pledged to keep up the pressure and that Adams would write additional articles on quacks and quackery.

Events in Washington, however, would dictate other action. Four days after "The Fundamental Fakes," the Senate on 21 February passed a pure food bill 63 to 4. Opponents were from the South, concerned about states' rights. Twenty-two senators abstained, including Aldrich, persuaded to be neutral by a threat from physicians and gentle arm-twisting by Roosevelt. The bill, weakened by amendment, went to the House where it began in the Interstate and Foreign Commerce Committee of Rep. William P. Hepburn of Iowa. The *New York Times* warned the bill faced the "last desperate resistance of its innumerable enemies."[18]

In the House Hepburn began to steer the pure food bill through the hearings. The sessions, which produced more than four hundred pages of testimony in two weeks, were followed by a nineteen-page report on patent medicines in which Representative Edwin Y. Webb of Shelby, North Carolina, who had folded his patent medicine bill into the pure food measure, was quoted. After the hearings, Adams helped Wiley and Representative James R. Mann of Chicago with the phrasing of a stronger patent medicine provision.[19]

Meanwhile, *Collier's* and Adams adopted a new tactic. On 10 March an Adams article on fraudulent food was announced. In "Food or Fraud?" subtitled "A Question for Congress," he attacked lobbyists who sought to stall the bill. While he and *Collier's* tried to unblock the legislation, another event produced an unlikely ally. Next to a 1 March *McClure's* ad in the *New York Times* for an Adams short story was another ad for a new novel, *The Jungle*, by Upton Sinclair.

Turned down for a serial by *Collier's* because of fear of libel and run in the socialist weekly *Appeal to Reason*, the novel about meat packing abuses was intended by Sinclair as a plea for socialist reform of working conditions but instead aroused the public about bad meat. "In other words, I aimed at the public's heart, and by accident I hit it in the stomach," Sinclair wrote seven months later. Roosevelt, incensed by the book, named a commission to investigate. The president also enlisted Senator Albert J. Beveridge of Indiana to add an amendment to the agricultural appropriations bill that would provide for meat inspection. This new approach, seeking regulation against adulterated meat, would directly affect pure food legislation and indirectly its companion patent medicine regulation. Purity became a key issue for an aroused public, a reform-minded Congress, and an aggressive president.[20]

Although Roosevelt's interest in the pure food and drug bill was heightened by his ardor over meat, he was cooling toward the muckrakers. The president was stung by articles in William Randolph Hearst's *Cosmopolitan* by David Graham Phillips on "The Treason of the Senate" that Roosevelt felt were demeaning. In a 17 March speech in the Gridiron Club off-the-record style he attacked muckraking. Then, prodded by favorable comment, he repeated his charges at the dedication of the House Office Building on 14 April.

Referring to *Pilgrim's Progress* by John Bunyan, the president, who had seen the exposure journalists as supporters and then as usurpers of his Progressivism, attacked them as grovelers in the muck. Noting the Interpreter's comments to Christiana, Roosevelt paraphrased: "You may recall the description of the Man with the Muckrake, the man who could look no way but downward, with a muckrake in his hands; who was offered a celestial crown for his muck-rake, but who would neither look up nor regard the crown he was offered, but continued to rake to himself the filth of the floor." Chiding what he saw as "mendacity" by unnamed muckrakers, he claimed there was an "epidemic of indiscriminate assault on character."[21]

Although Roosevelt later moderated his criticism of muckraking by claiming he was mostly concerned with Hearst, journalists Phillips and Steffens reacted as if gored, but not Adams, whose silence indicated his continuing disdain for Roosevelt. He, like fellow muckraker Charles Edward Russell, wore the label as he would a mantle. "All the Adams and Hopkins in him made him love the job of finding and exposing corporate sin. He wielded a mighty rake," Irwin wrote.[22]

The patent medicine lobby was not silent. The use of newspaper columns to bombard *Collier's* had been the tactic of the Proprietary Association, which never took legal action. In the *St. Louis Medical and Surgical Journal* an April editorial by A. H. Ohmann-Dumesnil called Adams a new Ananias. He traced the twenty-two cases of death caused by acetanilid in the "Subtle Poisons" article, labeling them "pipe dreams" and attempting to show other causes of death.[23] Despite Roosevelt's admonition that "the men with the muckrakes are often indispensable to the well-being of society, but only if they know when to stop raking the muck," Adams and *Collier's* kept up the pressure. *Collier's* announced 21 April a seventh article, "Warranted Harmless," would be published the following week. Delaying the second series on quacks, the article repeated earlier charges on deaths caused by acetanilid and on opium in headache powders and cough cures. This unplanned extra article may have been prompted as a public answer to Ohmann-Dumesnil or as a perceived need to push federal legislation in the House where Speaker Joseph G. Cannon had refused to have the bill considered although the committee reported it ready on 10 April.

Adams did not fight just from the sidelines for legislation. Although he had as a primary tenet the adage "He that hath eyes to see, let him see," he differed from many of his muckraking colleagues in that he took an active role in campaigning for legislative reform. Tarbell did not press for legislative action to break up Standard Oil, nor did Steffens ask for outside governmental intervention to correct municipal corruption. Adams had earlier said, "Once my profession succeeds in driving the foe into the open the fight is over for us," but as the crucial time neared in Washington, Adams joined the battle in the House. The legislation had been bottled up until *The Jungle* broke it loose.

Adams even had accepted a watered-down bill in the belief that a law would "give the public a chance to know, not to save fools from their folly."[24]

Adams went to Washington to conduct informal lobbying of the House when later in June the body wrestled with the pure food bill. Cannon, who had received a personal plea in late May from Roosevelt, let the bill come to the floor. Representative Mann, a member of the Commerce Committee and designated by Chairman Hepburn to manage the bill, reported to the House that he had consulted with Adams to compile a list of sixty-one dangerous patent medicines with drug content that should be included on their labels.[25] Mann also placed in the record letters Adams had received on nostrums.

In floor debate Representative James L. Slayden of Texas praised Adams for his "remarkable series of articles." Slayden said that Adams "did more, in my judgment, to advance this very much to be desired reform than the work of any other single man in the country." Adams also drew praise from Sereno E. Payne of his home district; Henry C. Adams of Madison, Wisconsin, former state dairy and food commissioner; and Webb. At one point Mann told the House that Adams had met with him in his House office and they had discussed Mann's successful strategy of accepting an early amendment that he had targeted for reversal as the vote neared.[26]

The House version, stronger than the Senate's, passed 23 June by 241 to 17, the opposition again coming from Southerners espousing states' rights. A Conference Committee resolved the differences in the bills, keeping the House's labeling of habit-forming drugs but removing provisions for setting standards and the providing of samples by nostrum makers. The compromise measure passed 29 June, and Roosevelt signed it the next day.

Success has many fathers. Historian Young said it best when, in assessing the campaign, he wrote, "At the end 'pure' came to mean an absence from meat of the nauseating ingredients Sinclair had alleged, an absence from processed foods of the poisonous preservatives Wiley had condemned, an absence from patent medicines of the dangerous narcotics Adams had excoriated."[27]

With the fight for federal legislation won Adams continued a campaign for state legislation. Although he had testified at a hearing for New York State legislation in March, the bill had been killed in May when a last-minute amendment meant the revised bill could not be printed in time for passage. Seldom discouraged, he fought personally and publicly for his beliefs. In his medical and patent medicine exposure writing he urged education as the means for continuing health progress. "It all resolves itself into a question of education: patient, unremitting instruction of the public through the press, the platform, the pulpit, and the schools." In July he addressed a pure food convention in Hartford, urging stronger state legislation, and wrote "Curbing the Great American Fraud" in *Collier's*, repeating the theme and tracing the successful campaign in Congress and reporting the "complete and overwhelming rout" of the Proprietary Association.[28]

In July Adams also opened his second series of four articles, this time aimed at medical quackery and quacks. Entitled "The Sure-Cure School," the first article concentrated on firms that offered remedies for those with cancer and tuberculosis. Unlike the patent medicines that were sold in drug stores, the mail-order remedies offered cures like the clay paste with which Doctor B. F. Bye made the "preposterous claim" of removing cancer. "His treatment wouldn't remove a wart or cure a mosquito bite," Adams asserted. He drew on his earlier exposés to attack Kilmer, whose Swamp Root he called "one of the most blatant of the patent-medicine swindles" and who ran a "CanCertorium" where Kilmer maintained he could cure cancer.

Besides the "sure cures" and quacks, he continued his relentless criticism of the press in the first article and increased the tempo in the second, "The Miracle Workers," on 4 August. Quoting from advertisements, he attacked healers and legitimate drug companies that made the frauds. He singled out radium that "having occupied the public mind and excited the public fancy, has furnished material for the lively commercial imaginations of the quacks." This element, the discovery of which brought the Nobel Prize in physics to the Curies in 1903, had been used by Adams in his fiction writing with White. Now he looked at the mysterious substance medically.

Radium Rings, Radiozone, and Radol were products that claimed to feature radium, believed to be effective in the treatment of cancer. Of Rupert Wells's Radol Adams reported that chemical analysis had shown it "contains exactly as much radium as dishwater does, and is about as efficacious for cancer or consumption." Young said that the liquid was an acid solution of quinine sulfate with alcohol that produced a bluish fluorescent glow that Wells attributed to radium.[29]

The third article, "The Specialist Humbug," ran 1 September and took on quacks who had specialized practices. Noting the quack "is but an exaggerated and grotesque imitation of the regular practitioner," Adams criticized "the medical guerrillas" for their lack of knowledge and their making diagnoses by mail.

"The Scavengers," the last article in the two-series "Great American Fraud" exposés, ran 22 September, almost one year after the first. His target was the claim to cure alcohol or drug addiction by mail. The thrust was against firms that offered help against addiction but whose compounds contained the very substances, such as morphine, they sought to allay. While concerned about "bracers" sold to alcoholics, he was critical of the "leeches of the uttermost slime" who provided a "vivid illustration of the value of the patent medicine clause in the pure food bill, requiring that the amount of habit-forming drug in any medicine be stated on the label." His reporting led to the only major error of the series, provided by a surprise source—Mark Twain.

Soon after the series began, Adams got a letter from Samuel Clemens complaining about testimonials used by the Oppenheimer Institute, an organization that offered a treatment for alcoholism. Adams went to see the writer on lower Fifth Avenue. Adams told Holbrook: "He hailed me genially and declared the *Collier's* articles were just what the doctor ordered. Then he unfolded what he said was the worst fraud of all, and asserted that it was being perpetrated—naturally enough, he added—by a religious outfit." Adams said he should have been wary because of Twain's antagonism to religious groups, but because he had investigated two drug-and-drink cures by the St. James Society and the St. Paul Association, he tended to believe the story. "I did some investigation after I left Mr. Clemens," Adams said, "but it turned out to be less than enough." One testimonial was from a bishop, who claimed it was a phony and received a correction. To Holbrook, Adams took responsibility: "Although Mark Twain was responsible for getting me into the mess, and expressed himself as most penitent, I blamed myself because, in my great faith in him, I did not investigate in my usual, and if I may say so, rather thorough manner."[30]

Adams's success on patent medicine legislation was not equaled by his attack on quacks. After the series had ended, the *Literary Digest*, which carried newspaper comment on public issues, was so concerned about the lack of discussion that it did a two-part synopsis of the articles. In *Collier's* Adams's last article was followed with a nonbylined "'Strictly Confidential,'" in which he looked at testimonial firms that collected tens of thousands of letters that then were sold to the nostrum makers. It was his last article on patent medicines in 1906.

In 1906 Adams was at the apex of his career as a muckraker. His *Collier's* series established him as a serious magazine writer. His stature was enhanced by the serialization of his and White's "The Mystery," which began in the May 1906 *American Illustrated Magazine* and continued in the renamed *American Magazine*.

Adams was not content just to be a muckraker. He remained dedicated to medical writing. His "Yellow Fever: A Problem Solved" ran in *McClure's* in

June 1906. His peculiar relationship with McClure continued as the publisher still printed his health articles and short stories and even considered him a member of the staff. When McClure was threatened by a possible lawsuit by the Beef Trust, he wrote Baker: "If they should sue us, my notion is to have Sullivan and Sam Adams, probably, and you take up the whole Beef Trust question, and mass together all the material possible." McClure also wanted Adams to write a series of articles, on the alcohol use worldwide and Sunday closings, for a new magazine he was planning.[31]

Adams did not write the articles nor did he become embroiled in a May palace revolt over the magazine's editorship, a title McClure emphatically retained. Junior partner John Phillips plus Tarbell, Baker, Steffens, and Albert Boyden broke away to buy the *American Magazine* in the summer of 1906. Although Adams had two pieces, his and White's serial and an essay on dynamite, in the first issue of the new *American* in October, he did not let the rarity of two bylined pieces sway him. He walked a line between the two camps.

Adams still planned to do "a great deal of free lance article writing for S. S.," according to Irwin, who joined *McClure's* on 1 June 1906 after distinguishing himself with his account of the April San Francisco earthquake. The *Sun* journalist knew what he was getting into after a talk with Adams on 1 May in which the older man warned him about the desperate state of *McClure's*. Irwin nonetheless looked at a position as managing editor with anticipation. "I fancy that Sam Adams and I will be the Steffens and Baker of the reorganization."[32] While Irwin replaced Steffens as managing editor, he did not check with Adams.

While Adams balanced his work between *McClure's* and the *American*, his primary source of publication remained *Collier's*. He was earning five hundred dollars per article plus five cents per word for editorials and occasional pieces in "Editorial Bulletin." The earliest record of his editorial writing showed *Collier's* paying him for a 2 December 1905 editorial. In editorials identifiable as his he wrote about public issues ranging from patent medicine practices to jury duty. He did sporadic editorial writing for *Collier's* for four years.[33]

Although he would make no further commitment to McClure, his editorial writing in *Collier's* led to a new venture. During the summer of 1906 he joined the new *Ridgway's* magazine as chief editorial writer. Planned by Erman Ridgway, the magazine, a forerunner of *Time*, was published in a fourteen-edition format in cities ranging from Boston to San Francisco and from New Orleans to Seattle. The magazine bore the subtitle "A Militant Weekly for God and

Country" and in its fourth edition outlined Adams's duties on the uniform editorial pages: "The District Editors, men of trained selective minds, telegraph the significant news of their sections to the editorial chief of staff, Samuel Hopkins Adams, who welds it into a compact and illuminating summary of comment upon the week's vital events."[34]

His shift to *Ridgway's* editorial writing produced a change in focus. His investigation of nostrums had showed many of the swindlers and quacks to be successful businessmen. Like Asa Soule in Rochester, they became leaders in their communities by generous donations. The power of these barons and the growing influence of business interests and the trusts concerned him.

Writing about twelve editorials a week beginning in October 1906, he occasionally focused on health topics, but the thrust was directed at trusts and increasing business power. For example, on 13 October, he wrote fifteen editorials including attacks on publisher Hearst and trusts, the involvement of a cardinal in politics, a railroad power grab, support of taxing the wealthy, the need for political scrutiny, and the People's Lobby. Week after week, he warned of the dangers of trusts taking over government. He remained optimistic on the ability of America to correct its ills, however, never questioning the system itself.

His belief in fundamental American institutions kept Adams from joining colleagues Steffens, Hapgood, and Russell in support of socialism. He remained a liberal Democrat, and although he might have thought of himself as a socialist in spirit, he did not adopt the philosophy of state ownership. Dismissing socialism as a "catchword" in *Ridgway's*, he did not offer socialistic solutions to the abuses he detailed but instead thought public opinion would produce reform, a false hope.

*Ridgway's* began to fall in November when the magazine cut back its fourteen-city format to a single edition in four cities. In the first issue of 1907 Adams ended his *Ridgway's* editorials. It was a small loss; he was established as an authority on public health, an emerging fiction writer, and a muckraker. Although he did not reach the status of Baker, Steffens, and Tarbell in muckraking assessments, he said later: "That was a good time, a lively time, and I guess we all were taking our lives in our hands. I don't know how many millions I've been sued for, but no trial ever came of it. Yes, a very good time, lots of fun."[35]

# 6

# WRITER
## 1907–1909

O N 25 JUNE 1906 in the lavish roof garden of Madison Square Garden, which he had designed, architect Sanford White was approached by Pittsburgh millionaire playboy Harry Kendall Thaw. At the nightclub with his wife, Charles Dana Gibson's model Florence Evelyn Nesbit, Thaw shot White at point-blank range, killing his wife's former lover. He was taken prisoner almost immediately afterward.[1]

As his brief tenure with *Ridgway's* magazine wound down, Adams in early 1907 took an assignment from the New York *World* to cover the sensational trial. When the Thaw case opened on 23 January 1907, Adams joined some eighty reporters, special writers, and artists assigned to the twelve-week murder case.

The *World's* coverage of the Monday-through-Friday trial included Adams's lead story, often set double column on page one and running over to the second page. The state presented its case on Monday, 4 February. Adams summarized in the next day's paper: "The entire accusation of the State consumed but a trifle more than two hours. In its cold measured logic, one heard the inexorable, remorseless dropping of weight upon weight into the scales of justice." Adams did not shy away from interjecting himself into the trial: "What a contrast when the defense had its inning. I have attended many murder trials, great and small, simple and intricate, in the past fifteen years, but in none have I heard a forecast of the defense, so wandering, so purposeless, so lame, halt and straggling as was the opening address of Thaw's counsel."

A highlight of the trial came on 7 February when Evelyn Nesbit Thaw took the stand. The woman's three days of testimony on her relationship with White were reported in detailed accounts that filled several pages of the *World*. President Roosevelt, among others, complained about what he called the "disgusting details" and asked the post office to consider excluding the offending publications from the mail. Will Irwin felt Adams was "sledging the adjectives while the *Sun* was telling the straight, plain tale" until Brazilian-born Inez Haynes Gillmore convinced Irwin that the reader "needs the emotionalism of the Sam Adams stuff" to show how the lawyers acted and the emotion of the defendant.[2]

Two months after the trial had begun, on Saturday, 23 March, and while the trial bogged down in a battle of psychiatrists debating Thaw's sanity, Adams's name appeared for the last time after thirty-eight bylined stories. His name was not on the stories of the summations nor when the jury failed to reach a verdict on 12 April. The exactness of the two-month duration of his stories may indicate that his assignment ran out. Or he may have wished to return to magazine writing because he did publish a scathing exposé on corruption, "The New York Police Force," in a late March *Collier's*. Or he may have bowed to the pressures of his personal life.

The professional commitments of his work with *Collier's* and then the long trial took a toll on the Adams marriage. Their trip to California in late 1904 was slated to last several months. Beth Adams, however, possibly finding life in the mission town of Santa Barbara as unexciting as in Auburn, returned east when she had a premonition about something happening to their daughter Katherine, who had indeed fallen on the stairs of the Auburn home.[3] Although they made the trip to Washington together in June 1905, Adams spent much of the rest of the year traveling alone on his patent medicine research, occasionally seeing Beth in New York.

By 1 July 1906 they no longer had a home listed in the New York directory, and later in July an Auburn newspaper reported they were at Quisisana on Owasco Lake with their daughters. Irwin said he and Adams discussed their respective marital difficulties on 3 October 1906 but later that month the Adamses visited friends, indicating they were still together. Then all mention of the couple disappeared. On 10 July 1907 they received a final decree of divorce, usually granted by interlocutory judgment three months earlier.[4]

Irwin provided sketchy details in a 1914 letter to Gillmore, indicating that the divorce was a messy affair. Irwin wrote: "As between Sam and Beth, I can't judge. Certainly none in that combination was without blame. There is in it besides all the modern tragedy which comes when one outgrows the other. I have always criticized Sam for the manner in which he got that divorce. He let his Puritanism run riot; and of course he was backed in it by his mother."[5]

The friendship between the men endured, however, and Irwin explained after the divorce: "It was a very different Sam with whom I walked the Bowery last night, through the scenes that thrilled out some of his great newspaper stories, and discussed the loss of enthusiasm and the broadening of view that comes as age creeps on. He is going to Paris for the winter."[6]

The breakup of the marriage produced an unusual family arrangement. Daughter Katherine Adell recalled that her sister Hester told her that the judge split custody of the two girls, with Katherine going with her mother and Hester telling the judge she would like to live with her grandmother. Katherine Adell said she and her mother immediately after the divorce had gone to California where Beth Adams's brother was living.[7] The two Hester Adamses remained in Auburn, with Adams buying 32 Chedell Place. His uncles Woolsey and Stephen Hopkins moved in with his mother and daughter.

The next year Adams tackled the Owasco Lake property, building a new house across the creek from the old bungalow. When Irwin visited in August 1909, he and Adams slept and wrote in the old cottage and ate and socialized in the new house that was "presided over by his mother. . . . Where Sam gets his positiveness, I know. There is something almost theatrical about his imperious way, and what she says goes, even with Sam, which is a quiet and humorous delight to me." The removal of Beth from Adams's life strengthened the already dominating position of his mother. From Irwin's visits to Auburn he gave occasional glimpses of her in letters to Gillmore. "For physique, she is big and heavy, she wears her iron gray hair in an eccentric fashion with the comb in the front, she is growing a short mustache, and you can see that she was splendidly pretty in her youth," Irwin wrote in 1909. By 1912 she was still running the floor business and earning eight hundred to one thousand dollars a year, an income comparable to an Auburn principal. Her financial security did not lessen her seriousness, as Irwin noted: "I can't find humor in her anywhere, nor wit, only deadly literalness. And to see her quarrel with Sam, missing all the point of his half-humorous back-quarreling, is a circus perpetual."[8]

With the young Hester in Auburn Adams shuttled monthly between central New York and New York City. In the city he joined the Players Club and established the Gramercy Park building as his mail address and meeting place when he was in New York. He was equally at home at the Dutch Treat Club's weekly luncheon of artists and writers or at dinner at the Cafe Boulevard or at the Hotel Brevoort where he and Irwin would celebrate a sale. He remained loyal to his old friends from *McClure's* and attended the *Sun* reunions where he was often called on to speak. In Auburn Adams also enjoyed the social

4. Wide Waters as seen from Owasco Lake. Samuel Hopkins Adams Collection. Syracuse University Library.

scene. While Irwin was in Auburn in August 1909, he was introduced at a dinner party to "our crowd." Assessing the inbred Auburnians, the New Yorker called the group "bromidically middle-class to the limit" although Adams "thinks they're pretty."[9]

As Irwin had indicated, in 1908 Adams left New York on 11 March for several months in Europe. He visited Copenhagen, where he got information on its pure-milk program, and Paris. After he returned from Europe, he published in late 1908 and early 1909 a light-hearted three-part series on France. In Paris he became friends with the Booth Tarkingtons and many years later recalled in a letter to Tarkington their visit to Salon des Independants but did not recollect Henri Matisse as being present, adding that he did remember seeing him in Gertrude Stein's studio.[10]

Adams returned to the United States for the summer but was on the move again in fall 1908, this time taking a trip in September to Venezuela for an asphalt company. Later he said he and the firm were unclear about the duties of his final job unconnected with writing. In Caracas he fell into a story as President Cipriano Castro fled a revolution. The New York Times interviewed Adams on his return in December, and then he wrote several articles for Collier's. In a later novel he used material concerning Castro's suppression of news about the bubonic plague and about the mob actions.[11]

Adams's 1905–6 muckraking momentum carried over into 1907 when he was paid $150 for a nonbylined *Collier's* article, "Aftermath," that appeared in January. Summing up the legal aspects of the patent medicine series, the article revealed that only one lawsuit, by Pink Pills for Pale People, was still pending and corrected the Mark Twain criticism of the Oppenheimer Institute treatment for alcoholics.

All was not well, however, with the Pure Food and Drug Act. One reason was that Wiley, given the task of enforcing the act, neglected the drug provisions.[12] In March 1907 Adams wrote Wiley that he found the general disposition was to evade the law as far as possible. Wiley responded 1 April, "Our experience is in accord with yours."[13] On 8 June Adams offered a pessimistic assessment of "Patent Medicines under the Pure Food Law" in *Collier's*. He noted that although some firms had gone out of business or changed their formulae, others blatantly labeled their compounds as containing cocaine, opium, and morphine, or ignored the new law. By July he wrote Wiley he was planning an investigation into nostrum makers and a short article on their operations under the law. A clerk answered by his letter, saying Wiley was out of the country.[14]

So instead of writing about the patent medicine operations, Adams did two articles criticizing the religious press for accepting patent medicine advertising. The minister's son wrote, "Religious! Their tongue is set on fire of hell!" The articles were extensively reprinted in the *Journal of the American Medical Association*, which adopted his title, "The Great American Fraud," in its continuing campaign against patent medicines. Although the religious articles ended his nostrum publication for the decade, in late 1909 he was writing on patent medicines for *Hampton's* magazine.

While his muckraking of patent medicines lessened, his medical reporting continued in *McClure's* and other magazines. His reputation as a health writer was so convincing that two publications claimed he had studied medicine.[15] His last work for *Ridgway's* was an article on Scranton's water supply in February 1907. The next month he again urged public action on "Typhoid: What Are We Going to Do about It?" in the *New York State Journal of Medicine*. He returned to *McClure's* with an article of praise, "Rochester's Pure-Milk Campaign." The article mirrored a widespread opposition to pasteurization and favored milk being pure and germ-free to start with.

In 1908 he wrote two more health articles for *McClure's* on public health officers and milk, drawing on his research in Copenhagen to show a model dairy. His articles sought to bolster public health by countering the public's apathy and by lessening the influence of business interests. He called for a comprehensive national health organization, more accurate reports of vital statistics, and higher appropriations for health departments. His health expertise earned him an assignment in 1909 as part of a social survey of Pittsburgh; his highly critical article, "Pittsburgh's Foregone Asset, the Public Health," appeared in *Charities and the Commons.*

Adams also was back muckraking with three 1909 articles on the "Art of Advertising" in which he discussed techniques, correspondence schools, free offers, and bait-and-switch methods. His *Collier's* advertising series took him almost two years to research, required a massive revision, and omitted his last article, which had been promoted as "The Publisher and the Press." His initial look at advertising would form a foundation for later work.

As he prepared his series and branched out into other endeavors, he did not slacken his editorial writing for *Collier's*. He was given the latitude to choose his topics, and in the summer of 1907 he wrote a muckraking editorial. If his patent medicine articles produced combat, his editorial about a Post Cereal Company advertisement created a war.

*Collier's* and Charles William Post had not been on good terms since the magazine had issued the edict in 1905 that it would no longer accept adver tisements "making claims to medicinal effects." In the same 4 November issue, on the same page as the editorial, was a one-column testimonial advertisement by the Postum Company in which a man said the drink cured him of the nervousness and heart trouble produced by coffee. Conde Nast, *Collier's* advertising director, notified the firm that it must change its copy in the future. Post refused, canceling his advertising in the magazine.[16]

The advertising claims continued in other publications, and another Post product, Grape-Nuts, claimed to ward off appendicitis. On 27 July 1907 Adams published in *Collier's* a condemnation of Grape-Nuts and Postum in an editorial entitled "Futility." The editorial, which Collier said was prepared by Adams "without consultation with any employee of *Collier's*—written solely on his own judgment and initiative," angered Post, who placed an advertisement, "The 'Yell-Oh' Man and One of his Ways" in newspapers throughout the country. The ad charged yellow journalism and blackmail because Post did not advertise in the magazine. Collier responded to the blackmail charge by suing Post for libel. In December 1910 a jury awarded Collier fifty thousand dollars, then the largest libel verdict in New York State, after a stormy trial.[17]

Adams was quick to take up his pen whenever he perceived an injustice. A protest came in 1909 when he was in Irwin's apartment at Washington

Square. As they were watching from a window a parade honoring Henry Hudson and Robert Fulton, police attacked a crowd of tenement dwellers. In a scathing letter to the *New York Times* the next day, 1 October, Adams belittled the handling of the immigrant crowd by the police, noting they used clubs on an elderly woman, on a mother with two little children, and on an Italian passerby.

When he was not getting angry over something, his independent course in writing was taking new forms. Beginning in 1906 he turned increasingly to fiction although he sought to maintain a balance between his story and nonfiction writing. In 1911 he said he expected to combine them someday into a novel that could tell the inside facts.[18]

He joined a growing list of journalists who made the transition from newspaper to fiction writing, including Ray Stannard Baker, Willa Cather, Stephen Crane, Richard Harding Davis, Theodore Dreiser, William Dean Howells, Jack London, David Graham Phillips, Mark Twain, and John Greenleaf Whittier. Late in life, Adams told an interviewer he wrote for no particular reader. He said he wrote, instead, for himself, for what he wanted to tell. "I've never written a line of fiction to give the world a message or float a banner."[19] Some early short stories belied the statement.

During the second half of the decade he published ten short stories, most of which had a crusading aspect. "A Matter of Principle" told an idealistic story of a Bowery waif who rejected life in a gang and was Adams's first magazine story that used his knowledge of the East Side. Another short story, "B. Jones, Butcher," told about a meat seller who battled the Beef Trust. Two stories had crusading themes on business corruption. "Balanced Account" told of a bribed juror who turned against a crooked contractor after his building collapsed, injuring the juror's wife. "Three Men" was an idealistic story about a mill owner, his son, and a laborer in an attack on exploitation.

He also used his medical knowledge in his fiction. Adams first had published in September 1905 a short story, "Last Resort," about a man who believed he had progressive paralysis but was tricked with a placebo into walking. He dealt with typhoid in "The Substitute" that told of a mother's search for her army son in a typhoid hospital at Montauk during the Spanish-American War. He combined a serious theme, the yellow fever epidemic in New Orleans, with a love story in "Medico-Strategist." In 1909 he used the scourge of tuberculosis in a Poe-like mystery story, "Grimsden House."

The mystery story was another type of writing that Adams had been developing. Near the end of 1904 or early in 1905, he used a story he had heard at

Hamilton College to write "Forsaken Mountain" for the *Collier's* short story contest, and the seventy-five hundred word story was chosen with sixty-eight others for publication. The story concerned two men stranded on a mountain where one died and the other, a sleepwalker, kept bringing the body back into the cabin, making the sleepwalker think the man was not dead. Sleepwalking fascinated Adams, and he wrote "The Adventures of a Somnambulist" based on his Hamilton roommate, Schuyler Brandt, in *American*.

As his short story publishing continued apace, his work with Stewart Edward White reached fruition with the book publication of *The Mystery* by McClure, Phillips, and Company. Illustrated by Will Crawford, *The Mystery* had a handsome cover with a pistol-brandishing, bare-footed seafarer sitting on top of a mysterious chest that figured prominently in the story.

The final version was in three parts. The first section told of the United States cruiser *Wolverine*'s discovery of the deserted schooner *Laughing Lass* in 1901, of putting a crew aboard her, having a mysterious light throw the compasses off, and then finding the schooner again with no one on it. The cruiser, however, did find a drifting dory with journalist Ralph Slade, who directed the ship to go to a volcanic island. The second section was Slade's account of a scientific expedition by the *Laughing Lass* led by Doctor Karl Schermerhorn. It told of the adventures on the island, including a seal hunt, a mutiny, a volcanic eruption, and a mysterious substance taken from the island in the doctor's chest. The final part returned to the present, and the reader learned the doctor's chest contained a powerful radium that drove men off the schooner and at the end dissolved the mystery ship.

The response of the critics to the combination of mystery and science story showed mixed reviews with the characterizations of the mutineers, likened to Robert Louis Stevenson's pirates, getting the most praise. Although no sales nor royalty reports remain, *The Mystery* did make *Bookman's* bookseller listings on three months. A lesser measure of success came from a letter inviting White and Adams to join an expedition, free of charge, to locate the mysterious island with its radioactive substance. Adams complained to *Bookman*: "White being notoriously a fireside loiterer, declined to go. Thus I lost my chance of untold riches."[20]

After *The Mystery* Adams decided to strike out on his own as a novelist. He turned to "The Flying Death," the serial in *McClure's*. Written originally in the form of two letters, two statements, and a telegram, "The Flying Death" told of the killing of a man by what seemed to be a surviving pteranodon, a prehistoric reptile. After a subsequent murder, a scientific justification for the beast's survival, and another attempted murder, the denouement revealed the murders were committed by a cousin of the first victim, a juggler who walked on his hands to create the impression of reptile tracks.

In the novel *The Flying Death* Adams expanded the cast of characters and the number of victims, added two love story elements, extended the episodic adventures, and even produced the creature in the final chapter, only to slay it. The result, Adams admitted, was that although it was a good short serial, it was a poor novel.[21]

According to the *Bookman* bookstore listings, *The Flying Death* placed fifth in Louisville in April. That was the only mention in the United States although the Canadian edition by Musson was on the list in May and June. Although certainly not a bestseller, the novel established Adams as an author.[22] For a dedication to *The Flying Death* he chose his roommate, Brandt, of whom he said, "In token of a friendship which, begun at old Hamilton, has endured and strengthened as only college friendships can, for an unbroken twenty years."

Indeed, in the first decade of the century Hamilton played an important role in Adams's life. Between graduation in 1891 and 1905 he made occasional forays to Clinton to attend Alpha Delta events and commencements and, when he became advertising manager of *McClure's*, to seek an assistant. Then in 1905 the Board of Trustees, under the leadership of Melancthon Woolsey Stryker, who had been replacing clergy members of the feeder college for seminaries with prominent alumni such as Senator Elihu Root and attorney Dan Burke of Utica, elected the muckraker as a member of the board. He was promptly named to the Press Committee.

After he became a trustee, he and his college friend Weaver in September 1905 established a '91 Hamilton Manuscript Prize to encourage "original literary effort." The winner of the first prize in 1906, with a rakish story entitled "The Precipice: A Story of Bohemia," was Alexander H. Woollcott. When Woollcott won the prize a second time in his senior year, he asked to see Adams. Adams met him on the library steps after, Adams recalled, "an odd figure came into view, crossing the campus with an undulated prance. The youth was clad in excessively wrinkled and bagged trousers, a misshapen corduroy coat, grimy sneakers, and a red fez with gilt tassel." Despite the attire Adams was impressed "with the owlish gravity of the eyes behind the large lenses, and an air not so much cocky as confident."[23]

After meeting Woollcott, Adams agreed to write a letter to former *Sun* newsman Carr Van Anda, managing editor of the *New York Times*, which was becoming a leading newspaper. Although Van Anda did not have an immediate opening, he hired Woollcott in the fall. Woollcott became a dramatic critic, and his relationship with Adams continued for the rest of his life.

The trustee election was not the only honor Adams received from his alma mater. The local chapter of Phi Beta Kappa in June 1907 elected him to membership, a high honor considering his academic record. He showed his pride by wearing the key in later years.[24]

Adams's success at Hamilton College was not mirrored in his relationship with *Collier's*. Beginning with his patent medicine series, he had published short stories, exposure articles, humor, and editorials in the magazine. With his advertising series running he was preparing a new look at patent medicines. Then Irwin reported to Gillmore in June 1909 that Collier, who inherited his father's business, had said "buying high-priced manuscripts was going to stop, which may be a notice of dismissal. In the Players at lunch I found Sam Adams and he'd just had his—Collier had called off three patent medicine articles already ordered. Sam was madder than a wet hen and talking suit. We held a grouch meeting that lasted most of the afternoon."[25]

Collier's move may have been prompted by the advertising series that cost more than six thousand dollars. After two editorials on 31 July 1909, Adams and *Collier's* severed connections. The break was complete. Irwin said in August: "Five libel suits have been filed against Sam's advertising series! Hapgood says plainly he's through with Sam. Can't afford the luxury of a man who can't write a straight article without roasts. I tried to talk for Sam, but it was no use!"[26]

Adams received three hundred dollars on his patent medicine articles and forty dollars for the two editorials as final payments, bringing his 1909 total from the magazine to $1,614, about half of the three to four thousand dollars he received the previous three years. Although beset by increasing financial woes, *Collier's* continued on its muckraking path. Adams, who had other markets such as *Everybody's* and *American*, went to Owasco Lake.[27]

At Quisisana the writer expanded the new house by adding a farmhouse as an ell to the back of the main structure. He entertained friends by bringing them by special boat to a shore dinner and joined his uncle Woolsey Hopkins as a speaker at the Owasco Lake Anglers. His theme was to be "Catching Fish with a Muckrake," but Adams, who said his fishing consisted of "waiting," declined to tell fish stories. Instead, he gave a lighthearted tale of talking to a seer who told him "when you have nothing to say, tell stories."[28]

Although the *Collier's* market was closed to Adams, Finley Peter Dunne of the *American* asked him to document a story Thomas Mott Osborne of Auburn

5. Samuel Hopkins Adams with an unknown friend fishing on Owasco Lake in front of Adams's summer home, Wide Waters. Samuel Hopkins Adams Collection. Courtesy of Syracuse University Library.

had told Adams during a train ride. It concerned a comment by Secretary of State Philander C. Knox, who in early 1909 succeeded Root, about politics being a dirty business, and Adams wrote the prison reformer for specifics. Ready to leave for the winter in California, Adams said Dunne wanted to use it, but Osborne was unable to locate the Knox speech. What Osborne needed was a detective, but it was Adams who would find one.[29]

# 7

# DETECTIVE
## 1910–1912

Y THE second decade of the twentieth century the detective story had become a staple in the nation's newspapers and magazines. Arthur Conan
Doyle had made his Sherlock Holmes stories a sought-after commodity, and
many American authors rushed to capitalize on the public's insatiable appetite
for more stories. Adams, who had written mystery stories but none with a de
tective, was ready for the challenge.

As he headed for California in January 1910, however, his thoughts were not
on detectives but on magazines. Along with his article criticizing enforcement
of the food and drug act in *Hampton's,* a fantasy short story, "Chosen Instrument," told about a violinist who meets a ghost. His "Romance of the Right-
of-Way" that combined business greed with humor cracked the *Saturday
Evening Post* market in May.

Political and business improprieties were Adams's nonfiction topics in 1910
as he returned to the concern he had expressed in the *Ridgway's* editorials.
After publishing "The Joke's on You" in which he detailed legislative trickery
in helping sugar, railroad, shipping, and petroleum monopolies, he wrote
"The Real Reason for High Prices" in which he sought to deal with the symptoms of a cost of living "swollen like river in the flood." He blamed Wall Street
and the monopolies for inflating prices to offset overcapitalization and urged
action, lest "the consumer become the consumed."

At last he proposed remedies for, rather than just giving the causes of, economic distress. His economic reform, however, was mired in the traditional
system and offered little new. He urged a countercentralization of power by
use of commissions to limit industrial and railroad capitalization and to tell

the trusts, "You shall not charge one fraction of a mill above what will give you a fair return on a fairly estimated investment."

The next year he continued his economic concern but returned to symptoms rather than cures. "Lemon in the Tariff" warned of a conspiracy by California growers to establish a lemon monopoly. An answer he rejected, as he had in *Ridgway's,* was socialism, which he said was "trying to befool the people by a catchword."[1]

His economic concerns lapped over into his detective story writing. Adams seized upon monopolies and political corruption as villains in his stories. For his detective hero he rejected a policeman, for whom he had little regard, and sought to create a distinct personality for the sleuth. His background as a police reporter and in investigating patent medicines had earned him a reputation that was mirrored in a 1909 identification in his *Auburn Daily Advertiser* as "author, detective, and writer of stories and magazine articles."[2] The character he devised was part alter ego and part wishful hoping.

To make his hero different from other American detectives he took the model of the British aristocrat and fashioned a self-sufficient man. His detective was Adrian Van Reypen Egerton Jones, whose given name initials A. V. R. E. produced Average Jones. He defined his detective as having the distinction of being inconspicuous. The setting for most of the stories was the fictional Cosmic Club at New York's Gramercy Park, a similar location to Adams's beloved Players Club. To Sherlock Holmes, Adams owed his modus operandi. Holmes had occasionally read the agony advertisements in newspapers, and Average Jones got the leads for his investigations from the ads in the paper for which he was an Ad-Visor. His hero also had Holmes's dilettantish interest in science. Science allowed Adams to arm his villains with a variety of weapons and provided his detective hero with the means to solve intricate cases.

With his detective elements in place Adams sought a market. He found the struggling *Success* magazine that was changing from covering the successful man to running public commentary and fiction by Zane Grey. Fiction was the responsibility of his former *Collier's* colleague Sam Merwin, who bought four Adams detective stories.

Adams's initial story, "The B-Flat Trombone," used science to uncover a plot to assassinate a politician by using a trombone to break a glass vial of acid suspended above explosives under a booby-trapped chair. He relied on his scientific knowledge of insects in his second story, "Red Dot," with a poisonous spider distinguished by a red dot on its back. His research on dangerous insects formed the basis not only for the tale but also for two nonfiction articles.

The "Red Dot" was tied to "Warring on Injurious Insects" in the *American* and "Poison Bugaboo" in *Everybody's*. The first article lauded the Department of Entomology for trying to stop the billion-dollar yearly destruction by insects including the boll-weevil and gypsy moth. The second sought to debunk the deadly reputations of snakes and insects, including the "Red Dot." Reaction to the second article was collected by government entomologist Leland O. Howard, whom Adams profiled the next year.[3] In "Red Dot" Adams also had the Canned Meat Trust indicted, a social theme of meat adulteration. American writers frequently inserted social statements into their detective stories.

The danger of great wealth was featured in the story, "Pin Pricks," in which he dealt with the threats of a blind man against a millionaire. He concluded the series with "The Mercy Sign," a long story in which Adams's knowledge of chemistry disclosed the handwritten word *mercy* was the formula for the deadly poison cyanide of cacodyl. While the Average Jones four-story series was running, *Success* said it hoped more would appear but "that depends on Mr. Adams."[4] Adams agreed to do more stories but moved his detective around.

When he was in California with White, Adams made a trip to Baja California. It produced an article, "Tenderfooting for Mountain Sheep," in *Sunset* and the locale for Average Jones in "Open Trail" in November. In "The Fire-Blue Necklace" Average Jones sought some missing jewelry. The story featured his use of real names, including his classmate George Weaver, a practice he would lessen in future work. As 1911 began, Average Jones tackled "The Man Who Spoke Latin," an off-beat story that would later intrigue anthologist-author "Ellery Queen." Adams switched the setting to Baltimore, where he had visited Johns Hopkins, and then sent his detective to New England to find the kidnapped son of a minister in "Big Print."

In February Adams sold the book rights to *Average Jones*. His publisher of the first two novels, McClure, was out of business by 1911. He may have found publishers Bobbs-Merrill through Sam Miller, a classmate, also in Indianapolis. Or the contract might have been the work of a literary agent, Carl Brandt.

Brandt was in his early twenties in 1911 but already had the courtliness of a Southern gentleman and the bawdy wit of a New Yorker. He and his brother, Erdman, were the sons of the house physician at the Homestead Hotel in Hot Springs, Virginia, but had gone to live with a Baptist clergyman and his wife because his father felt they were being spoiled by the wealthy Homestead guests. Orphaned at sixteen, Carl learned to live by his wits and to fight for what he wanted. With a handshake, Adams and Brandt, whom author Stephen

Birmingham called a shrewd and exceptionally graceful trader, formed a life-long alliance.[5]

For the book Adams added cross-references in the stories and transformed a detective Everett King story, "The Million-Dollar Dog," which he had sold independently to *Red Book Magazine,* into an Average Jones story of the discovery of a missing dog through beetles. He retitled "Flash-Light" to "The One Best Bet" in which he used the unusual detective theme he had employed in the first story of the trombone, that of preventive detection.

Adams sent the completed manuscript to Bobbs-Merrill, which paid five hundred dollars on receipt in April 1911 to go with the five hundred dollars upon the contract signing in February and five hundred dollars in October when *Average Jones* was published. The book sales were not strong enough to make *Bookman*'s revised "Book Mart" of the top six books in demand, but it sold 5,245 regular copies, 250 in Canada, and 2,000 cheap editions for a total of $930.50. The failure to make the $1,500 advance did not discourage Bobbs-Merrill, which probably still made money and must have felt the public was interested in the new detective.[6]

But Average Jones was no more. The short run of Average Jones was emblematic of detective story publishing in which most American writers produced only one or two collections of stories. After ten tales, Adams abandoned the detective to the later chagrin of anthologists Hugh Greene, Queen, and Howard Haycraft.[7] *Success* also vanished in 1912. The Ad-Visor title survived for another day. So did the detective format, but this time a scientific sleuth, Chester Kent, was in the *Sunday Magazine of the New York Tribune* newspaper.

Adams introduced the character in a short story, "The Message," in November 1911. Like Average Jones, Kent was an ordinary-looking man of independent wealth. Unlike Jones, he was a scientific professor and a secret adviser to the federal Department of Justice. Political and corporate corruption was present, but the story was a murder mystery in which three miscreants died while receiving a telephoned message. The villain used electricity to charge the phone receiver.

"The Message," billed as an entry in a prize story competition, set the scene for an announcement that a Chester Kent serial, "The Great Game," would begin in December. Daily for six weeks, excluding 31 December, the story of a mysterious manacled corpse unfolded. Set in a locale similar to Scituate, in Massachusetts, where Will Irwin and Inez Gillmore summered and Adams had visited, the story featured a romantic subplot and a cast of unusual characters including a mystic, an artist, and a mysterious Bohemian woman.

The final installment ran on 14 January 1912, and Adams signed a book contract 13 February with Bobbs-Merrill. After he put the novel together from the serial, he delivered the manuscript in May for September publication under its new title, *The Secret of Lonesome Cove*. Although *Average Jones* had received little critical notice, his new detective novel got the attention of more reviewers, not always to the good.[8] The sales of the novel were close to *Average Jones* as 5,562 regular, 350 Canadian, and 7,100 cheap editions were sold for a total royalty of $1,038.05, a second failure to equal another $1,500 advance.[9]

The new book did demonstrate his ability to exploit different markets. Initially run as serial in a newspaper magazine, the parts were put together as a novel, and then almost two years later the novel was taken apart and sold to newspapers as a serial, similar to *The Mystery* that had been serialized after it appeared in book form. Both competing newspapers in Auburn carried the serial of *Lonesome Cove*.

Before the book was published, Adams continued his stories with a two-parter, "Chester Kent Cures a Headache," involving attempted murder by dynamite. A fourth Kent story, "The Case of John Smith," about a man who was presumed murdered but who died accidentally, was announced on 8 September but did not run until 1 December, indicating a flagging interest in the detective.

It certainly ended Adams's interest in him. The Smith case was the last Chester Kent detective story. He enjoyed writing detective stories and even acting the part, such as when he told *Bookman* in January 1912 of a flaw in a Sherlock Holmes tale. Citing Adams's evidence, the magazine suggested Doyle abandon the form. It did not need to suggest the same to Adams, who wrote a newsman in 1916 that he had left the detective field. He said he had run out of plots.[10]

Adams channeled his writing energy into health. In his article "Guardians of the Public Health" in July 1908 Adams had been intrigued by the Chinese idea of preventive medicine in which an individual paid a physician to keep him well. He developed the concept for a four-part series, "The Health Master," in the stylish fashion magazine *Delineator*. In the series a wealthy family hired a Doctor Strong to protect them from various personal health threats. After the series, he began adding more examples of the health concerns. "Remade Lady" told how good diet and exercise programs could transform an individual. "Magic Lens, with Several Sequels" about proper eye care was followed by "Red Placard" on the need to quarantine households where diseases such as typhoid were present.

The need for public awareness of health dangers such as typhoid also was a theme in his nonfiction writing in which he attacked public health secrecy. In his medical writing Adams had been critical about the failure of communities and physicians to report disease threats. His concern was underscored by his belief that the public health and medical professions were so ineffectual that individuals had to seek help through voluntary groups. The groups needed informed citizens because, in his words, "in general, it is to the public-spirited citizen and not to the public-supported officeholder that we must look for leadership."[11]

In 1910, two years after his original article on public health in Pittsburgh, he returned to the city for *Survey* with "Tomfoolery with Public Health." He found political abuses and decried secrecy in public health. The initial typhoid article had detailed how an epidemic of the fever at Cornell University had been hushed by businessmen in Ithaca, and he had attacked the political and economic pressures that had delayed community action on yellow fever in New Orleans in 1905. He urged public disclosure in his "Guardians of the Public Health" in 1908 in which he saw widespread secrecy as "the national hygienic failing" caused by business exerting "a malign influence, and usually an incredibly stupid one." In "Tomfoolery," he attacked Pittsburgh's Health Department for not revealing the incidence of tuberculosis found in a house-to-house canvass by nurses.

From 1910 to 1912 Adams's magazine writing was prolific, more than thirty-five short stories and articles. He probably made between eight thousand and ten thousand dollars a year from book royalties, and sales of serials, short stories, and articles, some of which were published in a newly reopened market, *Collier's*.

Adams's return to *Collier's* in 1912 could have been caused by the magazine's successful defense against the United States School of Music, a firm named by Adams in his advertising series. The June 1911 trial had attracted attention, with New York newspapers assigning special reporters to cover the fifty-thousand-dollar suit. The jury, which reportedly was 10-2 in favor of the magazine, failed to reach a verdict. Seven months later Adams was back on the attack on a familiar topic.

Alerting the public was the goal of his return to patent medicines because many conditions that he had fought were uncorrected. The 1906 law had been weakened significantly, and patent medicine advertising continued to run in the nation's newspapers, often masquerading as news stories. In the 1910 Hampton's article "What Has Become of Our Pure Food Law?" Adams charged that the law had been subverted by Roosevelt's appointment of a Referee Board of Consulting Scientific Experts that had hamstrung Wiley's efforts. Since then, Wiley's friction with Secretary of Agriculture James Wilson had intensified, and the United States Supreme Court in May 1911 had ruled that although patent medicine labels must list ingredients, proprietors were free to claim for the product whatever cures or virtues they pleased. When Adams wrote in Hampton's, "It is the law that is being poisoned, and in its corruption every citizen is corrupted," he was stating one of his basic themes, the development of a dangerous conservatism created by governmental favor and judicial ignorance.

The Democratic Adams, who had little use for Republican William Howard Taft, still harbored a Progressive's impulse for reform. In "The Fraud Medicines Own Up" in a January Collier's the muckraker lashed out at the Supreme Court ruling, showing offending labels and demanding Congress take remedial action. He next reported on a cynical patent medicine salesman in "Tricks of the Trade," followed with "The Law, the Label, and the Liars" that dealt with the government political subversion of the law, taking Secretary Wilson to task and demanding the Department of Agriculture be purged. In "The Fraud above the Law" he detailed the operations of the Kilmer family of Binghamton, famous for the Swamp Root patent medicine.

Adams's steady work produced income that gave him a lifestyle that allowed the single man great latitude to travel, entertain, and set his own time schedule. Foreign travel was one indication of his resources although regular trips were no longer high on his agenda. After his two trips to Europe in 1908 and 1909, he traveled abroad in February 1912, hoping to link up with Irwin for a visit to Rome. His stay in London resulted in a light-hearted account in Collier's entitled "Votes (Whang!) for (Biff!) Women (Smash!!!)," telling of his experiences with store window–breaking suffragettes. It joined two other light travel articles during 1912: an account of a pickup baseball game south of the border and "Ingenuous Impressions," a humorous narrative of a motor tour of France.

In Paris he met with author Meredith Nicholson and Indianapolis friends. Irwin put off his Rome trip, and in mid-April Adams booked his return, on the

*Titanic.* At the last minute, he told Stewart Holbrook, he delayed his departure. "Before I left England a cabled report from the United States had me among those who went down with the ship. The canard survived repeated denials over several years." The near miss apparently slaked his thirst for Europe; he never returned.[12]

Back home, he found Wiley had resigned under fire. He also found the exposing of patent medicines and quackery was now being aggressively pursued by the American Medical Association under the leadership of Dr. Arthur J. Cramp. He had pushed the publication of Adams's *The Great American Fraud.* The last edition was published with a notice that "some of the nostrums and concerns described in earlier articles have gone out of existence; the composition of some preparations has changed, while the claims that were made for many of the products have been modified since Mr. Adams brought the matter to the attention of the public." With the loss of Wiley, the increased activist role by the AMA, and an amendment to the law, he turned to other matters.[13]

During the period Adams had to balance his marketplace in New York with his home in Auburn, which he tried to visit monthly for one week at a time. His daughter Hester was growing up, entertaining friends at a birthday party, taking dancing lessons, acting in a play, and during the summer having her friends visit Quisisana. Adams would fish for bass and play golf and tennis, occasionally in tournaments.

Sometimes he mixed business with pleasure. When Irwin wanted to do a series on the high cost of living for the *Saturday Evening Post*, Adams invited him to Auburn. Irwin was more critical of "our crowd," observing: "The general dense ignorance of the Bridge-playing, country-club, rich American Tory woman makes Darkest Africa look like the Athens of Pericles." Nonetheless, Irwin found helpful sources, including a young lawyer earning two thousand dollars a year, for his series.[14]

The friendship of Adams and Irwin was noted by Jesse Lynch Williams, who said that when Adams came to New York, "he lives and fights with his old friend, . . . Will Irwin." Although they argued politics, their levels of concern were different. As Progressives sought power in 1912, Irwin actively joined the Bull Moose campaign of Roosevelt. Adams, aloof to Taft and Roosevelt, did not join in the Progressive quest.[15] A Wilsonian Democrat, he limited his activity to voting.

From Irwin, Adams adopted his writing regimen of rising at about five, writing letters, having a light breakfast, working with a goal of one thousand words whether inspired or not, and then joining friends or exercising after noon. His friends in New York ranged from Franklin Pierce Adams—known as F. P. A. to those who read his "Conning Tower" column—to playwright A. E. Thomas, a former *Sun* reporter and frequent tennis opponent. In a sketch on Adams, Moses concluded, "The friends who talk with him are linked with him because of the battles they have fought together."[16]

Adams lent his name to various causes. Although he shunned an activist role, he was on the executive committee of the National Consumers League and a member of the National Committee for the Prevention of Tuberculosis, of the Committee of One Hundred on Public Health, and of the National Conference of Charities. He also joined the Authors' League of America, of which Irwin was an active member.

Although he gave mostly lip service to national groups, Adams actively participated on the Board of Trustees at Hamilton College. His alma mater remained close to his heart, but his participation was becoming more visceral. His roles took many forms. At a meeting of the New York alumni association in January 1910 he was accused of "taking liberties" by removing Lloyd Stryker from a list of nominees for its board. The action indicated a growing breach between Adams and the president, the father of Lloyd Stryker. On the board Adams led an override of President Melancthon Stryker in 1911 on the appointment of librarian Joseph Ibbotson.[17]

During the next few years he and the trustees grappled with a number of issues, including strengthening the power of the faculty, creating an alumni advisory council, revising entrance requirements, and updating the curriculum. Adams, who had been reappointed in 1912, was chairman of the centennial observation. To help with the centennial the college named four undergraduate aides. One was sophomore Carl Carmer, who first met Adams on the tennis courts as an opponent in a doubles match. "After two sets of chasing sharply angled balls," Carmer recalled, "we realized his tennis certainly wasn't cricket."[18] Over the years Adams and Carmer became close friends.

Hamilton also was a setting for a story in *American*, which he wrote to commemorate his twentieth reunion. The 1911 short story, "The Long Tryst," was based on a chance remark by Senator Root that Hamilton had once been co-educational. In college publications Adams said, "By what process of crystallization a short story plot formulates itself in the mind, is a matter beyond the explanation of any writer." Yet, in one of his few discussions of his creative process, he added, "For a year or more I had harbored the notion of writing a story, the scene of which should be laid on campus, and the plot of which should deal with the mysterious subpersonality revealed in somnambulism."[19]

The writing of the story took him several weeks, and the result was a mysterious tale of a young man named Donald Laurie who came to the college his great-grandfather had left in 1812 after being expelled for an indiscretion with a female student. During his sleepwalking Donald was seen with a young woman and at the end was found dead at her grave. The short story was one of his best and was in a 1929 anthology for college students by Blanche Colton Williams.[20]

Adams also went into the classroom. In January 1910 he told a Hamilton seminar in journalism that a newspaper like the New York *World* uninfluenced by paid interests and not susceptible to advertising influence was the most powerful enemy of corruption. That may have been prompted by his close association with Irwin, who wrote a fifteen-part series on newspapers in *Collier's*. Irwin said the articles had disappointed Adams "who favored straight muckraking" rather than Irwin's decision to forget "his original goal of merely muckraking in order to delve more deeply into the origins, purposes and principles of journalism."[21]

Adams was more than casually interested in the newspaper's role in society. When he had been a journalist on the *Sun*, he had toyed with using the reporter as a hero in fiction. After he left the newspaper, he said he "began to see the newspaper as it really is." The newspaper he saw was one controlled by the outside hidden influence of quack doctors, ward politicians, public utility magnates, newspaper proprietors, and millionaires who forced newspaper business managers to set news policies "in the interests of the till."[22] He remembered a critical 1909 speech in Rochester and his continued questioning of the policies of the press in running nostrum advertising.

As Progressive muckraking ebbed, Adams let it go unwept, choosing instead to put aside exposure reporting and take what he had learned about society, business, and people into long fiction. In his exposés he had written much showing the effects of medical frauds, governmental secrecy, and news manipulation but he said the novel form allowed him to address the causes. He knew there were things he could say in fiction that he had been unable to detail in his previous work.

Adams began drawing together the currents of his life — newspapers, patent medicine investigations, concern about great wealth and political corruption, and public health—into a coherent look at the world as he knew it. Moses later said, "If the novel is not, strictly speaking, the autobiography of Samuel Hopkins Adams, it is the reflection of his professional judgment, and the measure of his spiritual reach."[23]

Adams maintained a faith that idealism would triumph over corruption, as noted years later by the *New York Times*. Even in his Rochester speech, he said: "No body of workers are more capable and more loyal to the honor of their profession than journalists. The curse is not within, but it comes from the outside."[24]

To show the inner workings of the press he chose to have his hero buy a badly run upstate New York newspaper. To incorporate nostrums Adams modeled the hero's father into a patent medicine millionaire based on an old antagonist, Hartman of Peruna fame, with an added dose of the pioneer "medicine man" experiences of the father of John D. Rockefeller—the Rockefellers having lived many years earlier on the main road above Wide Waters. For his nostrum operation he used the Binghamton operations of the Kilmer family, known for its Swamp Root and cancer cures. He modeled the locale of the novel, the city of Worthington, on Rochester. Adams chose a title of *Whose Bread I Eat* from the old Scottish proverb: "Whose bread I eat—his song I sing" but agreed to a change to *The Clarion*, the name of his fictional newspaper.[25]

The hero was Harrington "Hal" Surtaine, who having returned from college and four years in Europe, was unaware of the corruption underlying the family fortune. Thus he was so concerned when his father's popular nostrum "Certina" was attacked by the city's newspaper that he bought the paper. To show the inner workings of the newspaper Adams introduced an old-timer, Ellis McGuire, who proclaimed that "buying a newspaper doesn't make a newspaper man" and then went on to teach Surtaine, and the reader, the business.[26]

Hal Surtaine became a crusading editor who vowed to print only the truth. From this idealistic premise of giving the news "without fear or favor,"[27] Adams showed the results by methodically isolating his hero and placing him in financial and personal jeopardy. Surtaine championed the efforts of Doctor Merritt, the city's health officer, in a typhoid epidemic in the tenements. Unfortunately, one of tenements was owned by the woman he loved, Esme Elliott, who had already been upset by Hal printing a story about an accident involving one of her close friends. Local businessmen preparing for Old Home

Week were outraged when the paper exposed the epidemic. Libel suits were threatened, advertising was withdrawn, and the building was dynamited by a mob, placing the paper on the verge of bankruptcy.

The young editor confronted his father and charged that the patent medicine business was "all lies! Lies and murders!"[28] Nonetheless, one of Adams's best characterizations was of the old charlatan, reflecting a grudging admiration for Hartman. The sympathetic portrayal was surprising for the hardened muckraker Adams, who, as 1912 ended, wrestled with his book's many themes, subplots, and characterizations.

# 8

# ROMANTIC
## 1913–1914

WHILE HIS NOVEL *The Clarion* preoccupied Adams professionally in 1913, his personal life was taking a dramatic turn. Letters between Irwin and Gillmore, whose own friendship was blossoming into romance, gave insights into Adams. She was not taken with Irwin's best friend but maintained a politeness balanced by her suspicions. In a perceptive 1910 letter she wrote from San Francisco where she spent considerable time during her separation before her divorce she had analyzed Adams: "Do you know I think, he spends most of his time trying to find congenial people to associate with? You see he's suffering from the ennui that comes to a man suddenly and swiftly released from domestic ties. . . . He'll be married before he knows it—he's just ripe for the first woman who interests him enough."[1]

Gillmore was wrong on her last point. A relationship between Adams and her younger sister, Edith "Daisy" Haynes Thompson, estranged from her husband, was thought by Irwin to be serious, but the friendship resulted only in her becoming Adams's typist. He was also linked with other women. An actress said she and the author were engaged. At a party Adams was accosted by another woman who said he had trifled with a friend while in England. But none were as serious as his infatuation with illustrator Rose O'Neill.

Adams became interested in the pretty and talented Rose O'Neill Wilson in January 1913 when, Thompson told Irwin, they "staid at her turkey trot party until three o'clock in the morning." Irwin further reported on the telephone call from Thompson: "She also said that Sam was so crushed on Rose that he was soft and mild to everyone—Jimmie Hooper said that he was even tender to him. By the way: Sam as you know is going to New Orleans to see the Mardi Gras and write it. He is taking a party; and Rose is going to join said party."[2]

The visit to New Orleans produced "Milady in Motley," a light-hearted account of the Mardi Gras. Although the article continued his development of humorous writing, much of his 1913 and 1914 writing had serious themes. One new market was Bok's popular *Ladies' Home Journal* where Adams attacked the making of false merchandise labels with "The Dishonest Paris Label." Asked to comment on Caroline Bartlett Crane's series on bad meat and worse politics, he reviewed the material in "U.S. Inspected and Passed" and demanded A. D. Melvin resign as the head of the Bureau of Animal Industry.

He also combined serious topics with a light-handed style in *Collier's*. In one article he championed physical exercise to counter the nervous strain of work. The May 1913 cover story, "My Business Partner—'Gym,'" was reprinted in booklet form by the Auburn Young Men's Christian Association. He took on railroad arrogance in a fictional cover story, "President and Passenger." In a "fairy tale" he recounted a trip full of abuse. His story showed his concern for the consumer extended beyond medicine and nostrums.

He returned to *Delineator* after eight months with a new "Health Master" story, "Grandma Sharpless Drives a Quack Out of Town." The reason for the revival was apparently his decision to collect the stories into a book. Bobbs-Merrill retained the first look at his books but was not interested, and Carl Brandt approached Houghton Mifflin of Boston, headed by director Ferris Greenslet and his aide, Roger L. Scaife, about the book. The two men encouraged Adams to do *The Health Master*.

Adams started with the initial *Delineator* series that had explained the Chinese plan, discussed milk, water, and air purity, explored the benefits of corrective surgery, and emphasized the key role of the druggist in the community. He added four more stories. He adapted a *Collier's* article, "Saving Hope in Cancer," and included three more stories that he sold to *Delineator*, "Grandma Sharpless," "House That Caught Cold," about the dangers of the common cold, and "When the *Star* Killed an Epidemic," in which he advanced a pet theory that "yellow journalism" newspapers were able to alert the public to health dangers.

He also wrote a story, "Plain Talk," based on an article, "Public Health and Public Hysteria," that he had published in *The Journal of the Public Health Association*. The article urged sex education to counter the public panic over venereal diseases. When, more than two years later, he continued the topic in a speech attacking quacks who preyed on venereal disease victims, *Survey* cheered him on. When later the *Saturday Evening Post* took up venereal disease, Adams's strong feelings led him to suggest that the chapter be offered to the magazine gratis. If offered, the *Post* did not use it.[3]

*The Health Master* was published in November 1913 with a dedication to Rochester's public health officer, Dr. George W. Goler, hired to keep the city well under the Chinese plan. Public health officers were real-life heroes to Adams, who urged they be scientists rather than political hacks. Although he conceded in an introductory note that the "best wisdom of to-day may be completely refuted by to-morrow's discovery," he considered the book a manual for good health. His faith in what he wrote was shown in an inscription penned in a copy to Stewart Edward White "with the pious hope that a life, guided in strict accord with the principles laid down herein, will enable him to die of old age, some time not earlier than the year of grace, 1974."[4]

The *New York Times* did not review the unusual book, but years later the medical magazine *MD* would laud Adams's "common sense approach to the care of contagious diseases, cancer and colds, the secrets of feminine beauty and sex education." Interest by the buying public was lukewarm, however; 2,437 copies were sold. Nonetheless, the book was a success for Houghton Mifflin, which had estimated 1,272 copies to break even. One reason was that Adams got only a $250 advance. Royalties on sales produced $383 over the years.[5] Although his total was considerably less than his $1,500 advances from Bobbs-Merrill, he and the Boston publisher would work together for almost ten years.

*The Health Master* was a continuation of Adams's wish to educate the people about health issues. In 1913 he got his chance to use a more systematic approach when he agreed to write a monthly health column for *McClure's*. The magazine, no longer under the control of S. S. McClure, offered Adams the opportunity "to teach people how to keep well."[6] The column, "Health; Public and Private," began in March 1913. But after three issues the new health column was dropped.

The magazine did carry in June a fiction piece by Adams, "Omitted From Publication," an adventure story about a lethal butterfly that Venezuelan officials, unable to verify, classified as existing only in folklore. Although the magazine ballyhooed the story as similar to Jack London and Rudyard Kipling tales as "one of the great inventions of fiction," he must have been irate about the end of his column because, after the story, his byline did not appear in *McClure's* again.

His third column had been on cancer, one of several articles he wrote on the subject in 1913. Concern about cancer had been mounting in the medical profession because of the lack of early detection. In the first months of 1913 Dr. Thomas Cullen of Baltimore had been named head of the Cancer Campaign of the Clinical Congress of the Surgeons of North America to bolster public education. Believing women were the key audience, Cullen went to Bok with an article that the editor rejected as too technical and too lurid. Bok said he wanted an article, but one written by a layman. Together, but independently, they chose Adams.

A terrapin dinner meeting in Baltimore was arranged to provide information for Adams on his way south to the Mardi Gras. He already had dealt with quack remedies for the disease, but concern about cancer had made it a public health problem. The topic so concerned him that when he spoke to the Syracuse Advertising Club in March, he chose to discuss cancer rather than advertising.

Adams produced a thirty-two-hundred-word essay "What Can We Do about Cancer?" for the May *Ladies' Home Journal.* He subscribed to the medical belief that most cancer was curable if detected early and if surgery was used. Cullen, to whom Adams sent the article for review, said: "It was graphically written, covered the subject perfectly, and all that I did was to cut down the percentage of recoveries in stomach cancer." Cullen estimated that the two-page article, which was reprinted almost in full by newspapers, reached eleven million readers within a few weeks. He quoted one surgeon who said, "Cullen, as a result of the *Ladies' Home Journal* article I had six early cases of cancer in a little over a week." After the article, Adams was summoned to the American Medical Association meeting in Minneapolis in June 1913. He was made an associate member in the AMA, an unusual honor for a layman.[7]

Adams also dealt with other health issues. He published "What Is the Matter with Your Stomach?" urging common sense instead of patent medicines in October 1913. The next month he discussed emotional depression brought on people by routine factory work in "Blue Mondays," based on material he had gathered at the AMA meeting and one of the few articles he wrote touching on mental health, a topic that Adams said the absence of medical knowledge made it difficult to write about.

Although Adams was working on a series on civic questions for *Collier's,* they were put aside in favor of a cover article, "Oxyfakery: The Tin-Can Sure-Fire School" in the 8 November 1913 issue. He exposed how the Oxypathor device was supposed to cure a number of diseases by forcing oxygen through the skin. The quack article was billed as the first of a series on fake remedies, but it produced a suit by Oxypathor. Norman Hapgood had left the magazine during the 1912 presidential race, and an editorial on 29 August 1914 revealed, at least in public, a new attitude: "When we reflect upon the aggregate millions of dollars that divers patent-medicine concerns have named as amounts we have damaged them, we are almost impressed by ourselves." The position was not matched by practice as the promised continuation never occurred.

Adams remained occupied by his private life. With illustrator O'Neill, achieving fame and considerable fortune as the designer of the Kewpie doll that made her the highest paid woman artist in the world,[8] Adams was "hard hit." Irwin said they would have wed "if the law hadn't stood in the way." Adams later said they parted after an incident in which she used him to make her estranged husband, Harry Leon Wilson, jealous.[9] By the end of 1913 Adams was a free agent. Enter Jane Peyton.

Jennie Van Norman was born in the 1870s to George Bosworth and Elizabeth Atkinson Van Norman in Spring Green, Wisconsin. Her father, a successful meat packer, in 1874 moved the family to Milwaukee and in 1893 opened a Chicago office, splitting his time between the cities. She had been married the previous year, on 26 October 1892 to Robert Curtis Brown, a physician in Milwaukee.

Life as a wife of a doctor was not enough, and she sought a career on the stage, a move opposed by her husband and her father. Undaunted, she adopted the stage name of Jane Peyton and caught the eye of actor-manager Otis Skinner. At the turn of the century Peyton left the Midwest, Doctor Brown, Milwaukee society, and her family as she headed for Broadway. Her father responded by disinheriting her.

The play was *Prince Otto*, a five-act romantic melodrama written by Skinner. Lasting for forty performances in the fall of 1900, the Manhattan introduction of Skinner brought accolades from the *New York Times*, but Peyton's debut drew no mention, even in the cast credits. Nonetheless, she won the role of Lady Fitz-Herbert in the Irish melodrama *Tom Moore* that opened in 1901. The *New York Times* commented that the play gave Peyton "little opportunity" but that she "is sufficiently distinguished in appearance to fill the role." The play ran forty-one performances.[10]

Another short run began on 31 May 1903 when she married musician-composer Arthur Cyril Gordon Weld, whom she may have met when he was a drama critic in Milwaukee and a conductor of its symphony orchestra. The monocled Weld directed musical comedies in New York. The marriage did not affect their careers and apparently dissolved into a separation.[11]

On the stage Peyton appeared in Weber and Fields's *Personal* in 1903 for thirty-eight performances. Although she was credited with acting in *The Earl of Pawtucket* with Lawrence D'Orsay in 1903 and *The Heir to the Hoorah* with Guy Bates Post in early 1906, her name did not appear in the cast lists, indicating fill-in or road performances. Unreported also was her performing with Ethel Barrymore, an appearance that her friend Alice Hills would recall many years later.[12]

In 1906 Peyton was in *The Three of Us*, which ran for 227 performances. Playing the part of Mrs. Tweed Bix, she was called by the *New York Times* "refreshingly buoyant and easy." She became sick, however, and went to Chicago ill and broke. She was pursued there by three suitors from New York. Irwin reported she explained her third marriage, to actor Guy Bates Post, by saying that she refused the first two proposals, "but Guy came on a day she was perfectly discouraged. And on impulse she married him."[13] They wed on 21 August 1907. Two months later her lawyers filed papers to have her marriage to Weld annulled.

After the short-run *The Worth of a Woman* in 1908, she took the role of Mrs. Jack Wilton in a play by J. Hartley Manners, *The Great John Ganton*. With an overpowering actor, George Fawcett, in the title role, a young actress, Laurette Taylor, came to audition. The reception was colder than the day in February 1909, with Peyton asking Manners: "Do you think I'm going to play second to that?" After Taylor's reading, Peyton complained: "But, Hartley, the girl has no voice!" She got the part, however, and the cast went to Chicago for a ten-week trial run during which the two women became friends with Peyton helping to care for her colleague's two children, Dwight and Marguerite.[14]

*The Great John Ganton* opened 3 May 1909 at the Lyric Theatre in New York. *The New York Times* called the plot hackneyed, raved about Fawcett, praised Taylor, and ignored Peyton. The play ran forty performances, but the friendship it spawned between the two actresses would continue for almost forty years. In later years Taylor offered this sketch of her friend: "She had a creamy skin, a delicate race-horse sort of nose, white, even teeth, a devastating dimple in her chin, and red-brown hair, eyes, and brows. . . . At first I didn't like Jane. I wondered how a woman with a deep, merry dimple in her chin could be so very determined. I learned, as I knew her better, that her determination about almost everything was right. And when it wasn't, people forgave her because of that dimple."[15]

Peyton's longest stage run as an actress began in March 1911 when she started rehearsals in William C. De Mille's *The Woman* produced by David Belasco, who also directed the play about corrupt political intrigue and the woman caught in it. Peyton was criticized by the *New York Times*, which said

6. Samuel Hopkins Adams, ca. 1910s.

she, "except in occasional moments, was unable to give expression in the important role of the woman in the case."[16] Despite the tough review audiences attended 254 performances.

The final New York play for Peyton was *We Are Seven*, which opened Christmas Eve 1913. She played a role that the New York *Tribune* called "a small part with few opportunities." The farce ran twenty-one performances and ended her acting career. Marguerite Taylor Courtney later wrote that Peyton used the theater more as a lever for her social life than as a profession. Now as the curtain rang down on one career, another had begun.[17]

Enter Samuel Hopkins Adams. In his early forties, he was described by Moses as "of solid build, a blond of the extremely clear skinned type, of medium height, and with a look that betokens alertness and aliveness." Behind the alertness Moses found "a man of intense earnestness" and noted he was "quick of speech, showing the rapidity of clear thinking, and the importance of a subject is measured by the length of silence before he answers. But when he does speak he loves plain talk. . . . And in talking with the man himself, one feels the all consuming force that guides his conversation."[18]

Exactly when Peyton and Adams met is uncertain. Adams, replying to a *Cleveland Press* questionnaire in 1920, said he met her at a dinner party in New York and in 1944 told the *New York Post* that the introduction was made by Ruth Hale, future wife of Heywood Broun. Irwin's first mention linking them was in early December 1913 when he wrote Gillmore: "The Chapman-Fosters gave a turkey trot party last week to which Sam took Jane Post. It must have been a hot party."[19]

Her marriage to Post had not gone well. She told Irwin in 1914 that within two weeks of the marriage in 1907 he "had shown that brutal temper which is her main indictment against Guy, and she didn't love him any more." By the end of December 1913 Irwin reported, "that damned old butterfly Sam is having some flirtation with Jane. He gave her as a Christmas present a set of glass—a silver decanter and flagons which cost some money, believe me." Adams went to Auburn for Christmas and became ill. He went back to New York, however, arriving "considerably the worse for wear" for a New Year's party for her adopted daughter, Mildred Post.[20]

Although Mildred Post had Guy Bates Post's name, she had been adopted by Jane Peyton after she had come east from her first marriage to Brown. Adams's grandson, Harlan, said that the actress went to an orphanage and chose the prettiest girl. That may be, but like many events concerning Adams, the background is more complex. Irwin reported the actress told him she went to an orphan asylum in Baltimore on impulse. When she found no child to her liking, the mother superior suggested she meet her personal favorite, who was in a Baltimore tenement with a Polish family. Peyton fell immediately in love with the four- or five-year-old and offered to adopt her, leaving her in the convent and paying for her board and educational expenses. Later, when the girl was about ten, typhoid struck her. On doctors' orders to get the girl to a high altitude, the actress took her to Switzerland. Peyton then returned to America and the stage to pay for the treatment and boarding.[21]

Now as 1913 closed, Mildred Post was back from her schooling in Europe. Adams attended the coming-out party, turning, with Peyton, the event into a dancing party. In the first months of 1914 the twosome made the rounds of a series of parties and dinners, making little attempt to hide their infatuation from their friends. Post conveniently was not in the picture because, beginning in January 1914, he had the starring role in the play *Omar, the Tentmaker* for an anticipated three-year run. While Post starred, Adams and Peyton played.

Meanwhile, Irwin and Gillmore were concerned about Adams's relationship with his children. In 1912, while staying in Auburn, Irwin had reported, "I am quartered in Hester's room with pictures of her mother and sister hanging over her bed to point the pathos of her baby situation." In January 1914 Gillmore contacted Beth Adams in Oakland. After a visit, Gillmore wrote both Irwin and Adams. Although those letters were not saved, Adams's reaction was recorded by Irwin in a letter to her: "Sam mentioned your letter yesterday. He said 'The way she wrote about Beth has given me a rather bad day.' In fact, ever since he has at intervals been sitting and gazing far to sea."[22] At the same time Adams wrote Gillmore a chatty letter in which he thanked her for her interest in Katherine, commenting her letters were the first personifying of her that he had had and asking her to check on music lessons for the girl. He also indicated no rapprochement with Beth.[23]

With Beth Adams out of the picture, Post tied up with his play, and Peyton's play *We Are Seven* closed, "the affair between Sam and Jane goes merrily on," Irwin wrote. In May Jane went to the Midwest to investigate her marital status. Meeting the lawyers who had filed the papers concerning her divorce from Weld after her marriage to Post, she reported that one attorney had said, "Madam, I am sorry to say that legally you have been living in adultery for six years. All you have to do is remarry Mr. Post." She asked, "But what if I don't want to marry Mr. Post?" He said, "In that case, simply tell him to go to Hell."

In telling the story to Irwin two months later Jane said: "Other women have to do messy things with detectives or go away for a year. I have only to walk out. Isn't that just my luck!"[24]

As Peyton sorted out her marital status, Adams sought to strengthen his relationship with Gillmore. After she had an operation, Adams sent her a cheery letter, telling her he had written an unsuccessful one-act play, he had declined two assignments to don a khaki suit and cover the American invasion of Vera Cruz in Mexico, and he was going to Owasco Lake for a summer of tennis and work including building a tennis court.[25]

Adams returned upstate and used his public speaking talents in May 1914 to come out publicly for women's suffrage. One week before the speech he sent a letter-to-the-editor to the *Auburn Citizen*, calling the National Association Opposed to Woman Suffrage to account. At a mass meeting on suffrage on 2 May in Utica he announced his retreat from "the safe and sane policy of silence." He traced his conversion to a serious episode years earlier. He reported he had investigated cotton goods manufacturing in Fall River, Massachusetts, and found the women living and working in squalor. He said, "If those women had a chance to register their opinion of those conditions by voting they might make some very marked changes."[26]

Buoyed by her trip, Peyton became more brazen. Irwin gave an update: "That affair of Jane's and Sam's is one of the damnedest I ever saw. . . . For three weeks before Sam left town he and Jane dined at Moquin's every evening. . . . As for Sam, while he has never said to me that he is in love with Jane, he makes no bones about taking it for granted in our conversations. Jane flirts with him and tries to make him jealous—and he gets jealous at the drop of a hat."[27]

Peyton's dying third marriage did not automatically mean her fourth to Adams. On 14 July Irwin reported she at last had told him about her and Adams and that she was "badly in love with him, but she is at present refusing to marry him. That great big boob hadn't any more sense than to suggest that she marry him and live with his mother and daughter in Auburn. . . . Jane has written back to him that marriage would be impossible on those terms." Irwin noted: "Mrs. Adams is a good deal of a devil and had a lot to do with the trouble between Sam and Beth." He said her influence on Hester had been so negative that Adams planned to send the girl to a convent school "to mend her manners."[28]

Adams contemplated leaving Auburn, and an alternative must have been Scituate, the coastal area thirty miles south of Boston that was a favorite of writers. Irwin had accompanied Adams to Scituate in September 1913 after promising Gillmore that he would not let him come alone. After the visit, Adams said that although he was tied to Owasco Lake because of his mother and Hester, "If it weren't for that I would build in Scituate." Such a move probably was not encouraged by Irwin and certainly was opposed by Gillmore.[29]

Although Gillmore would not welcome Adams as a neighbor, she was developing a tolerance for him. One thing that drew them closer together was her collection of antiques that fascinated Adams. Irwin recalled that during the period he and Adams lived together, first on Washington Square and then on Stuyvesant Square, he had furnished their quarters with early American furniture about which Adams complained: "There isn't a chair in this place that when you sit down in it doesn't reach out and bite you!" Irwin said, however, "Environment breaks down the sturdiest characters. Within three years, he was scouring the barns and attics . . . for hutch tables, six-legged highboys and Currier and Ives prints." Later Adams, admitting he must be "a peculiarly corruptible person," credited her with inoculating him with the virus of the antique "and it has since cost me thousands of dollars!" Adams would specialize in prints and old bottles.[30]

As Adams wrestled with what to do about Peyton's Auburn ultimatum and arranged to have his daughter Hester enter a private Engleside school in New Milford, Connecticut, Peyton was concerned with reputation. Afraid that Adams would be labeled a home-breaker, she said: "If you stay at home and grouch, it is all right. If you make yourself happy, it is all wrong."[31]

In August 1914 Irwin reported: "Sam has yielded the point about his mother and Auburn and everything. As I knew he would." Although Jane still was in doubt about marriage because of his mother, she told Irwin: "All the same, I'm crazy about Sam." Asking her point-blank whether she would marry Adams, Irwin said she replied, "Yes, of course I will, but don't tell Sam yet."[32]

As Adams's romantic life blossomed, he remained true to his craft. By 9 December 1913 he had thirty-five thousand words of *The Clarion* written and was working daily in an office at *Collier's*. In early 1914, while he was squiring Peyton in the evenings, he was furiously at work at Irwin's apartment. His dedication to his work was shown when Irwin reported on 22 January to Gillmore: "Sam strained his back in the gym the day before yesterday. He has been sitting in his bath robe, with a hot water bottle down his back, attached to his neck by a string. He is working like the Devil, working both morning and afternoon. He is about half finished, he says." Occasionally, Adams would write Houghton Mifflin with a new idea for promoting *The Health Master*, but his thoughts and fingers were at work on *The Clarion*.

"Sam finished the novel on the last day of March," Irwin reported to Gillmore, "that being the schedule he set for himself." On 2 April Adams sent the first eighteen chapters to Greenslet and the rest the next day after he received it from his typist.[33]

The end of the novel showed his sentimentality and idealism. Hal Surtaine and Esme Elliott were reconciled as she realized the dangers of her tenement and had it razed. Businessmen needed *The Clarion*'s circulation and resumed advertising. His father renounced patent medicines, and the paper's campaign against typhus was recognized by none other than the president, who agreed to attend Old Home Week. To Moses, who called the book "melodramatic, even middle class in its atmosphere," Adams explained his intention: "It is, in essence, a declaration of the faith that is in me, the faith that a newspaper can prosper against the pressure of adverse circumstances and influences by sticking to its primal concern of telling the news straightly."[34]

The first draft was enthusiastically received by Greenslet who read the 130,000 words in five hours and wrote Adams that he wanted to make him a proposal for "an A#1, man-sized, good book." Recognizing that "our Indianapolis friends" had first crack at it, he offered several suggestions, including making the heroine, Esme Elliott, more believable, and noted an inconsistency in the club membership of the hero, indicating that his fast read had not been a superficial one.[35]

Adams wrote back that he promised Bobbs-Merrill only the right to look at the manuscript. Greenslet accepted the delay, and a few days later the two agreed to let the Brandt office handle the contract. Adams's work was far from done. He rewrote the book after taking April off to start a new serial for *Delineator*. He spent five weeks reworking his novel. As he rewrote, he argued for a better cover illustration that he got, debated the caption under his picture, and sent a biography that he said could be cut.[36]

The initial reports from the book travelers indicated that advance orders for the novel would reach twenty thousand. Then the troubles began. First Harper & Brothers announced a novel by Will N. Harben entitled *The New Clarion*. Although the novel was about life in the Georgia hills, the similarity of titles worried Greenslet and must have irked Adams, who still liked his original title. The publisher, however, felt *The Clarion* would be a success based on advanced sales that were running even with those of Adams's friend Meredith Nicholson and ahead of the romantic writer Mary Roberts Rinehart.

Then there was the war in Europe. In July Austria-Hungary, one month after the assassination of Archduke Ferdinand, declared war on Serbia. Other nations quickly joined the war. On 12 August while asking for a copy of the book for a possible play by A. E. Thomas, Adams asked if the war would hurt his book sales. As the book was on the press 13 August, Greenslet replied, "You will be somewhat hit by it, I am afraid."

The war was affecting not only Adams. Irwin accepted an assignment from *Collier's* to cover the war and left for Europe 6 August. While Irwin was in Europe, Adams polished the serial for *Delineator*. His romance, "Little Miss Grouch," was based on a trans-Atlantic crossing. The plot of an heiress escaping an arranged marriage had the farcical twists and turns that Adams would employ many times in the years to come.

The serial also was sent to Houghton Mifflin in September. Greenslet said that the farce comedy was "mighty good of its kind—very juicy and amusing." Although he cautioned that it "will not solidify still further the solid reputation which I think 'The Clarion' is going to make for you," he offered to publish *Little Miss Grouch* at a lesser royalty. Scaife wrote Adams the next day that as light comedy it was delightful, but he expressed concern that Adams might turn out light comedy so fast as to congest the market. He said he felt an author should publish only one book a year and suggested Adams use a pseudonym. Adams replied that although he was willing to leave the question of pseudonymity open, *Delineator* wanted his name on the serial and offered $3,500 for the serial rights. Paid ten cents a word by *Delineator*, he earned $3,266.70 of the $3,500 maximum.[37]

*The Clarion* was published 10 October 1914 with a dedication to his father, Myron Adams, Jr., "who lived and died a soldier of ideals." Franklin Pierce Adams, who received an advance copy of the book, called it "a fine, brave book, and all people should read it, to know some truths about newspapers." When the newspaper reviews came out, all did not agree. The newspapers tended to be critical, whereas the magazines were more favorable. No review equaled the animosity of the editor of the Proprietary Association's *Standard Remedies*. The editor said Adams was "like a certain nasty breed of wooly dogs that delight to roll in filth and then sit down and rapturously smell themselves."[38]

At Binghamton, the home of the Kilmers of Swamp Root fame, the book received another reaction, a boycott. The Kilmers, who reportedly had bought up the issue of *Collier's* in which they had been featured, now sought to keep the book out of their city. Adams, the author, became Adams, the promoter. He penned "Why I Wrote 'The Clarion'" for the November *La Follette's Magazine*. He agreed to help *Book News Monthly* with its "Adams issue" scheduled for January. The magazine assigned Moses to interview Adams but wanted a more personal profile, and Adams suggested several writers, of whom Jesse Lynch Williams was selected. Adams urged the Binghamton boycott also be featured. Despite their efforts about Binghamton a local bookseller reported that only seven copies of the book were sold. "This is pretty poor business. In fact I calculate that it has cost us about $5.00 per copy to sell these books."[39] Binghamton notwithstanding, *The Clarion*, priced at $1.35, did sell.

The fears about *The New Clarion* appeared well founded after it got two mentions on *Bookman's* "Book Mart" in November 1914, but then it disappeared. *The Clarion* was listed in December, with Albany and Atlanta putting it number one. In January *Bookman* reported it was number one in Rochester and in Los Angeles where it maintained that position in February and March. By April it cracked into the top six books in demand, placing sixth. Although it never topped the list, the book was a financial success for Adams, who got forty-five hundred dollars in October 1914 in combined straight and subscription advances. In sum, during 1914 Adams had earned more than seventy-nine hundred dollars from the "Little Miss Grouch" serial, *Clarion* advances, and *Health Master* royalties, a sum more than the annual seventy-five hundred dollars salary of a congressman.

Adams was unable to take advantage of the lucrative serial market with *The Clarion*. Adams later said the frankness of the treatment kept the novel from the magazines. When *Publisher's Weekly*, however, which had called the book "one of the most real and vital among recent novels," took a year-end survey of booksellers on the best 1914 book, *The Clarion* got the most votes.[40]

He met in November with Moses, who found Adams "like a Bradstreets's directory he can tell you the standing of every paper's columns," attributed his knowledge of newspaper advertising to dealing with ad clubs, which were battling fraudulent advertising.[41] His continuing crusade for truth in advertising and *The Clarion* led to a surprising new venue.

On 15 November Adams wrote to Greenslet that he had contracted with the New York *Tribune* to write a series of ten articles on dishonest newspaper advertising, which he predicted would tie him up for two or three weeks. The newspaper's editors and its new general manager, Richard Waldo, who had been hired from *Good Housekeeping* in August, had been impressed by Adams's *Clarion* and believed he would help in the paper's campaign to clean up its advertising. Unaware of what the assignment would lead to, as was Adams, Greenslet replied that he was intrigued because "nearly all the distinguished men I know are being employed, one after the other, by that enterprising sheet."

As 1914 drew to a close, Adams and Greenslet were concerned about advertising *The Clarion*. Adams asked for more, and Greenslet said Houghton Mifflin had spent more than usual, but "we shan't let up if we see any sound response." Apparently satisfied, Adams went to Auburn to spend Christmas with his mother and daughter Hester, back from Connecticut for vacation.[42]

Then on 30 December Peyton asked the Illinois Supreme Court in Chicago to annul her marriage to Post on the basis it had been innocently bigamous. Her action in the Midwest and the *Tribune*'s plans for the Adams series in New York were to produce major changes in the life of the author, who was being his domestic best in Auburn.

# 9

# COLUMNIST
## 1915–1916

I N DECEMBER 1914 the New York *Tribune* began to ballyhoo the upcoming
Adams series on fraudulent and misleading newspaper advertising. The
campaign was the result of actions taken by the newspaper after a federal law
was enacted in 1912 to require distinct labeling of paid advertising and a state
statute in 1913 to make false advertising a crime. Neither law worked well, and
the *Tribune* vowed to bring more public support for the laws by educating the
consumer.

After an ill-fated try with a special investigative department, the newspaper
in 1914 made a pledge to "[e]nsure the trustworthiness of every advertisement"
by offering a guarantee on its advertised products, similar to the money-back
pledge by *Good Housekeeping* where *Tribune* general manager Richard Waldo
had worked.[1]

With a stated goal of ridding the paper of bad ads, the newspaper sought
to expose the fraudulent advertising. The campaign began at a time when government and newspapers were concerned about the credibility of circulation
figures and advertising claims. The Audit Bureau of Circulation had been
founded in 1914 to provide an independent audit of subscription claims. States
and newspapers were wrestling with laws or new guidelines to curb bad advertising. Although the Federal Trade Commission was established in 1914, its
original charge was to prevent business activities that were unfair or anticom-
petitive and to protect business rather than the consumer. Advertising was not
mentioned in the enabling legislation. As ad clubs, newspapers, and govern-
ments were taking their initial steps to combat false advertising, it was the New
York *Tribune,* once Horace Greeley's "Great Moral Organ," that took the lead.

On 28 December a three-column advertisement announced the Adams series aimed at "dishonest and unclean advertising." The ad, also placed in magazines, was headlined "Go to it, Adams—The sky's the limit!" and said: "We have given Adams a free hand. When he can best make a point by walloping a *Tribune* advertisement, he doesn't spare the rod." It offered free copies of the column to persons outside New York.

The first Adams column on 4 January set the tone as he stated the articles were not for the merchant but for the consumer. He promised to be specific in attacking such practices as markdowns and mislabeling of items such as German silver that was neither German nor silver. He foresaw that dishonest merchants would emit "the shrill howl of 'muckraking'" and pledged the "keep-off-the-grass sign does not wave above these columns."

After the introductory Monday column, Adams followed on Wednesday, attacking the curative claims of cottage cheese and, on Saturday, Hearst for accepting patent medicine advertising. This attack on patent medicines indicated that Adams's foray into consumer reporting was taking on a familiar target, but he later explained: "The prime purpose of this series is to instruct the public in the matter of improper advertising of all kinds with the view of protecting it against being swindled. As medical advertising is the most dangerously fraudulent, it naturally comes in for a great deal of my attention."[2]

If, however, readers thought Adams was using the advertising columns just for fresh attacks on nostrums, they were wrong. He was now concentrating on truth in advertising and wrote only sporadically about patent medicines and quackery. During the second week he blasted bunco advertising, including the use of foreign labels on domestic products such as furs, and then charged the Kosofsky brothers with appropriating reputable business firm names such as Filene's.

The columns not only brought praise from the public but also lawsuits from the merchants. One was by J. A. Kosofsky, who demanded a retraction or he would pursue a libel action. Legal threats did not deter Adams, who in the third week warned about so-called bargains and then attacked markdowns and markups in a column that produced a $250,000 suit by Isaac and Meyer Liberman. The Liberman suit brought comment from *Editor and Publisher* in its column on newspaper advertising called "A' Top o' the World." Representing the point of view of newspaper publishers, the trade magazine said the initial article and follow-ups "were all of them masterpieces of good copy." The magazine also noted an increase in the newspaper's circulation in and outside New York and that local advertising content "has improved marvelously."

By March the newspaper claimed its circulation had risen 97 percent in the city and its advertising had the only gain reported by any New York City morning newspaper.[3]

His critics saw the articles as mere promotion of the newspaper, but *Editor and Publisher* said, "It takes a lot of sand to start a thing of this kind." For Adams the series allowed him to champion the consumer and to express his optimism that papers could reform. Moses said his belief was "that the general tendency is upward and forward; not downward and backward."[4]

He led off the fourth week with a column prompted by a Hearst reaction to his earlier column. He criticized a *Tribune* advertisement for an electric vibrator that he claimed could not provide the cures it promised. Other columns warned about freak sizes, seconds, and off-color claims and praised honest advertising. He then attacked another newspaper, the *Globe*, for carrying false advertising by the Liberman brothers, who filed another suit bringing the Kosofsky and Liberman total to five hundred thousand dollars. Two of his last three columns criticized patent medicine testimonial ads and the relationship of nostrums and editors.

The column research and writing were wearing on Adams, who marked his forty-fourth birthday with friends on 26 January. The initial *Tribune* series ended 9 February after fourteen columns instead of the ten for which Adams had been contracted. An editor's note at the end said, "The public by its response has shown us that, as a newspaper topic, there is as big an issue in Clean Advertising as was ever found in Clean Politics." Ten years afterward Adams reflected on his original series, commenting "we had caught so many and such large fish by the tail, and were trailing or being trailed by so many more . . . that it was impossible to let go."[5]

He agreed to continue his columns after the newspaper promised an investigatory staff to help him. One factor in his decision might have been a generous, although unknown, amount the *Tribune* paid him. Another reason could have been a new celebrity status. As Greenslet said, he joined the *Tribune*'s stable of visible writers such as Franklin Pierce Adams, Heywood Broun, Alice Duer Miller, and Grantland Rice, whose sports reporting began at the same time as Adams's columns.

While the *Tribune* was running his consumer columns, "Little Miss Grouch" began a five-month run in *Delineator.* Further visibility came in the January "Adams issue" of *Book News Monthly* with the interview by Moses, a friendly sketch by Williams, and an account of the Binghamton boycott by H. K. Bishop. These, plus advertising by Houghton Mifflin, reinvigorated sales of

*The Clarion*. Although he said he had given up on the novel, he eventually added $1,217.31 to his original $4,500 royalty. For Houghton Mifflin, which had estimated 8,914 copies would cover costs, the final sales of 36,519 still fell short of expectations. The sales director maintained that without "the untimely outbreak of the European war, we should have sold 100,000 Clarion." But Adams suspected that the failure of the book to reach expectations would bring displeasure from the firm's business office.[6]

For the *Tribune* he resumed his column on 16 February with an attack on Fifth Avenue merchants, including rug dealer J. M. Harris, who promptly sued. Adams continued with columns on bad sales manners, ill-fitting made-to-order suits, tobacco ads, and comparative shopping. Of special interest was the 9 March column that reported the Kosofsky suit had been dropped, told of continuing claims by the cottage cheese maker, and refused to retract what was written about the vibrator.

Meanwhile, in early February he was on the road, stopping in Auburn, and then going to Rochester to speak to the Civic Club about fraudulent advertising but also to plug *The Clarion*. Back in New York, he found Irwin had returned to Europe from where he sent dispatches to the *Tribune*. Although Adams did a light-hearted analysis of the popular song "It's a Long Way to Tipperary" for "The Conning Tower," noting it depended on from where one started, he offered little public opinion on the European war, reflecting the neutrality stance of many Americans, including President Wilson.[7]

Peyton's trip west in late 1914 became successful when on 16 February the Supreme Court of Illinois in Chicago annulled her marriage with Post, citing her divorce from Weld came after her marriage to Post. Adams returned to Auburn in early March, evidently to tell his mother the news. On Thursday, 11 March, he and Peyton were married at the New York home of Josephine Chapman, who was the bridesmaid. Weaver came down from Utica to be best man. His mother, who entertained friends in Auburn the wedding eve, did not attend.[8]

Several hours after the wedding the couple sailed for the West Indies and South America. While they were in Venezuela, the couple took a train ride, and he wrote Franklin Pierce Adams: "La Guayra has the highest R.R. rate known: 40¢ per half mile, on the Harbor Corporation narrow gauge track. But if you try to get to land any other way the other sharks get you." The New York *Tribune* item prompted the *Auburn Citizen* to note: "Those honeymoon expenses always seem greater than ordinary."[9]

The Adams honeymoon was far from all play. In an 11 April letter from Caracas to Greenslet, who had written Adams his congratulations and asked if

Houghton Mifflin could start setting *Little Miss Grouch* in type from the magazine serial, Adams asked what the hurry was and disclosed he was working on the other light novel. Greenslet replied he was eager to read the new work and explained the reason he wanted to start setting *Little Miss Grouch* without new material was his travelers were predicting "a large fat sale." Adams's *Clarion* fears allayed, he told Greenslet to go ahead, admitting any attempt at padding was dangerous. In May Adams finished the draft of his new Caribbean novel, *The Unspeakable Perk*, and left a copy with a Caracas friend to check.[10]

Delayed by interruptions in travel because of the war, they returned in late May. The influence of a new wife was evident to Franklin Pierce Adams, who wrote 27 May about having seen the writer the day before: "I did note how he had changed the way he parted his hair; for he was wont to part it in the middle and now he drapes it upon the right side, and very handsome it makes him appear, too, and I asked him whether Jane, his wife, hath ordered him to change, and he said, yes; which shews how the blusteringest of us are the meekest."[11]

Several days later the Adamses went to Auburn to visit his mother on Chedell Place. His plan was to let his mother stay in the Chedell Place house while he and Jane Adams lived at Quisisana. He bought his new wife a wedding present of a tract of ten acres along the lake and then two years later another twenty-four acres that she began developing into a farm that would eventually total three hundred acres stretching up the hill from the lake property. "Jane always asked that her birthday presents be more land, and she gave father improvements in the house for his," Katherine Adell recalled.[12]

Before they left for Auburn in late May, Adams sent the manuscript of his Caribbean novel, *The Unspeakable Perk*, to Greenslet. The author said he was going ahead with the revision because a magazine was interested in a serial. Greenslet found it to be "a first-rate specimen of its kind." Cheered by Houghton Mifflin, he was shocked when *Everybody's* rejected the serial. He said the editors liked it, but his old employer Ridgway had ordered it killed because he said it had no message.[13]

If the sale of the serial was frustrating, his work with the *Tribune* continued apace. He had had a hiatus after a 30 March article on flimsy raincoats although the newspaper continued to market him through a booklet of the early columns, *The Adams Articles*, for which he wrote a foreword in which he said he was trying to let light shine on dubious advertising, not reform it.

Upon his return from his honeymoon Adams said, "I found the advertising fight I had started still raging, and was swiftly drawn back into it." True to its word, the *Tribune* had secured help for Adams by setting up a Bureau of Investigations charged with processing information that would be written up in a new column, the "Ad-Visor." *Editor and Publisher* headlined a story on the consumer service "Adams and His Tomahawk."[14]

Adams, using the title he had given his detective Average Jones, on 22 June outlined the purpose of the new department, to answer consumer complaints. The first double-column "Ad-Visor" appeared 28 June with "Conducted by Samuel Hopkins Adams." He also used material from the bureau for a Sunday article 4 July attacking Max H. Finkelstein's department store for false bargains. The *Tribune* liked it so much that it was reprinted the following Tuesday with a comment that Adams would have "one of his characteristically smashing articles on business fakes" every Sunday.[15]

With bylined columns on Sundays, anchored on the back page of the first section, and "Ad-Visor" columns two other days, week after week Adams flailed away at cut-the-price-upward jewelry stores, consumption cures, store window baiting, and vanity advertising. More and more these columns were product oriented, discussing misnamed watches, inferior straw hats, and "tailored" ready-made clothes. He was given carte blanche, so his topics ranged from refilled whiskey bottles to used cars. Adams's assessment in 1925 was, "The articles stirred up so much comment and more enmity; the experiment was at the time quite new in the field of journalism and has not since been followed, as far as I am aware, by any other important daily in this country."[16]

The popularity of his column put Adams on the speaking circuit, targeting bad advertising. Repeating what he had said at Rochester, he charged twenty-five dollars to Young Men's Christian Associations and fifty dollars to other groups. He was in demand, talking to the Association of National Advertisers in New York and to the Chamber of Commerce in Boston. His careful research for his column writing was not always present in his speeches. In the December address to the Boston Chamber he gave what *Editor and Publisher* reported was a "sensational speech." Adams attacked the Boston *Post* for taking "anything up to a plugged quarter" in advertising. The newspaper's management confronted Adams and asked him to come to its offices. There they showed him a file of rejected advertising. Adams backed down, reportedly saying, "I wish to say that I can see that it is the intention of the management of the *Post* to keep its columns free from fraudulent and objectionable advertising."[17]

In September Irwin was back from Europe and after meeting a returned Adams at the Players Club, they went to Jane Adams's apartment on Tenth

Street. Irwin wrote Gillmore, "Sam looks thin and Jane frazzled." Irwin added that his friend had not sold a magazine piece since returning from South America but was optimistic.[18] Adams finally did sell two health articles to the *Ladies' Home Journal*, offering practical advice on colds and a tuberculosis warning to women. He placed a short story, "Fairy Princess," in *Everybody's*, which also published his only other short magazine work, "Jitney Partners for the Dance," about a New York dance hall in which "slaves" worked for one quarter a dance.

*Little Miss Grouch* was published on 18 September 1915 with the extended title *A Narrative Based on the Private Log of Alexander Forsyth Smith's Maiden Transatlantic Crossing.* In the novel the hero, an inventor with an alias of haberdasher Sandy Daddleskink, met Cecily Wayne as she fled on the *Clan Macgregor* from an engagement arranged by her father, a millionaire. Together they dodged her father's detectives and a self-appointed chaperone. They sought to avoid legal entanglements by hiring a distinguished jurist for five dollars.

The reviewers embraced the new Adams novel as the nation began preaching war preparedness. Readers agreed. Sales of 20,014 copies came from 11,450 regular, 6,564 cheap, 1,000 Canadian, and 1,000 Australian copies. The demand was not enough to put the novel on *Bookman's* "Book Mart," but it made $1,922 in royalties. Although sales did not reach those of *The Clarion*, Greenslet offered a higher advance for *The Unspeakable Perk*, which was serialized in *Ainslee's* magazine. The reviews and sales encouraged Adams to make light fiction a staple in his writing regimen.[19]

Equally encouraging for him, *The Clarion* produced more than book royalties. Earlier in 1915 the sale of movie rights to *The Secret of Lonesome Cove* had been chilled by doubts that the film could get by the National Board of Censorship, probably because of the Bohemian heroine. But on 1 November the film rights of *The Clarion* were sold to Equitable (World) Motion Pictures for one thousand dollars, the first Adams sale to the movies.

At home a power struggle dominated his domestic life. Jane Adams was adapting to Auburn, entertaining at the Owasco Country Club and keeping his mother at arm's length. His daughter Hester, attending St. Margaret's School in Toronto, Canada, became a pawn in the struggle. After her grandmother had a tea for the teenager and her girlfriends on Chedell Place during Christmas vacation, Jane Adams held a house party at the lake for Hester, three other girls, and four boys, complete with sleigh ride, dinner, and dancing.

By the end of the year Jane Adams wrote her old confidant, Irwin, a triumphant letter that he sent on to Gillmore, who was stunned: "That letter of Jane's—which following your orders, I destroyed—was one of the most terrible I have ever read. The stark gloating cruelty of her attitude towards Mrs. Adams—and her pagan enjoyment of the fact that she has made Sam take that attitude too—and then asking you not to let Sam know—it was all fairly terrific, I thought."[20]

If Gillmore was not happy with Jane Adams, less than one month later, she was furious with Adams, whom she called a "lily-pollen." What infuriated her was a visit with Beth Adams and daughter Katherine in San Francisco during which she learned that he was giving the teenager only seven dollars a month and had canceled her music lessons. Although his daughter later said that the allowance then was "a lot for a kid" and that she was not very studious at the piano (a condition Adams had made when asking for the lessons), the situation upset Gillmore. Gillmore conceded, however, that Jane Adams had sent the girl a gown for Christmas and that Beth Adams "spoke very kindly of him, . . . [and] hoped it would mean happiness for Sam and was glad when I told her that Jane had reduced Sam's mother to subjection."[21]

Despite Gillmore's criticisms of the couple, any animosity dissipated when on 1 February 1916 Sam and Jane Adams joined sixteen other friends and relatives at the wedding of Irwin and Gillmore, whose divorce from Rufus Gillmore had been finalized. The next day the Irwins left for Europe to cover the battlefronts.

Still publicly silent on events overseas, Adams had his own war with Greenhut department store. A *Tribune* column on the store's merchandising was slated for Sunday, 6 February but was halted when the store obtained an injunction on Friday evening. While the *Tribune* fought the injunction, it published a booklet by Adams on *How It Works*, which included columns and examples of the newspaper's money-back guarantee. The newspaper also began house ads intended to show the independence of Adams from pressure from within the newspaper. "And when he comes to New York—well, do you think he writes like a man who could be urged, cajoled, threatened or wheedled into printing, or not printing anything against his desires?" a February ad asked.

While he waited for the court to act, he wrote columns warning on store guarantees, telling of a new unethical store, cautioning about classified advertisements for work at home, and returning to a favorite topic on nostrum testimonials. On 11 March a justice of the New York Supreme Court refused to make permanent the temporary injunction, ending the prior restraint. The *Tribune* the next week promoted the Greenhut column that ran 19 March, accusing the store of holding a fake sale. Three months later Greenhut sued the newspaper for five hundred thousand dollars on the promotional advertisement, a suit the store lost late in the year.

The Greenhut case did not cow Adams in the slightest. In a February 1916 speech at the Young Men's Christian Association in Middletown, Connecticut, he said that "a newspaper didn't belong to its advertisers but to its readers and that the double standard of morality in the editorial column and dishonesty in the advertising columns had got to go." This high moral stance was translated into specifics when *Editor and Publisher* in a March editorial, either in admiration or in dismay, reported Adams's reply to a request for no coverage by B. Altman's and Company, a large advertiser: "The *Tribune* is not edited by any advertiser, and advice and counsel such as are contained in the Altman letter are not taken in good part in this office."[22]

Not content with his public rebuke of Altman's, he did a Sunday column on the store 30 April. After Altman's discontinued advertising, he again returned to the battle with an "Ad-Visor" column in June. Although, after the Altman's column, he continued to discuss products such as shoes and jewelry, he must have crossed the line. In July the byline "Conducted by Samuel Hopkins Adams" was dropped from "Ad-Visor." His Sunday column ended regular publication 6 August 1916 with a piece on Harlem stores, finishing a thirteen-month run. Unwilling to abandon him entirely, the newspaper issued in September a new booklet of his columns, *Samuel Hopkins Adams on Fraudulent and Deceptive Advertising.*

Meanwhile, the filming of *The Clarion* had begun in January 1916 in Jacksonville, Florida. The release date was 21 February, and the *Tribune* reported that private viewings showed the mob scene to be "one of the most remarkable pictures ever taken." Agreeing that the mob scene was handled well, *Variety* added, "but the interiors were badly lighted or poorly developed." Adams said simply it was rotten. Still, the movie bug had bitten him despite his belief that any movie companies that were not made up of crooks were run by lunatics.[23]

The Adamses returned to Cayuga County in the middle of February after a month in New York, and a showdown between his wife and mother was prompted by Jane Adams's health. Although the lake property was fine most of the year, the central New York winters were something else. Adams had planned after his marriage to go to a warmer climate in the winter, and he would have been wiser to follow the plan. At the lake Jane Adams contracted pneumonia, and they had to move into Auburn. The presence of the two women under the same roof produced changes. Adams had his mother move around the corner to a room on Easterly Avenue and rented out the Chedell Place home when they were not using it. "They threw her out," his daughter Katherine Adell recalled.[24]

*The Unspeakable Perk* was published on 21 July. The story's hero was a mysterious entomologist named Perkins who wore goggles to disguise himself on the island of Caracuna. Like Doctor Strong in *The Health Master*, Perkins only had a surname from which he derived the sobriquet of "The Unspeakable Perk." The name was apt for the taciturn man, even when he met Polly Brewster of Utica, the daughter of a millionaire whose yacht was in the harbor. The plot featured the threat of bubonic plague and a quarantine, a Dutch man-of-war blockade, anti-American activities by the Hochwald minister (notably not German), a native insurrection, and leprosy, all of which enmeshed the young lovers in difficulties over which, predictably, they prevailed.

When some critics suggested Adams was wasting his time on light fiction, Houghton Mifflin agreed and urged Adams to make his next book a more serious effort. Although *Perk* was on *Bookman's* "Book Mart" list in the last three months of 1916, the novel never came close to the two leading fiction novels, *When a Man's a Man* by Harold Bell Wright, whose work was not appreciated by Adams, and *Mr. Britling Sees It Through* by H. G. Wells, whom Adams admired greatly. Sales of 9,914 regular copies were considerably higher than the Houghton Mifflin 3,686 estimated break-even point, and the advance and royalties eventually reached $2,515.[25]

Although he was frustrated at his plans to sell *Perk* for a film, he was successful in marketing his short stories to magazines. In March 1916 he had published "Our Square and the People in It" in *Everybody's*. He chose for the setting a fictional New York park. In it two characters conducted a courtship, sculptor Bonnie Lassie and Cyrus the Gaunt to whom she restored self-esteem, a metamorphic theme that was recurrent in his writing. Arthur Bartlett Maurice said the author created a composite of Stuyvesant Square, where he lived with Irwin, and Tompkins Square on New York's East Side. Adams's park was a "valiant green space" surrounded by slums.[26]

The initial "Our Square" in *Everybody's* intrigued *Collier's*, which contracted for a series of tales using the locale. Beginning in August, eight stories were in the magazine over a twelve-month period. In them he drew on his experiences as a reporter, noting he had "cherished in his mind the idea of set-

ting down, in a series of stories, the casual record of a quaint and lovable lo-
cality which I had known well on the east side of New York." The stories offered a response to former *Sun* colleagues who, Irwin said, "have told me
always that none of his short stories compare with his little newspaper tales
of the East Side."[27]

The stories were bought for $5,150 and this, added to Adams's other sales,
brought his total for 1916 to $8,630, not including what he earned from the *Tri-
bune*. Even his luck with the movies improved. Before the "Our Square" series began, Adams placed a short story, "Triumph," in *Collier's* for $500. The
story of a dying man who took the blame for a murder to shield a young
woman was bought by Universal Film Manufacturing Company for $500. Sold
for $250, also to Universal, was "A Letter to Nowhere," a short story sold orig-
inally to the Associated Sunday Magazine supplement. Despite the two sales
to the movies Adams had low regard for the film business. Sales of film rights
were just money.

During the late spring and summer Adams split his time between Central
New York and New York City. In June the Adamses announced the wedding
of Mildred Meredith Post to actor Douglas Jeffreys Wood on 25 May. They also
took his daughter Hester to Clinton for the Hamilton College commencement
and his trustee meeting. At an earlier meeting he had proposed the reorgan-
izing of the history and political economy departments and read a minority report on the faculty, both of which were probably disliked by President Stryker.

Stryker had been an outspoken critic of Roosevelt in 1912, but he supported
the former president's pro-Allies stand. When the *Lusitania* was sunk in May
1915, Stryker ordered the college flag not to be flown until the United States
had entered the war. Wheras Stryker was pro-Roosevelt, he was also fervently
anti-Wilson.

At the June trustee meeting Adams's minority report on the faculty was
adopted, but trouble developed when three days later President Stryker attacked Wilson in a speech. Present were Adams and Alexander Woollcott, who
later reported, "It was he and I who rose and stamped noisily out of the alumni
luncheon at Commencement when Dr. Stryker so far forgot himself as to
speak sneeringly of Wilson in his post-prandial discourse." Although trustee
chairman Elihu Root offered a mild rebuke to Stryker, Adams resigned from
the Board of Trustees of his beloved Hamilton.[28] It would be ten years before
his break with the college would be repaired.

Other changes were occurring in Adams's life. Evidently young Hester's
stint at the Canadian school was producing changes more acceptable to the

Adamses because they brought her to the lake after their return from Clinton. There she played her father's favorite game of tennis and entertained friends. The Adamses also established their annual Fourth of July house party, inviting nine guests. Even Jane Adams's attitude toward her husband's mother softened as the two Hesters went in late July to spend a month at the lake.

He returned to New York in October to do a piece on the World Series. He also went shopping after seeing an advertisement for a Gimbel Brothers' sixth birthday sale. After a break of more than two months, his column returned to the *Tribune* with a blistering attack on Gimbels department store. The store sued Adams and the newspaper for one million dollars. The *Tribune*, which had gained more than one million advertising lines and 65 percent in circulation in 1916, lost little time in issuing another pamphlet, *"Keeping the Faith"; Gimbel Brothers and the New York Tribune*, by Adams.

Although Gimbels lost, one suit was successful on 4 December when the rug merchant Harris, who had sued for fifty-thousand dollars, was awarded six cents after a two-week trial in which Adams testified. In 1925 Adams said that "the sum total of damages from suits aggregating some three million dollars was a modest six cents, a discouraging result to our opponents who had held the comfortable theory that advertising, good or bad, was nobody's business but the advertiser's."[29]

While Adams battled against false advertising, he enlisted in the fight against suppression. He joined other authors in supporting the publication of Theodore Dreiser's *The Genius*, which was under attack from the post office and the puritanical Comstock Society in a battle that had anti-German undertones.[30] He also got more involved in the 1916 presidential campaign. The liberal Democrat, who called himself politically independent, had been publicly silent during the three-cornered race of 1912. In the race between incumbent Wilson and Republican challenger Charles Evans Hughes, however, Adams joined fifty authors in supporting Wilson. A few days earlier the Publicity Bureau of the Democratic National Committee quoted him as saying Hughes was no more than "a hope in a fog" and, "Therefore, as an independent voter, I shall vote for President Wilson, because I wish to vote positively not negatively; constructively, not destructively; in the light, not in the dark; for a confidence, not a hope."[31] The victory by Wilson would have future effects on Adams, but for the present he turned to his next book.

Looking toward 1917, Greenslet in August 1916 asked Adams to write a "full-bodied opus." After speaking with Adams about *The Clarion*, Moses had predicted that "it would not surprise me to find him soon in another novel declaring those disintegrating forces in journalism which serve to undermine the editor who starts out with an honest policy." Adams replied to Greenslet that a long novel was a matter of finance and that he needed to sell a short serial and four or five short stories. He suggested Greenslet take a look at the "Our Square" stories on which *Collier's* was spending four thousand dollars to promote. Greenslet doggedly urged work on the "*opus*, for, whether published in 1917 or 1918, I think it is pretty near time you got about it."[32]

One month later Adams noted the newspaper novel would take one year of no income and he needed a six thousand dollar pot. Noting his experience with *The Clarion* indicated no serialization, he proposed the publishers pay fifteen hundred dollars on delivery of the manuscript and another fifteen hundred dollars on publication. Greenslet agreed enthusiastically.[33]

In early November Adams outlined his schedule for *Success*, planning to spend one month doing most of part 1, going to New York for magazine work, then visiting California to rest up before going full steam with a target of early fall 1917, unaware that personal and world events would upset his careful planning.[34]

# 10

# PROPAGANDIST
## 1917–1919

A S 1917 BEGAN, Adams was gathering the funds he needed for his novel *Success*. In the last months of 1916 and January 1917 he stocked his larder with five thousand dollars from magazines and movie rights. He added sixteen hundred dollars from *Collier's* for the light romance, "Enter Darcy," a four-part serial that featured another Adams metamorphosis, this time a young woman remade by an actress and an athletic trainer to become attractive, successful, and married. Another five hundred dollars came for the movie rights to the story "Orpheus." The "Our Square" series was concluded with the purchase for seven hundred dollars of a story about real estate dishonesty, but then fortune changed for Adams.

Before Sam and Jane Adams headed for California, he gave a talk on bad advertising in Auburn's Westminster Presbyterian Church despite a mix-up by the pastor, who had slated a wedding at the same time. The scheduling conflict should have warned him about what can happen to well-laid plans, but the Adamses left on 30 January for Cleveland, where he gave a speech, and then Indianapolis and Chicago, from which he did New York *Tribune* columns praising efforts in the cities to police advertising. On they went to the Southwest, and at the Grand Canyon he received word that his mother was seriously ill.

Returning to Auburn on 26 February, he found his mother conscious and able to recognize him but given only a few days to live. One week later, however, he wrote Scaife at Houghton Mifflin that his mother's condition remained the same and that the novel would be delayed because of the expenses. He reported he had accepted new *Tribune* work and now hoped to finish the novel in the fall. Scaife said if the novel did not progress well, the firm might consider a book of "Our Square" stories to fill in an off season.[1]

Hester Rose Hopkins Adams died 9 March at seventy-two. Adams spent a few days closing her rented room, including donating his father's official Civil War transcripts of the signals in the Battle of Mobile Bay to the Library of Congress. From the estate, to which he was sole heir, Adams received almost seven thousand dollars, mostly in stock not transferred until the end of the year.

On 15 March Sam and Jane Adams left again for California by way of New York. While there he wrote a *Tribune* column on the returned goods evil, in which he warned about the consumer footing the bill for returned merchandise. The newspaper asked him to follow his two city columns with a series on advertising practices by papers in other cities. The Adamses headed south and west, this time by a circuitous route. He wrote pieces from fourteen cities, including Baltimore, Washington, Atlanta, Shreveport, New Orleans, Dallas, Los Angeles, San Francisco, and Portland, Oregon. If the New York newspaper hoped to show that it was alone in its concern about fraudulent advertising, it was disappointed as he told not only of poor practices in other cities but also of successes. The Dallas *Dispatch* was so pleased with his column that it was reprinted in booklet form.[2]

Meanwhile, "The Meanest Man in Our Square" was published in the 24 March *Collier's*. Using a June 1916 *Tribune* column on Mary Murphy's experiences in dealing with real estate dishonesty in house buying, Adams stressed the need for legal aid societies. Like the other stories, the signatures of the "Our Square" series, which book critic Lewis Gannett later said "out-Henryed O. Henry,"[3] were his frequent poetry, social concerns, strong dialogue, and unusual characterizations such as Leon the Gnome, Dead-Man's Shoes, Pinney the Rat, and Terry the Cop, names similar to those that would be popularized by Damon Runyon twelve years later.

Greenslet, back from Europe after the United States entered the war on 6 April, followed up on Scaife's suggestion that Adams put the sketches into a book and wrote him on 20 April that he had made a proposal to agent Carl Brandt to publish *Our Square*. Adams, staying with Stewart Edward White at his new home in Burlingame and working on *Tribune* articles and short stories, accepted the proposal by the end of the month.

Although he was on his western trip when the country joined the Allies in World War I, he had shown during his stop in New York in March an interest in participation in the growing home-front activities. He attended a New York meeting of the Vigilantes, an association of writers and artists formed that month before America entered the Great War in April. The group was patterned on a British society of literati who provided propaganda favorable to the Allies. Although he was not a signer of the Vigilante pledge to abide by the general director's orders, he was an early contributor of a fable warning of the dangers of pacifism.[4]

After he spoke in May to the San Francisco Advertising Club on his findings in the city, the Adamses headed east. On 5 June they stopped in St. Louis where he covered and spoke at the convention of the Associated Advertising Clubs of the World. Adams heard how newspapers were supporting Liberty Loan and Red Cross drives, and he joined the war effort as soon as he got home. The local Red Cross had launched its campaign for forty thousand dollars, and he became head of publicity. He handled newspaper advertising, public speakers, and news coverage that raised more than forty-seven thousand dollars.

Throughout the summer Adams was busy writing up the *Tribune* series, which reported his findings in Arizona, Seattle, and Minneapolis and took him to Cleveland for his final city column. He also was editing *Our Square and the People in It*, delayed by a war-caused personnel shortage at Houghton Mifflin.

One welcome break came from a visit by Katherine Adams, who came east to visit her father and Jane Adams. At fifteen the girl was described by Gillmore as "a perfectly darling, very pretty little girl translation of Sam, even to Sam's amusing nose[.] But Katherine has her mother's eyes which are lovely in color—a deep blue." She went with her sister to Quisisana where things did not go well at first. "I brought some pretty dresses, but Jane had them dyed black," recalled Katherine Adell, probably because of the recent death of her grandmother. But the ever social Jane had a house party for the girls, and the ice thawed. On 21 July Katherine left for home after spending several weeks.[5]

When correcting book proofs in early August, Adams realized the original "Our Square" story in *Everybody's* had been omitted and had to edit the magazine copy before *Our Square and the People in It* was published 14 October. This lack of coordination led an alert *New York Times* critic to note that the Bonnie Lassie's first name was Carol in chapter 1 and Cecily in the last, but overall the *Times* was mostly positive.[6] The book took until February to get on *Bookman's* bestseller list. The main demand was in New York, and the book was listed four months. Equally importantly, the book made money, selling about six thousand copies, substantially more than Houghton Mifflin's breakeven point.[7]

Adams told Robert van Gelder in 1945 he considered the stories his best fiction and said, "Those stories are out of print now, but people still write remembering them and wanting to buy them." In the interview he told of his limited view of plots: "[T]here are only two basic plots: that for the adventure story of which mystery is an offshoot, and that for the love story."[8]

In early fall Adams went to Washington where his pen was enlisted in the national war effort by George Creel. A close friend of President Wilson, for whose reelection campaign he had marshaled support like that of Adams, he had been named in April as head of the Committee on Public Information. The committee, given almost dictatorial powers over the flow of information, had set up numerous subgroups. One, the Division of Syndicate Features, was charged with disseminating allied home-front propaganda to newspapers. To staff the division Creel called upon prominent American writers such as Adams's friends Tarkington and Nicholson and included muckrakers Baker and Tarbell. Creel estimated the features reached twelve million subscribers each month, or one-fourth of the population.[9]

Although Adams had come into the war late, he quickly bought into the growing nativism that targeted German-Americans, seen as agents of an alien state, but he broadened his attack to socialists, whose party was assailed as being dominated by individuals with pro-German leanings. On 5 September he wrote Greenslet that he would be putting in most of his time hunting pro-German and peace propaganda. From that moment until the war's end and beyond he dedicated most of his writing energy to the war despite Greenslet's appeal: "I am becoming convinced that we could do business with 'Success' in the fall of 1918. We ought not to skip a year without an Adams book—neither ought we to put in a boys' (or misses') size one again before 'Success.'"[10] For Adams Success was on the far horizon.

He had paid his own way to Washington to offer his services and was assigned a story on some captured German documents. In April 1916 the government had seized papers in the office of Wolfe von Igel, the undersecretary of the German Embassy, that purported to disclose a plot to blow up the Welland Canal between Lakes Erie and Ontario in Canada. Creel later wrote of Adams, "As a result of his skillful analysis of the papers taken from Von Igel by the Department of Justice, a page story went out that showed German intrigue down to the last sordid detail."[11] The Tribune ran the Von Igel story issued by the Committee on Public Information on 23 September 1917. Its placement minus a byline on the right side of page one was balanced by the second of three Adams articles on Hearst on the left.

Although the newspaper had continued its efforts on advertising, paying little attention to losing another six cents in a second libel suit, Waldo left the

*Tribune* on 1 September, and the next day Adams wrote a wrap-up column about his findings in the various cities he had visited.[12] Two weeks later he returned to the front page with his first "Who's Who Against America" column, intending to expose anti-Americanism and Hearst.

The post office had pushed the series, seeking to arouse public opinion against what it considered seditious utterances. The three Adams articles on "Herr William Randolph Hearst" attacked the New York *Journal* publisher and his growing empire of newspapers as having pro-German policies and as being the leading spirit of German propaganda. Post office hopes for prosecutions were dashed when Wilson replied 4 October to Postmaster General Albert Sidney Burlson on the Adams columns: "I have looked over them very carefully. It makes a tremendous case, of course, against Mr. Hearst, but there is nothing new about that and I am sorry to say there is nothing brought out in the articles which would seem to me to prove that Mr. Hearst had overstepped the bounds of law, outrageous as he has been."[13]

After Hearst, Adams criticized editor Abraham Cahan of the Yiddish socialistic daily *Forward* that had a circulation of more than one hundred thousand. He next fired another broadside against Hearst's International News Service. Then he took on editor Victor L. Berger of the Milwaukee *Leader,* a socialist daily, which he claimed got its inspiration from Hearst. He continued with Wisconsin Senator Robert M. La Follette, using the lawmaker's public comments to damn him, and ended his part of the series with a column asking, "Is Wisconsin Against America?" indicting what he called the state's anti-American phalanx.

Not only using the *Tribune* as an outlet, Adams pursued the theme of anti-Americanism in a four-part series entitled "Invaded America" in *Everybody's.* In the first article, "Poisoning the Press," he detailed through quotes the questionable conduct of the press, the pro-German foreign-language newspapers and Hearst. In the second article, on Wisconsin, he used some of the same information as in the *Tribune* but broadened his analysis to social, political, ethnic, and journalistic issues. In his third article he discussed what he called the process of Americanization in which he found some promising results in the Middle West. The fourth article had a similar theme, the assimilation of the alien, noting that one-third of the population was foreign-born or had foreign-born parents. Adams's optimism showed as he wrote, "If this war shall eventually unite the old America to the new America in a spirit of understanding, a bond or true national fellowship, it will be well worth the heaviest price that we may have to pay."

Adams finished his three years with the *Tribune* on 16 December when he returned to patent medicines with an exposé on the "stimulant" in nuxated iron peddled by two quacks armed with fake testimonials. The column also was his swan song with patent medicines as the war now occupied him and the public.

Sam and Jane Adams had returned in October 1917 from New York to Auburn where both joined committees for the first Liberty Loan Committee. Their efforts were assisted by the emergence of a special form of communication, the Four Minute Men. Before radio, the Committee on Public Information had organized the group as a speakers bureau. The Four Minute Men talked to audiences in the theaters and movie houses, publicizing the Liberty Loan drive with four-minute appeals. At the end of October Adams received one of the lowest payments of his career, a check for one dollar issued by the United States treasurer for Adams's salary as a "National Security and Defense Executive."[14] His employment as a dollar-a-year government employee was not a total loss for the free-lance writer, who was paid for many short stories. But the payment also reflected a new position.

When the Four Minute Men was two months old, Franklin McCormick Blair of Chicago became national director. Blair sought to expand the force of fifteen hundred speakers that had been credited for helping achieve the oversubscription of the national Liberty Loan goal of two million dollars by 52 percent. To help with the reorganization Blair set up a four-man National Advisory Council, which included Adams.[15]

Over the next year the Four Minute Men would grow to 75,000, and by the end of the war it was reported they had made more than seven-and-one-half million speeches to audiences totaling 134,454,515 people. His contribution to the organization was assessed by Blair in the *Four Minute Man News* bulletin to which Adams contributed an article on speech-making hints in April 1918: "Samuel Hopkins Adams was a most valuable addition to our staff. His advice and suggestions on all phases of what we were doing, but particularly on the bulletins, were of unestimable help. . . . Wherever he went he won recruits for us and left the local organizations immeasurably stronger and more enthusiastic."[16]

His greatest contribution, however, remained with his pen. He took his war duties seriously as his output of fiction was mostly devoted to war themes. "A Little Privacy" told of a private in the Home Guard who became a hero; "Orator of the Day," about a speaker for War Savings Stamps; "Three Days Leave," a romance between an army private and a colonel's daughter; and "The

Briber," about a young man and his sister who offered a local draft board a bribe to allow him to serve in the army. His last war fiction, a two-parter, "The Dodger Trail," was about German intrigue on the home front.

Adams returned to the *Saturday Evening Post* with a short story, "The Beggar's Purse." Subtitled "A Fairy Tale of Familiar Finance," the story told of a rich man who received from a beggar a magical wallet that controlled his money by refusing to open for unnecessary purchases. Over one day the man saved enough to buy two War Savings Stamps, learning "every time I spend a dollar I spend an extra quarter for vanity and a dime for timidity." He was asked for permission to reprint the story in pamphlet form. In a foreword Boston publishers Smith & Porter said the intent was to distribute a small number, but bulk orders from large firms were so great that a larger printing was ordered. The publisher said Adams asked that the books be furnished at cost in place of any royalties.[17]

Although he was paid for his fiction, no record of payment exists for "Fighting-Fit," an article in which he discussed medical preparedness at army camps, and "Private Smith Is Cordially Invited," about War Camp Community Service organizations that bolstered soldiers' morale. His need for money, however, may have led *Collier's* to pay seven hundred dollars for "Uncle Sam M.D." in which he discussed the preparedness of doctors in the army. Adams explained his war work in an October 1918 sketch prepared for *Collier's*: "Nowadays when I forsake the pig for the pen, it is mainly in the conscientious endeavor to earn the dollar a year which a recklessly extravagant Government pays me, or to write articles or fiction dealing with the one all engrossing subject, the war. But as soon as possible I revert to the job of raising food to Mr. Hoover's order."[18]

This assessment mirrored his modesty. Although in 1914 he had reluctantly talked with Moses, he shunned publicity. Neither Auburn newspaper mentioned his national war work. He did write the autobiographical sketch for *Collier's* and his publishers sent it to Charles Crittenden Baldwin for *The Men Who Make Our Novels*, issued in 1919 with the pseudonym George Gordon.

After his signing on as a dollar-a-year man, Adams often took to the road, such as to New England on government business in January 1918, to Hamilton College (his first reported return since his resignation as trustee) in February for Four Minute Men recruiting, and to Camp Devens in June. His efforts were not limited to government work. In July 1918 he was contacted by Van Wyck Brooks for a piece to go with a volume of cartoons by Louis Raemaekers. Enclosed was a cartoon showing the Kaiser hanging by his bound wrists from a cable running from the Eiffel Tower to the Washington Monument. Adams wrote a three-paragraph entry for the facing page in *America in the War*, called "Higher than a Sour Apple Tree" that decried the Kaiser's scorched earth policy in Europe as an "offense against generations unborn" for which, Adams said, he should hang on a gibbet.

At home he remained active, serving on the committee for the third Liberty Loan drive. He also put his wallet where his mouth was, giving $360 to the War Chest and investing the maximum $1,000 in War Savings Stamps. He offered his "best war story" at a Liberty Loan tea, about a German who said it was best to kill an Allied surgeon because a doctor could save five hundred soldiers.

Earlier, when the research for the Wisconsin articles had been done, Sam and Jane Adams spent an extended time in Wisconsin. The visit provided Adams the ammunition for his attacks on pro-German propaganda. Although his magazine work gave him considerable leeway in expressing his point of view, his findings in Wisconsin spurred him to turn to fiction to give a fuller account of the nature of the pro-German threat. One of his longest short stories, "Common Cause," bought by the *Saturday Evening Post*, told of German propaganda in the state of Centralia and the need for people to put aside their political differences to deal with it.

After Greenslet read an Adams copy of the "Common Cause" story, he wired in May 1918: "THE COMMON CAUSE IS WORTH BUILDING UP. COULD YOU MAKE IT FIFTY OR SIXTY THOUSAND WORDS AND INTRODUCE A SKIRT?" Adams replied he could deliver a book by September, starting the first of July and doing the first draft in five weeks. In June he received one thousand dollars for "Common Cause" from the magazine. Although he had hoped to sell it as a two- or three-part serial for more money, he was pleased with the *Post* placement because of the visibility offered.[19]

Concerning the novel, he said although he was using a newspaper environment, it was a war story. His intentions, however, were overwhelmed by his interest in the American newspaper as an institution and "its struggle to maintain its independence against the forces which seek to employ it as an agency for alien, and in this case un-American, propaganda." He admitted the theme was essentially the same as *The Clarion*, "that is, the persistent and perhaps inevitable effort to use the newspaper press for ulterior purposes and thus divert it from its proper function of informing public opinion."[20]

After his visit to Camp Devens, he met with Greenslet to go over the beginning and summary of the new novel. Agreement was reached for an advance of five hundred dollars. Scaife was particularly interested in the developing of the women's angle, noting the work of women's committees: "They are dabbling in politics too, and a great many of them would like to dabble more."[21]

In June Adams contracted with Gertrude Battles Lane of the *Woman's Home Companion* for "Whisperings," an article warning against the spreading of anti-American rumors. He sent the manuscript for six hundred dollars in early July and turned to his novel.[22] His work was complicated by the health of his flamboyant uncle Woolsey R. Hopkins, who had been stricken by a heart attack in March. Heart disease, which had killed Adams's father, made the active lawyer an invalid and kept Adams close at home.

Eager to prime his cash flow, he did go to New York in early September to seek magazine commissions and got contracts for more than $6,000. His orders were with *Collier's* for six articles totaling $3,500 and with *Everybody's* for four short stories on Washington for $2,650. He continued to rewrite his novel in September, cutting paragraphs except for the final chapter. He sent Greenslet the last batch of proofs on November 8, two days after his uncle died at sixty-seven.

The end of the war on 11 November came as a surprise to Adams, but he was quick to assess the effect of the armistice on his yet-to-be-published novel. In response to Greenslet, who wrote that the publishing had been delayed until after Christmas and told him the novel would be promoted "not as a war book, but as an #1 novel of Western newspaper life, with a certain amount of historic war interest," Adams agreed but reflected that the beginning of the war had hurt *The Clarion* and now the end might do the same to *Common Cause*.[23]

He was named to Cayuga County's Homecoming Reception Committee to welcome the twelve hundred returning veterans on the same day *Common Cause; A Novel of the War in America* was published, 25 January 1919. In view of Adams's and Greenslet's concerns about a war book it was surprising that neither seemed concerned about the subtitle. On that date, also, Houghton Mifflin paid $750 for advance orders in addition to the $500 advanced in September. "The book has made a substantial start, and everybody seems to like it," Greenslet wrote.[24]

The novel told of a young man, who used his inheritance to buy a corrupt daily newspaper. Like Hal Surtaine of *The Clarion*, Jeremy Robson was guided by a mentor, Andrew Galpin, an experienced newspaper man. Instead of patent medicines and public health suppressers as villains, "Deutschtum" was composed of pro-Germans seeking to establish a Little Germany in the midwestern state of Centralia. In the fight the newspaper had to deal with unhappy advertisers, corrupt politicians, and self-centered businessmen. At the end the newspaper was prosperous, the young couple married, and Robson became a United States senator.

His pat ending did not dissuade the reviewers from praise. Not only had Adams done his newspaper work well, but his account of Wisconsin prompted a state newspaper to adopt him as "a Wisconsin man" although it noted that he said the novel was "based upon the Wisconsin situation as I found it in 1917 and the early part of 1918." War-weary America, however, had tired of war stories, even if they had other themes. The novel never made the revised *Bookman* format of the top six books in demand at public libraries. When told by Brandt three months after the book was published that Scaife was disappointed by sales, Adams wrote he was not surprised by the sales after the armistice. Scaife replied he was disappointed because the book was good.[25]

The sales of *Common Cause* did surpass the total of *Our Square and the People in It*, totaling 7,578 copies, including 160 in Canada and 145 to war libraries. It more than doubled Houghton Mifflin's break-even point of 3,650 volumes and produced $1,793.12 in royalties. Despite his constant concern about money Adams did well in the war years. In 1917 his gross payments from magazines and book royalties were $9,204, more than his $8,630 in 1916. The 1918 gross was $9,768, with help from *Collier's* $3,500, and 1919 would be even better.

For much of the last month of 1918 and the first two of 1919 Adams was in Washington doing research for his *Collier's* articles and *Everybody's* short stories. Most of the *Collier's* articles were four articles called "Loose Leaves of Diplomacy." He also published "U.S. Adv.—An Experiment in Idealism" on how five million dollars was used to promote Liberty Loans. "The Color Scheme of War" and "Rx—American or German" discussed the German dye industry. For the *Everybody's* series of short stories on Washington, he had tales on bureaucracy in Washington, on war profiteering by a "spillionaire," on a romance in the Chemical Division, and on the changing postwar role of women in the nation's capital.[26]

His magazine nonfiction writing covered a variety of topics as the author sought his place in postwar America. In *Delineator* he had concentrated on health with "Famine—The New Threat Against the World" and "To Keep Europe Alive—Milk." Both articles urged America to use its resources to feed beleaguered Europe. In *Red Cross Magazine* his interest in medicine led him to explore the rehabilitation of wounded veterans.[27] In *Red Cross* also his

"Hand-Made Americans" in November discussed a naturalization class conducted by Utica publisher George Dunham, a graduate of Hamilton.

He developed one aspect of the rehabilitation programs for *Collier's* with "'Blinks'" about a government training program for veterans blinded by the war. Other articles for *Collier's* showed a weaning from wartime issues. Although his propaganda pen was silent on political matters involving the peace, he turned to theater and to labor, on the Winnipeg general sympathy strike. The magazine continued to promote him as its labor reporter and Carl Sandburg reported Adams in Chicago to research the Labor Party, but a strike by the *Collier's* typesetters later in the year may have chilled the topic. The magazine, however, did order a new series of six "Our Square" short stories for forty-nine hundred dollars.[28]

His fiction also was paying further benefits. The June 1919 sale of his serial "Enter Darcy" to Famous Players of the Lasky Corporation continued Adams's flirtation with the motion pictures. Although his "A Letter to Nowhere" never made it into film, his short story "Triumph" had become a Bluebird Photoplays film of the same name, made by Universal Films. He sold a two-part adventure-romance in the Caribbean, "'Excess Baggage,'" to Essanay Film Corporation for $750, but no record showed that it or "Orpheus" became films. His short story, "A Little Privacy," however, became a two-reel Universal Special under the title *Fighting Mad*, for which Brandt & Brandt recorded no sale. Adams may have donated his rights to the war effort. He certainly made up for it with his two thousand dollars for "Enter Darcy."[29]

The original serial was retitled *Wanted: A Husband*, with the scenario written by Clara S. Beranger, called one of the ablest continuity writers. Years later he called the film awful although he said he never saw it. The film, however, spurred the Houghton Mifflin sales manager to urge the serial be developed into a novel.[30]

He hoped to start *Success* in October and then take the draft to Hibernia, Florida, for six weeks in the winter. This left time between July and October, so he told Greenslet on 28 July that although his feelings would not be hurt if a plan to turn "Enter Darcy" into a novel were rejected, he would do it if they wished.

After Greenslet gave him a contract at the end of August, Adams promised the expanded version in a fortnight, but he did not finish the last chapter until 21 October. The delay may be attributed, in part, to his lifestyle. At home he continued recreational pursuits to counter his mornings of writing. A revival of community interest in tennis led him into a Labor Day tournament in which he won the city championship over Frank W. Moore, a member of the Auburn Theological Seminary and twenty years younger. "I only won because Frank had hurt his hand," Adams said many years later.[31]

Finished with writing the light novel, he shipped the manuscript to Houghton Mifflin. Adopting a practice of giving publishers and his agents authority to make any changes they wished after he had completed writing, he turned to discussing the illustrations. Instead of the originals, drawn by Fred Steele, the author suggested the Billie Burke still pictures from the film. When Greenslet saw the photographs, he warned they would "carnalize your tale." After getting them, Adams agreed and urged Steele to make Darcy more attractive.[32]

One concern he did not have at the end of the decade was money. In November he had published an article on the rising cost of living, "The Anxious Class," in *Pictorial Review*. In the article he defined the comfortable class as those two million families living on incomes of between $2,000 and $6,000 per year. By the end of 1919 his recorded earnings were $10,693. Not included was the sale of his Chedell Place house for $7,000 nor of the articles privately negotiated.

The Adamses spent Christmas 1919 getting ready to leave for Florida. Adams was eager to write more "Our Square" stories. America now looked forward to the next decade with a desire to return to normalcy after the Great War. He, too, hoped to find his "real book" as he returned to his *Success*. Both the nation and the writer would meet with unexpected results.

# 11

# CHRONICLER
## 1920–1924

As the Adamses settled in Hibernia for the winter in January 1920, he had his novel *Success* to complete. Jane Adams entertained visiting Northerners, partial to the Florida community on the St. John's River, ten miles south of Jacksonville. Despite guests his regimen of writing in the morning was zealously guarded by his wife until their social day began with tennis or lunch.

His fictional account of the story of Arthur Brisbane, Hearst's right-hand man, continued its interrupted path. In a letter to Greenslet, Adams on his forty-ninth birthday suggested a book of the new "Our Square" stories. Explaining that he was not working on *Success* because he still had one or two stories in the series to write for *Collier's*, he admitted that he also was working on a detective story. He promised, however, he would finish his short fiction in February and then tackle *Success*.[1]

Greenslet replied that the book of short stories should follow, not precede, *Success*, predicting advance orders of twenty thousand to fifty thousand for the novel, whereas the anthology would sell from five thousand to ten thousand. He warned that if the anthology were published first, it might cut the *Success* sales in half, but if the novel went first, the short story book sales might double. Saying the reasoning was sound, Adams turned to discussing the dreary Florida weather.[2]

January 1920 also marked the debut of the first of three Adams sports short stories on boxing in the *Saturday Evening Post*, the gamble of having selected the magazine for "Common Cause" in 1918 paying off. At a time when the Manassa Mauler, Jack Dempsey, was electrifying heavyweight boxing as champion, the stories featured trainer Andy Dunne, whom Adams had introduced in "Enter Darcy." Sports remained a theme for "Amateurs and Others" in *Red*

*Book Magazine.* Reminiscent of the 1919 Black Sox baseball scandal, it told of corruption and a minister who took the mound to save the day. *Red Book* also carried two mystery stories, including the detective story mentioned to Greenslet. "Doom River Red," about a sleepwalker falsely accused of a crime, was followed by "The Town That Wasn't" about a disappearing man and town.

*Collier's*, the *Saturday Evening Post*, and *Red Book Magazine* were not his only markets during the early part of the 1920s. He published two romances, featuring a butterfly in the *Ladies' Home Journal* and a botanist in Hibernia in the *Post.* Earlier the publishers of his "Miss Grouch" serial, the fashion magazine *Delineator*, ran an article using the fable of the ant and the grasshopper to urge people to buy their coal early.

Pleased by his return to *Delineator*, the new editor, Marie M. Meloney, privately negotiated another article, "Why Boys Leave Home," questioning whether they were quitters or pioneers. He also wrote a brief short story freelance, "Salvage," about a boy accused of breaking a streetlamp globe with a bean shooter but exonerated when the judge tried to duplicate the feat. Meloney, a former New York *Sun* staffer, bought the story, praising its compactness.[3]

While Adams was in Florida, the book based on "Enter Darcy" was published in April under the title of the film, *Wanted: A Husband.* The story featured Amanda Darcy Cole's transformation from a frump into a radiant woman. Her mentor was actress Gloria Greene, and the conversion was handled by athletic trainer Dunne. As he often did, he used locales he knew, and he transported Darcy to Boulder Brook on Lake Quam, a thin disguise for the Boulder Brook address of friends, the R. L. Beckwiths on Squam Lake in New Hampshire.

When sending Adams an advance copy in March, Scaife indicated his tepidness, saying, "I only hope that the book will sell up to its value because it is a diverting little story which I imagine you have written 'with your tongue in your cheek' as it were." It would eventually gross Adams $2,280 on sales of 13,308 copies, more than double *Our Square* and 6,000 more than *Common Cause.*[4]

He finished the rough draft of part 1 of *Success* on 15 April 1920. He estimated the book would be done in August and began part 2 in May after a stay in New York where he researched newspapers, sent an inscribed copy of *Wanted: A Husband* to Billie Burke, and nursed Jane Adams after an "unusually severe" tonsillectomy. He was cheered by *Everybody's* interest in part 1 of *Success*, which traced the early years of hero Errol Banneker as a railroad station agent in the Southwest.

Scaife was pleased that *Everybody* was "getting on the Band Wagon," but in June Adams reported that part 2 about Banneker's newspaper work in New York was not going well. He urged Scaife or Greenslet to come to the lake to talk it out, offering as further bait a meeting with penologist Thomas Mott Osborne, who was planning five books.[5] Neither Scaife nor Greenslet could come, and Adams enlisted Brandt's aid as he wrestled with the novel. He took out some of his frustration on the golf course before finally losing to Harold Ferris in a tournament. Although the Adamses had their usual houseful for the Fourth of July holiday, the rest of the summer of 1920 was devoted to *Success* and a few guests.

One guest was a young girl, Lydia Mead, whom Jane Adams had met through a mutual friend. In Moravia, a small village south of Owasco Lake, Jane asked the girl's mother to let her visit. "Mother, who thought I would be exposed to wild people, was reluctant," Lydia Mead Engelbert recalled. "After Jane promised, 'Mrs. Mead, we'd love to have Lydia come and I'll protect her like a daughter,' my mother relented." During the summers Lydia Mead was a frequent guest, and true to her word, Jane on occasion had the beautiful young teenager sleep on a lattice-work bed in her dressing room.[6]

The friendship produced an early education for Lydia Mead, who remembered the "scintillating breakfasts," the Sunday evening hymn singing with Jane leading and Adams playing the piano, and, most of all, the other guests. A special favorite of hers was illustrator Rae Irvin, who would do the first cover for the *New Yorker*. She also recalled Adams's old flame, Rose O'Neill, actor Otis Skinner, Stewart and Betty White, novelist Kathleen Norris, and critic Percy Hammond, but her fondest memories were of Jane Adams: "She was very handsome and always stood very erect. She had chestnut hair and eyes and never looked old. She swam in the lake every morning in the nude and everyone knew to stay out of the way. She was smart as a whip but did not let it show and would bring out the best in a person. Jane was especially understanding of people who had problems." Dinner was a big event, with often twenty people. Adams was deferential to his wife, who loved to make dramatic entrances. "Everyone drank a lot," Lydia Mead Engelbert recalled, "but Sam and Jane were very stable together in the midst of the ruckus. Sam was puritanical and didn't like overdrinking or coarse stories. I had a lovely time."

Adams shipped the draft of part 2 of *Success* to Brandt in late August, and Greenslet reported that he had heard from the agent "that it is the best piece of work you have ever done, and it is one of the best stories he has read in a long time." Saying that all departments were eagerly awaiting the book, he declared, "We are prepared to make it our leader for next spring or fall, whichever season it will be ready for." Adams said he would go over the third part with Brandt before visiting Scituate.[7]

He also tackled the serial version of part 1. *Everybody's* had turned it down, but Brandt persuaded *Pictorial Review* to run a three-part serial as "Enchantment." Adams had to incorporate the first and last parts of the novel to produce a strong ending. He said he regretted that the book would be delayed a year by the serial but said that he was getting five thousand dollars for it.

Although *Wanted: A Husband* did little for his literary stature that he was sure would be enhanced by *Success*, Adams's advice on writing remained a sought-after commodity. Osborne gave him a manuscript to review, and with his usual candor and an unusual amount of tact, Adams congratulated the prison reformer on having a real story and then criticized the work for mixing together fiction and fact, a dictum that he himself would violate later in the decade.[8]

As 1921 began, the easy pace of the previous winter in Hibernia was now replaced by an accelerated rate. He arose before dawn, got in at least two hours before breakfast, and then worked the rest of the morning. He also had a volunteer help with the typing as he rushed to get the final rewrite done. Back in Cayuga County in May, he finished ahead of schedule, leaving time for Franklin Pierce Adams to check over the journalistic part 2. After receiving the completed novel, Greenslet said the manuscript was "very much improved" and would be the firm's leading fall novel "with undivided interest and genuine enthusiasm." As the early copies came off the press, he and Houghton Mifflin mapped the advertising campaign. Adams was excited by the prospects for what he was sure would be a big seller.[9]

While he prepared in late 1921 to spend the winter in a New York apartment, he continued to communicate with his Houghton Mifflin colleagues, identifying reviewers, who like his friends, critic Hammond and dramatist Channing Pollock, he felt would help promote the novel. He also suggested a copy be sent to Upton Sinclair, who Adams said might view *Success* as backing for his own *Brass Check* novel about newspapering.

*Success* came out 14 October. The story of Banneker's rise from desert station agent to a position of power as a New York journalist and of his subsequent return to California was told in a long, if not big, book, the seven years of work having produced 553 pages. Although J. P. Gavit in *Literary Review* called the book "the best newspaper story I can recall," the *New York Times* was brutal in saying Adams had created a "fantastic" story with the guise of being a realist: "Yet what Mr. Adams has actually done is to produce a tour de force of unreality. His people are unreal; his conversations, of which heavy page succeeds heavy page, are unreal; his action is unreal."[10]

The day after the *New York Times* review, Scaife wrote Adams: "Can't you do something to the *Times*—take an axe, or a bomb, or even better, get someone to reply to that outrageous review of 'Success' which appeared in the last issue?" Adams said it was what one might expect of the *Times* and suggested the newspaper's pan be put in an ad along with favorable comments. It was but did little to help the lagging sales of *Success*.[11]

What went wrong with *Success?* Its length? Its mixed plots? Its characterizations? Several New York journalists were recognizable through their thin disguises. He admitted that Banneker's confidant Russell Edwards was based on socialist Charles Edward Russell. Others identified Gordon as Chester Lord, Richard W. Gaines as S. S. McClure, Poultney Masters as J. P. Morgan, Tertius Marrineal as Hearst, and, of course, Banneker as Brisbane. The characterizations may have been lost on unsophisticated readers but riled journalists such as Woollcott, who wrote a distressed denunciation of Adams's portrayal of drama critics.[12]

Or was it tone? The bleak book ended with the loner Banneker leaving the newspaper profession in disgust. The theme of the "outsider" in American society dominated his early novels. As scholar James Stanford Bradshaw has noted about the Adams newspaper novels, Surtaine in *The Clarion*, Robson in *Common Cause*, and Banneker in *Success* were ostracized by the people they sought to help, making them pariahs. The detective Average Jones, health officer Perkins in *The Unspeakable Perk*, and the frumpy Darcy Cole in *Wanted: A Husband* all moved on the fringes of society. Despite his involvement in literary and Auburn circles Adams was, as writer George Metcalf suggested, also an outsider. His irascible nature often irritated his close colleagues such as the Irwins, and semi-isolation at Wide Waters set him apart from Auburnians. Temperament even strained his professional relationships.[13]

His relationship with Houghton Mifflin began to darken in January 1922. Miffed by an apparent end of advertising for *Success*, he wrote an angry letter to Greenslet that although he was receiving word-of-mouth praise for the book, it needed more promotion. He said that he was falling far short of his goal of fifteen thousand dollars for the novel and charged the company had lost faith because of some of the reviews. Greenslet promptly explained that the firm had already spent 15 percent of sales on advertising, more than the average of

7 percent and the company's maximum of 10 percent. He said further the company was showing a loss of more than two thousand dollars because of advertising and printing expenses of the long novel. He promised, however, the firm would review its position and asked to meet with him in New York the following week.[14]

After the meeting between Adams and Greenslet, Scaife jumped in, saying the firm was ready to spend more on advertising although more from loyalty to Adams than from any belief the advertising would help. Denying his concern about the *Times* review indicated "cold feet," Scaife added, "We are with you as long as you are with us." Adams continued to stew and then thundered at Scaife about a Greenslet comment that the book was two kinds of story. Scaife asked to meet him in New York. After the meeting, Scaife offered an advertising promotion in Rochester. Adams declined to participate. The author softened, however, and praised Scaife for doing his best. He then discussed his next serious novel, a struggle between the old and young based on the du Ponts. Scaife, equally eager to bury the argument, said he was delighted with the book idea.[15]

Although Adams and Houghton Mifflin were chagrined by sales of the book, *Success* did eventually sell 22,632 regular editions with 10,000 cheaper editions by Grosset & Dunlap, plus 3,500 in Canada and 2,895 in Australia. The total was well above the break-even point the company needed to cover publication costs, and eventually his final gross was $8,020. Aside from money, his reputation was not damaged by the reviews, and a Minnesota professor, speaking on current fiction, in an Auburn lecture called *Success* a "first class wholesome American novel by a clean man."[16] That description of Adams would change.

When he and Houghton Mifflin discussed promoting *Success*, Greenslet had mentioned that Zelma Brandt, Carl Brandt's wife and colleague, said Adams was considering a book on alcohol. The fifty-year-old author, however, rejected the idea, saying, in a classic understatement on 27 October 1921 he might last to do one more novel.[17] Yet alcohol and the prohibition of its sale were themes in the early 1920s for Adams, an early backer of the prohibition movement, signing a petition of one thousand who asked Congress to ban the liquor trade. His idealism was not matched by performance.

He turned a blind eye on the ban when it came to his personal use. Katherine Adell said: "Father believed in following the law, but when it came to entertaining his guests, that was all right." In a 1920 questionnaire for the *Cleve-*

*land Press* he answered a query about his favorite hobby by saying, "Watching my friends violate the Volstead Act."[18]

Much of his nonfiction writing tried to deal with the contradictions; "On Sale Everywhere" in July 1921 discussed the nation's failure to comply with the law. It was followed by "My Bootlegger" in which he warned of the involvement of organized crime in the illegal acts. He was candid: "My bootlegger used to be a good citizen. So did I. He respected and obeyed the law. So did I. . . . He became an illicit seller and I became an illicit buyer. . . . We represent, I suppose, an abnormal condition of the body politic. My bootlegger is the symptom of it. I, I suspect, am the disease."

His willingness to speak out may have prompted *Leslie's Illustrated Weekly* to commission him to do an article in April 1922, analyzing information gathered by the magazine's questionnaire on Prohibition. He surmised the new law was neither established nor accepted. One year later he returned to the topic with "Science Has Its Say about Alcohol," citing statistics to provide the scientists' point of view about the abuse of alcohol. He quoted Dr. Raymond Pearl of Johns Hopkins, called the foremost American biological statistician, as saying the use of alcohol in moderation was not injurious to health. Adams concluded alcohol was a destroyer of souls rather than bodies, a position that produced a number of letters to *Collier's*.

The proposed book on Prohibition never developed because, as he wrote Maurice in April 1922, there was too much misinformation. Although he had an agreement in February for the book with Macmillan, he begged off, and Macmillan canceled the contract in May. His willingness to use new publishers had significance.[19]

Houghton Mifflin published *From a Bench in Our Square* in November 1922, with "Triumph" added to the *Collier's* seven stories. The *New York Times*, which had savaged *Success*, called the collection "interesting and diverting sketches" that would so please the readers they would want to read the first book. Noting that he used a method to "look deeply into the human heart and write about it in the colors of the finest possibilities which they see in its depths," the *Times* wondered how different his technique of "looking at life through the glasses of the optimist" was from the method of the younger generation, which was "interested only in colors that are dark and sinister."[20]

Writing, like America, was changing. Although Auburn dancing master J. Herbert Walsh after a visit to New York in 1921 announced jazz dancing was doomed, others did not agree. Sales of *From a Bench in Our Square* during

1922 and 1923 indicated changing tastes as the book sold 3,249 regular and 250 Canadian issues, barely more than half the sales of the original *Our Square* and considerably under the amount Greenslet had forecast. Adams grossed $873 from the book, and he sought new alternatives for his fiction.[21]

While Adams tried to adjust to the new times, Jane Adams showed that although she could be taken out of theater, theater could not be taken out of her. Her daughter, Mildred Post, had joined Laurette Taylor for a minor role in a February 1921 revival of Taylor's earlier success, *Peg o' My Heart*, and although Mildred disliked the theater, her work on the stage must have pleased her mother. The next year some gentle arm twisting by Osborne brought Jane back to theater as a director for the new Auburn Amateur Dramatic Club.

After directing several one-act plays, she took on the full-length farce, *A Pair of Sixes*, in November with Adams as a patent medicine maker, who "from makeup to mannerisms, was a delight in his character part of a drug company magnate." Osborne faded into the scenery, Jane directed for six years, and Adams retired.[22] After the play, they went to New York for the winter. While there, Adams was being amused by the sensation a new book *Flaming Youth*, by Warner Fabian, was creating.

As flappers, bootleg liquor, and spending excesses became rampant in the 1920s, authors such as Irwin were floundering in the new morality, unable to adapt to the Roaring Twenties. In a September 1920 letter to Meloney of *Delineator* Adams said he had talked with some college girls and had been startled by some of their views.[23] While in New York he had written an essay, "Apollyon vs. Pollyanna," for a *New Republic* supplement, "The Newspaper of Tomorrow." His warning of the dangers of censorship was heightened by his new book.

Unlike Irwin, he realized the potential for opening new vistas. He said later: "A young friend of mine kept a diary—quite a document it was. She showed it to me, and I asked if I could use some of it." With the diary as "a pretty accurate document on life," he created a family of young women caught up in the swirl of the decade. "Then I didn't want the source to get out, so I wrote it under the name of Fabian." Not only did he chronicle the mores of the new America, he invented a new author to write the story, Warner Fabian. The name was suggested by a woman in Philadelphia. "She made it up—she had some friends named Warner and some other friends named Fabian. I think I had to buy her a drink to pay for it," he revealed later. He gave Fabian the disguise of a family physician because the doctor "sees through the body into the soul."[24]

He told the story of the fictitious Fentriss sisters in Dorrisdale. When he was done, Adams said later, "I knew it was a book that could make a helluva lot of money, but I didn't want my name on it." He never mentioned the manuscript in correspondence with Houghton Mifflin, probably because the Boston firm would not have touched it.[25] Instead, Adams turned to New York publisher Horace Liveright.

Adams was known when he came to the brownstone house that was the home of Boni & Liveright at 61 West 48th Street, now part of the site of Radio City. But his manuscript was not, and it presented a gamble. Bennett Cerf, who joined Boni & Liveright on 1 November 1923, after working on Wall Street, said Liveright agreed to publish Adams's book because it was of the moment. "*Flaming Youth* was his kind of baby—a book about the flapper age," Cerf said of the novel, which he claimed Adams wrote "more or less as a joke."[26] Although Cerf sounded like an apologist, Adams, while admitting the writing was not his best, thought the theme of the rebellion of youth was so good that he used it for a dozen years under Fabian and his own name.

*Flaming Youth*, whose title came from Shakespeare's *Hamlet*, was published in January 1923. The critics were nearly unanimous in their condemnations. *Bookman* wrote: "Indubitably 'Flaming Youth,' though honest is shocking. We do not like it. It shocks *us*." After reviewing the plot, including the petting parties and a nude midnight swim, the *New York Times* asked, "Hot stuff, what?"[27]

Readers answered "yes" in droves as the book roared through sixteen printings in 1923. Although it did not appear on *Bookman's* list of ten top sellers and despite condemnation by critics and the clergy, *Flaming Youth* eventually sold 70,945 regular copies, 62,500 cheap editions, and 1,882 in Canada. Adams royalties were $500 on publication, $7,154 on 5 September 1923; $8,800 on 11 February 1924; and $2,821 on 7 October 1924. His total was $22,043 for the book. British editions by Stanley Paul sold more than 100,000 copies.

Promoted with big advertisements "with black, black type and eye-catching borders," the novel was, in Cerf's words, "The biggest of its kind until Scott Fitzgerald came along." One reader who appreciated *Flaming Youth* was Fitzgerald, whose *This Side of Paradise* had been published in 1920. After he received a copy of the novel inscribed by Warner Fabian, he wrote a letter to "Mr. X" in May 1923:

> Thanks ever so much for the copy of "Flaming Youth." I had of course been reading it as it appeared in Metropolitan and enjoying it immensely. It will be a great pleasure to start from the beginning and read it thru as I had missed several installments.

Who in the devil are you? Do you know at least a dozen people have asked me if I wrote it. I wish I had but I'm sure I didn't—so who did. Tell me immediately and oblige

Yours Admiringly + Gratefully
F Scott Fitzgerald[28]

Although the letter reached the Brandt & Brandt offices, no reply was recorded. The chances that Adams answered Fitzgerald's letter were slight because he and those around him guarded the identity of Fabian. Cerf recalled, "There was great speculation as to who Warner Fabian really was, but we kept the mystery going for a long, long time."[29] It was not until its 1947–49 edition that the *Readers' Guide to Periodical Literature* would list Fabian as a pseudonym for Adams.

Educated guesses, however, made the linkage. Cerf said that when a rumor reached a book buyer that Adams was Fabian, "an unsung hero from the Boni and Liveright sales staff convinced her in confidence that it really was Rudyard Kipling." As early as 1925, Baldwin in revising his Adams sketch in *The Men Who Make Our Novels* wrote: "Indeed, so great is his reputation for the light fantastic, he has been everywhere acclaimed the author of the decade's best flapper story, *Flaming Youth*."[30]

Although tame by current standards, *Flaming Youth* created such a sensation that it joined the Jazz Age and Roaring Twenties as describers of the time of the Lost Generation. If Fabian was shocking, the greatest shock came to his creator, Adams, when the Associated First National film company paid $14,000 for the movie rights to *Flaming Youth*. For Adams, who had recorded earning payments for his writings of $8,266 in 1920, $10,240 in 1921, and $10,292 in 1922, the sum was a bonanza. In 1923 he had $7,654 in book advances and royalties with the $14,000 for the film pushing him more than halfway to his biggest gross yearly income, without commissions deducted, of $38,942. And he had not reached his peak.

First National assigned John Francis Dillon to direct the screen version of *Flaming Youth* with Harry O. Hoyt doing the scenario. One of the company's new stars, Colleen Moore, was given the lead in the nine-reel feature film released 14 December 1923. The *New York Times* was surprised at the unusual leniency of the censor but attributed it to the artistic photography.[31]

*Bookman*, which had begun making comments on current novels in "The Bookman's Guide to Fiction," listed blurbs on *Flaming Youth* for twelve months. On the last month it also listed a new book: "SIEGE—Samuel Hopkins Adams—Boni, Liveright. Youth besieges family entrenched—it's no disparagement to say that a novel with such a theme has a 'Booth Tarkington' ring."[32]

Back in 1919 while Adams was doing *Success*, he shared his plans for his next book with Scaife and Greenslet. Maurice, who did a sketch of Adams for *Bookman*, said author Anne Parrish suggested the idea. Later, after talking with Meredith Nicholson, who had a similar idea but not the time, Adams liked his suggestion that he focus on the du Ponts. After he finally got to Wilmington, he discovered the du Ponts were not a suitable subject because the family had many admirable qualities. Instead, Adams switched the action to a New England mill town and created as a central character the grande dame Augusta Ruyland, modeled on his grandmother Hopkins and a fellow writer's mother.[33]

Correspondence in April 1922 had indicated that Houghton Mifflin would publish *Siege*. Adams promised Scaife first choice on the book, but the firm turned the book down. After a note from Adams on 3 November, letters between them ceased.[34] For *Siege*, Adams chose Fabian's publishers, Boni & Liveright.

While he worked on the manuscript, the Adamses had an uneventful 1923 summer at Wide Waters. Although he was in charge of tennis club planning, he did not participate in any tournaments, perhaps indicating a worsening hip condition. In the fall, after a visit to the Irwins in Scituate, Jane Adams again did a play. Two of Thomas Mott Osborne's sons, Lithgow and Charles Osborne, and their wives took roles as the friendship of one generation passed to the next, an occurrence that would form a pattern in Adams's life.

In 1923 he balanced his writing of *Siege* with demands for more Fabian work. He wrote a novelette, "Wandering Fires," in *Snappy Stories*, telling the story of Guerda Anthony, who sacrificed her reputation to protect a man from scandalmongers. Adams's own reputation may have suffered from a linkage with Fabian.

The *Saturday Evening Post* ran two of his stories in late 1922 and early 1923, "Poor Tessie" and "Vandorn's Hired Help." Then the *Post*, under the editorship of conservative George Lorimer, dried up as a market for his fiction. In August 1922 *Red Book* ran his "The Isle o' Dreams" and in March 1923 "The Eye of the Beholder." Then *Red Book* carried no stories for three years. Adams developed new markets. An early issue of *Liberty* ran a short story, "It Did Happen," about a woman who stole a car of a man looking for a wife. The sale opened a relationship that would last more than twenty years.

He also went to newspapers. His friend, Loring Pickering of the North American Newspaper Alliance, a syndicated feature service, asked him to do a piece on fictional characters he would invite to a dinner party. Adams's article ran fourth in a series, and in it he and the Bonnie Lassie of the *Our Square* made out the guest list, which included Mephistopheles sitting next to Pollyanna. Adams relegated himself to second butler.[35]

He sold to a secondary market, the *Chicago Sunday Tribune Magazine*, two short stories, and had a one-shot short story, "The Indissoluble Bond," in an anthology, *Marriage; Short Stories of Married Life by American Authors.* One market held up. *Collier's* in March 1923 ran "First Up Best Dressed," about actresses stranded in Chicago. It also ran two articles on public policy matters: an interview with a convict, who might have been in Auburn State Prison, on auto theft and an article on the deterioration of paper records in "Fade-Outs of History," urging preservation techniques for newspapers and the *Congressional Record*. The articles produced reaction, with *Literary Digest* reprinting the first and a reader commenting about the loss of printed records, "Praise the Lord!"[36] Adams must have said the same when *Collier's* bought the *Siege* serial for $12,500.

Although the muckraking movement had faded into World War I, he returned to public health writing with "Doubling the Guards on Health" in the May 1923 *World's Work*. He urged support for the efforts of public health officers and that they be trained professionals rather than recipients of political patronage. He was aware, however, the public health movement had accomplished many of its goals, and he turned to the medical profession.

Later in 1923 the *Ladies' Home Journal* began publishing a series by Adams on rural health care. In "The Vanishing Country Doctor" and "Why the Doctor Left" he examined the difficulty of luring medical graduates to rural practice. In the third article he proposed in "Medically Helpless" the establishment of state-supported rural hospitals with inexpensive care and national health insurance. This may have been too strong for the conservative magazine, or Fabian may have caught up, because a fourth article was never used. Adams's byline did not appear in the magazine again.

His discussions of alcohol and medical care were joined by three articles in 1924 on drug addiction. In "The Cruel Tragedy of 'Dope'" he called addiction a disease and attacked laws that made it a crime. "How People Become Drug Addicts" blamed wartime medical treatment. He ended the series by calling for legislation in "How to Stop the 'Dope' Peddler." With the drug series, Adams, for the most part, ended his medical writing.

The Adamses were in California when *Siege* was published in February 1924. The clash of generations featuring the powerful and lonely Augusta Ruyland received mixed reviews. *Bookman* carried book blurbs for five months, but it did not sell well, and at one place not at all. Cerf said Gimbels, which Adams had blasted in his *Tribune* column, refused to carry it: "But what amused us all, especially Sam, was that same store was selling *Flaming Youth* in great quantities."[37]

*Siege* eventually sold 12,576 regular edition copies, a little more than half of the sales for *Success*, and grossed Adams $3,114. This time Adams could not complain about advertising. When Scaife wrote him a friendly "My dear Sam" letter, asking how *Siege* had done, he said he wanted to know because "I am somewhat curious to know whether we were all dead wrong about it here." Adams explained his contract with Boni & Liveright guaranteed advertising that the publishers carried out without a complaint. He attributed the low sale to bad times in the book trade. Evidently unaware of Fabian's identity and Boni & Liveright making money on *Siege*, Scaife said Adams "put one over and I think Liveright shows his good sporting instincts." He ended, "Whether or not we ever publish anything else for you, I hope you will consider us as equally friendly and as keenly interested in your work as ever."[38]

Before leaving California, Adams received a letter from Auburnian Mildred Woodruff praising *Siege*, which pleased him. He told her Jane had x-rays taken of her back, which had been painful for a long time. Although they thought it was rheumatism, the San Francisco doctor said she had a dislocation of the spine and put her on a rack to stretch her out, producing instant relief.[39] The remedy was an iron brace, which Jane called a corset, that she would wear for years, adding to her regal poise. Her troubles, however, were not over.

Returning east in April 1924, he attended a meeting of the Brooklyn Alumni Association, honoring Woollcott, poet John Weaver, and himself. Meanwhile, in an Auburn home before a rehearsal for her next play, Jane decided to wash her hair and used an electric heater as a drier. A celluloid comb caught fire, igniting her hair and burning an area as big as a hand on top of her head.

The play was postponed only five days. The more lasting effect was that she would wear her hair in an upsweep for the rest of her life. Shaken by the accident, Adams canceled several writing projects. He was cheered up by a summer visit by Katherine Adams. Beth Adams had remarried in 1917 to architect Bertram Remmel, and now Katherine, who was at the University of California at Berkeley, was planning her own wedding to Milton Buckley. She recalled that Jane opposed the marriage and offered to send her to Europe if she would call it off. The familiar stratagem failed.[40]

In July, with the Irwins, the Adamses antiqued and visited across the lake with Gertrude and Ted Case, an inventor who was adding sound to motion pictures. Inez Irwin marveled at Jane's vitality after the head injury "and how she rises above it." At Wide Waters also were Mildred Post, whose husband had gone bankrupt, and Marian Richardson with her children, John and Elizabeth. The youngsters, called Buddy and Betty, drawings of whom by Jane Adams's friend, Maud Tousey Fangel, became the Quaker Oats children, would be "adopted" by the Adamses after the Richardson marriage ended.[41]

He continued to act on the popularity of Fabian. A return to the Dorrisdale of *Flaming Youth* produced *Sailors' Wives*, serialized in *Telling Tales*, "A Magazine of Speed, Spice and Sparkle." Although he used characters from the first book, he focused on the escapades of Carol Trent and Maxwell Slater in a suburban harbor town. Humorist Will Cuppy, who said he was prepared to sharpen "his ax with an eye, as ever, to the public welfare," told the New York *World* readers that to his chagrin he liked it: "When Dr. Fabian concentrates on cynical, improper and futuristic dialogue, he is priceless and deserves infinite royalties. When he becomes poetic and high-minded and above all lit up with pathetic prayers about womanhood and beautiful thoughts about the little water pixies in the hills and suchlike, he ought to be shot."[42]

The novel rated *Bookman* blurbs for three months, but its eventual sales of 26,970 regular edition copies fell far short of *Flaming Youth*. It had a total royalty and advances of $6,061, and his reported professional income rose to more than $46,000, close to the $50,000 salary of Yankee baseball hero Babe Ruth who hit forty-six home runs that year. More than half of Adams's reported income came from movie companies. He received $1,000 from Associated First National for a detailed synopsis of *Sailors' Wives* that was delivered for another $14,000. Although Adams had told Scaife that *Siege* "was not a good movie plot, because of the old lady being the principal character," Universal Pictures bought the rights for $10,000.[43] The increases in income did not affect Adams's parsimonious nature.

In answer to the Cleveland newspaper's questionnaire that asked what he would do with a million dollars if he had it to give away, Adams responded: "Salt it away in a very large barrel with a very small spigot."[44] The spigot dripped in September 1923 when he was an early donor of five dollars to the victims of a Japanese earthquake that killed two hundred thousand in Yokohama, and in late 1924 Sam and Jane Adams were separate contributors to the Community Chest. Earlier he was on the local executive committee to help raise one million dollars for the Woodrow Wilson Foundation.

Wilson was gone, and so was his successor, Warren Gamaliel Harding, who died 2 August 1923. The scandals of Harding's administration, however, were in the news in 1924. Frank Vanderlip's try to link the late president to an oil scandal through the sale of Harding's *Marion Star* was fizzling, but other charges were mounting.

When Baldwin updated the sketch of Adams for 1925, he led with "Fine! There is no other word for him—the picture of health, of good humor—an honest citizen." Baldwin urged "citizen" be marked because "he takes politics seriously and really believes that our governors should truly represent the best of which we are capable,"[45] a strange statement about Adams, publicly silent on politics since World War I. But now the reports of misdeeds in Washington were enticing him.

In a letter to Julian Street in April 1924 he was on the trail of the Harding scandals. He said he thought Vanderlip, a former banker who headed a citizens research bureau, must have material. After Jane Adams's accident intervened, he again wrote Street in May that he might write on Treasury Secretary Andrew W. Mellon, under fire for possible connections with commercial enterprises, for the North American Newspaper Alliance.[46] Although no record of a Mellon article was found, Adams's muckraker instinct was reawakening.

# 12

# SENSATIONALIST
## 1925–1929

DESPITE the concerns Adams had about scandal in Washington he concentrated in early 1925 on finishing a sequel to *Siege*. Spurred by a *Collier's* offer for a serial, he resurrected grande dame Augusta Ruyland but shifted the main character to her niece, Dorothea Selover. This led him initially to call the novel *Dorrie*, but like many titles, it changed to *The Piper's Fee*. He also was working on the third Warner Fabian novel, *Summer Widowers*, later retitled *Summer Bachelors*.

Although *Collier's* promised twenty-five hundred dollars for Adams's new serial, it did not buy *The Piper's Fee*. The reason was not given, but it could have been Dorothea Selover's cover-up of the illegitimate baby of Evelyn Ruyland by claiming the child as her own. On 27 August Zelma Brandt sent Liveright the finished novel with "We are rather doubtful that it will serialize, on account of the illegitimacy of the child in the story and Sam doesn't want to change that part." *Collier's* evidently tried to soothe the author because it bought a short story in May but did not run it for almost one year.[1]

Despite the loss of $2,500 from *Collier's*, Adams's royalties, movie rights, and the sale of the short story grossed him about $8,000 of the $18,000 he would eventually earn in 1925. Money from *Flaming Youth* kept coming from various sources. Records listed Fabian as the author for the Century Play Company edition and offered no indication that another author did the adaptation. From 1926 to 1933 Adams was paid 25 percent of the theater royalty for the play, a total of $2,471. Although a French edition of *Flaming Youth* was published without reports of payments, the British edition published by Stanley Paul and Company showed royalties in excess of $4,000.

The money was only as good as what it could buy. The Adamses began 1925 in New York where they took an apartment at 25 West Ninth Street. Their activities were noted: "Saml. Hopkins Adams and wife of Auburn (this State) are in town for the cold spell, doing a lot of entertaining and going to dinner and one thing and another, they being very popular members of the Younger Set." The item was in the first issue of a new magazine, the New Yorker, in which Adams would run a piece the second week and later articles and stories.[2]

In March they abandoned New York, going to California, where they visited the motion picture lot in which Siege was being filmed. The Adamses stayed in California for less than two months, returning to Auburn in May so that Jane could work on a play. Her interest in theater was more than equaled by Adams's passion for antiquing. His fascination was with Currier and Ives prints, which he eventually gave to Hamilton College.

In September they visited the Irwins at Scituate, where although he had given up competitive tennis, he played doubles, including five sets one day, golfed, and still had energy to go to a prize fight and then a dance. His interests were discussed by Baldwin in his 1925 sketch: "Mr. Adams is an amateur archer, an amateur farmer, an amateur collector of curios and what-not; and a genuine lover of life, of good horses, of the smell of the woods, the salt of the sea."[3]

He had finished The Piper's Fee in late August. Liveright had problems with the novel although not over the illegitimacy. Adams said Liveright objected to part of the structure of the book, and the author admitted he was right. Adams made the change, but Zelma Brandt was right about no serialization, and after Elks declined, she gave Liveright the go-ahead for the book.[4]

Although 1925 was the first year since 1918 no Adams or Fabian novel was published, two film adaptations were released to different reactions. Despite Adams's dire prediction about an old woman not being good film fare Siege was made by Danish screen director Sven Gade. It starred Virginia Valli and Eugene O'Brien, but Mary Alden, as Aunt Augusta Ruyland, stole the movie that would be called a "lost" classic. On the other lot, more than star Constance Bennett was needed to save Wandering Fires by Arrow Pictures that bought the rights for two thousand dollars and released the film in late 1925. Directed by Maurice Campbell, the film was considered "bantamweight principally because of the manner in which Campbell has handled it" by Variety.[5]

Adams continued to plumb the magazine market late in the year. Almost all his short stories were light romances. He also wrote a humorous article about the clash of chickens and automobiles, which Country Gentleman bought. The North American Newspaper Alliance bought an Adams essay that ran in June 1925, urging people to follow their dreams, such as joining the circus or capturing an elusive butterfly. In his essay he said he would like to learn to speak Russian, a surprising public pronouncement coming on the heels of the Red Scare during which radicals were deported, including Emma Goldman. Later he told his grandson: "Emma Goldman was the sexiest woman I ever met—on the inside."[6]

As he neared fifty-five, he wrote that he had a goal of living through the century to see the changes produced by the increase in leisure time. He added he had "a social curiosity to know what is going to develop in the relationship of man to woman, when woman gets an even fuller control of social relationships than she now enjoys," a theme that Adams and Fabian were developing with a string of strong heroines in the 1920s. His interest in science was in geothermatics, the conquering of disease and its effect on population, and the power that would be released when the atom was split.[7]

The Adamses were at Wide Waters in early 1926 so Jane could rehearse her next play. They were joined by the Irwins, who braved the central New York winter with predictable results. At first, Irwin reported it was "snowing beautifully" at Wide Waters, and Inez Irwin noted the lake was "like beryl," with a blue glow. Long walks, however, gave Inez a cold, and Irwin spent much of his time digging cars out of snowdrifts.[8]

They were also introduced to a prize Guernsey cow that had been bought in hopes of building a large herd for what was now known as Wide Waters Farm. The drain on their resources by the purchase of cattle may have led to the temporary collapse of the farm in March, forcing Adams to reorganize the operation. In June his modern chicken brooder caught fire, causing the deaths of eleven hundred chicks and a two-thousand-dollar loss. These were temporary problems, however. During the period Jane got more land, including a farmhouse that later they would use to handle the spillover of guests at Wide Waters. To finance the purchase she used as collateral part of the farm, leading to one of her husband's favorite quips. Asked if he had an interest in the farm, he responded, "Yes, in the mortgage."[9]

Jane's interest in country life included a friendship with Homer and Anna Champany, who owned a farm on Whiskey Lane that connected the Wide Waters driveway with East Lake Road. "Every spring my father would get a scraper to level off the road down to the shore property and do handyman jobs. He'd also keep his eye on the place while they were away," his daughter, Beatrice Champany, recalled.[10]

"My mother would help on the big parties, taking me along," she said, adding the Adamses "would find something for me to do in the kitchen." The young girl never got cash, but Adams would give her gifts such as scarves and tin boxes of imported candy. Equally generous to the girl was Jane Adams, whose "bubbling enthusiasm made you feel important. She was always very kind to me as a kid, interested in anything you wanted to talk about or show her. Her eyes talked." With Anna Champany, Adams shared a love of antiques, and when his new books came out, "he would always make sure he gave her an autographed copy." She recalled, however, how different he was from Jane. "He was a private person, a little grouchy and not at all interested in the farm."

7. Sam and Jane Adams on the back porch of the addition to the main house that provided him with an upstairs writing studio. An earlier addition, to their left, was an old farmhouse Adams also had attached to the main house. Samuel Hopkins Adams Collection. Courtesy of Syracuse University Library.

While Jane was developing the farm, he was expanding the main house. A spacious dining room was added with a bedroom, bath, and study for Adams above. A second-story porch with steps was built on the back to create a separate unit where he could have the isolation he needed for his writing. The fieldstone uprights and pink stucco crossovers beneath the large windows of the original house were matched in the addition. He was fond of saying the rock was imported from Canada, sometimes adding the glacier brought it.[11]

Jane followed the success of her play by agreeing to do another. Sam, however, was growing disenchanted with winter plays. After cast member Lithgow Osborne wrote his father that Adams was vowing that he would never spend another winter at Wide Waters, Osborne explained to a friend: "Sam is furious with Jane for attempting too much dramatics and having to come in for rehearsals."[12] She was not deterred. After the play in March, she was rehearsing another for a May production. In the fall she did her fourth play of the year. Slated for November, the play was postponed by the death on 20 October of Thomas Mott Osborne.

The year 1926 marked the thirty-fifth anniversary of Adams's graduation from Hamilton College. He invited the class of 1891 to Wide Waters before the official reunion. A gathering of fourteen of the twenty-seven graduates was attended by an *Auburn Citizen* reporter who went to a breakfast where the men reminisced about football, their campus activities, and their poor scholarship, which the reporter doubted because of the large number of Phi Beta Kappa keys around the table. He made no mention of an upcoming honor for one of the class.[13]

In June the Hamilton College trustees granted Adams an honorary doctor of letters degree. His old antagonist, former President Stryker, also proposed that he be added to the list for an opening on the Board of Trustees. If the move was an attempt by Stryker for revenge, it was successful because Adams lost not one but two votes for board seats. He had no recorded reaction to the votes, but he was delighted by the honorary degree, especially because the doctor of humane letters was more honorific than the doctor of literature degree he had thought he had received.

Jane's involvement in theater during 1926 gave him time to experiment with his writing, and he turned to the classics. In a letter to Joseph Ibbotson, Hamilton College librarian, he asked for information on Nero and for help with his Latin. He had already done a short parody for the *New Yorker* called "Our Own Lysistrata" bylined "S. H. A." with which he also was signing his letters. From the material he wrote the humorous story that *Pictorial Review* bought in

March. Later he would use the Roman motif for a story on gladiators, which *Collier's* bought for two thousand dollars, an amount that pleased him. Although he said *Collier's* wanted more, his last Roman story was in the *Chicago Sunday Tribune*.[14]

His short story work was joined by the publication in February 1926 of *The Piper's Fee*. The novel's reception by reviewers and the public must have indicated to Adams that the time had come for a new approach to his topics. The *New York Times* said his storytelling ability entitled him to "a respectable but not lofty place in his profession." The *Saturday Review of Literature* commented that if he were put in the company of other top storytellers, "he naturally looks a little out of place. . . . He is a showman, not an interpreter," a prophetic criticism.[15]

Readers echoed the complaints by buying fewer than half the number of regular copies that *Siege* had sold, an eventual 6,116. With 10,000 cheap editions, he still made money, recording $1,928 in payments, but scarcely a princely sum. Equally disappointing were the film rights for *The Piper's Fee*, sold in 1928 to Quality Distributing Company for $1,000. The film was not made, probably because the company felt it could not get the illegitimacy issue by the censors.

He finished the third revision of his Fabian *Summer Bachelors* in February 1926, announcing he was done with the book. The reason for his stand was his planning for his next novel as his craving for a "big" serious book continued. He told Maurice that his interest in the Harding scandals was revived on the golf course where the idea, setting, and plot of *Revelry* were born.[16]

The next month Zelma Brandt wrote Liveright for an advance of six thousand dollars, based on Adams's request for one thousand dollars a month, saying it would equal 20,000 copies at the standard 15 percent royalty. Liveright offered half, saying: "Good Lord, how many books sell anything like 20,000 copies?" Adams then offered to finance *Revelry* himself with the six thousand dollars used for advertising.[17]

He was ready for his task, Baldwin observed, noting: "He is utterly fearless and absolutely honest, with such a fund of information, such a wealth of experience, as is possible only to one who has been active, in present-day affairs, up to the minute, for thirty years." For aid with his project Adams turned to Street, whom he had helped with his writing and to whom he explained that he wanted his book to have a fictional setting but the basis would be the Harding clique.[18]

As he wrote the letter, he was struck with a thought that Street might be considering the same thing. His fears were allayed when Street wrote, "That's a bully idea, and I hadn't thought of it at all, so it's your'n as far as I am concerned." Street agreed to discuss his own experiences, suggested sources, and offered some impressions in a letter marked "Private, Personal, Confidential and then Some!"[19]

Adams knew what to do when he got to Washington, poring over reports of various investigations of the oil scandals, reading the *Congressional Record*, and talking to correspondents. His hopes of meeting with Street before and after his trip were dashed by Street being ill, but Adams had enough information. What he found was the president, eulogized after his unexpected death, had an administration whose corruption had been revealed in 1924 by congressional investigations. The probes uncovered several instances of graft tied to Secretary of Interior Albert B. Fall, accused of taking a bribe to arrange the transfer of government oil reserves at Teapot Dome to oil magnate Edward Doheny. Former attorney general and Harding kingmaker Harry Daugherty was also implicated. The investigations and journalistic reports failed, however, to arouse the public and the courts were mired. He had plenty to work with.

With a 15 September deadline for the completed book he set himself a frantic pace, explaining to Zelma Brandt that he had done a rough draft of the second chapter in two days and planned to write three chapters per week. As he wrote, she and Liveright argued over the title. Although *Revelry* won, his subtitle of "A Novel of the Time Just Beyond Ours" was not used, opening him to later criticism.[20]

Through the summer he wrote and rewrote the novel. The first draft was done longhand on legal-sized yellow sheets. "This is for mechanical reasons. I constantly make marginal and interlinear notes, besides keeping at my elbow a pad on which to set down ideas and schemes for the progress of the story," he wrote, adding it was vital to capture fugitive ideas, phrases, plot twists or apt words. "For these ephemerae are butterflies, indeed, and if one fails to pin them down, they will be out the window and off into the void forever."[21]

That summer they had a prolonged visit from the Franklin Pierce Adamses, beginning in July and stretching into September. Jane's red automobile, nicknamed Hester Prynne, was kept busy as Frank Adams ranged over the countryside, visiting a Latin teacher at Cornell University, going to see Auburn Prison, and finding that a bookstore in Cortland had never sold a copy of *An American Tragedy* despite Chester Gillette having worked in the town's skirt factory. For the guests at Wide Waters it was not all play and no work. Adams put three of them to typing *Revelry*. Marian Richardson, who was visiting with her children and had been hired by Brandt & Brandt, reported 2 August, "The darned old book is finished at last!" She said Frank Adams was doing some cutting on the manuscript.[22]

The Irwins arrived in September for the Wide Waters wedding of Mildred Post, who had ended her first marriage, to Atherton Harlan, a successful businessman and owner of a hundred-acre farm in New Canaan, Connecticut. Her marriage at twenty-eight to Harlan, fifty-five, produced a son, George Harlan, in late 1927. The birth of Adams's only grandson did not, however, soothe the strained relationship close relatives had with Jane Adams. Her daughter, although she liked Adams, felt her mother had abandoned her in Switzerland and often had clashes of wills with her. "Ath" Harlan did not get along with the former actress because, George Harlan said, his father "saw through Jane" and at one point warned his son, "I don't want you to marry anyone like your grandmother." Hester Adams was absent from the household in the 1920s because, according to her sister, she had been angered by Jane. Katherine Adell was awed by her and found visits a strain because Jane was so demanding. More distant Hopkins and Adams relatives, who saw her in small doses, were more positive.[23]

Although the Adamses may have had difficulties with their relatives, they threw their home and hearts open to the young such as Lydia Mead and Richardson's Buddy and Betty. Later in 1926 when he learned Richardson, recently married to Julian Wells, was going to Colorado, he moaned about not being able to see her children.[24] The Adamses attachment to the youngsters would lead them to take an active role in their futures.

With *Revelry* in the hands of Boni & Liveright on 11 August Adams contacted Ibbotson again on a new Latin short story but two weeks later wrote the librarian that his plans had shifted because he was going to California the latter part of September. He did not mention that he had a writing job with Famous Players-Lasky Corporation to do an original story for a film.[25]

Before he left for California, *Summer Bachelors* became his second novel published in 1926. Most reviewers found boring the story of New York stenographer Desideria Thomas's entry into the festive nightclub life where she captured the affections of single and married men. Only Lillian Hellman in a New York *Herald Tribune* gave it the same light treatment the author had. "Granting at the outset that 'Summer Bachelors' is plain trash, we can go on to state that it is excellent of its kind," she wrote and then ran through the plot,

ending with: "But let this not be condescension. The book is mightily interesting and even exciting—much better written than it should have been, and
put together with an excellent analysis of what the public reads."[26]

Readers agreed with her. While in California, Adams got periodic reports of
the "other book" that sold 19,060 regular, 5,007 cheap, and 1,904 Canadian
sales and grossed $4,946. The payments were in addition to the sale of film
rights to Cosmopolitan Producers for $20,000. Other things did not go well in
California.

Although he had expressed disdain for the movie business, the lure of seventy-five hundred dollars for an original story to be delivered six weeks after he
arrived was too tempting for Adams, who was promised another twenty-five
hundred dollars if the story was accepted. While in California the previous
year, he learned about the process of film making and said he met Hollywood
personalities, which may have led to the Famous Players offer. But his letters
to Zelma Brandt indicated that his disdain was reinforced.[27] If he did not like
Hollywood, the dissatisfaction was mutual. The twenty-five hundred dollars
payment on acceptance was never recorded, indicating a failure to produce an
acceptable script.

Although Adams was unsuccessful in Hollywood, Fabian's novels remained
a hot property. *Summer Bachelors* was released in late 1926 by the Fox Film
Corporation. With a scenario written by James Shelly Hamilton based on the
early title *Summer Widowers*, the film starred Madge Bellamy and was directed
by Allan Dwan, who would have a fifty-year career. Film chronicler Robert
Connelly said the motion picture had a "hint of naughtiness" but was a delightful comedy.[28]

When he was in California he was concerned with *Revelry*, upset first that
a postponement from a 25 September publication meant the book would miss
the publicity of the trial of former Attorney General Daugherty; he was further
annoyed when 25 October was not met, blaming Liveright's involvement with
Broadway for interfering with his publishing. When he learned the book
would miss the election, he threatened that Liveright might lose two authors
from his list.

Although she ignored thoughts of finding a new publisher, Zelma Brandt
was beginning to publicize *Revelry*. She compiled a list to generate a word-
of-mouth campaign in Washington. One was Burton Kline, an assistant to Secretary of Labor James J. Davis, who said he had gotten the secretary to read it
but that Davis would damn the book. He said the secretary had "slipped into

the trap that Adams sets for everybody" by taking the fiction as fact and had said it "ain't so."[29]

Distinguishing fact from fiction was, indeed, a challenge in the story of President Willis Markham, whom Adams described as "torpid, good-humored, complacent, friendly, indulgent to himself, obliging to others, as loyal as a Samurai, full of party piety, a hater of the word 'no,' faithful to his own code of private honor, and as standardized as a Ford car." The description was by Dan Lurrock, who resembled Daugherty and brought Markham from Michigan, instead of Ohio, to Washington.[30]

The novel opened with a poker party at the "Crow's Nest," similar to Harding's House on K Street, and introduced the characters, including Andy Grandy, a secretary as was Fall. At the end of the party Markham walked back to the White House and met Edith Westervelt, who supplied a romantic interest for Markham but was fictional in terms of Harding. After discovering that Gandy and others had been looting the government and betraying his trust, Markham, who had accidentally taken some poison that he coaxed from the suicidal Westervelt, despondently accepted a prolonged death. At the time rumors were circulating that Harding had not died a natural death, and the stunning ending added to the blurring of fact with fiction.

*Revelry* was published 10 November when Adams was with the Whites. After the release of the novel, Richardson reported from Brandt & Brandt: "The book has certainly created a furore around these parts. On November 10th I don't think anyone in the office did anything but send out copies of REVELRY and answer questions in regard to it. I am tickled to death."[31] One reason was that the publicity effort by Zelma Brandt received an unexpected boost from President Calvin Coolidge, vice president under Harding. Washington correspondents reported that *Revelry* was a topic at a 9 November luncheon given by the president for a half dozen Republican senators. Coolidge was reported as being annoyed by the publication.

Boni & Liveright jumped as if to starter's pistol, running a two-column advertisement the next day quoting the *World's* story and including excerpts from a positive review by Harry Hansen.[32] The *World* then followed up with another story that reported Coolidge, who had not read the book, asking at the luncheon whether any of the incidents in the book mentioned the White House and when told yes, replied: "I think it is scandalous." Adams was delighted by Coolidge's comment, telling Richardson: the adjective should be worth several thousand copies.[33]

Coolidge was not the only provider of unexpected, but welcome, publicity. In Washington the trial of Fall and Doheny for conspiracy in the Elks and Naval Reserve leases opened. When a prospective juror in the Teapot Dome trial was examined by Doheny's defense attorney, the *New York Times* on 23 November quoted a question: "Have you seen any articles in the newspapers a day before yesterday saying that the jurors were all reading that book, sitting up nights reading it?"

William A. Wolff seized on the testimony for an article, arranged by Zelma Brandt. He also used Coolidge's reaction and comments from senators. Montana Senator Thomas J. Walsh, who had begun the investigation, said although he did not like the book as a book, it might serve a purpose if it awakened the nation "from the apathy with which it received the facts brought forth from his investigation." Armed with the Wolff article, Zelma Brandt compiled a list of thirty-eight newspapers, mostly Democratic. Both Auburn newspapers used it, but others declined, such as the New York *World* that found itself in what *Bookman* called "a miniature civil war" over *Revelry*.[34]

Hansen had fired the first shot by calling *Revelry* a "daring and sensational political novel." He was followed by a mention by Franklin Pierce Adams, who said he found it "very interesting, and showing how human and corrupt be deemeth our politicks." The *World* columnist did not mention his work on the book. When Adams was in California he had suggested that *Revelry* be linked with a gossipy novel from England, *The Whispering Gallery*, also published by Boni & Liveright. That was what a *World* editorialist did, noting under "Scurrilous Books" that the British book had been withdrawn from publication in England and the same should happen in the United States to *Revelry*, which it called "nothing more than unwarranted scandal-mongering."[35]

Hansen blasted back at the editorial, conceding while the novel might be second rate and in poor taste, the author had the prerogative to use facts as he wished. "Literary history is filled with tales of authors using actual persons for their characters and getting into hot water as a result," he wrote, citing William Thackeray, Guy de Maupassant, Jonathan Swift and American authors Sinclair Lewis and Theodore Dreiser.[36]

Others reacted strongly to the *World*'s call for suppression of the novel. John Haynes Holmes, head of the nondenominational Community Church and editor of *Unity* magazine, wrote Boni & Liveright to urge the firm to ignore the challenge. He praised Adams for his "ruthless and therefore wholesome portrayal of the spirit, atmosphere, purpose and consequence, if not the precise facts, of the most corrupt administration this country has ever known."[37]

At the *World,* Heywood Broun, whose column shared the op ed page with Hansen and F. P. A., jumped into the debate. In his 21 December column he called *Revelry* a good novel and well worth reading. Written after Fall and Doheny had been acquitted, Broun wrote that he hoped *Revelry* "may very well serve to rouse more indignation at public corruption than did the Walsh investigation."

Armed with the six-thousand-dollar advertising budget from the unclaimed advance, Liveright told Zelma Brandt on 24 November: "I feel we must put ourselves on record as stating that we did some of the best work in our publishing career in our advance exploitation of the book, in our advertising since its publication, in our many special publicity efforts, and, what is more important, we are very well satisfied with the sale."

*Revelry* sold out three printings in three weeks, reaching ten thousand on 13 November, fifteen thousand by 22 November, and twenty-five thousand by the end of November when Adams went to Auburn to see Jane Adams's latest play. After a nine-inch snowfall accompanied by twelve-below-zero temperatures reminded him of the need to escape the Cayuga County winter, he bundled his wife up, allowed the hired help to return to the countryside, and on 27 December headed for New York.

The furor of the *World's* "civil war" had quieted after Broun's column, but one of the casualties may have been Sam Adams's friendship with Frank Adams. After the editorial calling for suppression of the novel, the columnist was silent, mentioning Adams only as a leading reporter of the 1890s. Sam and Jane Adams had dinner 12 January with the Irwins and the Frank Adamses. The Irwin diaries mention only that the talk was about a possible war with Mexico. Frank Adams's column noted the dinner with little comment. It became the last recorded meeting between the men.[38]

During the visit Adams was interviewed on why he had written *Revelry.* To John Farrar of *Bookman* Adams was defensive. "Why in thunder didn't someone do it before me? There the story was. As dramatic as anything." To the New York *World's* Harry Salpeter the author said, "The first duty of the novelist is to be interesting" and that if he had written the book as a muckraker rather than a novelist, it would have been more sensational. He added, "Nobody can attribute motives to me, except God and myself."[39]

Almost thirty years later when Adams was asked about the controversy over *Revelry,* he admitted: "That did raise considerable hell. I'm a very mild person and not usually given to raising it. But everything here could have been found in the *Congressional Record,* if anyone had looked."[40] From the beginning he was intent on exposing the corruption, and in that he was successful. Avoiding the corruption was different, and he did not suggest what an aroused public could do to counter scandals. He was, as the *Saturday Review of Literature* had said, a showman, not an interpreter.

In late 1926 and early 1927 Brandt & Brandt was actively seeking to sell both the movie and stage rights to the novel. Hopes for a film sale fell apart because Adams decided to wait, afraid that the Will Hays office would ban it. Robert Milton secured stage rights, with Maurine Watkins suggested for the stage version. She got the job after seeing Adams before he went south.

While he was in Florida, the second trial of Daugherty opened in New York. When a prospective foreman of the jury admitted that he had read *Revelry*, a defense attorney called the book "insidious fiction," a charge with which the United States attorney agreed. The next month the Cleveland Heights public library banned the book as "one we don't care to circulate."[41]

The second trial of Daugherty propelled the novel toward its final sales of 80,243 regular copies, 4,195 cheap editions, 5,133 in Canada, and 1,738 regular and 64 cheap copies of the Bretano edition in England. Although the more than 90,000 total sales were less than the 100,000 usually credited to Adams, advances and royalties eventually topped $23,000. Not listed were any payments to Adams for the stage version.[42]

One issue raised obliquely by *Revelry* was several mentions of plagiarism, a topic that dogged Adams as it did other authors. In 1916 *Bookman* had observed that "he has been accused of the theft of plots as often as the average writer, invariably by some aspiring genius who has not yet attained print, but who seems to suspect him of having read his or her mind through some process of telepathy." In a letter to Adams concerning *Revelry* a veiled reference to unidentified plagiarism charges was made by Upton Sinclair, who said he had read the novel with great interest and liked the story. Adams replied the plagiarism charge was absurd and dismissed it.[43]

After almost two months in Florida, the Adamses returned in March to New York to a flurry of parties while staying with the Irwins. The pace, however, was too much for Jane, who became ill. After a week in which she lost twenty-five pounds, he took his wife to central New York. While his wife rested, he watched the success of his novel and worked on his next project.

When Adams had done the plot outline for *Revelry*, he had included a key to the various thinly disguised characters. For the devotee of word puzzles and parlor games his next book was quick and easy. Using a parlor game, "Shedding Light," with a bow to "Twenty Questions," *Who and What* was subtitled

"A Book of Clues for the Clever." Played at Wide Waters and Scituate, the game consisted of describing a person, animal, or object such as George Washington, Rin-Tin-Tin, or a Ford automobile. The audience asked questions, leading to identification of the subject. Edited by Adams, who supplied an explanation of the game, the book had two hundred entries. He was helped by Maurice Hanline, who also contributed entries, as did authors, Auburnians, and Hamilton College faculty members. Comment on *Who and What*, published 6 September 1927 was favorable.[44]

The public, however, were disinterested in *Who and What*, buying only 1,318 copies in the United States and sixty-three in Canada. Boni & Liveright, which had given Adams a $500 signing advance and another $500 on delivery, recorded a loss of $798 on the book. There was always Fabian to soothe the bookkeepers, however, and on 28 June 1927 Adams signed a contract for his fourth Fabian novel, *Unforbidden Fruit*.

The excitement generated by the novel *Revelry* was rekindled with more smoke than fire by the stage version. The play opened in Philadelphia for previews before New York. To attorney Bernard R. Cohn *Revelry* was more than a play with mixed reviews. On the grounds that the play "flaunts the Federal Government and ridicules high officials" he sought an injunction to ban it. A judge refused to make the injunction permanent although he denounced the play as "false, base and indecent and slanderous of the dead." Despite the ruling the theater manager said the play was "so essentially unpatriotic" that he ordered it closed.[45]

Saying the injunction was good publicity, Adams invited Street to the New York opening. New York critics J. Brooks Atkinson of the *New York Times* and Woollcott of the *World* were unimpressed. In reviewing the season for 1927–28, which he said began promisingly and faded hopelessly, Burns Mantle said the expectation that *Revelry* "would create a furore" never developed. The play closed in six weeks after forty-eight performances.[46]

After spending January 1928 in New York, the Adamses again went west to visit for two months with the Whites. While they were in California, the film version of *Sailors' Wives*, the Fabian novel published in 1924, was released, starring Mary Astor as a girl going blind. The movie was called a "weak sister" by *Variety*, but it did concede that Astor carried herself well.[47]

The Adamses returned in April to Cayuga County where Jane began her new play. She also accepted a position, suggested by Lithgow Osborne, on the National Voluntary Committee of Women for the Association Against the Prohibition Amendment. Adams did not join until the next year, when he was one of 212 writers, cartoonists, and illustrators on the Writers and Artists Committee. Adams was listed as one of thirteen founders.

While Jane was busy, he was floundering. He had finished *Unforbidden Fruit* as a Fabian novel and sought a topic for his next book under his own name. A book on Prohibition never developed. After *Revelry* Adams seemed fascinated by government corruption and that of the Ulysses S. Grant administration, asking Ibbotson in April for material. The librarian, however, said another author was doing a biography on Grant, killing that idea. Instead he began *The Flagrant Years* about a young woman's adventures in the beauty shop business.

His long fiction was so pervasive that Adams nearly ignored the short story and article markets he had worked so hard to build up. It was not that he was unsuccessful, because in the March 1927 interview with *Bookman* he said: "I have failed to sell only two of my stories in all the time I've been writing."[48] He published only two romantic short stories during the late 1920s. They were joined by an article for *Harper's Monthly Magazine*, "Sabbatical Year for Marriage." Written a dozen years after his second marriage, the article analytically proposed that to avoid smothering each other, couples should spend some time away apart. The reaction of Jane Adams was unknown.

What was known from friends and relatives was their devotion to one another. The strong-willed and often irritable Adams was more than matched by the former actress who swore like a Marine sergeant and fondly referred to her husband as "the little bastard." Katherine Adell remembered them having arguing matches behind closed doors but without rancor. Mildred Harlan told her son that Jane Adams would read her husband the riot act as a sign of affection and that they adored each other. Nowhere in the Irwin diaries was a mention of a serious disagreement. At least part of the reason may have been that they had divergent interests with Adams enjoying bridge and antiquing and his wife involved with the Grange and community theater.[49]

In June visitors included Carl Brandt, no longer with Zelma Brandt, plus newcomers Sylvia Bernice Baumgarten and her new husband, author James Gould Cozzens. Raised in a middle-class Jewish home in New York, Baumgarten had joined Brandt & Brandt as a secretary, but Brandt recognized her talents and had her handle book rights. She rapidly got a reputation as one of the brightest and toughest literary agents in New York. She and Adams developed a close professional and personal relationship.

In June *Unforbidden Fruit* also was published. Set at a large women's college, the novel was called by Mark Sullivan "an even greater apotheosis of pruriency" than *Flaming Youth*. The story concentrated on the search for new experiences. The reviewers did not buy it, but readers did—18,627 regular copy sales with another 2,141 in Canada to produce a final total of advances and royalties of $5,973. The biggest financial benefit, however, came from its sale to Paramount Famous Players–Lasky Corporation for $17,000.[50]

Not all of Adams's earnings came from his work. Later in the year he joined 148 writers in backing Governor Al Smith for president against Herbert Hoover, who had an ardent backer in Irwin. Although Adams knew Hoover from Dutch Treat lunches, he pledged to work for Smith. His activity seemed to be limited to talking up Smith, but he was sure he was backing a loser and bet Lithgow Osborne one hundred dollars that Smith would not carry New York. The cocky Osborne suggested Adams simply donate the amount to Smith's campaign. Adams won.

After a summer of caring for Marguerite Taylor, who was recuperating from a back injury, he was troubled by a finger that was so affected by the cold in the fall that he wrapped it in flannel. The result was that the little finger of his left hand was amputated at the first joint because of the gout.

During 1928 Adams finished *The Flagrant Years*, and it became one of his biggest moneymakers. He received a serial contract with *Cosmopolitan* for $2,500 on signing and five monthly payments of $3,000, making $17,500 spread over 1928 and 1929. Paramount Famous Players–Lasky Corporation bought the film rights for $22,500 but apparently never made the movie. Liveright gave a $3,000 advance on the book, bringing the gross on *The Flagrant Years* to $43,000.

The sale of film rights, his Hollywood venture, and book royalties pushed his recorded earnings for 1926 to about $48,000, considerably more than, as a comparison, the $15,000 Irwin got that year. Irwin and Adams were closer in 1927, when Irwin had his peak year of $28,000 and Adams had about $24,000, of which $18,000 came from *Revelry* royalties. Irwin dipped in 1928 to less than $25,000, whereas Adams grossed almost $39,000, mostly from Fabian movie rights and *The Flagrant Years* serial. The serial money plus book royalties and movie rights put his recorded earnings at almost $54,000 in 1929, a year in which Irwin made slightly less than $20,000. A major contributor to Adams's highest gross thus far was another movie writing job. Despite his protestations that once was more than enough, Universal Pictures offered an irresistible double enticement: he could write a screenplay in the East and the offer was $20,000.[51]

The economic clouds were building, however, in 1929. In a letter to Adams, who had flirted with the idea of a novel about Atlantic City in November, Liveright proposed a book on Wall Street and told him in February 1929 without amplification, "We have a lot of work to do on it and we want to make a smash of it—before the smash in the market comes, which it surely will some time or other." Their discussion of various rights ended in February when Adams accepted the movie offer.[52] With that the Adamses left for Hibernia where he worked on a Fabian story for Universal until April.

That month the film *Wild Party*, adapted from the college novel *Unforbidden Fruit*, was released. Three writers did the adaptation, including John V. A. Weaver, a fellow Hamiltonian and husband of actress Peggy Wood before he died in 1938. Film historians Jay Nash and Stanley Ross said that although "the plot practically grows mold before the viewer's eyes," the film was fascinating because it was Clara Bow's first talking role and the second film of star Frederic March.[53]

*The Flagrant Years, A Novel of the Beauty Market* was published in May 1929. Reviewers with *Revelry* still in mind were expecting his beauty shop novel to be another muckraking-type exposé of what Adams said was a billion-and-one-half dollar business. Although the story of Consuelo Barrett's experiences as a beautician had tinges of exposé in the marketing of cosmetic products, the book was not meant to be an expanded patent medicine exposé or a *Tribune* consumer column.

Despite generally good reviews the novel sold 10,193 regular copies and 678 in Canada. The royalties did not quite reach the generous advance of three thousand dollars, bothering Adams. Although he took a personal hand in its promotion by speaking at a Brooklyn theater, he doubted Liveright was doing his best to advertise the novel. The struggling Liveright wrote Baumgarten that 1929 had been the worst book-selling season in fifteen years.[54]

The Irwins made their usual trip to Wide Waters in May when Irwin reported, "Sam's nerves going bad." A newcomer at the Adamses was Nancy Wilson Ross, a young writer who had married into an Auburn family. She was one of the writers who sought Adams's counsel and help in getting their work published. He asked Liveright to read her *Twice Two*. After he told Adams of little enthusiasm for the book, he complained that the marriage of his business manager, Julian Messner, meant he would have to keep his nose to the grindstone.[55]

After thanking Liveright for reading the Ross manuscript, Adams said he would be happier if he limited his other pursuits. An angry Liveright shot back: "I believe that my job is an executive and creative one and should not be a routine one in which regular hours should play much part. It is my job to create ideas and plans and it seems that in eleven years I've done pretty well at this."[56] That was too much for Adams, who went looking for a new publisher.

While Adams was working on a Fabian book for which he had a serial contract with *Romance* magazine, he tried a new topic. Brandt in June contacted Joseph W. Sears on the Adams book. Discouraged by the lack of current success of his light fiction, the author had begun a biography of Daniel Webster. Brandt offered Sears the biography and sweetened the deal with Fabian's *The Men in Her Life*, cutting all ties with Liveright.

As was his practice, Adams threw himself into his project on Webster, contacting Clarence Saunders Brigham of the American Antiquarian Society in Worcester, Massachusetts, beginning a long friendship. His work was interrupted at summer's end by a call from Hollywood for what he told Brigham was a six-week job, presumedly to make changes in *What Men Want* written earlier in the year.

The stock market crash in October, which cost Liveright his publishing business and caused the economically naïve Irwin continuing anguish, did not immediately affect the Adamses, who were visiting the Whites after the Hollywood stint. While in the San Francisco area, they probably saw Milton and Katherine Adams Buckley, who had married in 1925, and their new granddaughter, Elizabeth Buckley, born 23 March 1929. The world of Adams was changing.[57]

Back home in December 1929, Adams concentrated on the biography. As he did research and began writing, he was battling infirmities of his late fifties. His fingers were affected by gout, and the calcium deposit on his hip forced him to give up tennis and was worsening. He remained focused on his Webster project, however, which would shape the rest of his life.

# 13

# HISTORIAN
## 1930–1934

T HE MOST INTERESTING PERSON I know is Samuel Hopkins Adams, the
author. He is almost sixty years old, but just as active as if he were fifty.
Many a time I have watched him play set after set of tennis.

Mr. Adams is very amusing and is always wonderful at a party. I don't know
anyone by whom I would rather sit.

When he is writing he does not like to do things that make him think hard.
One of his favorite games when he is working is "sniff." I like to play it with him
very much; he gets so cross when he has to draw and he takes the game so
seriously.

I have read only one of his stories. It is called "For Those Who Walk in
Darkness." We all like Mr. Adams very much and I certainly hope he continues to live in Auburn for many years.[1]

This short essay by a young girl captured the essence of the man who, after
the writing of *Revelry* as a historical novel that was more novel than history,
sought to use history to bring to life Daniel Webster. To allow his favorite form
of character development, dialogue, he employed historical recreations to en-
liven the history. In a sketch for librarians Adams said his instinctive distrust of
oratory had led him to write about Webster. He also was eager to paint a sympathetic picture to offset the tarnished reputation of the Great Orator as he had
tried to do with the ill-used Harding.[2]

While wintering in Hibernia in January 1930, he continued his correspondence with librarian Ibbotson gathering information on the atmosphere of
Webster's Washington and asking his advice on whom to contact at the Library
of Congress. To Brigham at the American Antiquarian Society, however,
which he had visited before going to Florida, he confided in February that the

further he got into Webster's career, the less he liked him. The plan was to have Sears publish the biography and follow it with the latest Fabian novel, *The Men in Her Life*. Adams found biography was slow going, however, complaining in March he was puzzled by the necessity of sifting. Sears decided to give Adams extra time on Webster by publishing the Fabian book first.[3]

His struggles in the early months of 1930 were surpassed by the troubles of Liveright. In January the embattled publisher sent Adams a plaintive letter through Baumgarten. Unaware of the agreement with Sears, Liveright wrote: "I can't tell you how upset I am about the situation that seems to have arisen between us. A letter can't convey all that I want to say, but I do urge you not to make any decision about your next book before you talk to me. I am perfectly willing to make as big an advance as any other publisher would, and to agree to any sane business-like terms regarding the exploitation of the book."[4]

The defensive nature of the letter brought no sympathy from Baumgarten, who at Brandt & Brandt served writers, not publishers. She reported to Adams in forwarding Liveright's plea that she and Brandt had "howled over it, and I think it will afford you a good deal of amusement." The crash of the market plunged Liveright, who had lost money on his theatrical ventures, through the thin ice on which Cerf said he was always skating. He was forced out of his firm in late 1930. At that time other publishers sought the authors on the Liveright list. One was Cerf, who had bought the popular Modern Library from Liveright in 1925 and then opened Random House in 1928. He targeted three authors: Eugene O'Neill, whom he got after visiting him in Sea Island, Georgia; Robinson Jeffers, signed in California; and "quite bit later . . . Sam Adams."[5]

The Adamses came north in April, attending a *Flaming Youth* party in New York and visiting the Irwins. In early May they stayed with the Atherton Harlans in New Canaan where they discussed the collapse of Harlan's business in the crash. Adams himself was beginning to feel the squeeze, writing Baumgarten to ask when book money would be coming in because he could use it. Later in May, facing a June deadline on his taxes, he told her he would have to sell some stock or borrow money to meet the payment. His situation must have been far from desperate, however, because he did not draw on the Sears advance of three thousand dollars until late summer.

The search for new income dominated the efforts of both Baumgarten and Adams. She spent the first part of 1930 trying to get foreign rights on his books, a frustrating effort except for *The Flagrant Years*, which she finally got John Hamilton to publish in Britain. Adams pursued the possibility of a radio series on historical topics but balked at a contract with an option for his personal radio services, unwilling to make a binding commitment. Nothing came of the negotiations although he did a first short script on Nicholas Biddle. More successful were talks with the World Syndicate Publishing Company, which contracted for a low-priced reprint of *Unforbidden Fruit.* Efforts on other Adams books failed when World limited its project because of the bad publishing climate.

Meanwhile, Adams went to Worcester to see Brigham. While in New England, he was contacted by Baumgarten at Dartmouth College where he was using a collection of Webster letters. She told of an overture from owlish-looking Tom Smith who had been editorial assistant to Liveright and had become editor of the firm. Smith had written her asking for a meeting with Adams: "I simply do not want to go without an understanding, just as we do not want to hold him against his wishes. But I should like to be frank and helpful to Sam for personally I am very fond of him." Adams replied he welcomed the chance to see him.[6]

Besides writing and visiting his librarian friends, he went to the Syracuse Public Library to use reference works as he was finishing the biography in early July. While there he met a reporter whom he told he had destroyed the first part of his manuscript because "I found I was writing history and I wanted to picture the man." He further said, "Webster had a reputation of being both immoral and a drunkard, but if he was either of these I have found no evidence of it."[7]

The muckraker did try. When Ibbotson had suggested that he check a book on the social life in Washington, *Recollections,* by S. G. Goodrich, Adams asked if the author were Sara Goodrich, a miniature painter, who loaned Webster money and could have been his mistress. Ibbotson replied that the author was Samuel Griswold Goodrich, author of school books and popular history.[8]

As Adams was finishing *The Godlike Daniel,* a sobriquet that New England conservatives gave Webster, word reached Houghton Mifflin. Greenslet wrote Baumgarten: "I observe that Sam Adams, under at least one of his aliases, is changing publishers. . . . We still have a rather soft spot in our hard publishing heart for Sam and we also, as you know, have been looking around for a good book on Daniel Webster. Is Sam's already sold, or can we have a crack at it?"[9]

She replied that the book was contracted for and sent a copy of the letter to Adams, thinking he might be amused. Not so amusing was her report that World Publishing had sent copies of *Unforbidden Fruit* to Kresge in Boston, but it had refused to sell the book because, unknown to Brandt & Brandt, the

Watch and Ward Society had banned the original edition. Adams was un-sympathetic, replying that if World could not fulfill its contract, the publica-tion should be stopped.[10]

While he had censorship problems, Sears was also giving him headaches of a different nature. The Fabian novel *The Men in Her Life* and Adams's *The Godlike Daniel* were published almost simultaneously in October. Not only did he compete with himself *The Godlike Daniel* was also the victim of bad timing as Little, Brown and Company produced a two-volume *Daniel Webster* by scholar Claude Moore Fuess at the same time. As *Revelry* had been com-pared with the *Whispering Gallery*, the Adams biography was lumped with the Fuess work in several reviews and came off second best.[11]

Readers, facing a decision between what the New York *World* called Fuess's conservative "slow of pulse" authoritative treatment and Adams's interpreta-tive "aliveness" approach did not flock to buy *The Godlike Daniel*.[12] The book sold 1,340 copies that fell $2,046 short of the $3,000 advance by the financially strapped Sears. The loss was offset by the financial success of the Fabian *Men in Her Life*. The advance and royalties on 8,317 regular editions and 785 sales in Canada grossed $3,049 for Adams before Sears went bankrupt.

Although the *Christian Science Monitor* reviewer had been perplexed by not being able to decide if *The Godlike Daniel* was fiction or biography, Adams was hooked on history. Adams wrote Brigham, now director of the Society, of plans to tackle a historical novel on the Jackson administration focusing on Anne Royall and Peggy O'Neale Eaton. The sketch for librarians later ex-plained: "In conducting his research for *The Godlike Daniel* he found the pe-riod more and more fascinating. Peggy O'Neale particularly appealed to him because whatever she was, she was honest and forthright in a time when women were conscious prudes."[13] At about the same time he received a feeler from Baumgarten about a biography of Henry Clay for his first publisher, Bobbs-Merrill, but he had his next novel.

As the search for more income continued, Adams and Baumgarten sought to sell a book based on the Fabian film *What Men Want*. The motion picture itself was released by Universal in 1930 to a resounding thud. Later, Adams ad-mitted that he wished he could answer a blanket "No" to the question "Do you write with an eye on the movies?" He explained: "I once did that very thing. The resultant picture would be listed by any fair and competent critic among the ten worst of any year. I shall not make that mistake again."[14]

*What Men Want* was described by historians Nash and Ross: "Problems arise for a debonair playboy, Ellis, when his mistress swoons for another man,

[Ben] Lyon. When her sister comes to town, the plot thickens and becomes an edible stew." Attempts were made to sell the book to Sears in 1930 and Smith at Liveright in 1931, but Baumgarten warned Adams, "Please don't count on it, however, because it might not come through at all." She was correct, and it went into the dead-end B-file.[15]

While Baumgarten was working on the book end, Brandt sought to sell his work to the magazines. The Great Depression was having profound effects on the magazine market as smaller magazines were closing and larger ones were cutting back on space. In the dismal climate Brandt found Tower Publications. Records of Adams's short story sales in these years were sketchy because most of his work in Tower Publications was not collected or indexed. Many in 1930 were reprints of earlier stories. His reported earnings from his writings steadily declined in the first three full years of the depression. In 1930 his sales were more than $17,000, about $5,000 more than his colleague Irwin earned. Both men made about $12,400 in 1931 with Adams getting the bulk of his income from movie rights to *The Men in Her Life*. With no movie money coming in during 1932 Adams's recorded writing earnings fell to $4,500.[16]

Adams was aware of what was happening. In August 1930 he telephoned Irwin and said bankers had told him the situation would be worse next winter and spring and the economy would not come back until 1932. Irwin said he hoped "this is just Democratic pessimism" but fourteen years later added a notation in his diary, "on the contrary rank optimism!" Near the end of 1930 Irwin again saw Adams, who "spoke of pessimism of great bankers and economists. Hell of a fix."[17]

The troubled economic times and the changed public mood affected the Adamses. Jane Adams, with her understudy Katherine Morse, directed two one-act plays in January 1930. Morse, a 1926 graduate of Bryn Mawr College, increased her activity and one year later Jane announced her swan song. As with many in the theater, her retirement was delayed. She directed a one-act farce in January 1932 and a pantomime for the Christmas Basket and Clothes Relief Fund in December. When the Amateur Dramatic Club dissolved the next June into the Drama Guild, Jane Adams was not in the new group.

The depression did not alter their going in the early months of 1931 to Hibernia where Adams turned sixty in January. Nor was Adams cautious about economics. He turned down a Liveright offer to produce a cheap edition of *Revelry*, playing a hunch that he could get the firm to print more copies than the five thousand it was proposing. He was right; the Liveright firm doubled the number and raised his royalty from $250 to $500.

But there were no visits by the Irwins to Wide Waters or by the Adamses to Scituate. One event that could not be put aside was the fortieth reunion of the Hamilton College class of 1891. The Adamses had ten of the twenty-five surviving members of the class at Wide Waters in June. Another event that did not suffer from the economic times was the traditional Adams Fourth of July house party during which they filled the big and small lake houses. The fifteen guests included one other married couple, plus Marguerite Taylor, Lydia Mead, and other young people, showing a growing tendency by Adams to surround himself with the young.

In October 1931 the film version of *The Men in Her Life* was released by Columbia Pictures. Later Adams said the adaptation by Robert Riskin, a newspaperman and playwright who had been brought to Hollywood by director Frank Capra, bore little resemblance to his book. Strong performances by Charles Bickford and Lois Morin, however, saved the film in *Variety*'s view.[18]

Back in Hibernia in January 1932 Adams was finishing his book on Peggy Eaton amid distractions from afar. In February Harry Daugherty published a book, *The Inside Story of the Harding Tragedy*, intended to clear the president's name and his own. He was still smarting from *Revelry*. He said Adams was a disgrace to the family name and denied the existence of the House on K Street. Contacted by the New York *Evening Post* in Florida, Adams shot back, in part. "Mr. Daugherty says that I wrote 'Revelry' in fictional form to escape prosecution for criminal libel. Prosecution by whom? By himself? It is difficult to contemplate without unseemly mirth the prospect of Harry Daugherty prosecuting any one for libel in any court."[19]

More intimate was an argument that developed between Adams and his friend Lithgow Osborne. Once rebuffed, Nancy Wilson Ross had been successful in getting Liveright to publish *From Friday to Monday*. Set in the fictional city of Easterlin, the story featured the amorous adventures of Martin Truesdale. To Osborne, Easterlin was Auburn and Truesdale was himself. One Auburn woman remembered that the book took Auburn society by storm. "It was a hot topic," she recalled. In careful control the future diplomat wrote Adams, saying he had heard the author had advised Ross and had helped her to get the book published.[20]

Adams was alerted by Morse, working for Osborne as a secretary, about the intensity of his friend's feelings. He carefully explained that he had only brought the novel to the publisher's attention as he had with a book by Osborne's sister-in-law, Edith Osborne. He denied helping Ross write her book and said his friend was being too sensitive. After two exchanges of letters in which Adams repeated his position, Osborne backed off, saying they still disagreed but offering to look for an antique chest for Adams during his visit to Denmark.[21]

Despite his arguments with foe and friend and his financial squeeze he realized he was not the only one in tough times. He authorized Smith at Liveright to allow a young man to have *Who and What* free for newspaper use, much to the chagrin of Baumgarten, who commented, "I daresay, you will get your reward in Heaven." She also was pressing Smith for a three thousand dollar advance on the Peggy Eaton book, but Smith wrote that he was eager to publish the book but could only afford two thousand dollars because of the unpredictability of the market. Adams told her to accept the two thousand dollar offer because he had told Smith he could have the book on his own terms.[22]

At the same time he was writing Baumgarten about the Liveright contract and was preparing to leave for the North the latest Fabian book, *Week-End Girl*, was published by Macaulay, which Baumgarten had found to replace Sears. The story of Venetia Carr, who was a paid guest at weekend parties and repelled various advances until she met the right man, was released almost simultaneously as a film titled *Week-Ends Only* by the Fox Film Corporation. This time the stars, Joan Bennett and Lyon, could not help the adaptation by William Conselman.

The release of the film and the publication of the novel at the same time might have been rationalized on the basis that the publicity of each would help both. The film was panned, and the book sold 6,556 regular editions, a low for a Fabian novel. Augmented by 4,650 cheap copies and 226 in Canada, the book royalties still fell $929 short of the Macaulay advances of $2,500. The Fabian novels and film adaptations had lost their luster, endangering a main income source for Adams.

His priorities, however, did not shift. Hamilton College and his fraternity Alpha Delta Phi remained high on his agenda, so when he was asked to chair the program committee for the fraternity's centennial at its parent Hamilton College, he accepted. On Labor Day weekend the Adamses went to Clinton, entertained in a mansion, and participated in various events. He gave the welcoming speech to five hundred Alpha Delts, and Woollcott drove to Clinton and spoke.

After the centennial celebration, Adams faced the realities of reports that Liveright's business was shaky and was concerned about the Peggy Eaton book, the first part of which had been sent to the firm in March and the last part of which he was finishing. Baumgarten had not heard anything definite about Liveright's condition but, noting the firm would be all right or broke by spring, suggested they hold off delivering the rest of the manuscript until the last possible moment. She retrieved the first part and agreed with Adams the proposed title for the Tower serial of the Eaton book, "Invitation to Sin," was awful. Adams, who suggested "Dangerous Woman" and then changed to "Dangerous Lady," disbelieved that Tower's editorial director Hugh Weir had chosen such a title. The concern continued.[23]

If his writing was encountering bumps in the publishing road, politics offered Adams as a liberal Democrat some positive results. In 1930 he had been on a reception committee for a visit of Franklin Delano Roosevelt to Cayuga County, and when the New York governor ran for president, Adams quickly backed him. After Roosevelt's inauguration the next year, Adams accepted an appointment from W. Averell Harriman to the Cayuga County Re-Employment Committee of the National Recovery Administration. One week later he was master of ceremonies at Old Home Day at the West Niles Grange and heard conservative Republican Representative John Taber say, "The National Recovery Act won't work," explaining it would cause many difficulties for the small merchant. Adams replied that the act created "the greatest organization formed since war time, and to the efforts of this organization we must lend ourselves. . . . The N.R.A. is a march out of the valley of the depression, and a march in which we must all take part."[24]

His ardor for the Roosevelt presidency continued. More than one year later he told a Rochester newspaper: "I'm a strong New Dealer. I get a lot of enjoyment out of Franklin D. He's not afraid to be wrong, goes ahead on the theory we should have put into government a long time ago—the scientific use of the principle of trial and error. Unless we have the courage to break out new paths, our civilization will come to an end."[25]

On occasion Adams mixed politics with his social activities. Alice Hopkins Eyerman, a great-great-granddaughter of Samuel Miles Hopkins, remembered that on her first visit to Wide Waters in the fall of 1932 the license plates of the cars of others at the dinner had state seals. Adams had looked up his cousin in Ithaca where she and her husband, both of whom were in Cornell University's School of Architecture, had an apartment. "Cousin Sam, who wore glasses with a ribbon, invited us for a weekend and suggested we bring another couple to feel more comfortable." She remembered being greeted by Adams with a shaker of martinis. "It was a special evening. We had a lot of fun even though all the other people at the table were politicians."[26]

Politics aside, 1933 offered Adams a comeback in his writing and finances. Greenslet offered to read without obligation "Invitation to Sin," a title he called "not so hot, or too hot." Adams sent the letter to Baumgarten with a notation that he would welcome having the literary director read the book because his scholarship could be invaluable.[27]

Greenslet's reaction to the Peggy Eaton book was a three-page letter in which he called the book "a first-class job." He congratulated the author, saying he could not remember having seen "the tumult and shouting of the Jackson era anywhere better presented." He ended with suggestions for a better title of which *Bellona* was his favorite because "simple one-word titles of this sort take color from both advertising and talk about the book." Adams agreed the Roman goddess of war was appropriate. Baumgarten went along although she said it did not "fire me with enthusiasm." The book was put off until the financial status of Liveright was clearer.[28]

With the book stalled Adams continued to work the magazine market. Tower placed a mystery serial, "Bells at Night," in *Detective Story* and ran the renamed "Gorgeous Hussy" serial from the Peggy Eaton book in *Love* magazine. Adams also wrote two other stories, which he told his daughter Katherine Adell were based on a chance meeting with a young woman on a bus, probably during his March trip between Florida and New York the previous year. A short story about a forlorn young woman and a despairing young man who met on a bus was run as a one-page short story, "Last Trip," in a March 1933 *Collier's.* Dissatisfied that he had made the most of his material, he developed, along the same lines, "Night Bus" as a serial or a book. It was first published as a novelette. Baumgarten thought it should be a Fabian story, but Brandt insisted on an Adams byline.

"Night Bus" ran in the August 1933 *Cosmopolitan,* and one of its readers was film director Frank Capra. The story, which had similarities to the 1915 *Little Miss Grouch,* featured penniless inventor Peter Warne and spoiled heiress Elspeth Andrews who met on a bus trip from Miami to New York. She was fleeing from her father, and together they faced adventures that caused them to fall in love. Capra liked the story: "It had the smell of novelty." He showed it to screenwriter Robert Riskin, who agreed. Capra asked Columbia Pictures to check the asking price and was told the cost was "Buttons! We can buy it for five G's." Capra told the studio to buy it, and afterward studio head Harry Cohn told the two men to develop a shooting script. The result was *It Happened One Night.*[29]

The $5,000 for the film rights and $2,000 for the novelette pushed Adams's recorded earnings from his writing to about $12,500 in 1933, back to his 1931 level. Most of the rest came from his various offerings in Tower Publications, but "Night Bus" and its stepchild, *It Happened One Night*, were his financial godsends.

"A film about making *It Happened One Night* would have been funnier than the picture itself," Capra recalled in his autobiography. According to film historians Nash and Ross, the first right of refusal was given to Louis B. Mayer of Metro-Goldwyn-Mayer, but the Republican did not like the character of the tycoon father, and although he offered the stars Capra wanted, Robert Montgomery and Myrna Loy, both turned the script down. Capra's search for the female star led to Miriam Hopkins (Adams's personal choice), Margaret Sullivan, and Constance Bennett; all rejected the part of renamed Ellie Andrews. Finally, Capra got Claudette Colbert from Paramount after promising he would shoot the film in four weeks so she could spend Christmas with her friends in Sun Valley. For the male lead, Mayer sent Cohn a young actor who he felt was goldbricking and should be punished by having to do the film, Clark Gable.[30]

Riskin fashioned a plot, making the most of Adams's story, although the part of inventor Peter Warne, whom Gable played, was changed to a hard-bitten newspaper reporter. The part for Colbert was changed from a spoiled to a bored heiress. In deference to Cohn who had had ill luck with two other bus pictures, the bus was downplayed and the title changed. Many of Adams's already visual scenes, however, including the "walls of Jericho" sequences, and secondary characters remained and were strengthened for actors Alan Hale, Roscoe Karns, and Ward Bond. But it was the chemistry of the brusque Gable and the vulnerable Colbert that made the film the biggest "sleeper" in American cinema.[31]

The movie opened in February 1934 at Radio City Music Hall, and the critics were not sure what to make of it. The reviews were not bad, but certainly not raves. Radio City showed the film for one week instead of holding it over for the usual second week. The small Columbia Pictures had no large advertising budget or publicity gimmicks. Colbert seemed to be right when she told friends at Sun Valley after the four-week shoot: "Am I glad to be here. I've just finished the worst picture in the world!"[32] The Adams adaptation seemed to be following the path of recent Fabian films.

He also was having trouble getting the Eaton book published. On 5 May 1933 the *New York Times* reported the bankruptcy of Liveright, and he wrote Baumgarten to contact Greenslet. A couple of days later he sent her a note that he had received from Smith saying the firm was being reorganized, but Adams said that he wanted a financially sound publisher. She was firm, saying Liveright "can demand as much as they like—they shall not have it." Over the next months she, Greenslet, and Adams tried varied approaches to get the book from Liveright. Finally, after Liveright was reorganized under Arthur Pell and Smith, she got Smith to release it. On 1 November contracts were signed, and Adams returned to Houghton Mifflin.[33]

As the legal entanglements were being cleared, discussions returned to the title. Greenslet abandoned *Bellona,* and Adams proposed *Peggy Was a Lady,* which Baumgarten said was a "swell title for a sentimental ballad." After Greenslet said it "suggested either a juvenile or a very light sentimental novel from a female pen," they compromised on the serial title, *The Gorgeous Hussy.*[34]

With the title and legal issues settled Adams had three books in the works by the end of 1933, *Hussy,* an expanded *Night Bus,* and the latest Fabian, *Widow's Oats.* Despite his ailing hip Adams had remained active during 1933. While he was in Coconut Grove, he had checked out the southern operation of the Adirondack-Florida School, which the Osborne boys had attended.

One was Lithgow Osborne's youngest son, Frederik R-L. Osborne, who often visited Wide Waters. Maybe because he was Jane Adams's godson, he was forgiven his first meeting with him. After overhearing the former actress describe Adams in her usual earthy style, he was introduced to the author for the first time. "Oh, you are the great big goddamn fool," the boy said. Nonetheless, he became a playmate for George Harlan, and when he went to the Adirondack-Florida School, another new boy was Buddy Richardson, which may explain Adams's interest in the school. At Wide Waters Osborne found a warm, vibrant household that he found exciting because of the personalities. "Mrs. Adams was a little Auntie Mamish. I remember once when I was in their dining room, I accidentally broke a ruby and white glass on a shelf. Sam Adams got mad with considerable justice, but she just passed it off." Although the young Osborne found a welcoming house where a child could play with Adams's collection of mechanical coin banks, he said Adams was not the type of man "who would set you on his lap and read to you. He did not have the warmth of Jane Adams, and I was always in awe of him."[35]

Awe was a description that relatives and friends had of Adams. And probably no place engendered more awe than at the bridge table. If tournament golf and tennis were casualties of his physical infirmities, his combative nature still was present at bridge. He was fiercely competitive, Serrell Hillman later wrote, and brooked no chit-chat over the cards. "Once, as the first hand was being dealt, a young woman who was visiting Adams said brightly: 'My, it's so nice to be here!' Adams growled: 'If you want to gossip, let somebody else play bridge.'"[36] The game also challenged his volatile temper. One recipient was Marion Kennedy.

She spent summers across Owasco Lake at Ensenore. The wife of attorney Samuel V. Kennedy, Jr., the New Hampshire native came to Auburn's private Logan School. Her first memories of Adams were at a bridge table where he threw a deck of cards after she made the wrong lead. "I was very shy in those days, and so embarrassed. Several days later Sam invited me on an antiquing tour." Although he was critical of a glass dove the former New Englander bought, they became friends.[37]

Adams and Kennedy shared an interest in history and writing, and "he wanted to get me going, suggesting an outstanding editor to help me." Although she published a short story in *Story* magazine, she felt she could not make the time commitment he said was needed. She also had trouble in following Jane's suggestion she entertain more. When she did entertain "having the Adamses for dinner was scary," because Adams was so outspoken and Jane daunting. "I remember one Sunday supper when the Adamses arrived late, coming with three unexpected guests and armfuls of wine. The chicken cooked slowly and Sam stomped up and down the porch, saying 'I want my dinner!' But after he had a couple more martinis, it became one of the best parties I ever had."

The dinners at Wide Waters were elegant in their formality. Kennedy recalled that Jane would be stunning as she came sweeping into the room in her long velvet gown. "Although she was heavy-set, her feet were delicate and her dark eyes very sparkling," she said. "The dinner table was often so packed you did not have room for your elbows. The talk was light and you were expected to participate."

She recalled that overall the Adamses were "awfully nice to me." Although they surrounded themselves with beautiful and successful people, Adams had a special affinity with people who shared his interests and for women who were beautiful, in that order. Kennedy recalled taking an unattractive daughter of a friend to an Adams party with some trepidation. In what she called one of the biggest surprises of her life, "Sam was intrigued by the woman because of her interest in history and took her off into a corner where she opened up to him as she never had with anyone else."

Adams's hip did not stop him from traveling in 1933. He and Jane visited the Brandts in early August. Carl Brandt had divorced Zelma Brandt and in May 1931 married Carol Hill, who was a friend and lover of author John P. Marquand, a client and friend of Carl's. Later, in October, the Adamses went to Bryn Mawr, Pennsylvania, to visit the N. Myers Fitlers. Between trips, tennis occupied Adams. Although he had given up playing tennis, he donated gold and silver vases as trophies and umpired Auburn matches, taking the chair for a week.

The worsening hip that had made Adams almost a cripple with considerable pain kept them closer to home as 1934 approached. They went to New York for the winter. While they were there, *It Happened One Night* suddenly took off. Audiences identifying with the depression scenes and the escapism of a time when one-quarter of the work force was idle flocked to the picture. Critics remained mystified, but Adams, who later said of films that had been adapted from his work "some with a result so painful that I have been unable to sit through the presentation," liked *It Happened One Night*. He found it "improved in the adaptation, and was directed and acted with such artistry and verve that I should like to see it again."[38]

On a negative note he and Irwin in March attended the funeral of Weir, the *Tower* editor who had used his stories and serials. As often happened, the change of editors meant a closed market. *Liberty*, under Fulton Oursler, remained the only outlet for his magazine work, publishing one 1934 piece, a short-short story, "Fire."

His historical novel, *The Gorgeous Hussy*, was published in April 1934. The story of Peggy O'Neale, whose rise in Washington politics and society he had traced from when she was fourteen, chronicled the middle decades of the 1800s. He followed her through three marriages, one of which was to Secretary of War John H. Eaton, to an age when she realized her charm and beauty were gone. Along the way he offered sketches of the Andrew Jacksons, Webster, Clay, Royall, and especially John Randolph, whose characterization in the Webster biography critics had praised.

Although he later credited the book with teaching him how to do research and write history, he had approached the novel with "a broad license in the matter of dates." In "A Letter to the Meticulous Reader" preamble he explained: "Accuracy is the chain in which the writer of history is fettered, but the novelist's fidelity is of another and looser kind. He has fulfilled his whole duty to his subject in preserving the integrity of his *dramatis personae* and in presenting them against a background faithfully drawn."

Several critics had difficulties with Adams's license, but overall they gave the novel good marks. As the Adamses prepared to return to Cayuga County, sales of the book were strong. From 13 May to 17 June *The Gorgeous Hussy* made the New York *Herald Tribune Books* list of "What America is Reading," placing among the teens of the fiction rankings. The book also was on the "Best Sellers Here and Elsewhere" of the *New York Times* that canvassed the major city markets, showing strength in Washington, Atlanta, and New Orleans over eighteen weeks. In late August, to paraphrase the title of a new book on the list, it was *Goodbye, Mr. Adams*.[39]

Greenslet reported near the end of July that Houghton Mifflin had almost exhausted its first two printings, totaling 10,000 copies, and was ordering another "which, considering everything, is I think not so bad." He noted Adams had exceeded the $2,000 advance by $919.92. The book would sell 12,040 regular copies, almost tripling Houghton Mifflin's break-even point of 4,855 volumes. In addition it sold 12,750 cheap copies and 200 in Canada, totaling almost 25,000. His advance and royalties were $5,035.79, before commissions.[40]

The financial success of the historical novel during the depression was a real positive for Adams. It maintained his independence and offset reverses such as the foreclosure action on a Niles farm family that left Jane Adams holding a note for seven hundred dollars. Fortunately, their own Wide Waters Farm was doing well.

The farm was managed by Michael Kowal, who was in his twenties. Kowal received thirty-five dollars a month plus room and board, more than the going twenty-five-dollar rate in the area. The farm was run somewhat independently of the lake houses. Kowal said Jane Adams took an active interest in the farm, coming up the hill a couple of times a week to see how things were progressing and occasionally going for a horseback ride. "Mrs. Adams went out of her way to help the poor, paying for Christmas food baskets for some of the neighbors," Kowal said, adding that she left her rough language down at the lake.

"We kept an eye on the property while they were away, cut ice every spring, and put in the dock, but otherwise pretty much stuck to the farming," Kowal recalled. The fifteen to twenty tons of ice in two-hundred-pound chunks were packed in sawdust in an icehouse between the Adams property and industrialist Fred Emerson's summer home, Boscobel, to the south. The ice was for the kitchen, and "he also used it for the truck that came from Canada every spring loaded with booze."[41]

Wide Waters Farm offered the Adamses during the depression logistic support for their lifestyle. It provided fresh food and available help. On the farm, of which only about half of the three hundred acres was tillable because of its hilly location, they grew corn, hay, and oats. Part was sold, and part was used for the twenty-five to thirty cows. "We also sold milk to a dealer in Auburn,"

Kowal recalled. The sales of milk and crops kept the farm going, "but it didn't make them rich. Mr. Adams paid the bills," Kowal reported, adding that the author would come to the farm but was not involved in the operation. For Jane Adams the farm offered a diversion and for Adams, a concern for money.

The search for income continued. While *The Gorgeous Hussy* was selling, Baumgarten tried to place Adams's two other books. Although she had offered his Fabian novel, *Widow's Oats,* to Macaulay, she was cool about the book detailing the amorous adventures of older women who told a young physician why they had found men disappointing. Her criticism produced a mild protest from Adams although he then conceded she might be right. A few months later, with no word from Macaulay, he was concerned because the League of Decency was making a fuss that might hurt the lucrative movie end of the Fabian books. Confident that the League would overreach, he asked her to call the book back.[42]

The book version of "Night Bus" was a tough sell. After Liveright turned it down, Baumgarten turned to the publisher of other Adams seventy-five-cent editions, Grosset & Dunlap. Alexander Grosset said publication would come too late because the film had been released. She then tried Julian Messner, who had left Liveright to form his own firm. Messner offered no advance, and Adams countered by asking a ten-cent per copy royalty. After gentle pestering from Baumgarten, Messner finally rejected it despite Adams's offer of his new novelette.

That novelette, "In Person," was bought in July by RKO Radio Pictures for twenty-five thousand dollars and was serialized in *Motion Picture* in 1935. The whopping film payment may have led Adams to suggest "A Long Yell for Nero" be offered as a Christmas edition. The realistic Baumgarten said she would try but felt it was too short for even a small book.[43] She was right. And Adams knew it. Over the years, his correspondence showed an abiding faith in the business judgment of his literary editor and an interest in the publishing success of her husband. Like other women, he treated her as an equal, constantly asking her opinion, welcoming her criticisms, and occasionally dueling with her on artistic matters.

The summer of 1934 began uneventfully with the Adamses moving into Wide Waters in late May, and the Atherton Harlans arriving with their son, George, on 2 June. Adams attended commencement at Hamilton and in early August spent several days in Washington. The Adamses went in mid-August to the Adirondacks. But all was not well.

On 26 September in a letter to Ibbotson he revealed that Jane Adams had been seriously ill for a month with nerve exhaustion, but four days earlier Irwin wrote in his diary that he had received a letter from him saying that Jane had a brain disease that caused partial or complete loss of the power to use or understand words. In November Adams wrote Woollcott thanking him for his article in the *New Yorker* on Adams's battle with Charles William Post. He then told of Jane's illness and his own plans to have an operation followed by eight weeks in a plaster cast.[44]

During a September trip to New York Adams sought the advice of a surgeon on an operation for his ailing hip. He suggested Adams have the operation closer to home and mentioned Rochester. When Adams said he knew no surgeons in his boyhood home, he was told of Howard Prince. Adams met with Dr. Prince, a jovial heavy-set man whose tastes ranged from cooking to chemistry to fishing. A friendship between Adams and the doctor developed that would last the rest of Prince's life.

Before going to Rochester for the operation, he made a trip to New York where he, Baumgarten, and a representative of Saalfield Publishing Company reached an agreement to publish "Night Bus" under the title of *It Happened One Night* in a dime version to be sold in chain stores. Adams was to receive a quarter-of-a-penny a copy with an advance on royalties of one hundred thousand books of $250. The payment capped 1934 in which Adams's recorded earnings were almost $30,500, a good rainy-day fund.

He went under Prince's knife on 10 December to correct a growth of bone inside the right hip joint, which had shortened the leg, making walking awkward and painful. Later a Hamilton College classmate gave Adams's account in a newsletter: "Dr. Howard Prince chiseled the bone out of the joint, fixed the joint solid, hammered a steel nail into it; cut a flange of bone, nailed that into place with two spikes, and closed me up. I was under the knife 2 1/2 hours. Came out without shock or even sickness and at no time suffered any pain in the operated leg. B U T they stuck me in a plaster cast; there to sweat and itch for eight weeks, and that was a modified form of hell."[45]

Jane Adams was at her husband's side, but when he felt well enough to give an interview to a Rochester newspaper, she went to Auburn to arrange his transfer. On 23 December he was taken from Rochester General Hospital to Auburn City Hospital to continue his recovery. Ahead for the sixty-three-year-old author lay the first period of extended inactivity in writing since he had graduated from college.

# 14

# SERIALIST
## 1935–1939

ENCASED in a body cast from armpit to toe and lying on a board in Auburn City Hospital, Adams took to his environment like a duck to a desert. Although he could write occasional letters, he was unable to do any major writing for weeks.

Brandt had urged him to use a Dictaphone, and that might have made him productive during his immobility. He had rejected the idea, however, saying his words became stilted. Although he used typists, he admitted: "A secretary, or even a stenographer, fatally gets between me and my work. That intervening personality not only induces in me a painful self-consciousness, but it also lessens my sense of the reality of the characters which I am striving to create."[1]

Gone also was the privacy of creative isolation he needed to write. One of the reasons he enjoyed Wide Waters, one mile from the main road and ten from Auburn, was the lack of casual morning visitors. Now he sought companionship and, when Brandt mentioned that he might come up for a day, Adams was quick to suggest dates. After Adams wrote again, telling of his boredom and use of codeine to help him sleep, Brandt came to Auburn.[2] Another friend rallied to the cause as Irwin on the way to Detroit got off the train in Syracuse. After seeing Adams and his physician, Wilfred Sefton, Irwin continued his trip with a Sefton pledge to keep him informed.

His surgeon, Howard Prince, came on 3 February after an x-ray the day before showed the bone was knit, and the cast was removed. Not only was the cast gone but so was the rainy-day fund. Later he estimated the three "shingle nails" that immobilized his hip had cost six hundred dollars each. His worries were eased by Lilla Worthington, who handled film rights for Brandt &

Brandt, that Metro-Goldwyn-Mayer had paid fifteen hundred dollars for an option on the possible purchase of *The Gorgeous Hussy* at fifteen thousand dollars. For three weeks he remained in the hospital, conducting business and reporting his progress to Brandt & Brandt. Then he went to Fred Emerson's Auburn home.

In the meantime he had been making slight changes in the page proofs of *It Happened One Night* to fit the film's still pictures that he coveted and eventually got. One of the "least pretentious pictures of the year" also did well. *It Happened One Night* swept the top categories of the Academy Awards while he was at Emerson's. It won best picture, and director Capra, actor Gable, actress Colbert, and adapter Riskin were voted the best in their respective categories. Adams' initial reaction concerned Saalfield not having the book out to take advantage of the publicity.

Another concern was mirrored in a *Citizen-Advertiser* editorial the next day: "This is an extraordinary record for a single motion picture. Auburnians, however, may find something ironical in the fact that about the only person connected with 'It Happened One Night' who didn't get a blue ribbon or something is the man who wrote the story—Mr. Adams."[3]

The main chore for Adams in the spring was to regain his ability to walk, and the effort took so much of his energy that he turned down two thousand dollars for an article on the Pulitzer-Hearst newspaper battle, an assignment he called easy. Earlier he had tentatively accepted an invitation from Percy Waxman of *Cosmopolitan* to the annual Dutch Treat Club dinner in early April. With the goal set he hobbled around Emerson's and on 17 March reported that he had put his bad foot to the ground.

He wrote a piece on hospital mental wards and an article on George Catlin, a painter of Indian life, furnishing six of his prints to go with it. Although on 21 March Sefton said he could not hope to be walking in two weeks, he booked a hotel suite that would allow the female members of Brandt & Brandt to properly visit him.

As his departure on 4 April neared, Sefton urged him to go because he was afraid he was becoming too dependent. One on whom he relied was Jane Adams, who, along with her own illness, had been through his ordeal and was feeling the strain. She had only been away for a few days in February, but she followed the doctor's orders and let Adams go to New York alone.

In New York Brandt shepherded him around, marveling at his ability to get in and out of taxicabs backwards. He took him to the Dutch Treat dinner, where Adams saw Irwin, who visited his friend at the Chatham the next day.

Coming to the hotel also were his friends from Brandt & Brandt, representatives of his publishers, and editors such as Fulton Oursler of *Liberty*. He had lunch with his daughter, Hester Adams, who was about to graduate from Columbia University with a library science degree, and had a cocktail party for his friends.

All went well because "everybody looks after a two-crutch man," except when it came to the hotel bathtub. "I got myself in with a great deal of pride and insufficient plans for getting out again." While he was stuck in the tub, pleas to those passing brought retorts but no help until he hurled a bar of soap through the transom, an act that produced the house detective and rescue. "The experience was salutary. It taught me that I might as well abandon self-consciousness and face new conditions without embarrassment."[4]

Back at Emerson's home, he was still suffering discomfort, physically and artistically. An editor at the *American* said his hospital story was not only unpleasant but also Adams was "cock-eyed" for thinking any psychopathic ward would allow patients to wander freely. Adams said small hospitals had wards for the temporarily mental and nervous, but he grumbled that it could be made a love story. He ordered the story held for future discussion. In a rare case of disobedience Brandt replied: "I'm going on with the story. The *American* didn't feaze me in the slightest. Also, I'm dead set against any goodness and light in it."[5] Several months later he placed it with *Cosmopolitan*.

His stay in Auburn was interrupted by word from the Century Club in New York that he had won a drawing to have a portrait done by one of the artists on exhibit at the club. In early May he went to New York without fanfare to choose the painter, Gordon Stevenson, whom he invited to Wide Waters during the summer. Back at the lake, he tackled his latest serial, "Perfect Specimen."

Still using a crutch, he picked up speed as Decoration Day arrived. He noted with interest the casting of Ginger Rogers, in her first starring role after dancing with Fred Astaire, for *In Person*, which had become a musical comedy about the saving of a movie star from an agoraphobic attack through the efforts of a young man, played by George Brent.

Adams turned to another revision of *Widow's Oats*, and at the same time "Perfect Specimen" began its tortuous path through the *Cosmopolitan* editors, who noted that it showed the masculine side of "Night Bus." He agreed to change the serial into a novelette, but as he labored, he made a plea to Brandt to keep the *Cosmopolitan* editors away after they had telephoned, asking for

8. Sam and Jane Adams at the fireplace in their living room at Wide Waters in the 1940s. Behind them is a portrait painted by Gordon Stevenson that is now in Burke Library at Hamilton College. Samuel Hopkins Adams Collection. Courtesy of Syracuse University Library.

outlines and synopses, which he disliked to do under any circumstances. Brandt assured him: "They did not mean to ride herd on you; it was all done in a grand mistaken spirit of good fellowship."[6]

Rewriting was part of his craft, and he welcomed it: "Fiction very seldom deteriorates in the process of rewriting. The only definite rule I follow is to try to write less with each revision." His main argument with the *Cosmopolitan* editors was not the rewriting but their interrupting his routine. Even a change of location did not alter his routine. On a September fishing trip to Canada, he did a horse racing story in two days in the combination living and dining room amid distractions and was proud the story ran in *Collier's* Christmas edition.[7]

During the summer of 1935 Wide Waters was abuzz. Among the visitors were author Carl Carmer and his wife, Betty. Carmer came to discuss Finger Lakes history. In August five Adams cousins were followed by children's book author Mary Fitler and her husband. Then there was portrait painter Stevenson who came with his wife on 13 July for a job that Adams estimated would take two weeks. He proved to be an unhappy subject, reporting on 22 July the portrait was taking too much time. When Irwin visited 24 August, Stevenson was still painting.[8]

While Irwin was visiting, Worthington's sixteen-month effort to sell *The Gorgeous Hussy* to motion pictures paid off when MGM bought the rights for ten thousand dollars. In September Joan Crawford was signed for the film. Worthington thought "she will be terrible," and he agreed. The sale of *Hussy* offset attempts to sell the film rights to *Widow's Oats* to Samuel Goldwyn, who turned it down because a studio reader found it "rather censorable."[9] "Perfect Specimen" seemed destined for a similar fate when Warner Brothers said no.

Although film rights on "Perfect Specimen" were elusive, Greenslet suggested that Houghton Mifflin might publish a book version of the serial. Adams doubted the firm would be interested in a light comedy but okayed a reading. After one month, Adams asked Baumgarten to send Smith at Liveright the magazine proofs because he suspected Greenslet would turn it down. Indeed, he found the serial a "little light" and said it would not help Adams's reputation. Smith, however, said it was "a charming piece of entertainment" and published it.[10]

The $10,000 for *The Gorgeous Hussy* from MGM plus $5,000 from *Cosmopolitan* for "Perfect Specimen" put his recorded earnings at more than $21,000 for 1935, when Irwin's income was about $8,000. His concerns over money after his operation were further lessened in July when some stock he owned was retired. In July, also Saalfield finally published *It Happened One Night* in what Baumgarten called "a distinct anti-climax." The book eventually sold 198,175 copies and netted him about $500 in quarter-of-a-penny royalty payments. His last Fabian novel, *Widow's Oats*, was published later in 1935, but sales were 1,803 regular and 1,244 cheap copies and fell $411 short of the $1,000 advance from Macaulay.[11]

One magazine that remained open to Adams was Oursler's *Liberty*. In July he contacted Brandt about a serial, "The Five Million Dollar Mystery," based on an idea from Franklin Delano Roosevelt, about a man who disappeared with five million dollars in securities that he used to live on undetected. Six installments were to be written by six authors. Brandt accepted, "thereby probably woefully exceeding my authority." Adams agreed to do the second installment. After receiving the first chapter by Rupert Hughes, Adams by 25 August finished the first half of his part and by 30 August completed his six thousand word installment. He confided to Brandt that he would like to rework Hughes's first installment.[12]

He got his wish. Oursler liked Adams's part so much he contacted Hughes about having Adams edit the first part, offering $100 in addition to his initial $750. Telling Brandt that it was $500 worth of work, Adams agreed because he liked Oursler and considered doing it good policy. Given a week because the installments were coming in, he reworked the first part. He did such a good job, according to Oursler, that the editor had to do some rearranging because otherwise readers would have known the first part was not by Hughes. The serial appeared as a book, *The President's Mystery Story*, at the end of the year. A film the following year got good reviews.[13]

In late September Adams went to Rochester, where x-rays taken of his hip confirmed it was in good shape. He abandoned his crutch for a cane. He returned to his boyhood home the next month to visit Prince, and while there, he told a journalist that Sinclair Lewis was the best living American novelist and that he was going to Hollywood just for "fun."[14]

When she learned he was going to California, Worthington tried to set Adams up with a writing job on *The Gorgeous Hussy* film. In Hollywood for one week, he was more concerned about the difficulty in selling his books to films. He was convinced it was caused by seeking out buyers rather than letting them come to him. He decided to play it coy. He met with Worthington's contact but refused to go onto the studio's turf, turning down a luncheon at MGM. He did meet with Crawford and was pleased to find *The Gorgeous Hussy* on her coffee table. He was not so happy when he found, while she was out of the room, that the pages remained uncut.[15] His latest Hollywood flirtation over, the Adamses went traveling.

During his California trip he saw an ailing Lincoln Steffens, who reported that the former muckraker was a cripple. Adams wrote a friend, however, that he was practicing golf approach shots and that he could manage fairly well without shaking his shingle nails loose. At the same time the film *In Person* opened. Worthington saw a screening and warned him not to go. Her opinion was supported by Jane Adams, who said Brent was bad and Ginger Rogers coarse. Although later he said he never saw the picture but added it to *What Men Want* as another of the Ten Worst Pictures,[16] Adams hoped that publicity from the film would sell "Perfect Specimen." He went back to Los Angeles, but the asking price of twenty-five thousand dollars brought no takers. Then they headed east.

In New York he persuaded Brandt to replace his California agent with Rosalie Stewart, whom he had met in Hollywood. He also gave Brandt a new serial about film making, "Maiden Effort," which *Cosmopolitan* rejected as too long. Further he was contacted by Greenslet, who reported that Grosset & Dunlap wanted a cheap version of *The Gorgeous Hussy* to take advantage of the upcoming film but wanted to eliminate the final section to save printing costs. Although Adams could have used the money, he replied that he did not want the book mutilated. His all-or-nothing proposal was echoed by Baumgarten, and Greenslet relented.

Liveright brought out *Perfect Specimen* in February 1936. The story featured a young heir whom his grandmother tried to develop educationally into the perfect specimen. When he escaped his caged life, a young woman took him on another chase story, similar to *It Happened One Night*. A strong start prompted Liveright to order a second printing of 2,500 copies. The magic of "Night Bus" was gone. Readers bought 2,733 regular editions. Another 2,184 Grosset & Dunlap cheap copies were sold the next year, bringing the total to almost 5,000. It fell $465 short of the $1,000 advance although reprints eventually produced a gross of $1,292.

Despite his difficulty with the book market he developed the serial on film making into a novel, *Maiden Effort*. Smith at Liveright, burned by advancing $1,000 for *Perfect Specimen*, offered an advance of only $250. Adams considered it too small and withdrew the book for revision. His attention, however, was now on a new serial suggested to Oursler by Bill Lengel, who had been at *Liberty* before becoming eastern story editor for Columbia Pictures. The romantic story, "Whispers," about a businessman who encountered love, corporate intrigue, an illegitimate pregnancy, and adventures that included being shot and almost bombed, presented a considerable challenge for Adams.

In the first installment he had to deal with the business aspects, bogging down the action. Both Brandt and Oursler had trouble with the story, and Adams revised the first part. He predicted the rest would be easier. Later in July, however, he was losing sleep trying to arrange his material. On it went for the rest of summer with rewrites and rearranging. He did not have any better luck with his short stories.

Marie Meloney, now with *This Week,* had bought a light romance, but all others were stalled until Brandt sold an old Fabian story to *College Humor* for $100. The editor, however, decided he did not want to run the story and asked Brandt for a substitute. A shrewd Brandt & Brandt employee, Alma Levin, shipped him the Adams hospital romance "West to East" but demanded an extra $150 to use it as a Fabian story, terms to which the grateful editor agreed. Supportive of the efforts of the firm's junior employees, Adams said she had done brilliantly. The price was low but welcome in the first half of 1936 in which his sales were less than $1,500.

His low writing income was supplemented by money from the investments of the sixty-five-year-old. The Social Security Act had passed the year before, but to Adams, survival meant self-reliance. In "How I Write" he said, "Writers who wait for inspiration presently find themselves in the bread-line, unless supported by worshipful relatives. Lacking relatives sufficiently affluent (or worshipful) to maintain me in the style to which I have become accustomed, and having no special taste for bread, I work regularly."[17]

Signs that the continuing depression was having an impact on their lifestyle were not evident as the Adamses continued their costly entertaining during the summer of 1936. The parade of visitors included Carmer, who had written an upstate New York historical novel, *Listen for the Lonesome Drum,* which Adams praised in a review. Marian Richardson Wells with Betty and Buddy Richardson came from the West Coast and were guests at many parties. A June party was given by Jane for her farm manager, Kowal, who married an Auburn woman. The next year, because his wife did not care for farming, Kowal moved to Auburn. Later he tried to buy land from Jane, who declined to sell any of her precious farm.[18]

June also marked the forty-fifth reunion of the Hamilton Class of 1891, and Adams invited ten members to Wide Waters where they reminisced before going to commencement. The big event of the summer, however, was a showing of *The Gorgeous Hussy* in Auburn. Friends turned the event into a gala dinner. At the theater he autographed books and spoke at intermission. His fears that Crawford would butcher his "Hussy" were not evident in his praising of her sympathetic interpretation. He also lauded the all-star MGM cast, including Beulah Bondi, who got an Academy Award nomination for her Rachel Jackson, the wife of Lionel Barrymore's Andrew Jackson.[19]

The enthusiasm in Auburn was not mirrored across the country as *The Gorgeous Hussy* was a box-office disappointment. Nonetheless, the release of the film caused Grosset & Dunlap to coordinate its publishing of an intact version of the novel. "It is about the best looking dollar book I have ever seen," Adams told Baumgarten.[20] The release of *The Gorgeous Hussy* film may also have spurred Hollywood interest in Adams. Worthington had died in the spring, and Brandt shifted the eager Collier Young to handle motion picture rights. He went to California and replaced Stewart, who had botched a deal with Pioneer Pictures for *Perfect Specimen* in May. He reinterested Warner Brothers, and a seventy-five-hundred-dollar offer was quickly accepted.

As the 1936 election campaign heated, Adams was deluged with requests. Knight Publications, recalling *Revelry*, asked if he would do a contemporary political novel, and he scrawled on the letter a note to Baumgarten that his writing would be from the New Deal angle. She said that Knight was a small operation and urged him to let her find a decent publisher, but he dropped the idea. Next he was contacted by H. W. March, a Boston politician, asking for a book on Huey Long. Adams told him he was a committed New Dealer but their ideas on Long might be similar. He told Brandt, however, that if March wanted a Republican campaign document against Roosevelt, he was not interested. March backed out. Greenslet reported Sinclair Lewis had suggested a novel on the Revolution from the Tory point of view. Adams said it would require extensive research time and declined as he finished "Whispers."[21]

Exhausted by his work on "Whispers," he left hectic Wide Waters for Vermont to visit Woollcott at Neshobe Island on Lake Bomoseen. Woollcott, whom he had tried to lure to Wide Waters earlier in 1936 and who had said he would see Adams "totter" at commencement, had bought half of the island for a permanent home. He ran it with other Algonquin Roundtable members such as Beatrice and George Kaufman, Alice Duer Miller, and Dorothy Parker somewhat as a cooperative. He charged fees, which could have irked Adams, whose own entertaining was extensive without recompense, but Adams accepted the charge. They would make regular visits to the island.[22]

Another visit with the Otis Skinners may have led to Cornelia Otis Skinner coming to Auburn in October for a performance of monologues. In No-

9. Members of the Hamilton College class of '91 gather in 1936 at Wide Waters before going to Clinton for their reunion. Seated, from left, are William P. Shepard, H. Platt Osborne, Robert N. Brockway, and George M. Weaver; standing, from left, George V. Edwards, Percy L. Wight, Albert E. Stuart, Jane Adams, Clarence W. Mason, Aurelian Post, Samuel Hopkins Adams, and Thomas L. Coventry. Courtesy of Hamilton College.

vember Adams went to Syracuse to bring William Beebe for a lecture on his underwater experiences in a bathysphere. He drove Beebe in his new Packard automobile, bought with his winnings from bets that Roosevelt would defeat Alf Landon and a trade-in on his Terraplane for a net cost of $41.50.

While Adams had been in New England, he was phoned by the hustling Young with a Paramount offer to adapt the shooting script of a film starring Colbert into a ten-part serial for magazines or newspapers. By now an accomplished serialist, Adams accepted the new challenge for $2,250. The film, *Maid of Salem*, was a costumed drama of the witch trials in Massachusetts. The deadline was tight because Paramount wanted the job done in less than one month. It sent the script on 29 September with an 15 October deadline for the first part. By 7 October Brandt said the first two parts "are darned swell" and that "you excell at hellish jobs." One week later he said the next two installments were "elegant."

Adams sent the last installment on 21 October, and on 5 November Young reported Robert Gillam wanted only minor changes, but one week later Gillam threw a brick. Young said Paramount, concerned about putting Colbert in a puritan costume, wanted the serial to indicate that the historical film was modern entertainment with fewer "prithees" and by "speeding it up." Adams agreed to remove the archaisms but was at a loss on how to speed up the story. After a meeting in New York in December, he finished his revisions. Young reported in the middle of February he had not seen it published.

As Adams had been beginning the "Maid of Salem" serial, Brandt reported the Canadian *Maclean's Magazine* would pay one thousand dollars for a five-part "Maiden Effort" serial. Adams jumped at the offer, even allowing cuts. The novel had already been bought by Smith for five hundred dollars. Such luck did not come to "Whispers." More than one month after he sent Brandt the final copy for Oursler, Adams asked his agent for the bad news. Brandt confirmed his suspicions but said it was a good serial. After *Cosmopolitan* rejected it, he tried *Delineator*, whose acerbic editor Oscar Graeve said: "I read and read and read without attaining even a prickle of a sensation. Besides this isn't a short serial. It's full length and I wouldn't care to cut it because then I'd have to read it."[23] Young did no better on the film rights. He was contacted by MGM, but Adams said Lengel at Columbia deserved first crack. Both studios turned it down.

Despite his sales difficulties and early financial doldrums Adams ended 1936 by grossing about thirteen thousand dollars, an amount that allowed the Adamses to go south for the winter. They sought some place new and chose a month in Sanibel, Florida, after a weekend at Beaufort, South Carolina. Years later, he described his introduction to the Southern town of about three thousand inhabitants: "The spell was cast as we turned off the main route, pursuing the vague report of an old and quiet city out among the sea islands. . . . The approach to Beaufort threads through broad marshlands and across shining rivers. There are far vistas of wooded islets, unpeopled and unapproachable across the high-waving reeds of the morasses. The effect is strangely other-worldly."[24]

At Beaufort with its mighty oaks and chinaberry trees laden with gray Spanish moss, they took a one-floor, five-room house in Colony Gardens, owned by

Katherine Gleason. Her sister, librarian Eleanor Gleason of Rochester, became a close friend. In March 1937 he wrote Brandt that Jane loved Colony Gardens. With that they became permanent winter residents.[25]

While he found his winter niche, his insecurity about his writing resurfaced. He finished polishing the *Maiden Effort* book. To Brandt he confided his concern that he was written out and compared himself with Sam Merwin, whose death the previous October had stunned him. Brandt said Merwin "was a sick man for years and he had no energy or real wish to achieve." He likened Adams to Tarkington, saying, "Your work is growing in depth and understanding." After urging him to keep writing to break the jinx, he said, "Let me hear no more of this nonsense, old behemoth!"[26]

Then the agent struck a deal with Ben Hibbs of *Country Gentleman* for a story by Adams, saying that the order for a serial proved "how little stock I took in the idea that you were not knocking 'em down in the middle of the alley." After discussions on a mobile trailer serial, they agreed on a romance involving the winning of a lottery in the first installment, a trip to Bermuda in the second, and an ending in New York in the third. Adams made plans to go to the island while writing the first installment.[27]

Along with writing the installment of twelve thousand words, a length that was new to him, he continued a barrage of short stories that bounced between him and Brandt & Brandt. None sold. After sending a revision of a story, Adams said if it did not sell, he was done with short stories for a while. Then Brandt sold a banking article to *American Cavalcade* for five hundred dollars and within days placed a romance for another five hundred dollars with *Liberty*. Adams predicted with the sale of another story and the *Country Gentleman* serial his confidence would return.

Hibbs's initial reaction to the first installment of the "Both Over Twenty-One" serial was positive, and in April 1937 Adams went by ship to Bermuda for four days to gather atmosphere for the second installment. News of his Bermuda trip brought requests from RKO Pictures and Columbia and Liveright to see the serial, but all were put off while he pushed to complete the rough draft in May. He was buoyed by the back-to-back sale of two more short stories to *This Week* and *Pictorial Review*. On 31 May he sent the completed manuscript of "Both Over Twenty-One," thanking Brandt and Young for their suggestions, most of which he had used.

After his visit to Bermuda, Liveright published *Maiden Effort.* The comic novel featured a young woman discovered by the president of Purity Pictures. The preliminary shooting of "Virgin Effort" was at a lake cottage, similar to

Wide Waters, near Moldavia in the Finger Lakes. The filming brought together the Hollywood types of Gloria Glamour and Moby Dickstein in adventures and misadventures. Readers were unexcited, buying 2,557 copies,
short of the five hundred dollars advance.

The Adamses returned to Wide Waters in mid-May where he learned *Country Gentleman* had rejected "Both Over Twenty-One." A bewildered Brandt
thought it was because the editors already had read the first part of the story
so they found it dull. Adams admitted it was a blow because he needed the
money but conceded it was part of the game. He blamed his cuts in revising
the serial and began adapting the long installments for another magazine's
shorter requirements.

As "Both Over Twenty-One" began its path following the ill-fated serial
"Whispers," an infected eye did not stop him from doing an article based on
a lithopedion, a fetus that has calcified in the body of the mother. He had first
mentioned the stone baby of the Cherry Valley region of New York State to
Carmer and then to *American Cavalcade* editor Tom Costain, who told Brandt
he was cool to the idea. Adams still did the piece, but it joined another unsold
article that he had written while in Florida on a man who caught snakes for
a living.

His trailer story was still active when Brandt was contacted by *Liberty*'s
Oursler, who tentatively agreed to publish "Both Over Twenty-One" but also
had a special job for Adams. Using an idea from Frederick Collins, Oursler
outlined a ten-installment story to be written and signed by Adams for ten
thousand dollars, of which Adams would get seventy-five hundred and Collins,
twenty-five hundred.

Adams began writing "The World Goes to Smash," a title that suggested the
growing tension in Europe. For the muckraker who had little to say publicly
on foreign and domestic events after the reelection of Roosevelt in 1936, however, the story was of organized crime taking over government and creating a
horrific second Civil War in 1940 with overtones about the dangers of dicta-
torship. While he was at Scituate, he visited Oursler in Boston, having luncheon with Tom Dewey, whose crime-busting activities in New York resembled
Adams's serial hero, and using Oursler's library to bone up on Floyd Gibbons's
*Napoleon.*

After he finished "The World Goes to Smash," Adams returned to "Both
Over Twenty-One," completing the revision for Oursler in mid-November.
Early in December Graeve, who had joined *Liberty* as fiction editor, rejected
the revised serial. Brandt was furious. Baumgarten had better luck with the

book rights to "The World Goes to Smash." Although she thought after reading the first three installments that it might be too hectic for Houghton Mifflin, in November she sent it to Greenslet, who made an offer in early December that was quickly accepted.

The magazine market remained tough, but Brandt sold one short-short story to *Liberty*. When the dialogue story that featured banter of a man and woman looking at a mink coat in a store window appeared, Richard Waldo said the revelation that they were husband and wife caused "a whale of response from the Waldo family." He asked if Adams had any stories for the McClure Newspaper Syndicate. A search of the Brandt & Brandt B-file found nine inactive stories, bringing his unsold stories, active and inactive, to about fifteen as of August 1937, close to the number he sold during the decade.[28]

While Adams was riding a roller-coaster with his writing, Jane came out of retirement to direct a community theater revival. Then they went to New York, missing the showing of *Perfect Specimen*. The male version of *It Happened One Night* drew raves from *Variety*, which praised stars Errol Flynn and Joan Blondell, supporting actors Edward Everett Horton and May Robson, and director Michael Curtiz.[29]

In Beaufort he finished *The World Goes Smash* in January 1938. For recreation they played golf and enjoyed the companionship of George Weaver, who had become a winter resident. One of the benefits of the early years in Beaufort was the employment by the Adamses of a black couple, Preston and Mae Huff. He was a chauffeur and handyman while she cooked meals their guests praised. When the Adamses went north, they were joined by the Huffs. "While most people in the South treated blacks like palms in the corner," George Metcalf, later author of *Black Profiles*, recalled, "Preston and Mae became members of the family. There was great affection between them."[30]

With additions came losses. Young went to California in February and got a seventy-five-hundred-dollar offer for *Both Over Twenty-One* from Warners, which Adams, suspicious of Hollywood, rejected because he wanted ten thousand dollars. It was the last offer. A further blow came when Young accepted a position in Hollywood. The job change by Young, with whom Adams had developed a close relationship, including loaning the younger man the cherished cape he wore to New York theater openings, put him in gloom. Brandt, whom Irwin called "a professional optimist," reassured Adams everything would be all right.[31]

Everything, however, was not all right. After Adams came to New York in March, Brandt sent an impassioned letter to Oursler with a plea asking him to reconsider "Both Over Twenty-One" because it was "a sort of turning point" for Adams, saying "at this particular point in his life, failure to put this over with you would do him irreparable harm." Oursler replied he could see no way to reverse the decision.[32]

The publication of *The World Goes Smash* in May brought negative reviews. Readers, bombarded by war news, chose not to escape to more horror, buying 2,061 regular editions, 2,500 cheap copies, and 125 in Canada. It had to sell 2,687 regular copies before advertising costs and fell $1,492 short of the $1,000 advance.[33]

In bad shape financially the Adamses reached Wide Waters in late May, and there he found a letter waiting from Greenslet, rejecting *Whispers*. A telephone call to Irwin revealed that his friend was so broke he could not visit as planned in June. Then Irwin sold a story for one hundred dollars, and he and Inez Irwin hopped a train to Wide Waters for the Fourth of July party. At the lake Irwin joined Adams in a tensome that played Emerson's golf course, up the hill from his Boscobel summer home.

One of the caddies for the five-hole course was Legare Hole, whose family lived on the Emerson summer property from 1934 to 1940. He and his brother, Robert, would often carry four bags apiece around the hillside course for the aging duffers. "Mr. Adams was a natural athlete," Hole recalled, "and darned good for his physical condition." He explained Adams could not bend over and "I'm not sure how good his eyes were when the ball was 120 yards out. However, he was good at putting and his shots were straight." The atmosphere was relaxed. "Nobody, including Mr. Adams, took the game too seriously and because the pace was slow, they talked a lot. Mr. Adams had a great sense of humor."[34]

Hole remembered occasionally going to Wide Waters where he found Jane Adams "always great around kids, very warm, gracious, and interested in us." He said she was "delightfully outspoken and enjoyed kidding around. She and Sam had a great camaraderie." That comradeship extended to the guests at Wide Waters. In late July friends from Philadelphia dropped in, and on the porch of the little cottage Adams told Frank and Kit Frazier that he had an idea for a new book. With two current manuscripts unsold, *Whispers* being read by Smith, now at McBride, and *Both Over Twenty-One* being mulled by Arthur Pell at Liveright, he was thinking of a return look at Harding. The casual conversation did not go unheeded.

After returning from the Adamses, Frazier tried the idea on his colleagues at the J. B. Lippincott Company, and they were excited and asked him to find out how large an advance would be required for a book for autumn 1939. Estimating three months for research and a trip to Washington and three months for writing, he set the advance at three thousand dollars.

Since he had written *Revelry*, a number of books had been published on Harding, including a generally discredited diary by Gaston Means, a book attacking Harding's morals by Nan Britton, and the self-serving autobiography by Daugherty. As rights with Lippincott dragged on, Adams was concerned about having time for the book. At the same time he was jarred by Smith, who rejected *Whispers* and suggested it be submitted to Pell at Liveright. Pell was already asking Adams to lengthen *Both Over Twenty-One*, something he would not do.

While his books were stalled, he saw Betty Richardson off to nearby Wells College and continued to churn out short stories, but Brandt's lack of success at selling them led Adams to try the *New Yorker*, which bought his stone baby article. He also found a Syracuse University doctoral student, Harold F. Alderfer, had done a dissertation on Harding. The discovery made him revise his proposal to Lippincott, saying that he would have to pay Alderfer one thousand dollars for his help. Estimating that his research time had been halved but having already spent considerable time on the book, he suggested that he would need a return of five thousand dollars.[35]

The five thousand dollars cooled Lippincott, and Baumgarten contacted Greenslet. Enthused after receiving a prospectus from Adams, he called a meeting of his executive committee at which he noted the advance would require the sale of eleven thousand copies but likened its potential success to Ike Hoover's *42 Years in the White House*, which sold thirty-five thousand in three months. One thing concerned Greenslet, who wrote Adams: "I think it is important to avoid the typical muckraking tone and method of T. R.'s time. As I see it, you are writing history, documented, well-considered, wise history." Although Adams agreed, his muckraking spirit produced a caveat that some prominent figures "I shall handle without gloves. In this way, I believe, we can get all the effectiveness of muckraking, where the rake is called for, without using the method."[36]

Confronted by animosity from sources such as Will Hays, by the burning of some of Harding's papers by his wife, and by the sealing of others by the Harding Memorial Association that would not give the papers to the Ohio Historical Society until 1964, he resorted to a ten-day Ohio trip to Columbus, Marion, and Cleveland. He told Brandt that it was fun to be on the trail again. He amassed material from his trip, from letters he wrote to friends ranging from William Allen White to Norman Thomas, from meeting with sources such as journalist Oswald Garrison Villard, and from Brandt, Baumgarten, and Greenslet contacting other people for information.[37]

At Beaufort Adams began his writing about Harding, setting a deadline of late March for the rough draft. He was doing twelve hundred words a day with a work schedule of getting up at 6:00, working until 12:30, later typing what he had written, and often checking references in the evening. By 13 February he had finished the first half, and Baumgarten reported: "The HARDING is going to be grand. The convention chapter had me fascinated."[38]

While Adams worked on Harding, Pell published *Both Over Twenty-One* and the first surge of fourteen hundred sales caused him to order a second printing. The romance of an heiress posing as a secretary and a young millionaire pretending to be a milkman on a prize trip to Bermuda eventually sold more than thirty-four hundred regular edition and five thousand cheap copies for a total gross of $401, including the $300 advance. In addition the book was serialized in the *Toronto Star Weekly* for $741.

The writing of the Harding book took longer than he predicted, and he missed his end-of-March goal by about two months. Despite the five one-thousand-dollar monthly payments of the advance, money was tight with little other writing revenue coming in. Even the sale of a golf story to the *Maclean's Magazine* did not cheer him. A hope was the serialization of the Harding book, but instead he spun off two parts, a piece on Means and an article on a suppressed book by William Estabrook Chancellor about the reported black blood in Harding's genealogy. When an editor rejected the Chancellor story as too dangerous, Adams exploded. In a letter to Brandt he accused his agent of not working hard enough to sell his stories. He threatened to use another agent and withdrew the Chancellor article.[39]

Brandt, who earlier had warned of changes in the magazine market, including the folding of *Pictorial Review*, reassured him: "Sure you have a license to growl, but you don't bite me. After all, I'm right in there growling with you. What editors do to you that's lousy, they do to me also." He listed nine stories and the thirteen to nineteen magazines they had been sent to. Brandt, who for the most part had insulated Adams's ego from the stream of rejections, admitted: "When I first read your letter I was mad as hops." He explained he let the matter simmer for a few days, "and I'm not unhappy any more. I can see how nervous and tired you are after this long job and I'm content to have you take it out on me. Gosh, what else am I here for?" Reassured by Brandt of "my affection for you, my gratitude, and my pride in you and your work," Adams said he would not consider any other agents.[40] Although Brandt sold a college romance to *Canadian Home Journal*, Adams did use an alien agent—himself. He independently sold the Chancellor article to the *New Yorker*.

He finished the first draft of the Harding book in May 1939 and headed north with a stop in Washington, telling Baumgarten that he wished she could keep Greenslet at bay until he finished revisions by 1 July. She and Greenslet, who said the final chapters were better than expected, searched for a title, agreeing on *The Incredible Era* with the subtitle *The Life and Times of Warren Gamaliel Harding*. Adams in Cayuga County began the revision, pledging massive cuts.

With a goal of revising two chapters every three days, he set to work. When Baumgarten read the early revisions, she was shocked, saying the chapters read "like a report rather than the swell story it really is." He said that he would be more careful about compression in the future. The pace of his work during the late spring and summer was hectic as Greenslet hoped to publish the book between 20 September and 10 October to have it established by the holidays. In early August, one month after his original deadline, he was still at work, finding footnotes and the index, with which he was unfamiliar, slow. He also continued rewriting and rearranging because he said it was important that the book be as good as he could make it. Working seven to twelve hours a day, he was still battling the index in September.[41]

His concern about accuracy led him to visit Aldeifei in July and to send chapters to Irwin and Senator William E. Borah for review. One person he did not contact was former Attorney General Daugherty, who chastised Adams in a lengthy correspondence with Ray Baker Harris, also planning a Harding book. Daugherty, convinced that Adams was trying to rehabilitate his reputation from *Revelry*, finally wrote Houghton Mifflin, warning that the book would damage its reputation, but Greenslet stood by the book.[42]

With *The Incredible Era* finished the Adamses went to New York where he signed a contract with Pell for the publication of *Whispers* by Liveright. Inez Irwin had dinner with Jane Adams, of whom she was becoming more critical, saying her friend "as usual contributes a vacuum." While the women dined, Adams and Irwin went to the Players, where Irwin noted in his diary: "Sam very violent and positive over war—Chamberlain and Hitler are equally naughty and Germany's going to win." In March Adams had told Baumgarten the radio news looked like war. She said that Brandt thought Adams was all wrong on the war but noted it might be wishful on the agent's part.[43]

Still wary, Adams told a Rochester newspaper in November that although he was a supporter of Roosevelt, he hoped the president would not seek reelection in 1940. He did say he would vote for him if he ran. He warned about the freedom of spirit being repressed "if the war gets any nearer" and had doubts about neutrality keeping the "war spirit out of America." Several weeks later, he decried what he saw as the subtle dangers of English propaganda: "If we go to war again, we should go with clear conviction and a clear conscience."[44]

In Rochester he met *Democrat & Chronicle* columnist Henry Clune. Baumgarten had arranged the visit with Clune, an author also represented by Brandt & Brandt. A rapport developed between the two men, with Clune writing the first of numerous columns on the author and Adams championing the young man who, he told Baumgarten, was scared to death she would drop him. Nervous about what Adams had told Clune, she was relieved by a Clune letter she quoted: "I have always been afraid of big shot writers because I have heard so much about their temperamental break-outs, etc. But he is one of the nicest and most kindly men I have ever met."[45]

In that first column Clune predicted Adams's new book seemed destined to be a bestseller. He was wrong. *The Incredible Era* fell far short of Greenslet's early estimates. Published 9 June, the book started out with advance sales of twenty-five hundred, which Greenslet had hoped would reach five or six thousand. Although it received mostly positive reviews, it eventually sold about seven thousand copies, falling more than twenty-seven-hundred dollars short of the five-thousand-dollar advance.[46]

The advance provided almost all of his recorded income for 1939, about $5,500, a little more than double what he had earned in 1938. Both were well under his writing income of $21,500 in 1937. An apparent casualty of the downturn in income was the Wide Waters farm. After the Kowals had left for Auburn, Jane enlisted the Champanys. They closed their home on Whiskey Lane and moved to the farmhouse. After two or three years, Beatrice Champany recalled, they returned home. She was uncertain of the reason, but it was probably a decision to sell the livestock and lease the land to tenants.[47]

The 1930s were troublesome for Adams. The effects of the depression on his traditional markets caused consternation. As his Fabian novels lost popularity, his Webster and Harding biographies failed to sell well. He relied on light fiction, riding *It Happened One Night* until it, too, played out. Despite his success with *The Gorgeous Hussy* the disappointment over *The Incredible Era* turned him back to a familiar form. With an eye on a serial he started a mystery called *Tambay Gold,* using South Carolina as the locale. He wrote

Brandt that Baumgarten, whom he addressed in letters as "B.B.," would be unhappy that he was doing fiction, but he wanted to see if his imagination was still working.[48]

Brandt shared his letter with Baumgarten, who wrote she was "pretty indignant," adding "a first rate novelist ought to be writing first rate novels instead of putting his time in on so-called light fiction." He conceded she might be right because he had no great opinion of what he had been writing and admitted it was pot boiling.[49]

As he sought to have the rough draft of *Tambay Gold* done before heading south, he mixed play with his work. He went to Hamilton College where he told an English composition class, "Forget about spelling and punctuation; proofreaders can do that," but when the students applauded wildly, Adams, whose own spelling and punctuation seldom erred, added, "Perhaps, I've overstated the case."[50] He met his deadline on the draft of the South Carolina book and wrote Baumgarten from Beaufort two days after Christmas to ask her to ship him a manuscript that Greenslet had been after him for more than one year to tackle. It was the first novel by a physician, Frank Slaughter.

# 15

# GHOSTWRITER
## 1940–1942

FRANK G. SLAUGHTER, a young doctor in Jacksonville, Florida, had a practice in medicine but a passion for writing. Although he had written upwards of one hundred thousand words per year, beginning in 1938, he had sold only one short story by 1940. He and four other physicians owned Riverside Hospital, "one of the few group clinics in the country and group practice was looked down upon generally by individual practitioners," he said. The enmity led the surgeon to study medical economics. He used his findings in a novel, "partly autobiographical and intimately concerned with medical problems in the Thirties." A local librarian who read the manuscript mentioned it to Lee Barker, a salesman-editor for Houghton Mifflin.[1]

Adams had been contacted in November 1938 by Greenslet about collaborating on the Slaughter novel. In the midst of his Harding book Adams had put off any involvement. One year later, he received a letter from Barker that Slaughter was writing a second novel, leaving the first available. With *The Incredible Era* on the stands, Adams asked to see the manuscript.

After he read Slaughter's manuscript, he was surprised Houghton Mifflin had not published it as it was. He then pointed out weaknesses in characterization and saw a need to cut the academic material and develop collateral drama and romance. He told Baumgarten that Slaughter should be easy to work with because he could write. In a letter to Slaughter, Adams was equally enthusiastic, his only concern being that the doctor was too close to the clinical side of medicine to see it from the reader's view.[2]

Adopting a technique he had learned at McClure, Phillips, and Company, he got opinions on the readability of the medicalese from Houghton Mifflin readers, from Brandt and Baumgarten, and eventually from a nurse and Jane

Adams. Reports on his own work, *Tambay Gold*, were not good. Brandt was blunt: "It sprawls, Sam. It sprawls like hell!" Baumgarten noted eight plot lines to Brandt with the admonition: "And if you show this to Sam, I know perfectly well that he will never speak to me again." Instead Brandt used them in an overall critique to Adams, who promised to rewrite the book.[3]

After celebrating his sixty-ninth birthday at a plantation party, Adams received Houghton Mifflin's offer of fifteen hundred dollars, with him getting 60 percent and Slaughter 40. Because Adams was strapped for cash, however, Baumgarten suggested he get the full advance of fifteen hundred dollars with Slaughter getting his share from the royalties. Adams agreed as long as Slaughter would not think of him as a money-grabber.

Still waiting for a Houghton Mifflin decision on the new terms, he was pleased by a comeback of *The Incredible Era* in the New York *Herald Tribune*'s "What America Is Reading." With the minimum of three mentions needed, the book made the list twice. Reacting like a person in a desert seeing a mirage, he asked Greenslet for renewed advertising. Saying the company had spent seven thousand dollars, about a dollar a book and should have sold twenty-one thousand copies for the money, Greenslet refused to invest more. He blamed a shift in reading after the outbreak of the European war but added: "Are we downhearted? No!" He cautioned, however, the doctor book market might be oversold.[4]

Ignoring Greenslet's caution, Adams quoted to Baumgarten the comment on not being downhearted. His own assessment of the failure of *The Incredible Era* to sell had been different. In an earlier letter to librarian Lewis Stieg at Hamilton College he observed that he may have been too gentle. He told Baumgarten that the issue of political control of medicine in the Slaughter book had to be preserved.

The next day Baumgarten lowered the boom. Houghton Mifflin had bowed out of publishing the Slaughter novel. Although Slaughter said it was because Adams had not met *The Incredible Era* advance, Baumgarten said the company feared what Adams proposed to do would be too complicated and expensive. She remained positive, saying that Costain — at Doubleday, Doran after his *American Cavalcade* folded — would be a possibility. Adams replied that he was not perturbed but amazed at what he considered almost bad faith by Houghton Mifflin and told her to contact Costain. A condition was one he had told Barker, that his name not appear on the book because he felt it would weaken the medical credibility. With that, he turned to revising *Tambay Gold*.

Meanwhile, his business romance, *Whispers,* was published by Pell at Liveright. The story of Parke Gerritt's return to Barriston and his involvement in the small city's financial affairs was called "a good yarn" by the *Herald Tribune,* but sales mirrored Greenslet's comment about the changing nature of readership, eventually selling 2,223 copies, almost 1,400 fewer than *Both Over Twenty-One* the previous year.[5]

While Baumgarten and Cozzens were on a Southern vacation and at the Adamses in early March, Brandt wired her that Costain wanted the Slaughter book. Although the issue of state medicine was agreed on, Costain asked for Adams's name on the book and a deadline of three months. Adams balked at both, and Costain relented.

The Beaufort that Baumgarten and Cozzens found had changed from the sleepy town the Adamses had discovered. Because of its proximity to the Marine Corps base at Parris Island, the community was full of officers and their wives. At Colony Gardens they befriended a young writer, Tom Belden, whom Adams encouraged with his work and as a bridge partner. Belden recalled the Adamses shared an impishness. Once a real estate man who liked to get celebrities together arranged a visit by Countess Mary Annette Russell, an English novelist who wrote as "Elizabeth" and had moved to Charleston. "She arrived with two great wolfhounds and apologized that the bitch was still up in Charleston. Sam and Jane rode that one. They loved to set up a situation and have fun with it." One situation they did not set up.[6]

On Sunday morning, 10 March, Adams was at his desk when he smelled smoke. He went to investigate and found the flames were up the flue in the big room and through the loft. Fortunately, it was on the weekend when Colony Gardens was full of marine officers visiting their wives, and a dozen of them plus an army colonel and Belden responded to the calls for help. Belden remembered, "We got everything out including the refrigerator." Belden said he even rescued the telephone. Later actress Peggy Wood, in a short promotional sketch on Adams, wrote that the dramatic Jane Adams called her friend Martha Elliott from a tree:

> "From a *what?*" gasped the friend.
> "A tree," replied Mrs. Adams. "Our house burned to the ground this morning, and the only thing we could drag out in time was the telephone. My kind neighbor has hauled it to safety and hung it and the wires on a tree."
> "Neighbor?" asked the friend. "Where was Sam?"
> "Oh, he's gone next door to write. He hadn't finished his stint when the fire broke out."[7]

The fire had repercussions. Adams, who escaped in his night apparel, caught a cold, and the Adamses were separated. She lived with Eleanor Gleason, and he slept in a storeroom and worked in Belden's apartment. Nonetheless, he was amused by a local account that identified him as author of *Incredible Eros*. The fire and its aftermath did not daunt their spirits; the next Saturday they gave a cocktail party for their helpers.[8]

Easter found Adams done with the revised version of *Tambay Gold* and finishing a story on a brimstone sign painter for the *New Yorker* while Jane Adams went to church. Waiting for Costain's editorial board to okay a contract for the Slaughter novel, he told Baumgarten he really had to do the book, even if he had to borrow the money. That was unnecessary because Doubleday, Doran issued a contract on the same terms as Houghton Mifflin.

Still money was tight. In early March he wrote Brandt that he was too broke to come up to New York for the annual Dutch Treat show unless the agent could sell a short story. On Monday, 1 April, Brandt sold a short story about a gossip columnist whose good deed saved a young woman from scandal to *Liberty* for four hundred dollars and urged him to come to Dutch Treat on Friday. But it was too late for Adams, who had put aside *Tambay Gold*, which both Brandt and Baumgarten said needed still more work, and had scheduled a meeting with Slaughter in Florida.

He went to Hibernia in early April. Slaughter recalled driving down from Jacksonville to a riverfront estate where "we would hash out medical scenes, which I would then write at night." They worked three to four hours a day for one week, and Slaughter wrote Baumgarten that Adams would do an excellent job. He said he wanted to give Adams credit but he preferred anonymity. Adams did the first of the three parts of *That None Should Die* before leaving Beaufort in May. Slaughter made a few technical changes and said it was "unusually complete and very interesting." Costain was also enthused, saying: "Sam has made an entirely different story. I think he is doing a swell job."[9] At Wide Waters, Adams sent a draft of the second part to Costain.

The summer brought a more hectic social pace, including the Fourth of July party and acting as "adoptive parents" for Betty and Buddy Richardson. She had left Wells College after her first year and, at the urgings of the Adamses, had gone to learn secretarial skills at Finch College. Estranged from her own father, she sought Adams's advice. "He treated us as intelligent people and was stimulated by the young," she recalled. "Jane Adams was very warm and loving, highly humorous, but would not put up with any nonsense."

In a sense, the Richardsons "adopted" the Adamses as much as the Adamses "adopted" them.[10]

Never one to abandon his literary children, Adams wrote Greenslet when *The Incredible Era* was not listed on a promotional piece. Greenslet responded that the book was played out, but Houghton Mifflin was considering a cheap edition the next year. Adams welcomed the possibility, seeing a chance to update the book. The Eagle Edition was not published, however, perhaps because of Adams's incorrect assessment that Americans should and could avoid involvement in the war.[11]

A more immediate concern for Adams was *That None Should Die*. After a parley with Costain and Slaughter at Wide Waters in July, Adams revised the novel in early August, employing Betty Richardson for the typing. But the novel estimated at 200,000 words had to be cut to 160,000. That job fell to Costain, and when Costain urged him to speed up the first chapter and work on the government control part, Adams put his pen down, saying his work was done and Costain should handle changes in his future editing. Adams turned his attention to two other Slaughter manuscripts, *Stepping Stones*, which he felt held promise, and a historical manuscript on Ignaz Phillip Semmelweis that did not. Then the Adamses headed for Alexander Woollcott's.

At Neshobe Island Woollcott was waging war with Arthur Hays Sulzberger, whose *New York Times* supported Wendell Willkie over Roosevelt. Sulzberger had asked at one point: "Where is the excellent, objective drama critic I used to know?" Woollcott shot back, "To answer you explicitly he is on an island in a lake in Vermont and his guests at the moment—Samuel Hopkins Adams, Ethel Barrymore, and Thornton Wilder—all happen to be vehemently pro-Roosevelt and it would be impossible for him to get up an argument around here."[12]

Certainly not from Adams. Surrounded in Cayuga County by Republican friends except for the Osbornes, he was interested in the 1940 presidential race. Despite his initial concerns about a Roosevelt third term he remained a committed New Dealer. "When his Auburn friends came to Wide Waters, he would put the picture of Roosevelt under the couch," Betty Richardson Steele recalled.[13] But they certainly knew where he stood and he had bets of seventy-five dollars and eight lobsters on the election.

While at Woollcott's the Adamses met authors Paul and Lilly Bonner, whom they invited to Wide Waters in October. Before they arrived, Adams read a piece by Bonner and offered criticism as he continued to help his fellow authors. He worked with columnist Clune whose satire *Monkey on a Stick* he praised but whose latest novel he felt needed work. He also offered Baumgarten a tactful analysis of Cozzens's *Ask Me Tomorrow*, including a page of corrections, helped historian Allan Nevins with some Rockefeller family background, and corresponded with Henry L. Mencken concerning alcohol experiments with chickens by Raymond Pearl of Johns Hopkins. He declined, however, to give Brandt a comment on Stewart Edward White's psychical *Unobstructed Universe*, saying it was too heavy for him.[14]

During the Bonners' visit Jane Adams battled a case of gallstones. Her doctor was Albert A. Getman of Syracuse, an old friend and a graduate of Hamilton College, who was also Woollcott's physician. He urged her to slow down and to go on a rigorous diet. Her activities were limited to trying to promote the work of a pair of young married artists, Letterio Calapai and his wife, whom she was housing in the farm, a move Adams favored because it kept her from worrying about herself.

He was having his own troubles. A reoccurrence of gout attacked his right ring finger, curtailing his working. A first operation did not alleviate the "most hellish pain" but did not keep him from voting for Roosevelt. The gout, however, forbade him the lobsters he had won and continued to plague him, forcing him into the hospital to have the finger drained. He was amused when the Associated Press asked for hourly reports on his condition but not when the wire service noted that it had no data on Adams since his retirement. He left the hospital for Thanksgiving but afterward returned to have the finger amputated at the first joint.

While Adams was incapacitated from his operation, the proofs of *That None Should Die* arrived. Unable to write with his right hand and groggy from drugs, he asked Katherine Morse Messenger, who was working for the Auburn newspaper, to help. "He and my mother were soul mates," her son Ray Messenger recalled, noting that she was ever ready to assist Adams. She battled through the snowdrifts of an early winter to find him distraught over new cuts Costain had made in the first chapter.[15]

Wiring Baumgarten that Costain had removed essential details, he demanded that the material be restored and threatened to hold up the proofs until assured it was done. At the same time he wrote Slaughter to get his support, but the young surgeon, eager to publish his first novel, passed the controversy to Baumgarten. Adams took matters in his own hands, or those of Kay Messenger, restoring some material after receiving a letter from Costain urging him to consider carefully before adding anything that would slow the first chapter. Costain also said he wanted to see him on his visit to New York to discuss another book.[16]

The trip to New York that had originally been planned as a week of theater and music was reduced to a short trip from the Atherton Harlans, who had moved to New Hope, Pennsylvania. The operation and recuperation had sapped Adams's vitality because, as he had told Brandt at the beginning of the year, his previous amputation had caused five times the suffering of his hip operation. In New York they had a quiet dinner with the Irwins on 17 December. Inez Irwin noted his arm was in a sling and that he was now minus parts of fingers on both hands, and Irwin wrote in his diary: "He's pretty shaken with it all."[17]

The finger's refusal to heal during the first two months of 1941 caused him to limit his writing to the revision of *Tambay Gold*. To add to his woes he was becoming increasingly concerned about the United States being drawn into the European war. He was sure if the British fell, every Latin-American nation would run to the conquering Nazis.

Costain visited Beaufort in February, and Adams gave him the latest version of *Tambay Gold* to deliver to Baumgarten. He may also have given Costain another manuscript at this time. Adams then turned to an article on Beaufort and a short story about a young man who conned a physician into hospitalizing him on a bet he could get a room on a football weekend, which was sold to *Liberty* later in the spring. Before that Adams had sold "A Sack of Snakes," the article he had written in early 1937 about a young man who collected rattlesnakes, to the *New Yorker* in a deepening relationship with the magazine and its editor, Harold Ross. Ross, whom Cerf called the greatest magazine editor but "very naive and very prudish," was a stickler for accuracy, and Adams grumbled about authenticating facts but had respect for the commitment to accuracy.[18]

His continued low rate of placement in the magazine market was a concern for Brandt. Despite the sale of the short story to *Liberty* the agent concentrated on the *Reader's Digest*, where DeWitt Wallace was having success not only in reprinting articles that had already appeared but in buying original work that he would then place in other magazines before reprinting them. After a number of frustrations Brandt wrote to the *Digest's* Burt McBride, who had seen the *New Yorker* article on the snakes and requested an Adams story, asking him to write the author with details on what he wanted. "Quite off the record Sam has been pretty ill off and on this winter and he also is getting a little oldish. The stuff hasn't got the same flexibility that it used to have and I don't want to have you encourage him to do something which will get kicked in the puss," Brandt wrote soon after Adams's seventieth birthday.[19]

His Beaufort article, "College Without Walls," about a philanthropic group, however, was rejected by the *Reader's Digest* despite Adams removing a portion concerning restrictions on blacks using a public park. He cut the part at Brandt's insistence, one of the few concessions Adams made of this nature. He was a realist, knowing and accepting that in the 1940s some topics, such as the pregnancy in *Whispers*, cost him sales. Quickly assimilated in the plantation society, Adams insisted, according to Serrell Hillman, that his liberal visitors from the North avoid racial discussions with his prosegregationist Southern friends as a social compromise. Nonetheless, the Gullah culture of the blacks in Beaufort fascinated him, and he wrote about it often. His relationship with his black servants, the Preston Huffs, was described by his friends as one of mu-

10. Sam and Jane Adams having breakfast in bed, served by Preston Huff, at Wide Waters in the 1940s. Samuel Hopkins Adams Collection. Courtesy of Syracuse University Library.

tual need. "Both men were very self-confident and secure in the relationship. If you knew Sam, you knew Preston," Ray Messenger, who did odd jobs at Wide Waters, recalled. "Sam would delegate certain things that Preston would take care of. Preston made sure things went the way Sam wanted them."[20]

The rejection by the *Reader's Digest* of "College Without Walls" led Brandt to try the *Saturday Evening Post,* often the first market contacted although it had not run any Adams work since 1923. In what must have been a surprise to everyone, Stuart Rose bought the expunged article to run "as a filler somewhere in the back of the book" for two hundred dollars.[21]

11. Samuel Hopkins Adams with three Hamilton College football players, Pete Hatch, Army Hoch, and Sonny Dale, in September 1940, the fiftieth anniversary of the college's first team, on which Adams played. Courtesy of Hamilton College.

12. Samuel Hopkins Adams working at a typewriter at Hamilton College during his fiftieth reunion when he wrote a class remembrance in 1941. Courtesy of Hamilton College.

Before the Adamses left Beaufort, he went to Jacksonville to see Slaughter about *Stepping Stones* and returned to the golf course where his initial attempt caused his finger stump to look like a ripe plum. His optimism about his and Jane's improving health was offset by an increasing and deepening worry over Woollcott, who had returned to the stage in *The Man Who Came to Dinner* despite Getman's earlier warnings about his heart. Adams's attempts to see his friend at the Hamilton College commencement were unsuccessful.

Hamilton College was high on his list as the Adamses returned north in May. He had written on the fiftieth anniversary of his football team for the October 1940 *Hamilton Alumni Review* and agreed to write a history of the class of 1891 for its fiftieth reunion in June with an assist from George Weaver. The reminiscence of his college days devoted an unusual amount of space to his growing preoccupation with the use of language of bygone days. In June three businessmen, three ministers, three professors, and one author from the class of 1891, adopting the motto "Preppy in Ninety-One and Still Growing Strong," gathered at Wide Waters. Afterward a heavy-set Adams with thinning white hair marched behind the class flag and spoke at the alumni luncheon.

After his reunion he met with Costain and Slaughter on the new book at Wide Waters in late June. As Adams saw it, the problem with *Stepping Stones*,

13. Samuel Hopkins Adams marching with Percy L. Wight behind the banner carried by Albert E. Stuart (in academic garb) and Robert N. Brockway at their fiftieth reunion at Hamilton College. Courtesy of Hamilton College.

a study of medical deterioration in which a young doctor attains success at too great a price, was that Slaughter saw himself as the doctor and he did not want to destroy him. They were spurred on by the success of *That None Should Die*, which had been selected by the Book League for twenty-five hundred dollars and had sold three thousand copies before publication in March. By June the total was estimated at from seven thousand to ten thousand copies. At the meeting, not only did Costain retreat on his request for a deletion in the first chapter after Adams said if the suicide attempt was gone, so was he, but also sought a third book, "Salvation, O! Salvation" on faith healing, with Adams's name.

After the business meeting, Laurette Taylor, who had been a success in *Outward Bound* in 1939 but had been inactive since, descended on Wide Waters. The teenage George Harlan met the once trim actress with her gigantic hat and eight trunks at the train station. "The huge woman enfolded me in feathers and fat," he remembered. Although she was having a problem with alcohol, she stayed on the wagon until a trip to Owasco Country Club where she visited the bar and got "drunker than a lord," Harlan reported, "and then she began to mimic the country club type. Jane Adams took it for about a half hour and then rose—She would not get up even in the presence of the queen—and announced, 'Laurette, we are going home' and Laurette wilted."[22]

Although she had come for a weekend, Taylor was still at Wide Waters six weeks later. Harlan's memory of her as a delightful person with self-deprecating Irish wit and ebullience came through in some sketches she was writing, and Adams sought to spur her to work harder. He himself was trying to meet a 1 September deadline for *Stepping Stones*. In Jacksonville Slaughter was working on other novels, a series of mystery stories, notes for the Adams healer book, and a play. Shortly thereafter the Adamses received bad news.

On a visit to her oculist on 9 September, Jane learned she had cataracts in both eyes and had to wait for them to develop before an operation. She took the news with courage, Adams wrote Woollcott the next day. His friend replied, "Tell her I ache for her and that when she needs someone to come and read aloud to her I will respond as to a three alarm fire." He also said, "the unreliability of the old Woollcott ticker" had prompted him to resign from the Hamilton College board of trustees, adding that he did not need to defend his action to a man who had "flounced off the Board in what we so underestimated you as to call your prime."[23]

Jane's eyes coupled with some back trouble for Adams produced a disastrous trip to the Irwins at Scituate in mid-September. Inez Irwin was miffed at Adams doing Double-Crostics all one evening, and Irwin grumbled about having to turn over his room to Adams so he could work on the medical novel. When the Adamses left after one week during which Inez Irwin said all was boredom, she wrote in her diary: "Freedom!"[24] It marked their last visit to Scituate. They returned to Wide Waters for the wedding of Lydia Mead, who was living in New York, to Dutch importer Henri Engelbert.

The final title of the novel was *Spencer Brade, M.D.*, and by the end of September he hoped his work was about over because he wanted to work on his own novel. Although Brandt sold the mystery short story "Office Butterfly" that he had written in May 1938 to *Esquire*, his work on short pieces was lessening to a trickle. Brandt's appeals for a short-short story during the summer went unanswered. When *Coronet* wanted a piece on patent medicines, Adams turned it down as too little money for too much work.

Although Baumgarten was racking up a string of rejections for *Tambay Gold*, which she wanted to place somewhere other than Liveright, she had better success with the Newspaper Enterprise Association, which bought a thirty-chapter serial of the novel for four hundred dollars. Further success came from the unexpected sales of reprint rights to novels. He accepted an offer from Stanley Paul in Britain for a flat fifty pounds per Fabian title. Another purchase was for a radio version of *The Gorgeous Hussy* for one thousand dollars by the *Cavalcade of America*.

World events were far from cheery. In 1940 he had prepared updated biographical material for *Twentieth Century Authors*, stating: "If I were to repeat my career, I could ask nothing better than the life of a professional writer. It permits freedom of thought, action, and mode of existence, and this in an era when individual choice, threatened as it is throughout an imperiled world, has never been so precious." The European war in late 1941 was creeping closer as Cayuga County's young men joined or were drafted into the service. His concern about the United States getting caught in the war without knowledge of its commitments led him to join America First in October 1941. His support for the noninterventionist group consisted only of lending his name to its national committee.[25]

Adams's membership in America First drew the attention of the Federal Bureau of Investigation. Although Adams was not the subject of an investigation, he was indexed with thirty cross-references in the files of other individuals, organizations, events, and activities.[26] An FBI report on the America First organization listed members of the national committee in a 19 November 1941 newsletter, including Adams and Charles A. Lindbergh. When a fellow writer later commented that the organization was "patently Fascist," Adams wrote him that while fascists were in the organization, many members saw it representing not fascism but liberalism.[27] The thought of being labeled a fascist must have appalled the liberal Adams. During the war he drew the FBI's attention by joining a number of organizations opposed to fascism.

Although he was in America First, like other Democrats he was a supporter of Roosevelt. The organization disbanded when, as a tank battalion drilled in Auburn, the Japanese attacked Pearl Harbor on 7 December 1941. The Adamses were on their way south to Beaufort, and he wrote Baumgarten that he was depressed by the news. She agreed: "It is a bitter experience to learn from, but we'll make out. I saw Will Irwin the other day and he said that we were simply having the first Bull Run over again."[28]

He reached his winter home, reluctantly facing the major jobs of writing "Salvation O! Salvation" and of working with Slaughter on the physician's next book. Then his life was thrown into a new tizzy. In late November Kenneth McKenna of MGM approached Cerf about having an author adapt the script of *The Harvey Girls*, based on the Harvey railroad restaurants, into a novel. Cerf said he had an author in mind and approached Brandt. "I had known and admired Sam since his days at Liveright and had always wanted to publish him, but I never managed this until I presented him with a wonderful idea for a historical novel about the American West," Cerf said later. Brandt shipped the script to Adams, who agreed but suggested terms that McKenna rejected. After Cerf backed Adams, the impasse was broken, and Cerf wrote McKenna, "I have a hunch that Adams is going to do a story that will be really important both for us and for you."[29]

Having written off *The Harvey Girls* as just another Hollywood disappointment, Adams was notified of the decision in late-December and immediately began to plot the book, facing a 1 June deadline. The plan was for the novel to be published 1 September, before the film was scheduled for release, and he arranged to go to California for a story conference early in 1942. As 1941 was closing, Brandt and Baumgarten gave possible directions the story could go and urged him to let the Hollywood studio take the lead. He said he would listen and then do the story his own way.

He entered the first full year of America's participation in World War II dealing with heavy airline usage, the problems of blackouts, and the possibility of volunteering as a coastal lookout. After a visit by Slaughter, he went to Los Angeles. In Hollywood his initial reaction was that the studio people could not be nicer, and he gave them an outline of the characters and the romantic development. Several days later, however, he found they were still courteous and considerate, but noncommittal. After they decided further talks were unneeded until the structure of the story was set, he left. The most useful result of the visit was a chance meeting with a studio commissary waitress who had been a Harvey girl for seventeen years.

He and Brandt's West Coast representative, Louis E. Swarts, enjoyed each other, but the lawyer wrote Brandt that he was concerned about credit being given William Rankin and Eleanore Griffin, who had written the original story. Brandt, however, said he had assurance from MGM that the studio had novelization rights. Swarts remained cautionary about possible future plagiarism charges. After dismissing the warning from Swarts, Adams went to Chicago to meet the Harvey people. He talked with Byron Harvey and representatives of the Santa Fe Railroad. Because the studio had a contract clause that gave the Harvey interests approval of the book, he had to woo the son of Fred Harvey, an okay he secured by adding an epilogue featuring him. Armed with background and atmospheric information, he faced the chore of writing a seventy-five-thousand-word book in four months.[30]

Back after six thousand miles in three weeks, Adams wrote Greenslet, nonchalantly asking him why Houghton Mifflin had declined the first Slaughter book. Greenslet cited a difference in editorial opinion and urged him to enjoy the bass fishing around Beaufort. It was the last business correspondence between the two men.[31] Another old friend, Tom Smith, also made his curtain call in an emotional letter asking Baumgarten about *Tambay Gold*. Before she answered, Smith had died, and she sent the manuscript to Julian Messner, the former Liveright sales manager, who had broken away to form his own firm. Adams, saddened by the death of Smith but glad to shift from Pell at Liveright, agreed to the Messner terms although he was amused by a request for an option on his next three light novels.

He set out on *The Harvey Girls* at breakneck speed, writing the two introductory chapters of six thousand words in two days. He conceded it was not his best but kept writing, leaving himself as much time for revision as possible. The plot followed three Harvey waitresses in the western town of Sandrock where they were contrasted with the saloon girls of the Alhambra. The atmosphere of 1890 and the social effect were the key elements with which he struggled. The novel consumed him, and he put aside Slaughter who was working on two new novels.

He had done one-quarter of *The Harvey Girls* by mid-February and hoped to be half done by 1 April. His work taxed him, but when Weaver, who had retired from his textile factory fifteen years earlier, took over a department in a Utica war plant, Adams told Woollcott he wished he could get into the war effort but said for the first time he was aware of his physical disability.[32]

He was cheered up by a visit from Costain, who reported that *Spencer Brade, M.D.* had an advance sale of almost seven thousand, but Adams was noncommittal about "Salvation O! Salvation" and the next book by Slaughter, who had applied to go into the army. Baumgarten responded to Adams's lack of enthusiasm, noting that the second doctor novel would sell about ten thousand copies, making his share, under a new fifty-fifty split, between twenty-five hundred and three thousand dollars, including the serial sale. She asked him, however, only to think about another Slaughter book.

On *The Harvey Girls* Adams finished the rough draft, except for the epilogue chapter, by the end of March, well ahead of schedule. Throughout April he revised the novel at the pace of one chapter a day, planning to bring the manuscript to Brandt and Baumgarten on 1 May. He figured that would leave one month for revisions. He also was cooling to a future writing relationship with Slaughter, who considered Adams an editor. Baumgarten, trying to keep Cerf at bay over *The Harvey Girls*, told Slaughter that Adams was too busy on his present project to do anything else.

But the hint was not enough. Two months later Slaughter wrote Adams, who had thought that Baumgarten or Costain had informed the doctor of the end of the relationship. Eager not to hurt the feelings of Slaughter, he urged that something definite and quick be done. Baumgarten wrote Slaughter, reporting to Adams that the doctor was "not even slightly hurt" and later that he had a new collaborator. Adams retained the rights to "Salvation O! Salvation" but never wrote it.[33]

While he was finishing *The Harvey Girls*, he took an assignment from the *New Yorker* for a historical sketch of Palmyra, New York. His preliminary research for "Home Town of a Prophet" on Mormonism also dealt with his beloved Erie Canal and his grandfather Myron Adams. On 29 May he sent the finished *Harvey Girls* to Baumgarten and told her he was eager to start his next novel, focusing on Palmyra. "It was fifty years since I had been there," he wrote of the town. "Something about the place went straight to my heart." He knew he could use his grandfather's canal stories, his own knowledge of canal lore, his love for earlier language, additional research, and the help of friends.[34]

While he plotted the new book, Doubleday, Doran and Company published *The Book of Ariel* by "Anonymous." Written in the first person, the book featured a long-lasting clandestine love affair between scientist Stanton Kennedy and a woman named Ariel, many years his junior, that ended when he helped her die before she was ravaged by cancer. Later it was revealed that Adams had a blind contract with Costain, who received the income and then forwarded the unknown amount to Adams. Why he masked the places and persons and chose the unorthodox method of publication is open to conjecture. Who was Ariel? Did he simply want to write a novel in the French mode? Was it to cover an illicit relationship? Did he seek to avoid possible false identifications? Was Adams, who belonged to an association to promote euthanasia, worried that the action to assist a terminally ill Ariel was too real?[35]

Adams's co-conspirator, Costain, had been eager to have an Adams book but had only used his work under the Slaughter name and the anonymous

*Book of Ariel.* The canal book offered a new opportunity, and he offered a contract with a twenty-five-hundred-dollar advance for the historical novel in
which Adams planned to show the effect of the coming of the canal on a Western New York community.

He approached *Canal Town* with the same tenacity he had shown almost
forty years earlier when researching patent medicines. He enlisted librarians
as helpers, collected one hundred pages of notes during a week's stay in
Rochester, and avoided Walter D. Edmonds's territory of a later canal era
pictured in *Erie Water.* As the information accumulated, he concentrated on
the townspeople along the waterway rather than the canal itself, using as his
culminating drama his *New Yorker* tale of the stone fetus that he had found
at Albany Medical College before it was placed at Cooperstown.

While he was writing and researching, he stayed close to home. A lack of
mobility because of gasoline and tire rationing restricted the Fourth of July
party to nearby friends. He was unable to visit Woollcott, about whose health
he was increasingly concerned. He had urged mutual friend Jo Hennessey to
keep Woollcott off the stage and away from activities that might strain his heart.
Woollcott replied he was being "docile as hell."[36] Almost one month later,
when Adams learned Woollcott had been in the hospital, he wrote again, reporting that Jane Adams's eyesight was worsening but that she was preparing
for a wedding. A somber Woollcott said "even in my most buoyant moments
I never quite admitted that this business of living was worth a candle." Adams
said his view was nearly scandalous.[37]

The wedding was an unexpected event. Betty Richardson came from New
York for a July holiday at Wide Waters and was joined by a visitor from the West
Coast. Several days later Adams announced in loco parentis her engagement
to Richard Steele of Pasadena. The engagement was short. Adams reported the
house was in pandemonium as the wedding neared, and he was thinking of
moving to the farmhouse for the duration. Nine days later the couple exchanged vows before 150 guests, mostly women. "It was a large wedding for
wartime," Betty Richardson Steele recalled. "It was beautiful, a real Jane
Adams production."[38]

After the wedding, he returned to reading *Harvey Girls* proofs and working
on *Canal Town.* Besides getting help from his librarian friends, he asked them
to read parts of the manuscript and in September went to Utica, Worcester, Albany, and New York with a side trip to see Edmonds in Boonville, New York.
"I liked him very much," Edmonds said fifty years later. He remembered that
he and his wife were amused as Adams toured their home and commented on

the furniture: "This is trash, this is okay, and this is good." Edmonds said Adams did careful research but that they did not use history as historians but rather to create readable books: "We were different kinds of writers who wrote different kinds of books." He noted Adams had come from the competitive world of reporting, whereas he had not.[39]

*The Harvey Girls* and *Tambay Gold* were published almost simultaneously in October, marking the third and fourth books in which Adams had published during 1942. Although *Tambay Gold* had a string of motion picture rejections, the novel drew surprisingly good reviews. The story featured Mom Baumer, an ex-carnival queen, whom he said in a foreword he had met on a number of occasions. In a first-person story told by her, the woman ran a trailer-diner that she parked at an impoverished plantation called Tambay Acres. There she dispensed food from her Feederia and common-sense advice for the problems of the plantation owner and others ranging from football players and Gullahs to a professor digging for Indian relics or possibly gold. The sales of *Tambay Gold* were weak, with the regular edition selling 2,523, about half of what Messner had estimated. The royalties met the $300 advance but were augmented by a 25 cent reprint of 130,000 copies that produced $650 and later another 50,000, another $250.[40]

*The Harvey Girls* did considerably better in its regular edition. Cerf reported that the demand on its initial run of four thousand copies had taken Random House by surprise. A second printing of three thousand went so rapidly that a third printing of twenty-five hundred was on the way as of 16 November. Adams was amazed because he did not think much of the hurried book.[41]

The fast start was not sustained, and Cerf reported in mid-December: "The book continues to sell well, although truth to tell, all books of fiction are overshadowed this season by war stories and humorous items." The book eventually sold 8,354 copies, and a cheaper edition published in 1944 sold 50,589 copies, producing a total royalty of more than fifty-four hundred dollars. This was along with the five thousand dollars for movie rights under the unusual MGM contract that also provided another five thousand dollars upon publication. A third five thousand dollars that was promised if the book was serialized was never paid when, because of the tight timing, Brandt was unable to find a buyer. After two years of relatively little writing income, about twenty-five hundred dollars in 1940 and twenty-three hundred dollars in 1941, his earnings in 1942, mostly from *The Harvey Girls*, were about thirteen thousand dollars, more than the twelve thousand dollars Lithgow Osborne was receiving as New York conservation commissioner. Nonetheless, he was eager, for income tax purposes, to delay payments, such as the *Canal Town* one-thousand-dollar advance, until 1943.[42]

His progress on *Canal Town* was steady, but not pressured. In November the Adamses headed south, stopping in New York, where he met with Costain about the completed part 1 of *Canal Town* and with Cerf, who was already asking Adams for another book. The meeting with Cerf put the two men on a first-name basis. Not going so well was the discussion with Costain. The initial reactions of Baumgarten and Costain to *Canal Town* had been differing opinions on how priggish the physician hero was. Even before the meeting, however, Adams had indicated that if Costain were unhappy, he would not hold him to the contract. After the New York meeting, Costain urged more action early in the story and other major changes. Adams promised to try.

After New York, the Adamses went to Beaufort, where Jane wangled a telephone although he said that it was practically useless for long-distance calls because of Parris Island. The phone was not the only wartime difficulty. He reported no bacon, no butter, and little meat, and although Jane became the confessed "Queen of the Blacks" for her dealings with the black market, he predicted a diet of oysters, crabs, and clams.[43]

The war also had other effects on Adams. Limited by his age and a lack of mobility, Adams tried to contribute to the war effort by doing what he did best, writing an article urging citizen committees to police speed limits so valuable rubber would not be wasted. *Collier's* reacted that it hoped the nation would not have to have "vigilanteism on a national scale." He had more success when Julian Street, Jr., of the Defense Savings Staff of the Treasury Department asked for his World War I *Saturday Evening Post* story "The Beggar's Purse." The tale on savings stamps was a radio script for *The Treasury Star Parade*.[44]

"The Corpse at the Table," a short story that had worn a tortuous path between New York and Wide Waters, was rejected by the *Reader's Digest* in July. The next month the magazine had a change of mind and bought the horror story for $750, placed it in *Saturday Review of Literature*, and reprinted it the next month. As 1942 ended, DeWitt Wallace reviewed stories in his *Reader's Digest* for the year and declared a $500 "dividend" bonus for "The Corpse at the Table," the largest amount for any of Brandt's clients. Adams said it was a "mighty pleasant" New Year's surprise, little realizing the ramifications of the Wallace gesture.[45]

# 16

# BIOGRAPHER
## 1943–1945

As 1942 was ending, Adams was contacted by Alexander Woollcott to be one of ten authors helping on a book of American prose and verse ranging from the Declaration of Independence to William Allen White's editorial tribute to his deceased daughter. Woollcott got the idea for *As We Were* from Felix Frankfurter, intending it for use by the literate American soldier. Adams accepted initially, sending suggestions. As he went to Beaufort, however, he realized a lack of suitable libraries was a handicap and notified Woollcott not to count on him but continued to offer possible entries.[1] Then on 23 January 1943, while Woollcott was making a broadcast, he was stricken with a cerebral hemorrhage. The death of the author, actor, dramatic critic, and radio personality would have a major effect on Adams.

The Adamses settled into their winter home in Colony Gardens with Adams pleased with the *Reader's Digest* bonus and Jane Adams foraging for precious meat. The situation was such that when he received a live possum at a birthday party marking his seventy-second, he pledged to eat it. At Colony Gardens Adams noted everyone else in the complex was a navy dentist. Mails were slow and gasoline rationing a curse.

He was working on his rewrite of the first part of *Canal Town* when Brandt relayed a *Reader's Digest* request for a remembrance piece on Woollcott. Mindful of the graciousness of editor Wallace, he began contacting friends of Woollcott for anecdotes. He wrapped up the novel's first of two parts while he waited for responses and then wrote the character sketch in one week. Wallace paid fifteen hundred dollars for it but decided to combine it with others into a composite article put together by his associate editor, Henry Morton Robinson.

Returning to *Canal Town*, Adams was displeased by suggestions from Baumgarten and Costain that slowed his writing of the second part. Then came a telegram from Frank Taylor of the publishers Reynal & Hitchcock that Adams quoted to Baumgarten: "We are working on a project for a really distinguished book embodying the life, times, and letters of Alexander Woollcott, the book to be much more than conventional biography. . . . All points to you as key man in picture."[2]

Adams told her he wanted to do the biography. He said if he took the job, it would mean a forty-eight-hour week, but it was worth a try. Taylor had persuaded his publishers that Adams was the choice after he canvassed members of the Algonquin Round Table, the social group of which Woollcott was a member. "Thornton Wilder said there was only one writer for the job—Samuel Hopkins Adams," Taylor recalled, adding, "Writers in those days were not as anxious as they are today to write revelations of their friends."[3]

Knowing of Adams mainly as a muckraker, Taylor reluctantly called him after sending the telegram and agreed on a meeting in Beaufort. Together they mapped out the biography, but when Adams asked Taylor to suggest an advance, the figure was fifteen hundred dollars. Facing six to seven months work, he countered with five thousand dollars, and the negotiations went to Baumgarten and the publisher. By the end of the month, she had a deal at five thousand with twenty-five hundred on delivery and a like amount on publication, with the proviso Adams could draw up to twenty-five hundred dollars at will. They also agreed Jo Hennessey, who had suggested Adams to Reynal & Hitchcock, would get five hundred dollars for his help.

With Brandt ill from viral pneumonia, Alma Levin Pritchard returned to the firm and sold *Spencer Brade, M.D.* to A. B. Ljus of Stockholm for $150 and 10 percent on sales over three thousand, "which I guess isn't bad for Sweden."[4] Later Baumgarten sold *That None Should Die* for $100 to Ljus, who handled Norwegian, Danish, and German rights as well. The seemingly piddling sales of foreign rights would have importance.

After the Taylor visit, Adams tackled *Canal Town* with renewed vigor, encouraged by Baumgarten and spurred by the knowledge he must get it in shape before beginning the Woollcott biography. By late April he finished almost all of it. After sending out more letters asking for personal recollections of Woollcott, he headed north. In New York he found winter had not been kind to his friends. Brandt was still recovering from pneumonia, and Will Irwin had suffered a heart attack, so most of Adams's time was spent with Robinson, whose article on Woollcott had been published under an Adams byline for an additional six hundred dollars. It was his only byline in 1943 except for a serialization of *The Harvey Girls* in five newspapers by Richard Waldo's syndicate.

Costain read most of the second part of *Canal Town* in May and told Baumgarten he saw serious problems but asked her to wait until Adams finished. In June he wrote Adams that the ending was not fully developed. The author agreed to expand the end, but before he finished, Costain wrote again, saying Adams had taken the wrong approach on the novel. Costain wanted less atmospheric background and more dramatic action. He ended with "I am so convinced that this way of doing it is wrong that I am risking your everlasting ire by saying that the novel should not be published as it stands. . . . A major operation is called for."[5]

Ire was what Costain expected, and ire was what he got. Adams wrote Baumgarten that Costain wanted a novel of his own, written by Adams. Facing the prospect of losing two years' work and of a budget crisis because he hoped the *Canal Town* money would finance the biography, he vowed he would go ahead and finish his story, not Costain's. The unflappable Baumgarten said he could draw on the Reynal & Hitchcock advance for *Woollcott* and began seeking another publisher for *Canal Town*.[6]

But Adams stewed. He gave the completed book to Taylor during the Fourth of July party at Wide Waters. Baumgarten, who had promised Random House a reading, was cool to Reynal & Hitchcock publishing the novel. Admitting he thought *The Harvey Girls* was a singular effort and he had forgotten Cerf's overtures, Adams confessed he should leave business matters alone.

After Reynal & Hitchcock turned down *Canal Town*, Adams got it back, made changes suggested by Taylor, and sent it to Baumgarten who, after a slight detour to Julian Messner, relayed it to Random House. Within one month, she wired Adams: "RANDOM ENTHUSIASTIC ABOUT BOOK ACCEPTING ON SAME TERMS AS DOUBLEDAY CONTRACT." Editor Belle Becker of Random wrote, "The manuscript has everything, and that in itself entails a minor criticism, namely, that there is an embarrassment of riches." She said the book would have to be cut but promised not to touch what she called the fascinating regional history. Aware of paper restrictions because of the war, he readily agreed.[7]

With the Random signing Baumgarten asked Costain to cancel his contract, and he requested its return from Adams. Grumbling, Adams mellowed enough later to send a Christmas card to Costain, who Brandt said was caught in office politics and remained loyal to Adams. Loyalty and politics of a different nature concerned Adams. As the seventy-eighth Congress convened in 1943, he joined more than one thousand signers to urge the Dies Committee be terminated. Adams criticized the House Un-American Activities Committee chaired by Representative Martin Dies because it was "a forum for the proponents of intolerance and hatred." His criticism of the committee, combined with his joining seven hundred as a signer of a full-page advertisement by the National Council of American-Soviet Friendship seeking the establishment of a second front against fascist Germany in 1943, was not ignored by the FBI. The bureau also collected information on his lending his name to the American Committee for Spanish Freedom that opposed the fascist Francisco Franco and on his joining three hundred signers of an appeal by the Council for Pan-American Democracy for Argentina, calling for Juan Peron to release thousands of antifascists in 1945. "When the question of basic human rights was under fire," George Metcalf wrote, "it drew from him the same emotions that a firefighter feels when he hears the bell and strips for action. He was a fighter and woe to that person who challenged his beliefs."[8]

A visit by Taylor to Wide Waters was a highlight of the 1943 summer. Taylor recalled the extraordinary presence of Jane Adams, the awful martinis, and the discussions about Woollcott. "Jane Adams had a generous spirit equaled by strong opinions, handled with wit. I never knew what kind of an actress she

14. Sam and Jane Adams playing backgammon at Wide Waters. This was one of their favorite photographs and was featured on a 1940s Christmas card. Samuel Hopkins Adams Collection. Courtesy of Syracuse University Library.

was, but she had beautiful legs and wore masses of jewelry like a gypsy. She swore like a trouper and called Sam 'the old prune,' her favorite loving term. She gave her love to those around her, especially the young."[9]

As good as Jane was, that bad were the martinis served on the porch of the old house. "Sam would put raspberries or whatever fruit was in season in them and ruin a very good martini," Taylor said, seconded by Kennedy who said some guests discreetly would dump them off the porch. Nonetheless, the martinis, made in a stainless steel shaker with a plunging device that Adams felt would not dilute the drink too much, were as much a part of Wide Waters as the Adamses. "I must have made eight million drinks," George Harlan said.[10]

15. Samuel Hopkins Adams with his grandson George Harlan at Hamilton College in 1945. Courtesy of Hamilton College.

A main topic of conversation between Taylor and Adams was how to deal with Woollcott's mumps and the possibility of sterility. "In those days there was no talk about homosexuality and Sam tried to walk around it, but we had long arguments about how to handle the mumps." At the end, as he had done with the question of possible black blood in Harding, he devoted part of his biography to the unresolved question.

After Woollcott's death he had been cremated, and a memorial service was held in New York with internment planned at Hamilton College later. Together with Hennessey, Adams contacted Woollcott's friends, and about twenty gathered on 15 July in a cemetery on the campus. After the ceremony, Taylor and Hennessey went to Wide Waters to discuss the biography, for which Adams was amassing information. After answers to his queries came in from friends such as Ross, Tarkington, and John T. Winterich, Adams began writing, using the patchwork method of a chapter here and a chapter there. He sent a chapter to New York in September, and although Baumgarten liked it, she said with her usual candor that his mixing of history and biography had produced writing that matched the period of which he was writing. He assured her that he would resolve it in the rewriting.

Despite putting all other writing aside for Woollcott he found a place in the war effort. The Cayuga County Civilian Mobilization Office had asked for volunteers to handle gasoline rationing books, and in August Adams answered the call although Hennessey asked, "Aren't you heaping on coals with your job on the ration board?" Adams worked some afternoons and all day during busy times. Wide Waters remained low-keyed that summer with Mildred Harlan spending the season. Her husband was gravely ill, and in October Atherton Harlan died. The family stayed at Wide Waters until Election Day and then spent six weeks with Mildred Harlan at New Hope.[11]

The Woollcott responses kept coming from editors such as Wallace, writers such as Marie Belloc Lowndes, and show business personalities such as actress Peggy Wood. The actress added to her letter: "I do wish I could see you when you are in town for you have a place of deep affection in my heart." Additionally, new information came from Robinson and Hennessey. Fortunately for Adams, who had a January deadline, Reynal & Hitchcock decided to postpone the book until the next fall to avoid competition with a book of Woollcott letters.[12]

*Canal Town* was done in August when he added a dedication: "To the Memory of DEACON ABNER ADAMS who did his bit, made his pile and left his name upon a section of the Big Ditch, this book is piously inscribed by his great-grandson." Cerf wrote Adams that he was delighted to have him back with Random House.

After dropping the family off in New Hope, he went to Baltimore to meet with Woollcott's brother and his wife. They were joined at dinner by H. L. Mencken. Afterward in his diary, Mencken, who said Adams was beginning to look old, wondered, "why a man with such serious writing behind him should devote himself to the career of so shallow a fellow is hard to make out." Others had similar concerns. One was a fellow author, who answered an Adams query with a terse "Dear Samuel Hopkins Adams: Yes, I'm in New York, but I want no part of Woollcott, dead or alive. Sorry. Edna Ferber." John Winkler, who had worked with Woollcott on the *New York Times*, wrote, "holy hell cats, who ever persuaded you that poor fat thwarted Alec W. was worthy of a real biog.? . . . Selah and good luck to you in yr. attempt to make a Man of a mouse." The answer to Winkler's question was Jane Adams. Adams, who said he found Woollcott a singular character deserving interpretation, could have had second thoughts, but Katherine Adell said Jane had an affinity with Woollcott, and the former actress urged her husband to do the book.[13]

After his visit to Baltimore, he went to New York where he met with the Cozzenses, his publishers, and various sources for the Woollcott biography, including columnist Danton Walker who said he conferred with Adams many times in person and by mail. Later Adams estimated he sent one thousand letters and talked about Woollcott "to, I should guess, 500 people." He returned to New Hope on weekends exhausted, complaining that New York was too much for an old man.[14]

In mid-December 1943 the Adamses left for Beaufort where they found a house to rent in the overcrowded community. They were lucky to get the small house in a newly developed area called Hundred Pines where Martha Elliott lived. Preston and Mae Huff still retained their Beaufort home, and Jane had to do housework, but she did not like it. Living next to Martha Elliott pleased the Adamses, and the feeling was mutual. "Jane was one of the most loving people I have ever known," Elliott said, recalling their long talks when Jane would come over with a bottle of sherry after her husband, attorney William Elliott, had left for work. She also praised Adams: "Sam would draw you out, build you up. He was as interested in your opinion as anyone's."[15]

Adams tackled the *Canal Town* proofs and comments from Random House's Saxe Commins, a former Rochester dentist. Adams was concerned with accuracy and wanted to take every precaution against error, noting experts were waiting for any historical mistake. He said the younger man had done a fine job on the proofs already. He was encouraged by a report from Becker and quoted part to Baumgarten: "'The chorus of enthusiasm, which started out as a solo, is swelling and everyone who has been lucky enough to read *Canal Town* is certain that we have a potential best seller on the list.'"[16]

Attempts to sell it to the motion pictures, however, seemed headed nowhere as Twentieth Century-Fox admitted candidly the stone baby was something the Hays office would not approve. In February a story editor for RKO Radio Pictures told Alma Pritchard at Brandt & Brandt that she was unable to budge the studio above a fifteen thousand dollar offer. Adams, noting *A Tree Grows in Brooklyn* had been sold for somewhere around fifty thousand dollars, suggested that they wait until the book was published. Pritchard said the gamble "seems to me well worth taking."[17] It was not.

With the proofs to *Canal Town* done, he turned to the Woollcott biography, the rough draft of which he hoped to have done in Beaufort. He was hampered by cold weather that depleted the heating oil in his rented house. He told Tarkington he was presenting arguments to the rationing board for more oil. Fortunately, the weather turned warmer and he continued to write eighteen hundred to two thousand words a day, sending ten chapters to Baumgarten by the end of January.[18]

Armed with the first six chapters, Taylor in early February visited Adams. During their discussions Taylor noted that *Canal Town* was going to sell at $2.50, a low price Adams had insisted on with Becker but about which he now had second thoughts. Afraid the book trade would not respect a book issued at a low price, a frantic Adams wrote Baumgarten, taking the blame and urging a $2.75 price. She replied with good news and bad news. The good news was "a shocking confession to make, but in rare instances I over-ride your express intentions and the truth is that the retail price of CANAL TOWN is $2.75." The bad news was Cerf had heard that Messner had had a crack at the book and was hurt that he had not followed Costain. She said she had assured Cerf that he would get Adams's next novel and that had calmed him.[19]

Adams wrote Cerf, however, tracing the events and adding that he did not want to be under suspicion. Cerf thanked him and said: "I hope I will never have to ask you to submit your future novels to us first—that you will take for granted that Random House is now your fiction publisher and wants to continue in that capacity indefinitely."[20] With one minor exception, Adams's parade of different publishers was over.

His relationship with Baumgarten also reached a new plateau. Her admission that she "in rare instances" made decisions without consulting him brought the expected blast. Uncowed, she replied: "If I seem to take too much on my-self, I know you will always remember that sometimes decisions are called for on the spot and sometimes, of course, I feel it is better to keep it all a dark secret from you until it is all over. I am afraid I am too old to reform."[21] He accepted her explanation without a whimper.

Despite his heavy work on Woollcott, with which he was about half-finished by March, he was at the Beaufort rationing board three days a week. He also was stymied by the slowness of Hennessey to furnish needed Woollcott letters. To increase his anxiety, he told Baumgarten in March that the author death rate was startling. He mentioned Irvin Cobb, Joseph Lincoln, and Hendrik Willem Van Loon, but he could have added Tarbell and William Allen White, both of whom died in January. He answered such bad news by working even harder, passing one hundred thousand words and entering the homestretch. After the proofs of the letters arrived, he balanced the gathering of information from sources with writing two thousand words a day.

Encouraging news came from Cerf, who in late March sent him the au-thor's copies of *Canal Town*, slated for 24 April "come hell or high water." Not-ing wartime restrictions caused manufacturing problems, Cerf said the book looked "pretty fine" and ordered a printing of fifteen thousand copies. Two weeks before the release advance sales were eleven thousand.[22]

The acute paper situation also was affecting the biography. Curtice Hitch-cock liked the book but said it was running long. Conceding the contract was for between 100,000 and 200,000 words, he urged a goal of fewer than 150,000. Somewhat distressed because Taylor had said more than 165,000, Adams aimed at 160,000. The result was closer to 170,000.

The Adamses left Beaufort in mid-April. He spent ten days in New York on Woollcott and *Canal Town* business. Although he refused to autograph the book in bookstores, he did a radio show with Mary Margaret McBride. He also met with various Random House people, who had good news. The advance sale of *Canal Town* was about thirteen thousand, and the Peoples Book Club made it the September–October selection for a fifteen thousand dollar guar-antee of which he received half. Another topic was the reviews.

Noting that the story of Dr. Horace Amlie and his labors against malaria, dysentery, and typhoid in part 1 was linked with the development of the wild canal town in part 2, Catharine Brody of the *New York Times* said the plot pro-gressed from the early "whimsy" into "a first-class medical mystery drama." She said although Adams had followed in Edmonds's footsteps, he "managed to stake out a field of his own." Adams, whose historiography had begun with the traditional elitism history of Webster, Eaton, and Harding and changed to the social history of the Harvey operation, now used the "bottom up" history based on old records, papers, and letters for his regional history. The result, Carmer said, revealed "the same kind of fondness for the eager, rough, sentimental people of our early days as did Mark Twain." His comments came days after the Americans and their allies landed at Normandy. It was not surprising that later in 1944 the Council of Books in Wartime printed 150,000 copies of the novel as a pocket-size Armed Services edition or that Adams received letters from servicemen in Italy, Brazil, and India.[23]

As the movement to draft Roosevelt for a fourth term developed in 1944, Adams was contacted by *Life* magazine for a feature article on election slanders in the past. Although he anticipated the job would take most of July, he accepted the commission and rushed to finish the biography, which by the middle of June was essentially done except for the final chapter covering Woollcott's death and obituaries.

Whether as a duty or an ego booster, he kept a date in Palmyra. The barge *Blue Star* had been converted into a "Bond Showboat" for the Fifth War Loan drive. In Palmyra, Adams was the honored guest. He extolled: "Our great grandfathers so believed in this nation that they bought the bonds by which the project could be undertaken. Those bonds did not pay much interest as War Bonds do today, but they carried plenty of faith and populism. There is an old saying, 'Money talks.' Well, today there is a new saying, 'Money fights.'"[24]

New also were some guests at the Adams party on the Fourth of July weekend. One recalled Jane's comment on the remaining aged golf foursome, including Adams and William H. Seward, at Owasco Country Club: "Those old goats—there's only six good eyes, five good legs, and seven good arms in the whole bunch of them." Faced with a dwindling number of friends because of the deaths of older ones and wartime demands on the young, Adams widened their circle to include his new publishing colleagues and their friends, Frances and Joseph Merriam, Frank and Nan Taylor, Akin and Peggy French, Albert Erskine, and William and Beth Scherman, all in their thirties.[25]

A promotion manager of Simon & Schuster's new Sears Peoples Book Club, Scherman recalled his first meeting about *Canal Town*: "Peggy French and I from the Book Club and Fran Merriam, then p.r. director of Random House, sat on little gold chairs in a nice room at the Waldorf with Adams and talked about promotion for the book. . . . He invited us to Wide Waters for his regular big Fourth of July party there, and that invitation (augmented by frequent Labor Day weekends as well) continued almost to his death."

The representatives from Peoples Book Club had good news about *Canal Town*, predicting that sales would go over two hundred thousand and saying Sears Roebuck was featuring it on its Christmas list. As he continued patching the biography, he turned to the *Life* article. He went to Cornell University for four days and in early August had finished his article on a history of presidential campaign smears. He was ready to go to New York or the American Antiquarian Society if the magazine wanted more material, but *Life* bought the article for fifteen hundred dollars, saying it would make any necessary changes.

Pleased by *Life*'s price that was five hundred dollars more than he expected, he braced for a visit from Taylor to go over the Woollcott book. He told Baumgarten that the book was about as he wanted it, but she made suggestions to Taylor to fix an unevenness in the writing by unraveling many of the inverted sentences and lessening the overuse of words such as *status*, *thus*, and *dubbed*. Taylor arrived with ten pages of notes. Afterward, Adams began revising the book, a task that continued into October.[26]

The slow progress on the biography was offset throughout the summer by the popularity of *Canal Town*. The novel had made the *Herald Tribune*'s "What America Is Reading" four times in May and June. Cerf reported in July that the novel "goes romping on," selling 255 copies in two days and crossing the 25,000 mark. When Adams expressed concern about not being on the best-seller lists more, Cerf said: "I know that it has sold far better than a lot of titles that are actually on the blooming things. They don't mean anything anyhow."[27]    •

As the regular edition continued selling, the Peoples Book Club was issuing its Sears Roebuck promotion for the novel. A pamphlet was prepared, including a discussion of *Canal Town*, a short piece by Adams on why he wrote the book, a biographical sketch of Adams by Robert Linscott, whom Cerf had hired from Houghton Mifflin, and another on Jane Adams by Laurette Taylor. Linscott's personality profile noted: "Sam Adams likes people and music, games, thick steaks and old-fashioned strawberry shortcake, biscuity with lots of berries. He dislikes spiders and thunderstorms (both of which scare the daylights out of him), ham, lemon pie and snobs."[28]

Random House's extensive advertising campaign for *Canal Town* ended in mid-September when Cerf reported to Baumgarten that the stock was running out and the company could not reprint the book in 1944 because "We have less paper than the ladies' room in Moscow Union Terminal." Telling Cerf that "it breaks my heart to tell Sam that there can't be any further printings," she softened the news to Adams by reporting the sale of *The Harvey Girls* in Britain.[29]

The popular success of *Canal Town* prompted him to recall the boyhood stories of his great aunt Sarah Bradford about touring actors on the canal, and he suggested the idea to Cerf as a follow-up novel. In July he reported Cerf's reaction, quoting the publisher: "'I hasten to tell you that I think your idea for a book about the adventures of an old-time theatrical company is Double-A, 4-Star, and a mile wide.'"[30]

As was his practice in fiction, Adams began his book by starting an alphabetically indexed ledger, in which he listed his characters. In a piece he wrote for the Dallas *Times-Herald*, he explained: "As soon as my plot is outlined, I list my characters from Arbuthnot to Zillendorfer. Whenever a notion strikes me as something that McSorley might have said to Xavasour, or a happy phrase of characterization for Viola Farthingale, I jot it down on a piece of paper . . . for transfer to my ledger. Unless I do this, it is likely to escape me."[31]

In late September Brandt, just returned from Hollywood, wrote that Clark Gable had expressly asked Adams to prepare an original story for him. Brandt said it would be a four- or five-page treatment for which Metro-Goldwyn-Mayer "might make a proposition which may make our eyes bug out." The only restriction was Gable's insistence that his war record not be used to exploit him or the film. Although an admiring Adams said the Gable prohibition showed him quite a man, the author told Brandt he had nothing in mind that would fit the Gable personality. He said he could not let MGM pay his expenses to New York on the chance.

With his statement to Brandt, Adams conceded that his difficulties with *Whispers* and *Tambay Gold* had ended his reliance on light fiction. Although he would occasionally dabble in the form in the years ahead, the bulk of his writing effort, after the Woollcott biography, would concentrate on history.

October was busy with Jane Adams going to Milwaukee to see her sister before her eye operation and with Adams researching at the American Antiquarian Society. They left Wide Waters shortly after the election. He had been worried until weeks before the election that Thomas E. Dewey would win and was pleased Roosevelt got his fourth term. The Adamses went to New York where they saw Lithgow Osborne, who had returned from London, as ambassador to Norway-in-exile. Adams also gave an interview in which he saw a fallow time coming in American literature, like that after the Revolutionary and Civil wars. He did add: "So far, this war has produced some extra good reporting. John Hersey's 'A Bell for Adano,' for instance. It's exceptional fictional reporting—a notable contribution."[32]

Jane went into the Presbyterian Hospital on 16 November for the cataract operation on her right eye. The recovery required her to lie motionless for two weeks for fear any jarring might cause a hemorrhage in the eyeball. For the first four days she was also forbidden to talk, causing Adams to muse about the outpouring of language when the restrictions were lifted. Armed with nonfiction books, he read to her, and the Brandts loaned her a radio. After she spent two weeks in the hospital, the surgery was called a success, and she was moved to a hotel.

While his wife recovered, he tried to wrap up the Woollcott biography, still looking for chapters to be returned by some readers. Attempts to serialize the biography were negative at two magazines, but in late November Brandt sold two parts, the chapter on Woollcott as a dramatic critic and a piece on his experiences on radio, to *Harper's* magazine for three hundred dollars each. Condensed versions later would be printed by Omnibook and *Liberty*.

On 9 December, using vocational gasoline granted by the ration board, the Adamses headed for Beaufort with Preston Huff driving. Jane was examined by a Charleston oculist who found her vision was excellent but was unable to fit her with glasses because the eye still had redness around the wound. She wore a patch, was unable to read or write, and was bored. The author also was bored, with the Woollcott book, and wrote Taylor he was making no more changes except for error.

One correction was demanded by George S. Kaufman, who had heard Adams had told about how Woollcott had joked with Kaufman's wife, Beatrice, about getting the playwright out of the way. Kaufman did not think its humor was apparent and demanded the paragraph be eliminated. Adams refused but did revise it.[33]

As the Adamses waited for Jane's eye to lose its inflammation, they settled into their new quarters, the Michael Hokes home near downtown Beaufort. Calling the house, named Windymarsh, too big and too expensive, Adams had little choice because all available apartments and smaller houses were taken. On the Beaufort River, across from Colony Gardens, Windymarsh featured porches on three sides and large oak trees on the spacious grounds. The plan was to use the first floor while renting out the rooms above to help defray the costs. Fortunately, across the street was the Tidalholm Inn to whose managers Adams offered overflow space.

Adams was uneasy about money as he tried to match his royalty payments with his income tax obligations. In early January he had sixty dollars in his account, having put his spare cash into war bonds. Faced with a cash-flow crisis, he was relieved when a Peoples Book Club check of seventy-five hundred dollars got to him by the tax deadline, along with a Random House royalty payment of about fifty-seven hundred dollars. When his next quarterly tax payment in March caused him concern, Baumgarten urged him not to fret because estimates did not have to be "absolutely accurate," to which he replied that if someone went too far under, the taxmen would ask impertinent questions.[34]

If his money woes were easily solved, the success of *Canal Town* dizzied Adams as he sought to keep the different publishers straight. The regular Random House edition, ended because of the shortage of paper, topped 26,000 sold. A dollar version published by the World Book, the Peoples Book Club edition, and the armed services overseas edition were joined by a British edition. In the mix was the Sears-Roebuck promotion, and taken together the novel sold about 350,000 copies.

As he celebrated his seventy-fourth birthday at a plantation dinner, he was reading proof on the Woollcott biography. He told Brandt that as soon as he finished the proofs he would begin the new novel, using some seventy pages of notes. He also read Edmonds's book on early circus life, *Chad Hanna*, to avoid any hint of plagiarism. Indeed, he was becoming increasingly enmeshed in legal concerns dealing with his writing. He had changed part of the Woollcott book to meet Kaufman's threat of libel, and earlier Brandt & Brandt had beaten off a charge of plagiarism from Clifford Funkhouser and Lyman Anson, who had published a story on the Fred Harvey organization in the September 1940 *American Mercury*. In July 1942 the authors claimed Adams used material from a source who had gotten it from them. A review of the articles and Adams's manuscript by a New York City law firm found no basis in the claim. More legal headaches, however, lay in the future.[35]

They enjoyed the Hokes's stately house. The effects of the war were present in their entertaining as the Adamses were eager hosts to a Red Cross visit of ten hospital cases from marines on nearby Parris Island. He remained concerned about the war, predicting the collapse of Germany, army by army, and a longer war against Japan. He was especially concerned that Buddy Richardson would go to the Pacific as a B-29 pilot.

As he stewed about the war and had an active social life, Adams was slow to write his theatrical novel. When he did, the going was tough, as he was swamped with detail but regretted that he had less information about actors than Edmonds had had about circus people. Nonetheless, he wrote one thousand words a day with no definite deadline. Despite distractions, by early April he had thirty-five thousand words written and reached fifty thousand words by the end of April when they left for Wide Waters.

The Adamses arrived in Cayuga County about 7 May, V-E Day, as the war in Europe ended. He was kept busy by the mail generated by *Canal Town* and increased by reactions to the two Woollcott excerpts that had been in *Harper's* and advance copies of the biography. One was Mencken, with whom Adams had been corresponding about language usage. Despite his earlier negative comments about the book Mencken told Adams that he had a good biography and if anyone said he had wasted his time, "invite him (or her) to kiss both your arse and mine."[36]

Reynal & Hitchcock set an advertising budget of ten thousand dollars for *A. Woollcott: His Life and His World* that cheered Baumgarten and Adams. The firm also blanketed his friends and acquaintances with invitations to a 4 June reception. During their stay at the Hotel Seymour they invited friends to their suite for a party described by Serrell Hillman: "Adams was the forgotten man at his own party. He dashed about his hotel room, serving food and drink, as his witty but imperious wife barked orders at him. Finally he could stand no more. With a martini pitcher in one hand and sandwiches in the other, he stopped short in the center of the room and squeaked: 'Don't keep saying 'Sam! Sam! Sam!'"[37]

The Reynal & Hitchcock cocktail party in the Algonquin Hotel's Rose Room that Adams said could accommodate comfortably about 125 people was attended by about 400. The crowd came in waves, Adams told Brigham, who was not there. Missing also was Irwin, bedridden after a second heart attack. Adams's own health was relatively good, but he wrote a friend he would probably have to trade in his cane for a crutch the next year.[38]

While they were in New York, the reviews of the biography began to appear. Although Adams considered the notices extraordinary, Stanley Walker was a prognosticator when he said in the *Herald Tribune Weekly Book Review*: "It is a friendly biography done with Mr. Adams' usual competence and skill, yet it is inevitable that many of Woollcott's admirers will regard parts of it as unfair." Indeed, the book had problems. Richard Watts, Jr., in the *New Republic* had raised the issue of the tone of the biography, saying Adams "makes no attempt to conceal the defects of his hero in any of his innumerable fields of endeavor. In fact, although the work is friendly, there are times when it appears that Mr. Adams finds relish in pointing out the multitudinous frailties of the critic and actor." Round Table member Dorothy Parker was harsher, saying she saw "a strange little underlay of meanness through all of it."[39]

Adams accepted the Parker review as what he expected. The *New Yorker* review by Edmund Wilson, however, enraged him. Although Wilson thought the biography was written in good spirit, he complained: "The writing of Mr. Adams himself is rather blurry and clumsy, . . ." It is not true, as he seems to imply, that Woollcott was wrong in protesting, in a letter to Ira Gershwin, against the use of "disinterested" in the sense of "uninterested." Adams raged to Baumgarten that Wilson should look up "disinterested." A letter to Ross brought a response from the *New Yorker* editor that Wilson "operates *behind* the dictionary and his remarks on 'uninterested' were undoubtedly written in the knowledge that the dictionary, too, was wrong." Ross also said he had read part, with Henry Miller's paean to his wife, *All Our Lives: Alice Duer Miller*, but admitted that "reading about two dead pals at once was too much." Several reviewers handled the books together and, in the *New York Times Book Review* Adams gave a mixed review of the biography of his fellow *Tribune* columnist and friend, who had died of cancer in 1942.[40]

Oblivious readers put Woollcott on "What America Is Reading" in the *Herald Tribune* for twenty-two weeks, finishing third on 29 July behind two war books, Bill Maudlin's *Up Front* and Ernie Pyle's *Brave Men*. Many of the weeks he trailed Cerf's humor book *Try and Stop Me*, and Adams asked Cerf if that was any way for a publisher to treat one of his authors.

All the publicity concerning the biography brought Adams higher visibility. Columbia Pictures asked for copies of *From a Bench in Our Square* and *Average Jones*. John T. W. Martin sought to adapt *Average Jones* as a radio detective. Impressed by the sales start, Hitchcock asked whether he might do another biography, and Adams asked Baumgarten for a bibliography on Heywood Broun, who had died in 1939. Brandt sold to *Liberty* a humorous mystery story, "Aunt Minnie and the Accessory after the Fact," that would become a favorite of anthologists, including Maureen Daly, who called the tale of a murderer who got rid of the weapon with a cat "an amusing, carefully paced suspense story." His magazine work, however, now had a secondary role to his books.[41]

Before he returned to his thespians, the Adamses celebrated the Fourth of July with a dozen houseguests, including eight of the young publishing group and Weaver. A party grew from twenty-five to fifty to sixty-five to ninety, in-

16. Samuel Hopkins Adams in 1945 signing copies of his biography of Alexander Woollcott at Hamilton College, from which both men graduated. Courtesy of Hamilton College.

cluding a number of returning servicemen. Adams hired the wife of a local attorney to handle his correspondence, which was growing to alarming proportions.

While the social life kept him busy in the evenings, his service on the ration board continued to occupy three afternoons a week. After a Syracuse reporter interviewed Adams, who was working the counter and typing ration coupons for gasoline and sugar, the *Herald-Journal* editorialized that he deserved a salute: "He modestly remarks that in taking time off from his writing and contributing his services to the local rationing board he is only doing what millions of other Americans are doing, by trying to help in this difficult war period. But his fine attitude is a reminder to the rest of us that we are still at war and that patriots should stay on the job until victory is done."[42]

Adams had told Baumgarten that he was returning to his novel on 12 July, but Woollcott would not let him alone. Several reviewers had mentioned that Adams's use of so many specifics opened him to further revision. Sure enough, incoming letters offered corrections, additional information, and new material. Baumgarten suggested he compile them in a *New Yorker* article, an idea that Adams said Ross would not entertain. He asked for a set of proofs for a future edition, but Baumgarten urged he make his corrections in the British edition.

Hamish Hamilton had offered a two hundred pound advance for the British biography, with one hitch, that some offending passages be deleted. Adams was adamant in opposing those affecting Woollcott's sexual slant. Baumgarten agreed that Hamilton was being "perfectly idiotic" to request the deletions. Two months later Hamilton agreed to publish the book on Adams's terms.[43]

Try as Adams might to concentrate on his novel, he continued to be diverted. He talked at his alma mater, during which he said *Canal Town* was his best work and *Revelry* his most satisfying. Then he got a proposal by the Hearst Sunday publication *American Weekly* for a series of articles on barbiturates. After a phone call with Brandt, he agreed to do twelve thousand words for three thousand dollars. In September he finished the four articles warning about dangerous sleeping pills and urging legislation to classify them as narcotics. *American Weekly* ran "Slaves of the Devil's Capsule" later that year, and Representative Edith Nourse Rogers of Massachusetts placed the first two articles in the *Congressional Record*.[44]

Swamped with Woollcott letters, he still was receiving mail on *Canal Town* from homesick service men who had been reading the Service edition, and he felt those letters one had to answer. The thought of more letters concerning the *American Weekly* series led him to ask Brandt to have the magazine handle correspondence. The wily Brandt demanded the magazine pay extra if Adams handled the mail, closing the issue. Not all, however, was well in the Adams-Brandt relationship.

Citing the *Harvey Girls* job and the *American Weekly* articles, Adams complained to Brandt that he believed the agent had consistently underrated his market value. In both cases he argued he had gotten higher fees than his agents had proposed. Brandt replied authors seldom had the overall picture but because he was his "very dear friend as well as my client," he would answer his points. One by one he explained how the prices were arrived at and said it was Adams's responsibility to say what he would work for. Sheepishly, Adams admitted he was wrong on *The Harvey Girls* and blamed his growing deafness on the telephone for a misunderstanding on the *American Weekly* price and apologized.[45]

Adams and Brandt shared the same skepticism concerning Hollywood, but Carol Brandt was more positive. Louis B. Mayer had made her a general representative of MGM at a salary of seventy-five thousand dollars, which Adams told Lithgow Osborne reportedly made her the highest paid woman executive in the world. Quickly she targeted Adams's slowly developing new theatrical novel. On behalf of his wife Brandt asked the author for a synopsis for a possible prepublication deal.

Responding that he thought it was another form of movie bunk, Adams nonetheless said that if Carol wanted it, she could have it. In a postscript he added that the story would be written as a novel without any other consideration. Reassured by Brandt, the author did a two-page outline. When the studio declined, Brandt asked his wife to write Adams: "You know how Sam is. He said nothing will come of this and he will scream."[46]

Carol Brandt wrote Adams, "For whatever it may be worth to you, darling, you put a big feather in a small cap and for that I am grateful." He replied he would be sore if it were not she or if he did not feel a debt to the studio for *The Harvey Girls*. At her request, he sent her an early draft of the novel, and in December terms were proposed but went nowhere. An exasperated Adams told a frustrated Carl Brandt he had confidence in him and would abide by any terms he made.[47]

Labor Day was relaxed for the Adamses with friends from Utica. It was just as well for Jane, who was beset by new and old problems in the late summer. A friend reported that she had severe attacks of asthma but that she "is magnificently courageous about it all, and I fear sees far less than she will admit." George Metcalf recalled that when Jane went to Owasco Country Club, she took his wife's arm and asked her to identify people for her.[48]

Then, as she was dressing for her 28 October birthday party, she collapsed. Both arms were helpless, and Adams said there seemed to be some paralysis. Although a stroke was feared, the doctor said it was nervous spasm produced by exhaustion. Strength returned to both arms, although her right hand remained weak, and Adams was concerned about a small embolism. The crisis passed, but Edith Osborne wrote the Lithgow Osbornes: "I have not seen her; her voice on the telephone is very thick and queer: She has not made much sense all summer, she does not finish any sentence she begins."[49]

Adams wrapped up the corrections on the Woollcott biography, and Baumgarten sent them to Taylor at Reynal & Hitchcock. Taylor, looking at all the changes, called Adams and begged not to have to reset the type. Adams, who

17. Samuel Hopkins Adams reading on a sofa in his living room at Wide Waters in the 1940s. Samuel Hopkins Adams Collection. Courtesy of Syracuse University Library.

sold more than forty-eight thousand copies for which he grossed more than twenty-seven thousand dollars, agreed. The corrections were sent to Hamilton, who included them in the British edition that sold more than eight thousand copies, grossing about two thousand dollars.

With Woollcott done, Adams turned back to his yet untitled novel about the 1830 theatrical troupe. In late September he told Cerf he had done about sixty thousand words, but if he could save forty thousand of them he would be doing well. Cerf cheered him on, saying this time paper restrictions would not hold them down.

The Adamses left Wide Waters on Election Day and went to New York, where they saw Irwin, who noted Jane's sight was spotty. They went to a preview of *The Harvey Girls* film, however, and dined with various friends, including the Brandts. Adams renewed his acquaintance with Costain, whose new book he praised. In December they went south, stopping in Meggett, South Carolina, so she could visit her doctor, John A. Boone, who sentenced Jane to a stern regimen of little activity. Jane, shaken by her seizure, agreed to follow her doctor's orders.

Facing what he believed would be a bleak winter, news on the financial front occupied him. His gross income from his writing in 1945 was more than thirty-two thousand dollars, almost three times the 1944 total of more than eleven thousand dollars and more than four times higher than the 1943 total of almost seven thousand dollars. At times of cash-flow problems, he did borrow on occasion. In a rare glimpse at his personal finances, he took a twenty-five-thousand-dollar loan in September to buy a new issue of bonds. He said the amount matched his total available assets he could make liquid.[50]

Startling news came from foreign rights, to which Adams had paid little heed. He did put off the payment from Hamilton for the British Woollcott because of the onerous 50 percent British tax. In September a Swedish check of eleven hundred dollars came as a Slaughter royalty. But that was an appetizer. In November Brandt & Brandt had a caller. Adams in mid-December told Lithgow Osborne what happened to his and Slaughter's first novel. Soon after its publication in Denmark the Germans stopped translations but permitted books already published. *That None Should Die* was the only important fiction available and became an all-time bestseller in Denmark. In November 1945 the Copenhagen publisher told Brandt & Brandt that as soon as the money could be released the authors would get fifteen thousand dollars in royalties.[51]

Under the original 60–40 percentage split arrangement on the first Slaughter novel, Adams's share was nine thousand dollars on the 115,000 copies in
Denmark where a sale of 10,000 was considered successful. Buoyed by the
news, they settled in their winter quarters. The enforced boredom of Jane, forbidden even from having her usual Christmas party, got results. Although her
hand still was weak, Adams said on 28 December he was cheerful because her
eye was beginning to show vision.

The cheer would not last long.

# 17

# REGIONALIST
## 1946–1949

Adams celebrated his seventy-fifth birthday in January 1946. It was the first full year after America's participation in World War II and a time of rising inflation and concerns about the threats of communism. It was also the worst year of Adams's life.

As 1946 began he was planning to write a chapter in an anthology dealing with the time between the two world wars. Before leaving for New York to do research, he finished the first part of his regional novel, on the traveling thespians, despite being pessimistic because of MGM's reluctance to consider it as a film. In New York he talked with Herbert Hoover to get additional information on the last days of Harding. He also met with *Life* editors who suggested several projects if he would postpone his novel, something he refused to do.

As January ended, a deal was struck between Random House and Western Printing & Lithography for a twenty-five cent Dell Book edition of *The Harvey Girls*, planned to take advantage of the film, finally released late in 1945, three years after his rush job. When the film reached Beaufort in April, Adams would not go, saying he had had his fill at a preview in New York. Nonetheless, the Johnny Mercer and Harry Warren music with "On the Atchison, Topeka and the Santa Fe" that won an Academy Award and an all-star cast led by Judy Garland earned an unexpectedly high five million dollars on its first run. Its credits listed five authors of the screenplay, Adams as author of the novel, and Eleanore Griffin and William Rankin as authors of the original story.

When the contracts had been drawn for *The Harvey Girls* novel in 1941, a film executive had suggested Adams give credit to Griffin and Rankin in his novel, an idea that Brandt had dismissed. In 1945 Rankin wrote a six-page, single-spaced letter to Adams at Random House, giving background on his writing of the story that Swarts had warned Brandt and Adams about in early 1942. Claiming he had not contacted Adams earlier because he was in the marines, Rankin went through similarities in plot and character names, demanding that he receive credit for his work that he said MGM had bought for fifteen thousand dollars. After the studio proposed language for a reply, Brandt, on behalf of Adams, wrote Rankin that the studio had bought all rights to the story by Rankin's admission and owned the material. Rankin was not to be denied, accusing Adams of an elaboration on his story. When the film began playing in the major markets, Rankin saw it in Los Angeles. Noting he had been given credit for the original story, he wrote Adams in January 1946 to threaten a plagiarism suit. Adams told Brandt he threw the letter in the wastebasket without replying.[1]

With "The Timely Death of President Harding" done, Adams returned to his theatrical novel. In March he was in full swing, and by month's end in the homestretch of the second draft. He suggested several titles, *Flag in the Forest*, *Wayside Flag*, or *Flag by the Wayside*, all referring to the barnstormers hanging a banner to announce performances. Baumgarten immediately seized on *Banner by the Wayside*, a title he said was much better.

His own troubles were not easily solved. His right hip, the one with three shingle nails, refused to support his weight, and he switched to the anticipated crutch, initially conceding any hope of continuing his golf. But one month later, with Huff caddying and holding his crutch while he shot, he was able to play. Because Jane was limited from attending parties, they entertained at home, and he found his expenses increasing. Along with his usual estimated tax woes, inflation and shortages were concerns as he complained he had to pay fifteen dollars for a turkey. He feared an end to governmental controls would result in inflation and a buyers' strike. He was also unhappy with world events, including a call for a naval buildup and the management of the atom bomb.

In late April the *Saturday Review* of Literature published a poll of twenty literary critics on their predictions for the 1945 Pulitzer Prizes in letters. In biography, the critics saw a race between A. *Woollcott: His Life and His World* with six votes and Richard Wright's *Black Boy* with five. Although Adams had won the Critics' Circle award for being first on its list, the Pulitzer jury gave the biography prize posthumously to Linnie Marsh Wolfe's *Son of the Wilderness*, on naturalist John Muir, a book no reviewer had mentioned.[2]

Having finished the first draft of *Banner by the Wayside* before he left Beaufort, he tackled the rewrite at Wide Waters. On 13 June he reported to Cerf that he had rewritten parts of it many times, but he expected the vultures at Random House to tear at its entrails. Cerf replied, "We are not vultures here at Random House as you unhappily suggest—just little bluebirds looking for happiness and novels by Samuel Hopkins Adams." Becker got the manuscript from Baumgarten after Adams wrote both women that it was for their reading only. Baumgarten did a quick read of the parts she had not seen before and left on vacation. Becker was enthusiastic about the novel, hoping to see Adams when he came to do a radio show at the end of the month.[3]

On their way north from Beaufort the Adamses had stopped in New York. Adams asked Scherman to stop by, cautioning him that Jane was finding the city too much. In Cayuga County her doctor in late May said that her heart was good and her general health improved, but she tired easily, On 25 June while she was in her dressing room, she grabbed the back of her head and collapsed.[4]

Adams wired Brandt that Jane was seriously ill with an embolism and to cancel a CBS appearance on *Invitation to Learning*. Brandt telegraphed he and Carol would help in any way. The next day Adams wrote her chances were very small because the brain area involved was so great and the absorption of the clot was almost nil.

Others quickly rallied to Adams's crisis. Mildred and George Harlan arrived. Emerson made his Auburn home available so Adams could be nearer Mercy Hospital, the Roman Catholic hospital that specialized in extended care. Becker, whom he had also notified on 26 June, said that she would get his manuscript to Baumgarten when she returned from vacation. Adams told Brandt that everything was being done that could be, urging him not to come upstate, even if Jane should die.[5]

On 30 June he reported to Brandt his wife was breathing easier but was growing progressively weaker. He included a list of their friends in New York who should be notified when she died. Then, the same day, the remarkable vitality that Jane had displayed throughout her life brought her out of her semiconscious state. "This is a hell of a place. I want to go home to Mae and Preston," she told a nurse.

The encouraging news prompted Becker to write with many suggestions on the novel and Cerf to send a cheery letter, not knowing that the next day she had lapsed back into unconsciousness and a consultation had offered no hope. The doctor was also worried about Adams, insisting that he go back to work.

In answer to a letter from Baumgarten, who had returned to the office where she got the news, he said on 12 July he would resume work on the novel the next week.[6]

At work, Adams suggested an idea for a mystery symposium for *Ellery Queen Magazine*, corresponded with Mencken on a word usage question, and met with Frank Taylor, who was staying with an Auburn couple and who proposed the novel be *Banner at the Crossroads*. Baumgarten stuck by her title and told Adams only some cutting was needed and promised they would pitch in.

For the rest of July Jane lay in the hospital attended by nurses around the clock. Adams said it was a daily heartbreak, knowing she could never speak to or know him again. Although he had trouble concentrating on the novel, he cut a Charleston chapter he admitted he had written to attract a movie offer. But, because he had not heard from Cerf about it, he had self-doubts and expressed concern whether Random House still wished to publish the novel.

Becker gently reminded him of his admonition against having anyone else look at the manuscript but said Cerf had been delighted by her report on the novel. Baumgarten, whose letter closings changed from the usual "as ever" to "love," jumped in to apologize for the oversight in getting a contract and said she would draw one at once. She also reported that Doubleday wanted a biography of Tarkington, who had died on 19 May, and asked if he would be interested in having his name suggested to Tarkington's widow. Aware the Tarkingtons' long-time secretary thought the Woollcott biography had been too cruel, he said he would not consider the book if she had any say, and the matter was dropped.[7]

During August Jane remained the same, and he asked Brandt to notify friends to omit flowers. Instead, he urged, they should donate to Hunger Incorporated or Food for Friendship. He busied himself by hosting Jane's sister, Alma Wait from Milwaukee, and buying from Anna Champany a coverlet that Baumgarten wanted. And as if Jane's illness were not enough, he heard in August that Stewart Edward White was dying from cancer in California. On 20 August Jane had a second hemorrhage, and he told Baumgarten that every time the telephone rang he shivered. He also said the hospitalization of his wife was costing more than one thousand dollars a month and he would be out of funds in three months. She responded by arranging for him to draw the *Banner by the Wayside* advance of twenty-five hundred dollars if he needed it, and when at the end of the month he again complained, she said Brandt & Brandt cashier Frieda Markel had "dug up $1,800 in cheap edition royalties from Random House."[8]

18. Sam and Jane Adams on the bridge over the creek that separated the main and little houses at Wide Waters. Samuel Hopkins Adams Collection. Courtesy of Syracuse University Library.

Despite his travails Adams returned to *Banner by the Wayside*. Spurred by Becker, who reported the book was scheduled for spring "if you and I roll up our sleeves and get to work," he set 15 September as a deadline to get the completed manuscript to her. He suggested she come to Wide Waters, an invitation she accepted while assuring "in spite of our little author-editor game nothing will be done to the book which does not meet with your approval." Friday, 6 September, he sent her the manuscript except for the final chapters, promising them the following Monday. The day before, he had told Brandt that Jane was low but she had rallied before.[9] This time there was no rally.

Jane Adams died early Sunday morning, 8 September, with the cause of death listed as a cerebral hemorrhage. Quickly, Adams and Brandt notified their respective lists although Adams reported difficulty in locating people on Sunday. Irwin, who was in New York where he was working on rehearsals of a play, wrote "Thank God for this relief to poor Sam," in his diary, lamenting that he would be unable to attend the Tuesday services because of the play. Becker received a Sunday letter from Adams, ever mindful of his responsibilities, telling her that Jane had died and it would be several days before he could complete the manuscript.[10]

The death brought an outpouring of sympathy. Walter Winchell aired her death on Sunday night, producing a flood of telegrams. Adams appreciated a *Citizen-Advertiser* editorial by Lithgow Osborne that ended, "One felt that she achieved personal happiness for herself by personally creating it for others."[11]

The funeral services were at Wide Waters Tuesday. The evening before, Adams had told Mildred Harlan: "Mil, I want to go down to the funeral home and see Jane again." Now a strong west wind came off the lake to whip the flowers as Ibbotson offered a prayer under a sunny sky. Afterward her ashes were scattered in Owasco Lake.[12] Weaver stayed at Wide Waters as Adams tackled the mountain of mail and the concluding chapters of *Banner by the Wayside*. Although Becker had told him not to worry about the end of the novel, he told her work was the best antidote to grief. The letters and telegrams offered a bigger challenge.

His friend William DeWitt suggested that they go fishing in Canada, and the author readily accepted the opportunity to get away on 20 September. Having set himself a deadline, by 15 September he had written 150 notes. By 18 September the total was 250 and the next day more than 300. While he wrote his notes, his long-time friend Stewart Edward White died from cancer. But all was not darkness. Auburn friends in honor of Jane organized a memorial fund for the Penn School at Beaufort. Preston and Mae Huff's daughter, Jonnie Mae, had graduated from the school in May.

After his return from Canada, he received word that his daughter Katherine had remarried on 30 September. Divorced from Milton Buckley in the 1930s, she had remained on the West Coast where she wed navy captain Cecil C. Adell, chief of staff to the commander of Naval Experimental Operations at Norfolk, Virginia. Telling his daughter that her marriage was the best news he had received in a long time, Adams prepared for Becker's visit to do the final *Banner by the Wayside* editing. He suggested to Baumgarten that she come to referee, but she replied she could not and warned she would probably side with Becker four of five times anyway. Becker visited in October, and afterward he admitted she had done a good job on his story. He enclosed a dedication that said simply "In Memoriam" and within one week sent the revised manuscript.[13]

His financial woes had been lessened by the ending of expenses at the hospital that had cost him more than twenty-five hundred dollars from 4 July through September. Under terms of her will Adams was to receive life use of the dividend income from more than six thousand dollars worth of stocks, and her estate also showed holdings of forty-five hundred dollars in government savings bonds bought in 1942. He also planned to sell the farm when the lease ran out the following spring.

His mood received a boost in October when the American Antiquarian Society elected him to membership upon recommendation of its director, Brigham. This unexpected honor was accepted by Adams, who, despite his success with regional history, was planning a novel on modern Washington.[14] During the summer the Senate War Investigating Committee had begun looking at profiteering by munitions makers but had broadened the topic to the practices of those with government contracts. Stories about influence peddling, illegal loans, and price gouging reawakened Adams's muckraking spirit. A mellower Adams decided, however, to tell his story of greed and power not with the indignation of exposure reporting but with the humor of satire.

He left Wide Waters after Election Day and headed for New York. One of his targets was Cerf, whose new offices were so luxurious that Adams called them Palazzio Randome. There he outlined for Cerf, Becker, and Linscott the plot of the Washington novel. He also received the good news that *Banner by the Wayside* had been selected by the Dollar Book Club for June, but the news about the magazines was not good. He had said he did not think the novel could be sold for a serial, but Brandt had sent it to the *Saturday Evening Post* and the *Ladies Home Journal,* with negative results. Earlier his agent had shelved the mystery symposium idea after two detective magazines turned it down.

Adams was more successful with a short essay on the Roman playwright Terence's statement, "I am a man; nothing that concerns mankind is alien to me," that Brandt sold to *This Week* for its "Words to Live By" series. Noting the adage was "touched with fire," Adams wrote: "Never before has the message of solidarity been so gravely needed. We are living at a time when creeds and ideologies vary and clash. But the gospel of human sympathy is universal and eternal." The piece was reprinted the next year in the first *Words to Live By* anthology under the title "The Brotherhood of Man."

Less immediate results came from an article Adams wrote while his wife was dying. When former Auburnian Earl Cohen in 1943 had written *Harriet Tubman* under the pen name of Earl Conrad, the author had acknowledged Adams's help in gathering material on the conductor of the Underground Railroad. Lewis Gannett of the New York *Herald Tribune* reviewed the Conrad book, and Adams wrote a three-paragraph reminiscence on Tubman that Gannett used. In August 1945 Adams expanded the Tubman sketch, suggesting to Brandt it be a "Most Unforgettable Character I Have Met" in the *Reader's Digest.* Brandt liked the story but returned it with "they were afraid of it. They haven't yet got themselves to do a negro as an Unforgettable Character." More than one year later the *New Yorker* published "A Slave in the Family," which the Auburn newspaper called a deft and touching portrait.[15]

While Adams was in New York, Laurette Taylor was gravely ill with a throat ailment that was sapping her strength. On 7 December she died at sixty-two. Adams, who had been friends with the actress during the good and bad times, later would write an assessment that showed a remarkable similarity to his own philosophy: "She had a double standard of morality. Her friends might do as they pleased. She never sat in judgment on them. Their behavior was their own business. For herself it was different. She could be startling free of speech. But her conduct was circumspect to the verge of being puritanical."[16]

As he went south, he stopped at Norfolk where he visited with his daughter Katherine Adell and her new husband. In Beaufort he began the Washington novel. He was encouraged by Cerf, who said he had read his regional novel and "Long may the Adams banner wave by the Random House wayside!" On 11 January Adams told Cerf he was on the second chapter of his new novel and that it was going to be such a stinker that it might be picked up by

Books for Brothels Club. The punster Cerf shot back: "If it is a bawdy as you say it is, maybe we can print it uniform with The Brothels Karamazov and sell the two books as a boxed set."[17]

Adams quickly settled into his routine of writing in the mornings, playing golf in the afternoons, going to cocktail parties, and playing bridge in the evenings. It was not all pleasure. His oldest friend, Weaver, had a heart attack, and Adams visited him daily in the hospital. Word from California was that Marian Richardson was dying of cancer. Nonetheless, he kept at work. By the end of January he had done fifteen thousand words on his novel and by 7 February was at twenty-five thousand. He set a goal of a dozen chapters by March when he went to New York so Becker could read it before her two-month vacation in Europe.

Becker, meanwhile, was working with Random House's Allan Ullman, who had replaced Frances Merriam, on publicity for *Banner by the Wayside*. A suggestion that he go on a barnstorming tour upstate was rejected by Adams, but he did agree to autograph copies after its 10 March publication. He remained firm on a pledge the previous year to make no more speeches. Coming to New York, Adams did a McBride radio interview and was pleased by the early reports that showed the novel was selling well.

The reviews praised the novel that told the story of tomboy Endurance "Durie" Andrews, a foundling educated by a bookseller, and Jans Quintard, expelled from Harvard College, who both joined the Thalia Dramatic Company, touring the Erie Canal. Their adventures culminated in a battle against a cholera epidemic. Edmonds argued that he would not swap the book "for a basket-full of our modern, hard-boiled, realistic, poetic-dramatic, or psychological masterpieces; for it would seem that S.H.A. has clung onto a cussed, cantankerous idea that one ought to get entertainment and fun out of a book."[18]

*Banner by the Wayside* sold 17,000 copies by late March, and Cerf told Baumgarten "the way fiction is selling this Spring, I think that is good." The optimism faded as the book remained stuck on the figure despite heavy Random House advertising. In its final accounting the novel sold slightly more than the 17,000 regular copies but had almost 190,000 book club sales for total Adams royalties of more than thirty thousand dollars.[19]

Back in Beaufort he was receiving recognition as an authority on upstate New York lore. The publishers of Glyndon G. Van Deusen's *Thurlow Weed: Wizard of the Lobby* asked Adams for comment, and he praised the book about the political mentor of Secretary of State William H. Seward of Auburn. Metcalf remembered he had urged Adams to write a book on Seward, but he had been reluctant to tackle an Auburnian. Metcalf had joined the *Citizen-Advertiser* as editorial writer, but his interest in Republican politics prompted the Democratic Osbornes to make him a columnist and to hire August Heckscher as an editorial writer. Both men became part of an informal circle of literary protégés of Adams.

The circle included writers such as Metcalf, Heckscher, and Kennedy, who Messenger reported "is plugging away at her typewriter, determined to prove to herself and to Sam Adams that she has a dramatic sense." Messenger said Adams had read one piece and told Kennedy, "At last you have learned how to tell a story." He also remained interested in columnist Clune, who did a book of Rochester sketches in *Main Street Beat* later in the year. Another author he encouraged was Conrad, whose *Jim Crow America* he found disturbing reading.[20]

His concern for his writer friends took many forms. To some, such as Lydia Mead Engelbert, he offered personal counsel, urging her to write a book on her experiences in running a factory in New York City. She published *Maid to Order* in 1940 and followed it with another humorous book, *Little Oscar's First Raid*, in 1942. He was also supportive of the writing of a relative, Harriet McD. Daniels, who at seventy decided to write historical fiction. Adams linked her up with Baumgarten, who helped her publish *Nine Mile Swamp* in 1941 and *Muller Hill* in 1943. Baumgarten reported in June 1947 that the Clinton resident had finished a new draft of another novel, pleasing Adams.[21]

He was always ready to offer suggestions to other writers he did not know well. When he read *Lost Men of American History* in which he was included in chapters on muckraking and Harding, Adams wrote Stewart Hall Holbrook offering minor corrections on the book, which he called delightful, and ending with his customary invitation to visit Wide Waters.

While Adams often offered criticism, he also was able to take it. When Brigham wrote him a laudatory letter concerning *Banner by the Wayside* but correcting a misspelling of the Maelzell collection at the American Antiquarian Society, Adams replied that sort of thing was exasperating. Brigham also asked about a reference in his book to a brochure, and he readily admitted that he had created it from his imagination in his fictional handling of the 1832 cholera epidemic. Adams urged him to check an article that he had written for *New York Folklore Quarterly*, which was not fiction.[22]

Adams also coupled the 1832 cholera epidemic with his grandfather in a story "My Grandfather and the Plague" that he sold to the *New Yorker*. The story had come from a suggestion by Ross, who had liked *Canal Town*, and had asked Adams, "You know as damn much about that country as you pretend to?" After he said that he did, Ross suggested some reminiscences of his childhood days, and Adams introduced the first of his grandfather stories.[23]

By early April 1947 Adams had written fifty thousand words of his Washington novel and faced major revisions. His work was challenged by a series of other offers. He rejected a suggestion in January for a book on the Finger Lakes. In February a friend had written of having dinner with Auburn native John Foster Dulles, and the talk had been about the scandals of the United Nations Relief and Rehabilitation Administration. Although Lithgow Osborne had been deputy director of the agency, Adams wrote Brandt that it sounded tempting. Brandt replied sharply to the aging muckraker, "The last thing that we want to have you do is get mixed up with the UNRRA's scandal."[24]

19. Samuel Hopkins Adams reading in his bed at Wide Waters. The picture on the wall behind him is of his daughter Katherine. Samuel Hopkins Adams Collection. Courtesy of Syracuse University Library.

Adams came north in early May. In New York he contacted Taylor, who had earlier in the year been pushing Adams to do a biography on Mencken, the Broun biography having vanished into the air. Taylor and Albert Erskine, however, left Reynal & Hitchcock in an editorial shuffle after the death of Hitchcock the previous year. They joined Random House in what Cerf called "putting all of Adams's eggs in one basket." Reynal & Hitchcock was still interested in Broun and Mencken, but Adams was noncommittal.[25]

At Wide Waters, he found life without Jane far from dull. Betty Steele came from California for a week of nightly parties. Then he went to Washington to do research on his novel with an assist from Elmer Davis and to New York for a radio show. He returned for Hamilton College's commencement, but his Fourth of July party fell apart when Mary Margaret McBride got the flu, author Vincent Sheean went on a bender, the young New York group was otherwise occupied, and Cerf's wife, actress and writer Phyllis Fraser, whom he had married in 1940, vetoed flying up because of recent crashes.

Mutual respect warmed the relationship between Cerf and Adams. Although the author grumbled about the publisher's percentage of secondary rights, he enjoyed the banter with Cerf. When the publisher asked Adams's permission to use him "as a token of affection" in an anecdote for his 5 July "Trade Winds" column in the *Saturday Review of Literature*, Adams agreed. Placed in a nudist colony, Adams reportedly said when asked how he knew it was the butler who greeted him: "Well, it certainly wasn't the maid." He assured Betty Steele the story was 100 percent imaginary and explained that Cerf was his friend as well as his publisher so it did not matter. When the *Reader's Digest* picked up the item, Adams asked Cerf for a cut of the hundred dollars he had collected, offering to settle for a drink.[26]

Any disappointment with the collapse of the Fourth of July party was assuaged by a two-week visit by Hester Adams and Cecil and Katherine Adell with her daughter, Elizabeth Buckley, and Cecil's adopted son, Randall Adell. He told Baumgarten the two sisters had not seen one another for more than twenty years. The death of Jane and the Adells' relocation in the East opened the Wide Waters door to his two daughters, with whom he had corresponded monthly, enclosing a check for each. While they were there, he began a massive rewrite of his Washington novel, called *Plunder*.

When Taylor had visited in late June, the two men discussed an Adams idea for a History of American Morals. Adams said he was too old to write it but would provide an outline for an honorarium. Taylor took the proposal to Cerf, who liked it and whose partner, Donald Klopfer, confirmed Adams's suggestion for an author, Stewart Holbrook. When Holbrook accepted his invitation in August, Adams developed a rapport with the younger man and interested him in the morals book. Later he would bow out because of other commitments, and Adams and Random House then chose Dixon Wecter.

Adams remained focused on *Plunder*. He finished the second draft in August and shipped it to Becker. Eager to get the book done before he left for a vacation in California in November to see the Steele family, he awaited her suggestions. Written more than one decade before Dwight David Eisenhower's warning about the military-industrial complex, the story of crooked Martin Strabo, a wheeler-dealer in Washington who believed money could buy anyone, had a theme of government by contract in which Strabo practically ran the government. The involved plot, set in the early 1950s, featured a fraud, Protectowear, that Strabo marketed as being able to withstand atomic radiation; the Committee on Dangerous Tendencies modeled on the House Un-American Activities Committee; a loose love story involving Strabo's mistress-secretary; and an attempt to fix the Army–Navy football game that was Strabo's eventual undoing. Becker, who said the book was in the muckraker class but not a serious exposé, had major problems with muddled themes, unmotivated characters, and length.

After meeting with Becker, Adams said he had enough rewriting to do to keep him busy until 1949 after the presidential election. In New York Becker reported: "It is tough, sometimes vulgar and cheap, occasionally sardonic and witty (I hope we've eliminated the slapstick from the humor), always readable in Sam's gay, sprightly style. I definitely think it will have popular appeal." She sent him a bottle of Burgundy with the advice not to rush the rewrite, but he was at work.[27]

Adams kept at *Plunder* throughout October. His planned vacation on the West Coast included taking *Plunder* with him and working eight hours a day the first week. By mid-November done with the revision, he began touring. He made a regular visit with Auburn geologist Levi and Dorothy Noble in Death Valley, where he was enchanted by a trip to the peaks of the Panamint Range, and saw the Harwood Whites in Santa Barbara, where he discussed with Stewart Edward White's brother a proposed biography that Adams said would have some amazing material. White later abandoned the project when he found too much disagreeable material about his brother.

Adams's flight home took him twenty hours, which he called hellish. Hellish also was a new problem for *Plunder*. Random House was concerned that one chapter was like the play *Born Yesterday*. Adams admitted it was but said it was not Garson Kanin but Euclid who devised the triangle. Despite several similarities of plot as well as language that the publishers' attorney urged be deleted, Random pushed ahead because of the then-current procurement scandals involving General Bennett Meyers.

Adams stayed in Cayuga County long enough to write Brigham that he was eager to get at his next novel, which he had decided would again be set in up-state New York. He asked the director for information on factory conditions in central New York around 1835. He spent most of December in New Hope where he was telephoned by Cerf, who had read *Plunder* and objected to Strabo's use of "Ah tit." In an internal memorandum Cerf suggested "Ah foo" or "Ah poop," along with criticisms about the editing and the need to fix the football chapter. Adams finally offered "Ah, poopity" and left for Beaufort.[28]

*Plunder* followed him to South Carolina. Saxe Commins, who had taken over the final edit from an ailing Becker, reported having trouble with the foot-ball chapter that he said "will be disbelieved by football fans." Indignant be-cause Cerf had promised no further changes without his okay and that his football credentials had been questioned, Adams demanded the chapter be re-turned. Telling Baumgarten the Random House lawyer had changed the text because he disliked the phraseology, he vowed to stop publication of the book if there were any more interference.[29]

He was equally angry in his letter to Commins. Assuring Adams that no changes would be made without his permission, Commins replied: "Noth-ing could be further from my mind than to do violence to your work. You ought to know that, Sam. I have too much respect for you as a person, and for your long and honorable devotion to literature." Adams replied that he was not being personal. On one thing they agreed—Baumgarten. "In my book," Com-mins wrote, "she is not only the best agent in the business, but one of the most intelligent, sympathetic and dependable human beings I know." Adams agreed, saying she was tops in his book, both as an agent and as a person.[30] To-gether with Baumgarten and Becker, Adams and Commins worked on the proofs for the remainder of January, arguing over footnotes that concerned a lawyer because of libel. When *Plunder* was done, Adams turned to his factory novel called *Sunrise to Sunset*, a title based on the working hours of the early mills.

An unexpected problem for Adams was money; this time it was not too lit-tle, but too much. In early 1947 Baumgarten had set up a monthly payment schedule for the Danish royalties. He received about six hundred dollars a month, the closest thing to a salary he had had in more than thirty years. In late 1947 he received almost five thousand dollars from the regular edition of *Banner by the Wayside* but was stunned when Peoples Book Club in January 1948 sent more than twenty-one thousand dollars on 187,428 copies. It was seven thousand dollars more than the contract called for and put him into the 59 percent federal income tax bracket. Added was a British payment of seventeen hundred dollars on Woollcott after England agreed to give refunds to American authors on taxes. Reminding Baumgarten one could avoid but not evade the income tax, he said he did not want any more money in 1948 and asked his *Plunder* advance be put off. In March 1948 his main pleasure from Baumgarten's report that Penguin Books had bought Woollcott for a reprint edition was that the income would not come in until 1949.

Other news from the North was bad. He was shocked by the death of Percy Waxman on 15 January. Then on 24 February Irwin died of a cerebral occlusion. Adams's close friend had been working on a history of the Union League Club, and he offered to finish it when in New York for the *Plunder* launch. Although he said he was doing it as a tribute to Irwin and because Inez Irwin needed the money, Brandt indicated he should not become involved, advice that the author took. Another friend was on his mind. In late January he heard from Daniels that she had abandoned her novel after Knopf had rejected it. Adams promised to look at it in New York.

New York had allure for a young friend. Heckscher left his Auburn position to join the New York *Herald Tribune* as an editorial writer. He kept his summer home in Auburn and recalled, "He had been against my leaving the newspaper in Auburn, fearing I would be caught in the trap of convention in the big city, but once I had gone, he was avid for the latest literary gossip, and at the same time a sensitive and caring friend."[31]

While Adams was struggling with his new novel, *Sunrise to Sunset*, he complained about his unproductive winter. One suggestion he rejected. When Holbrook mentioned a book on himself, he replied that so many other things and people interested him more. He went to New York in late March for the release of *Plunder*, which had been delayed from 5 March to 12 April. Early advertising for the original date had produced sales of seven thousand by late February, which Baumgarten called "simply wonderful." By 8 March Becker reported the sales were around ten thousand, adding, "Isn't that terrific?" She said the reviews had excellent quotable lines as sales neared fourteen thousand, but critics had limited enthusiasm.[32]

While Adams was in New York, he met with Brandt, who queried *Collier's* about an article on the Pure Food and Drug Act. The magazine was not interested. Attempts to sell a slave hunting article, a war leave story, and the Harding chapter to a magazine before its publication in the anthology *Aspirin Age* were unsuccessful. The inability to sell his stories may have prompted him to accept a commissioned job. When he returned to New York in May on his way to Wide Waters, he told Baumgarten he had agreed to do a history of the Auburn Savings Bank, of which his friend William H. Seward, grandson of the secretary of state, was president. The bank agreed to pay two thousand dollars for the booklet to commemorate its one hundredth anniversary.

Life on Owasco Lake was slow paced as he balanced work on his new novel with the bank history. On 31 July he was recognized by the New York State Historical Association with an honorary fellowship for his regional novels. The main speaker in Syracuse was historian Allan Nevins, and the next day Adams wrote Baumgarten that all he had to do was rise and smirk. He put aside *Sunrise to Sunset* in mid-August because he was getting stale on it, but in September he resumed. In the meantime he was finishing the bank history when, on 11 September, his neighbor Emerson died from pneumonia. For the Auburn newspaper Adams wrote, "I can think of Fred Emerson only as a friend whom I loved."[33]

Still high on Adams's agenda was his proposal for the history of American morals book, for which he had put together a preliminary outline. With Taylor acting as an intermediary, he tried to arrange terms with Cerf, but Random House was reluctant to close the deal until Wecter signed a contract. The arrangement was further complicated by Taylor leaving Random House in September to take a motion picture producer position in California. When Adams headed for a return visit to the West Coast, a meeting with Wecter was a priority.

He left in early November after voting for Tom Dewey over Harry S Truman and against his Republican representative, John Taber. Earlier in the year Adams had expressed concern that the Democratic Truman was pushing toward war. Taber, who had helped him with information for *Plunder*, was opposed in an Adams letter to the editor that said honesty and respectable intentions were no longer enough reason for continued support for the Republican legislator who had earned the sobriquet of "Meat-Ax John" on the House Appropriations Committee. His choices lost, and Taber kept winning until retiring in 1963 after forty years.

In California he visited the Steeles at Balboa Island. Although they had urged him to stay with them the previous year, he said his crippled condition made hotel stays more comfortable because he needed some valeting. Using fellow Hamiltonian Stephen Royce's Huntington Hotel as a base, Adams met with Wecter, who was ready to sign the morals book contract. Thinking ahead to another new book, he wrote Cerf asking if he could get him access to the *Police Gazette* files from the 1890s.[34]

While Adams was in the West, he was informed by Brandt that *Good Housekeeping* wanted him, for $750, to write a short piece on the decline in American workers' pride in their products. He wrote the article in early December after he returned east. He then spent a few days with the Dutton Nobles in Auburn before he went south. Noble was his lawyer, and the purpose of the visit was to sell 55.45 acres of the farm for sixty-five hundred dollars to the Girl Scouts for a new campsite.

In Beaufort he settled into a rented ranch house next to the Elliotts at Hundred Pines and was eager for a response by Baumgarten to part 1 of *Sunrise to Sunset*. Saying she knew he did not want editorial comments until she saw more of the book, she returned the manuscript with "I had fun reading it." As Adams went to work, Cerf wrote, "We are all glad to hear the famous Adams nose is back at the grindstone." Promising physical, spiritual, or financial help, Cerf said he hoped "you will keep it there so tightly that we'll be able to see the sparks all the way up here in New York."[35]

Weaver was also in Beaufort, but deteriorating health put him in the hospital for half the winter. "I took him driving whenever he would go, but most of the time he was not even up to that effort," Adams told Ibbotson. The wretched and unhappy Weaver went back north early. In April Weaver's sister wired Adams that he had died. He wrote her how much he would miss his oldest close friend. As when Jane died, his concern was with the living. Noting the world was in a state of desperate want, he said he was sending a contribution to Cooperative for American Relief Everywhere (CARE) in Weaver's memory. Two months later he remained concerned about the war's aftermath, joining 250 Americans, including Cerf and former Auburnian Allen W. Dulles, in asking Congress to pass the McGrath-Neery Bill to allow displaced persons into the country.[36]

As he worked on *Sunrise to Sunset* in Beaufort, the magazine market reopened. He sold an article to *True* in February for $750. When he was within hailing distance of the end of his novel the next month, he was contacted by

*Holiday* to do an article on the Finger Lakes. Brandt, miffed at being bypassed but always willing to stroke editors, made arrangements with associate editor Harry Sions, who promised to help with the research and asked for an outline.

The potential new relationship with *Holiday* had come, Adams believed, from a recommendation by the award-winning illustrator Letterio Calapai, the artist whom Jane had let use the farmhouse in 1940. When Adams met Sions in New York in May, they agreed on the Finger Lakes article, but a possible article about the commercial crabbing industry in South Carolina was turned down. Brandt was quick to submit it to Ben Hibbs at the *Saturday Evening Post*, and Hibbs responded favorably.[37] Adams also pressed Brandt to sell "The Criminal and the Genius" to *This Week*. The editors were dubious about the account of two men who suffered brain injuries after which one, Gaston Means, became a crook and the other, Clayton Halsey Sharpe, a brilliant physicist, and asked for changes.

Brandt also introduced Adams to William D. Kennedy, publications director for the *Ford Times*. They agreed that Adams would write a sketch of Beaufort for the "Favorite Towns" series. With the magazine projects in hand he went to Wide Waters where he finished his rewrite of part 1 of *Sunrise to Sunset* and shipped it off to Becker. Calling it "a gay and romantic novel with solid historical background," she said: "I think this book is no better and, I hope, no worse than" *Canal Town* and *Banner by the Wayside*. She asked if they would publish the book about the development of cotton mills and factories, the exploitation of female labor, and the establishment of humane labor laws. On her analysis Cerf scrawled: "Sure thing. Do we negotiate a contract now or wait? And should I write to SHA?"[38]

Cerf did write: "The Beauteous Belle Becker just tripped downstairs (and when the Beauteous Belle trips downstairs you can hear her for a considerable distance) to give me the welcome news that the new Samuel Hopkins Adams historical romance is in active preparation. I am delighted." Adams replied that he was writing the final chapter before taking some time off.[39]

He then went to Ithaca for the convention of Alpha Delta Phi. There he was impressed by the writing of a young man he urged Brandt to contact, reminding his agent that he had brought his attention to another writer, Dorothy Sayers. The effort was unsuccessful. After the Fourth of July, he went to Cooperstown for a seminar on American culture sponsored by the New York State Historical Association. He had been approached about doing the seminar by its director, Louis Jones, through Cornell Professor Harold Thompson, head of the New York State Folklore Society. Thompson, author of a 1937 sketch of Adams for the *Hamilton Alumni Review*, was also a participant in the seminar, as were Carmer, Edmonds, and Constance Noyes Robertson, who had written *Fire Bell in the Night*. Jones said that Adams was especially drawn to the attractive Robertson, who lived with her husband, Miles, near Utica.[40]

Adams's role at the seminar was relaxed. He had planned to spend a day or two but remained all ten days as he went to classes in the morning and spoke when he wanted to, worked on his writing in the afternoon, took swims in the pool, and partied. Back at Wide Waters, the houses were packed on weekends with guests totaling eight, fourteen, and, on Labor Day Adams said he did not dare count them. The expenses of the heavy entertaining concerned Mildred Harlan, who went to Adams. He said to cut back and then invited more guests, her son George recalled. Adams explained that having Wide Waters only made sense if one's friends were around to enjoy it.[41]

In his work he concentrated on magazine pieces. He wrote and rewrote the crabbing article for the *Saturday Evening Post*, did early research on the Finger Lakes article for *Holiday*, wrote a *New Yorker* piece about his grandfather Adams's dread of trains, and revised the Means article. On 26 August, two days after Adams sold the *New Yorker* piece for $550, Brandt wired that he had sold the commercial crabbing article to the *Post* for $1,500 and the Means piece to *This Week* for $500. "What a day," Brandt concluded. Adams praised Brandt for the handsome price for the crab article but groused he was getting too rich for income tax purposes. Brandt replied: "Don't worry about getting too rich. This year's riches are next year's chicken feed."[42]

His bank history was published without fanfare during the summer. Becker came on Labor Day to work on *Sunrise to Sunset*. She proposed the strengthening of characters and making some cuts, suggestions he adopted. He told Brandt he hoped to have the manuscript done by 1 October when he would tackle the Finger Lakes article for *Holiday*. Working with Kay Messenger as his typist, who he said was good and had found many minor errors, Adams missed his deadline by about one month.

Although he hoped to get the Finger Lakes article done before he left, he was still working on it as he headed south after Thanksgiving. During his stop in New York he met with attorney Samuel D. Cohen of MGM concerning the filing of a lawsuit against the studio over *The Harvey Girls*. On 19 December Adams obliquely reported to Brandt that the MGM hearing was over and there were no hard feelings and few hard questions. With that no further mention was made of Rankin. Adams also saw Sions on the *Holiday* story and met with Brandt, who had read his *New Yorker* piece about his grandfather Adams and early railroads that he had called, "a gem, my friend, a gem!" Adams said that he was "glad you liked the skit about Grandpa. The *New Yorker* has just accepted another and appears to want more."[43]

The story that the *New Yorker* accepted was "Grandfather and the Montague Collar" about a Troy woman's invention of a detachable collar, adapted from a chapter of *Sunrise to Sunset*. The story's success was not matched by the novel. In mid-November Becker reported Linscott, trying to get the Fiction Book Club interested, said the editor thought the book was too long by about 50,000 words. Becker said cuts from the 168,000 words might produce a better book. "Please, Sam dear, after your first explosion, will you sit down and consider all the recommendations carefully? . . . I look forward eagerly and hopefully to a non-combative mood and response from you, darling."[44]

He moaned about cutting fifty thousand words and noted that several times he had made book club changes to no avail. Cerf jumped in: "I am sorry to hear your new opus is undergoing the usual prenatal pains. . . . I hope you are not feeling too badly about the circumcision work; everyone says it is one of your best stories in years." Adams and Becker worked on the book, cutting twenty-five thousand words. Complimenting Becker on her job of editing, Adams said it was a real achievement. But, true to his predictions, the Fiction Book Club turned it down.[45]

While Adams was in New York, Brandt confirmed a deal with *Ford Times* for an article on Beaufort, but the ever-alert and honest Adams reported that he had seen an article in the magazine on the town and offered to do an article on the amateur sport of crabbing instead. The red-faced editor and Brandt agreed to the substitution, and Adams whipped it off during his trip south.

At Beaufort he faced a mound of Christmas mail and shipped the Finger Lakes article to Sions just before Christmas. Then he found a July letter from Kennedy at *Ford Times* saying the earlier story on Beaufort was brief and they wanted a longer piece. Adams also began an article on a single-scull boat race scandal, suggested a *Holiday* article on the Inland Waterway, and plotted a grandfather story for the *New Yorker*.

Despite his heavy magazine agenda and averaging a party a day in Beaufort, Adams was mulling his next novel using *Police Gazette* material from the 1890s and puzzling over how to handle another book that Cerf had persuaded him to write.

# 18

# JUVENILIST
## 1950–1953

A T SEVENTY-EIGHT Adams reached the midpoint of the twentieth century doing what Carl Brandt described as "all the things that certainly a man in his late fifties would consider to a degree pretty heavy going."[1] His magazine work in January supported Brandt's view.

The *Saturday Evening Post* ran his commercial crabbing article with color photographs that Adams praised. The article's local appeal was shown by his election as president emeritus of the Beaufort Board of Trade *in perpetuum* and by the owner of a crabbing company ordering fifty thousand reprints.

*Holiday* wanted only minor changes in his Finger Lakes article with more anecdotes. Editor Sions called his article on the single-scull scandal a "beautifully done story." He was beginning a third article on the Inland Waterway that Brandt urged not be a travel piece.[2] The *Ford Times* bought the recreational crabbing article and awaited the article on Beaufort for which Adams said he wanted new material.

*Nation's Business* was waiting for an article by Adams on how he coped with infirmity. Long urged by Brandt to write about his lameness, he agreed, saying one should make the best of infirmities without evasion or embarrassment. He said the difficulty in writing the article was to avoid being egotistic and self-pitying and asked Brandt to eliminate any maudlin references.

The *New Yorker* pleased Adams with its response to "Grandfather and the Montague Collar." He reported to Brandt a quote from Ross: "I've just read the proof on the story of your grandfather's collar, and I think it's a dandy, a story to be proud of." The magazine's continuing interest in Adams led to a special writer's contract that carried a retainer fee of one hundred dollars and

20. Samuel Hopkins Adams portrait in 1950. Courtesy of Hamilton College.

an increase in rate of 25 percent in return for first refusal on any story within the range of the magazine. The contract went into force in October 1949, but Adams delayed telling Brandt until January, assuring him the range was limited. Brandt said the one disadvantage might be the reaction of other magazines.[3]

Besides magazine work, *Sunrise to Sunset* was almost done. When Becker told him the Fiction Book Club had turned down the book, she fretted: "I suppose now you can send me a thousand I-told-you-so's." He passed off the book club action and added he had so much magazine work he might never write another book.[4] Cerf disagreed.

While vacationing in Provincetown, Phyllis Cerf had been unable to find "an exciting book on the Pilgrims" and had urged Cerf to publish books for children that would expand on what they were learning in school. After reading children's books to his two young sons, Cerf developed the idea of a series of Landmark books. Each would deal with a great episode in American history targeted at the nine-to-sixteen age group. He also decided to use known authors rather than those who specialized in children's books. From Cerf's list of ten potential titles, *The Pony Express* was accepted in late 1949 by Adams, who stopped at the Library of Congress for research materials on his way south in December. In the contract Adams asked for and received an outright twenty-five hundred dollars rather than a per copy royalty.

After Brandt read Adams's article on his infirmity, he said he was so excited that he wanted "to do something radical about it." Bypassing *Nation's Business*, he tried the *Reader's Digest*, whose Wallace declined because of its similarity to other committed stories. So Brandt sent it to Stuart Rose at the *Saturday Evening Post*, which bought it for nine hundred dollars.[5]

Adams was surprised by the sale to the *Post* and congratulated Brandt. His cheering was tempered. Telling Becker he never liked writing about himself, he confided that he agreed to do the article for *Nation's Business* because nobody he knew read the magazine. He added that everyone he knew read the *Post*.[6]

The juvenile book remained a concern. He wrote Ibbotson about *The Pony Express*, asking for suggestions on material, and also told his friend who had lost a leg that he had contacted a Hollywood firm to send him information about his aluminum crutch. Katherine Adell explained that her father often used a wooden crutch around the house and his metal crutch, which was doubly adjustable, when he went out—unless, he told Martha Elliott, the event was not "worth the party crutch."[7]

And he did go out. He wrote Brandt in February there was danger that he might die of an overdose of parties. He preferred to entertain over dinner, and although he said he did not care for cocktail parties, he went. Between being guest and host, he told Brandt he had only one vacant evening that week. Hillman wrote, "For Adams, a day that didn't include parties was a day lost. He was as generous a guest as he was a host. He was a fine, salty conversationalist with a sharp sense of social responsibility. He frequently tried to appear crotchety,

21. Samuel Hopkins Adams in the 1950s working with his pen and bottle of ink in this photograph by Phyllis Cerf. Courtesy of Hamilton College.

irascible, and crusty, but the pose fooled nobody. Nobody could be more courtly with pretty women—and Adams was always surrounded by them."[8]

Later interviewer Jessica Wellner would observe that Adams, who ended his letters to Cerf with a reference to his pretty Phyllis, had the wonderful knack "of making a pretty woman feel prettier and a plain one attractive." Noting that late in his life Adams could no longer rise to greet a woman, she commented "his manner has such grace that he gives the effect of doing so." The mutual attraction of Adams and Phyllis Cerf was not unusual. Adams's attraction to pretty women was reciprocated. "I can count on the fingers of both hands the men I knew who liked women and felt comfortable with them. He was one," Frank Taylor's former wife Nan Abell recalled, "and women felt comfortable with him and knew he was not out to make them."[9]

Peggy French recalled: "Sam was very complex and had a quality that set him apart whether it was partying, conversation or his relationships with women. He was like a prism in that one could look at different sides and see different things." She and Abell remembered a formality at Wide Waters, a code that did not allow "hanky-panky" or overdrinking. "He was a Puritan with no apologies," French said.[10]

In February he went by private plane to visit the Adells at Key West where he finished the proofs on *Sunrise to Sunset.* On the return trip the plane developed engine trouble and had to set down at an abandoned airstrip. Adams told new Hamilton College President Robert Ward McEwen the plane landed in a series of hops and he wondered whether he was getting too old for such escapades.[11]

At Beaufort he turned to his history of the Pony Express. Efforts to get information from Columbia Pictures, which had done *Cody of the Pony Express,* proved fruitless, but Brigham came to the rescue. The director sent material in March. Within one month Adams, beating his personal deadline of 1 May and Random House's 1 July, sent Brandt the book that he said might also be good for a serial sale.

Although Brandt was dubious about a magazine serial, Adams was in the catbird seat with improved health, visits from friends such as former *Collier's* editor Harford Powell, and a steady cash flow. When Becker sent him a "love and kisses" letter asking him to be her valentine but with an admonition to "attend to business," he told her he had sold four thousand dollars in articles to the magazines and had orders for some three thousand dollars more. Then the *Saturday Evening Post* threw him a curve.

22. Samuel Hopkins Adams at Hamilton College with President Robert McEwen, standing, and college Secretary Wallace Johnson. Courtesy of Hamilton College.

The magazine had printed in April its 27 May issue containing his article on infirmities with a new title. Although the headlines usually went with the proofs, this time it was written afterward and read, "Old Age — I Spit in Its Eye!" When a mortified Adams learned of the wording, he contacted Brandt, who on 21 April called Stuart Rose to complain, only to find the headline was not only on the story but on the cover. He reported to Adams it was too late to do anything.

Adams shot off a letter to the *Post*'s Ben Hibbs, saying he recognized Hibbs's right to change the title but not his right to use the first person to commit him to a cheap, vulgar, and blatant statement. The more he thought about it, the angrier he got, losing sleep and making the ultimate move of forbidding Brandt to sell any of his work to the magazine again. After Adams said he did not know when he had felt so hurt and shamed, the agent went to Philadelphia to see Hibbs, but to no avail. Later, as the magazine was to come out, Adams threatened an injunction to stop its distribution, indicating the depth of his sense of humiliation.[12]

The crafty Brandt sought to soothe the anger by suggesting something he knew would please Adams. He offered to visit Wide Waters that summer, and Adams quickly rose to the bait, sending his summer schedule. Brandt also offered Adams unexpected good news, the sale of the serial rights to *The Pony Express* juvenile to *Blue Book* for six hundred dollars under the title "The Mail Goes Through." With *The Pony Express* done, Adams began to make plans for New York, where *Sunrise to Sunset* was scheduled for May release.

Just before he headed north, the Rochester Museum of Arts and Sciences gave nonresident fellowships to a woman and, in absentia, six men, including Adams for his "achievements as a writer of distinction and preserver of America's historical tradition." *Sunrise to Sunset* was published on 26 May, the day after being selected as an October alternate of the Dollar Book Club. The story centered on Troy and its cotton mills where young millworker Obedience "Becky" Webb married her boss, Gurdon Stockwell. The marriage, by which the mill owner attempted to atone for the near rape of the girl, was doomed by the girl's love of another and Stockwell's involvement with a pregnant girl who was seeking an abortion and fell off a cliff. Intermixed with the already complicated plot were revivalism, an attempted lynching, the standard canal brawl, and the murder of Stockwell that allowed the girl to marry the other man, the maker of the Montague detachable collar.[13]

Reviews were positive. For the *New York Times* Carmer praised the scholarship, saying: "Mr. Adams' researches in our past extend much further than the usual 'background reading' which most authors of historical fiction regard as sufficient for their purposes. Few scholars are as aware as he of the history of American word usages, or for that matter of the modes of thought that prevailed in the nation's early decades." Adams was pleased the book was reviewed by Carmer, who the year before had called Adams's review of his *Dark Trees in the Wind* a "humdinger." Saying he knew if Carmer did not like the book he would not have agreed to review it, Adams cheered the review.[14]

One critic got the attention of the FBI, which indexed a review from the *Daily Worker*. Robert Friedman praised Adams's view of the "savage exploitation and intolerable regimentation of the women" and the greed of the unfeeling mill owner. "Unfortunately, Mr. Adams has not taken his theme seriously," Friedman wrote.[15]

He did take promotion of his new novel seriously, having pledged to Becker he would do anything to boost the book. Although Ullman told him that autograph parties had little value, he went to a White Plains bookstore where Hester Adams was working. He then headed for another promotion. Cerf had arranged a trip to Elmira and then a weekend at Wide Waters where, he told Adams, "think of all the time you'll have to bawl me out to your heart's content!" After Elmira, they went to Owasco Lake, and Cerf said the parties "exhausted everybody but the seventy-nine-year-old author himself. When last seen, Sam, like Oliver Twist, was still hollering for more."[16]

In sending a thank-you gift of books for Adams's guest rooms, Cerf reported sales of *Sunrise to Sunset* were "off to a very good start indeed." On 18 June the novel began twelve weeks on the *Herald Tribune*'s "What America Is Reading," breaking into the top ten twice. The last in a trilogy of adult novels on the Erie Canal eventually sold more than fifteen thousand regular copies and, with a Bantam Books edition royalty, grossed seventeen thousand dollars.[17]

Although Random House had paid Adams one thousand dollars in January for the American morals book that Wecter was scheduled to write, he was stunned in late June to learn that Wecter had died from heart disease. Telling Baumgarten that he should return the money, Adams wrote Cerf to propose several possible authors. Cerf wrote him not to worry and then told Baumgarten: "I appreciate Sam's concern about the $1,000.00 advance he received (I think he's a very remarkable man!) but since we made the deal with him in good faith, I don't see why he should suffer because it went awry."[18]

Going awry also was his magazine work. The *Saturday Evening Post* article with a half-page photograph of him pulling on his sock using two pieces of long cord and a long-handled shoehorn brought him a blizzard of mail from distressed people. He finished the Waterways article for *Holiday*, but Sions reported he was considerably disappointed because it "lacks the old Adams gusto, warmth and sharpness." Brandt urged Adams to personalize the story and promised to help in early August. While at Wide Waters, Brandt wrote Sions that Adams would rewrite the article when in Beaufort. Adams was also concerned that *Holiday* had not run his boat race story, but Sions, who said the magazine "measures time not by the minutes or the hours, but by months and years," assured him that it would appear.[19]

*The Pony Express* was published in late October. The debut of the book, in which Adams admitted in the foreword that he was presenting in broad outline the character and atmosphere of the enterprise because of scanty, vague, and contradictory information, with nine other Landmark juveniles went unnoticed in his hometown newspaper. The *New York Times* and *Herald Tribune* reviewed the series as a unit.[20]

Committed to the concept, Cerf sought to enlist Adams for another juvenile history for a second ten-book series. After Cerf visited Hamilton College

23. Samuel Hopkins Adams with publisher Bennett Cerf at Hamilton College in 1950. Charles T. Beeching '52 looks on. Courtesy of Hamilton College.

for a speech on book publishing, Adams told Baumgarten that the advance sale on *The Pony Express* was twenty thousand and he was willing to do another. The topic for the next Landmark book was the Santa Fe Trail. Concerned it might parallel his work on the Pony Express, he agreed with the proviso that he could go to another topic if he chose. He also noted that the Santa Fe Trail would be difficult, but Cerf replied it would be an easy job: "You'll toss it off in a week or two."[21]

Adams again turned to Brigham for information on the Santa Fe Trail while thanking him for his help on *The Pony Express*. The author reported the series and his book seemed to be successes. He was right. To even Cerf's surprise the first series had taken off. And the best seller was *The Pony Express* for which Adams had negotiated that lump sum payment. Several years later Cleveland Amory, substituting for Cerf on his "Trade Winds" column, told the story. The initial twenty-five hundred dollars was equaled and then doubled in months. As Cerf saw what was happening, he asked Adams for the contract back. The publisher tore it up and instituted a royalty of ten cents per copy, producing a princely sum by mid-1954, when sales topped 110,000, and adding about two thousand dollars a year for the rest of Adams's life. Later Adams thanked Cerf for not holding him to the foolish contract.[22]

Before *The Pony Express* money came in, Adams was so strapped for cash that he canceled his annual fishing trip to Canada and told Katherine Adell he was not sure he could afford to come to Key West. He refused, however, to put off the annual battle of Hamilton against Union in mid-November that had special significance because it was the sixtieth anniversary of their first football confrontation.

Throughout the fall he planned for the football game reunion, assigning himself the task of collecting two members of the old team and agreeing to speak informally with students at the Alpha Delta Phi house. His talk, in which he urged writers to make reading a continuous habit as a background for color and character and to study Somerset Maugham for his storytelling and Earnest Hemingway for his story structure, was more successful than the football game. He and three colleagues from the first football team sat on the sidelines to view a Hamilton 26–19 loss.

After the game he went south. He sent Preston and Mae Huff ahead in one car and then drove himself south to the chagrin of his friends. He arrived in Beaufort about one week before Christmas and was shocked on 23 December when his close friend, Bill Elliott, suffered a stroke next door to his bungalow at Hundred Pines. At three o'clock in the afternoon the forty-four-year-old attorney died without regaining consciousness.

His spirits were lifted by an eightieth birthday party arranged in Beaufort. Eighty persons were invited for eighty minutes of cocktails and eighty minutes of choice wines and foods for a price of $8.80 per person. After he hosted a dinner the night before, he went to a luncheon given by the marine commandant at Parris Island where Adams was serenaded by the post band's "Happy Birthday." After the luncheon he attended a basketball game with Quantico, whose commanding officer was Frank Hart. He with his wife, Katherine, were particular friends. Since before World War II, Adams had considered the marines his brothers in arms, he later told Cerf.[23]

A highlight came from a series of telegrams, including those from the Brandts, the Cerfs, the John Foster Dulleses in Japan, Marquand, Peggy Wood, and movie stars. Brandt had requested possible comments by featured players in Adams's adaptations, and messages came from Lionel Barrymore, George Brent, Joan Crawford, Clark Gable, Judy Garland, and Errol Flynn, who described himself as a "not so Perfect Specimen." Claudette Colbert sent two. Adams thanked the assemblage "with overflowing heart" and then played the piano for an hour as his friends made requests. In a letter to Clune, Adams said the party "was great fun, but doesn't compensate for being 80. What could!"[24]

The partying went on for several days until he found himself in a Charleston hospital to have a bladder condition checked. Afterward the parade of visitors was constant as he worked with materials sent to him by Brigham for *The Santa Fe Trail*. He went to New York in early March but again had health problems that caused him to collapse at the home of a friend. He downplayed the incident, preferring to discuss his pleasure at being made a life member of the Dutch Treat Club. Back in Beaufort, his miseries continued as a car bumped him. Although shaken by the mishap, he kept writing.

The *New Yorker* market was steady. He sold four grandfather stories, and a story about a Cardiff Giant-like hoax at Taughannock Falls, near Ithaca, was bought but not used. One grandfather story that was not accepted by the *New Yorker* was the story of a visit by a feminist, and Adams suggested that Brandt sell the story to Mabel Souvaine at *Woman's Day*, who had been asking for one of the tales. He also did the story about his boyhood in the Finger Lakes, finishing it in January so he could devote February to *The Santa Fe Trail*. Adams sent the juvenile manuscript to Brandt in March after working on it six to eight hours a day. While Brandt was selling the serial rights of the new juvenile to *Blue Book*, Adams struggled with the Waterways piece for *Holiday*, wrapping it up in June.

Cerf had been unable to attend Adams's birthday party because he was in the West, including a stop with Holbrook, whose work Adams admired. One author for whom he had little regard was William Faulkner, winner of the 1949 Nobel Prize for Literature. To Holbrook, Adams said he had never considered Faulkner first rate because he gained his celebrity status more from his vices than his virtues. Cerf disagreed. In a February "Trade Winds" column, he reprinted his client Faulkner's "magnificent" Nobel acceptance speech. Faulkner said in part: "I feel that this award was not made to me as a man but to my life's work—a life's work in the agony and sweat of human spirit, not for glory and least of all for profit but to create out of the materials of the human spirit something which did not exist before." He urged young writers to bear the "same anguish and travail" he had suffered. Cerf sent Adams the column. Adams replied the speech was drivel and asked if writing were any more agonizing than digging a sewer ditch. He decried the professional self-pity.[25]

Cerf was unbowed, replying: "I couldn't disagree with you more thoroughly about Faulkner's Nobel Prize speech. I thought it was wonderful." Later in April when he reported *The Pony Express* had reached thirty-two thousand and "is going like wildfire," Cerf added a postscript: "For the sake of your own reputation, don't go around telling other people what you think of that Faulkner Nobel Prize speech. You are a minority of one." The Faulkner speech stuck in Adams's craw, however, and in his last interview for the Associated Press the author spoke out, telling Wellner about the Faulkner speech: "Certainly writing is work, hard work. But so is any craft. I rewrite everything at least three times. But painful? For a writer to pity himself—to indicate that writing is painful—is hypocritical; it's a damned pose."[26]

An author he continued to hold in high regard was Carmer. He had hoped the Carmers would visit him in Beaufort, but changes in plans put off a meeting until May when Adams stopped at their home at Irvington-on-Hudson on the way to Wide Waters. While there he landed in the hospital again. More positively, Carmer, editor for John C. Winston's Adventure Book series, asked him to do a juvenile novel.

He reluctantly accepted a fiction book paralleling the Santa Fe juvenile but following the adventures of a twelve-year-old boy in the old Southwest. He outlined the plot to Brandt, asking about a serial sale. His agent said *Blue Book* in using his first two youth books considered them factual, simple, and clear narratives and would not be interested in an ordinary juvenile, quickly adding, "I mean, ordinary in scope, not in treatment by the Old Master!"[27]

When Adams got to Cayuga County about the first of June, there were changes. His senior golfing partner, William H. Seward III, was gone, having died at eighty-six. Metcalf was a Republican state senator. Jeff Kilborne was buying Emerson's summer home, Boscobel, and moving across the lake to be Adams's neighbor. The move strengthened his kinship with Kilborne, a farm implement dealer in Moravia and owner of twelve farms. A gregarious sportsman, the agribusinessman held game dinners, raised domesticated wild ducks, and had enjoyed the good life year-round at Ensenore. His marriage had ended in divorce after World War II, giving him freedom to travel. "Jeff was devoted to Sam," Kilborne's neighbor Marion Kennedy recalled.[28]

Adams also faced changes. Earlier, he had written Kilborne that he needed a slight operation for a hernia. After he met with a surgeon in Auburn, he was told he had a double hernia, involving two operations, five days apart. Brandt, who had had hernia surgery, said the operation was not dangerous, simply uncomfortable. Adams postponed it until fall.[29] Although told by his doctor to take life easy, he went to Hamilton College for his sixtieth reunion and to Cooperstown for the annual seminar in July. He also worked on his novel and in August did research in New York.

For the *New Yorker* he wrote "Grandfather Breaks a Strike" that an editor said cast his grandfather Adams in a bad light with "a somewhat disagreeable effect." Brandt agreed and suggested Adams shelve it, and the author agreed. His next story was an adventurous foray, this time into science fiction. In the "Isle of Blight," he dealt with bacteriological warfare that defoliated part of an island. It was turned down by the fiction editor of *Cosmopolitan* because it seemed "a little too far-fetched and fantastic to me to be credible." By December Brandt had six rejections, and it took until February 1952 to sell it to the ninth magazine contacted, *Fantastic Stories*, for two hundred dollars.[30]

Just before his operation on 2 October he shipped Baumgarten the first part of his New York City novel, saying he did not have time to straighten out the chapters. On 4 October the *Citizen-Advertiser* reported he was "recovering from a minor operation." Baumgarten wrote on 11 October saying how delighted everyone was to hear he was doing well and she found the early chapters of the novel "great good fun." Then she offered suggestions, including a warning about his first-person approach. From Cerf he received a package of books and an offer to "vent any possible crankiness on me personally the next time you blow into the office."[31]

During Adams's hospital stay his *Santa Fe Trail* was published. "The two books you've done for Landmarks are really perfection in their line," Cerf wrote and began negotiating for a third. Eyeing the Canadian market, Cerf said the Random House office could get background on the Royal Canadian Mounted Police, but if material were not found, another book could be substituted.[32]

Adams's expected early release from the hospital was stalled by internal complications, and it was thirty-three days before Mildred Harlan could take him home on 2 November. Although his condition remained up and down, he left Wide Waters in November. When he reached Beaufort, Adams had a rash that annoyed him because he could not write and scratch at the same time.

By the end of 1951 he was still being tormented by the itch and taking drugs so he could sleep at night but vowed to Brandt that he would return to his New York novel the first of the year. His juvenile book on the Royal Canadian Mounted Police was stalled. Cerf in November had assured the author, "Stick with me, kid, and I will have you eating caviar and filet mignon for breakfast every day," but in late December he said he had written his Canadian office "bawling the hell out of them for their delay." Adams remained lukewarm about the Mounties while being supportive of the series.[33]

He was more annoyed by a threat from Clifford Funkhouser, who renewed his claim on *The Harvey Girls*. Although William Rankin's claims had been taken care of, Funkhouser revived his claims pushed aside in 1942. A trial began in November 1951 in Kansas City, Missouri, and produced a half million words in a federal suit against Loew's for two million dollars. On 30 July 1952 the judge ruled no copyright infringement or plagiarism because ideas could not be copyrighted. Although Adams was not directly involved, the decision noted little similarity between the story by Funkhouser and the novel by Adams, or for that matter much similarity between the novel and the screenplay. The United States Supreme Court declined to hear the case on 14 October 1954, ending the controversy.[34]

True to his word to Brandt, Adams again began tackling his New York novel in 1952, warning Baumgarten she was going to have a tough time with it. She said she was eager to start. He took the novel with him when he went to Key West to spend the bulk of February with Katherine Adell and her husband, who was planning to retire from the navy in June.

"Father wanted to know if Cecil wished to take over the farm when he retired, but Cec was more interested in attending the Wharton School," Adams's daughter recalled. That decision opened the way for the sale of the remaining portion, but he said he would not sell his lake property while he remained above ground. In June he sold the farm for ten thousand dollars.[35]

His health continued to be a concern. After a forty-year association, Brandt recognized he could no longer push his friend. When Clara Savage Littledale of *Parents' Magazine* inquired about a short opener for the magazine, Brandt told her Adams was working on a novel, explaining: "He's a wonderful guy, as you probably know, but he can't do two things at once when in the past I used to count on him doing four or five!" Saying "it does seem almost too much to ask him for anything these days," Littledale told Brandt she could wait.[36]

Brandt got an optimistic report from Harold J. Michel, who visited Adams in March after seeing him on the way south "when his appearance was a real shock to us." When Adams returned from Key West, he saw a specialist in Charleston because a bladder infection continued. The news was discouraging. The infection was incurable except by another operation. Because the condition was not progressive, he hoped to have the novel done before the surgery in the summer. Lest Baumgarten or Brandt feel sorry for him, he noted an average of four dinner parties a week despite his legs being annoyingly weak.[37]

His next juvenile for Random House produced a new challenge. In January he had turned down the book on the Mounties despite Cerf's assurance that it would be a success like *The Pony Express* that led sales with more than forty-eight thousand and *The Santa Fe Trail* that had sold twenty thousand in two months. In April he told Baumgarten that Random House wanted him to do his next youth book on the Erie Canal. There were problems, however. The Erie Canal book had been assigned to Carmer, who because of repeated attacks of pneumonia and the flu had postponed it five times, causing the publishers to suggest it to Adams. After an offended Carmer wrote him, Adams told him to go ahead with the book. But he was torn between his friendship with Carmer and his sense of debt to Random House because of Cerf's generosity.[38]

Adams was still wrestling with his dilemma as he headed north. He dined with the Cerfs and then went to the Carmers. While at Irvington-on-Hudson, he and Carmer hammered out a deal, with Adams agreeing once again to do the Winston book and Carmer relinquishing his interest in the Erie Canal juvenile. Adams and Mildred Harlan went to Wide Waters on Decoration Day and then he went into a Syracuse hospital for tests while she went to her apartment in New York, but she was to return quickly. The results of the tests showed a severe bladder infection, and the urologist wanted an earlier operation than the July date Adams sought.

Adams wrote Baumgarten that because his impending operation had an element of risk, she should turn over his novel to someone if he died. She replied she had no suggestions on the book and added: "Other eventualities I simply refuse to recognize." He remained fatalistic. Just before the surgery he suggested Edmonds for the Erie Canal book if he should not survive. He came through the major surgery with little trouble, however, although Ibbotson had a similar operation three days after his and died from shock. "We all know and believe you are indestructible and for that we are all very grateful," Baumgarten replied. Cerf was equally optimistic: "I'd like to see the doctor that could get the better of a tough old buzzard like you."[39]

Although he was unable to do much work because of insomnia, Adams entertained the Random House group over the Fourth of July. Clune followed with a three-day visit that prompted "A Privilege," a column lauding Adams's versatility as shown in his conversations on the Korean war, baseball, medicine, history, countryside lore, politics, art, the stock market, women, writing, and reading. Adams told Clune the greatest novel was *War and Peace*, the greatest novelist, Honore de Balzac, and the best modern novel, *The Great Gatsby*.[40]

Added to Adams's entertaining costs, the hospitalization produced a shock to his cash flow that, as usual, was unable to handle sudden expenses. In July the author wrote Baumgarten that his medical bills were heavy: nurses, eighty-four dollars a week each plus the charges of the anesthesiologist, operating room, x-rays, drugs, and seventeen-dollar-a-day hospital room. Baumgarten agreed: "Medical expenses are appalling. I don't blame you for stirring us up." His anxiety was eased by a Random House royalty payment for *The Pony Express* of more than one thousand dollars and the sale of a grandfather story to the *New Yorker* for twelve hundred dollars. Further royalties of more than three thousand dollars came from *The Santa Fe Trail* and *Sunrise to Sunset*.[41]

The grandfather story was an Asa Soule character sketch. The acceptance by the *New Yorker* was a boost to Adams's morale, which he said had been low since the previous winter. He told Baumgarten the magazine was enthusiastic about the Soule story and that the twelve hundred dollars was double what he had gotten for his previous story.

After the Clune visit, Adams went to Cooperstown for the New York State Historical Association seminar. His participation was welcome, and a colleague, Clifford K. Shipton, later wrote: "He would refuse to present formal lectures like the rest of us, but would 'answer questions' from his vast store of memory and experience; the session was never long enough. At Cooperstown he impressed upon a whole academic generation the fact that a very distinguished and highly successful author could be sweet, gentle, and truly modest."[42]

Although Baumgarten had wanted him to concentrate on the New York novel before tackling the Erie Canal history, he sent her the novel with the intention of putting it aside until he could be more objective. After reading the manuscript, she relented while assuring him she saw value in it. Turning to the Erie Canal, Adams contacted Brigham for material on pre-canal events and the building of the canal, explaining he needed to be as careful of the facts as if he were writing adult history. He further enlisted the help of Edmonds, who brought his Erie Canal notebooks to Wide Waters. He also asked McEwen to bend the college library rules to bring a canal governance book to the Labor Day party.

Before McEwen visited, Adams entertained Carl and Carol Brandt and their friend John P. Marquand. When he heard of the possibility of his fellow author coming, he invited the erudite, Harvard-educated New Englander to visit. Marquand, twenty-two years younger than Adams, was an established writer. His early feature articles had been in the New York *Tribune* of Adams's day, but his *The Late George Apley* and its 1938 Pulitzer Prize established him as a serious novelist. His success with later novels and the popular Mr. Moto stories and books hid a tormented personal life. He had been married to Christina Sedgwick, and after their 1935 divorce she had married Adams's Beaufort friend Harford Powell. Marquand had a long lover's relationship with Carol Brandt and was a client of Carl Brandt, creating an overt triangle.

It was Carl Brandt who telephoned about including Marquand in the Wide Waters party. When Marquand arrived, Adams was concerned that a sprained back, for which Marquand got osteopathic help in Auburn and slept with a tailboard of a truck under his mattress, meant his fellow author did not have a good time. A letter from Marquand allayed his fear. "When I was with you at Auburn I felt for the first time in many years completely at home as a weekend guest. . . . The reason, of course, is that you have an understanding of people and of guests besides, and that your house is made both for entertaining and for peace of mind." Adams gave him a permanent invitation to Wide Waters.[43]

Adams tried to pry Bennett and Phyllis Cerf out of Mount Kisco. Instead, Cerf urged Adams in July to visit them later in the year. The publisher also reported *The Pony Express* still led Landmark books and a new World series was signing up authors such as his friend Nancy Wilson Ross. Ross had continued a string of successful books after her controversial *From Friday to Monday*. In a 1950 column in the New York *Herald Tribune Book Review* she credited Adams with teaching her the craftsmanship of writing as "my literary godfather."[44]

He accepted Cerf's invitation in September but put off his visit because of swollen legs. He assured his publisher, however, he been hard at work on the Erie Canal and expected to start the actual writing the next day. His third juvenile posed problems. A week into the project he found he was mired in detail. When Baumgarten offered to read the opening chapter in October, he asked why just one chapter. He was worried about how to keep it interesting and how much political and economic detail to include. Although Baumgarten edited the beginning chapters, it was a thirteen-year-old, Ray Messenger, who came to Adams's rescue.

"I read the manuscript three times," Messenger recalled, "and I told him there was too much grandpa Adams." Adams, who reported to Baumgarten that the boy was intelligent and not afraid to express his opinion, added his criticisms paralleled hers. Saying she was pleased to have her comments confirmed, she said: "I always knew that my mentality was just about the 13 year old class." In appreciation, Adams dedicated *The Erie Canal* with "To Ray Stillson Messenger, II, whose critical point of view has been a valuable guide to the author, this book is inscribed." A regret was that the book was released after the boy's 27 October birthday.[45]

Adams's swollen legs did not stop him from going to Geneva, New York, for a dinner hosted by writer and former *McClure's* editor George S. Brooks, who had just retired as Democratic mayor of Groton. Much of the talk by those present, including columnist Clune, was of the campaign between Democrat Adlai E. Stevenson and Republican Dwight D. Eisenhower. Adams continued his opposition to national Democratic leadership. "I'm a Democrat," Adams said, "but I think it's time we were kicked out of Washington."[46]

He continued to support causes he thought were just. In 1951 he had renewed his opposition to Spain's Franco by signing a leaflet issued by the Joint Anti-Fascist Refugee Committee opposing United States military and economic aid to the repressive government. In 1952 he was one of 280 national figures who appealed to the president to grant amnesty to those convicted under the anti-communist Smith Act. Truman ignored both pleas, which were collected by the FBI. The bureau also, with the help of the post office, thwarted an attempt by Adams to get a copy of *China Reconstructs*, which was intercepted and returned to Hong Kong.[47]

Washington, however, was also kind to him. Telling Baumgarten he was about to become a national monument, he explained that in January he would get $560 in a lump sum and then $80 a month tax-free. He said it had something to do with self-employment. He said he had paid $81 a year extra tax and got back $960.[48]

The impending government payment was good news for Adams, who made about ten thousand dollars from his writing in 1952, about half of the amount he had earned the year before and about two thousand dollars less than he got in 1950. Evidently earnings from his securities helped because in November 1952 he instructed further payments be deferred until 1953 when, he said, he would need them. Part of the reason was that the *New Yorker* renewed his contract to his surprise because he had published so little in the magazine during the past year. Although the renewal was only for one hundred dollars, it also brought with it bonuses based on sales and generous cost-of-living allowances that often were in the hundreds of dollars quarterly.[49]

Adams finished *The Erie Canal* in November and met with Baumgarten and children's book editor Louise Bonino in New York to go over the manuscript. Bonino's initial reaction was good, but two weeks later she said she was concerned because the book lacked personalities. Adams had noted the same difficulty earlier to Brandt, but Baumgarten was reassuring in saying the nature of the topic did not have a personality to emphasize.

In Beaufort he did the revisions on the juvenile, ending in December. He then turned to an article on Edisto, an island community north of Beaufort, for which Brandt had gotten an order from the Ford publications. He was slowed by his doctor's orders after overworking to the point of collapse, but quickly rebounded and finished the article by mid-January.

Most of the winter was spent on his fourth juvenile, *Wagons to the Wilderness*, for Winston. Although the story was fiction and took place on the familiar Santa Fe Trail, he felt he was short of background material. By March, however, he reported that the book was coming so easily he was afraid it was no good. He continued writing a chapter a day and found that the twenty-five thousand word limit was not enough. Baumgarten got Winston to agree to thirty-five thousand words. By mid-April he was working double time to finish the book before heading north. He mailed the manuscript before he left and received word on the way north that Winston had accepted the manuscript and sent it to Carmer, who wanted to do whatever cutting was necessary.

At Wide Waters insomnia kept him under the care of a doctor, who forbade a trip to hot New York in August. Instead, Adams sent Baumgarten a call to come to Owasco Lake for a discussion of his New York *Police Gazette* novel, offering to pay her expenses. She answered his call by agreeing to drive up for a day with her husband, Cozzens, whom Adams had congratulated on his 1949 Pulitzer Prize for fiction awarded for his *Guard of Honor.* After her visit, he told Brandt that he accepted her revisional ideas although he was not sure he could work out a happy ending that she proposed.

As he toiled on the novel, the Labor Day party brought the Carmers, Charleston author Jo Pinckney, and Irita Van Doren. His friendship with Irita Van Doren, editor of the New York *Herald Tribune Book Review,* had begun when she was married to historian Carl Van Doren and continued when she was a lover of Wendell Willkie. Their communication ranged from light banter to intellectual sharing. In a letter after Labor Day he thanked her for a yellow patterned necktie, commented on Wolfgang Lanewiesche's review of Charles Lindbergh's *The Spirit of St. Louis,* on which she had asked his opinion, and then informed her of progress on his novel, and lastly complimented her on her charm.[50]

A reunion with the Brandts and Marquand was enlarged to include fifteen-year-old Vicky Brandt on Columbus Day weekend, along with Gertrude Case. The widow of Ted Case had been "adopted" by the Adamses after his death in 1944. Before, during, and after the long weekend one of the topics was the possibility of Marquand spending the winter in Beaufort. Adams made the arrangements, but his friend wrote that his doctors insisted he go to the warmer climate of Grenada.

In late July Cerf had invited him "when you fly southward with the rest of the geese." Cerf was now a panelist on the popular television show *What's My Line?* and in August had guessed that a woman, a fishhook inspector who worked for Adams's friend, William DeWitt in Auburn, was a ghostwriter for Adams. He was delighted when Cerf got him six tickets to the show. Cerf also asked if he wanted anyone special at a party they were giving for him, and Adams said he would like to see the John Herseys again. Before Adams left Cayuga County, he was visited by Bill and Peggy Wood Walling. In New York he and Mildred Harlan took Carol and Vicky Brandt and August Heckscher, who had just become chief editorial writer with the *Herald Tribune,* and his wife, Claude, to the television show.

With Cerf he discussed business. Adams had new interest in the American morals book after Marquand suggested Frederick Lewis Allen. He pressed Cerf to allow him to contact Allen. Cerf agreed but was more interested in a World Landmark book. Adams proposed Erasmus after his novel, and Cerf seemed amiable but urged Adams to do a history of the Hatfield-McCoy feud as his next landmark.

Adams's *The Erie Canal* was published at the end of October. Purchases of the book continued Adams's success with juveniles as it sold more than twelve thousand copies in 1953, more than seven thousand in 1954, more than four thousand in 1955 and 1956, and continued selling for the rest of his life. Added to these were ten thousand specially bound school library copies and almost four thousand Book of the Month Club Young Readers of America copies. Late in 1952 the Book of the Month Club started a youth series and picked *The Pony Express* for $1,150 and then added *The Santa Fe Trail*. The two books were also sold in a Landmark subscription set by the Peoples Book Club with a $750 guarantee. His 1953 writing earned more than $16,000.

In Beaufort, after his two South Carolina stories were published in November, "Carolina Cruise" in *Holiday* and "Edisto, the Tranquil Isle" in *Ford Times*, he became a local hero, but his best compliment of 1953 came from Frank and Nan Taylor, who named their fourth son, born on 13 November, Adams Edward Taylor in his honor. The active social life of Beaufort kept Adams busy during the holidays, but he made Brandt a resolution to finish his novel in short order. His resolution would end up like most people's.[51]

# 19

# GRANDFATHER
## 1954–1955

Money worries, a bogged-down novel, an unwanted topic for his next juvenile book, and declining health challenged Adams and his optimism as he turned eight-three in early 1954. Seldom thrown off stride, he moved forward by looking back.

Despite having his usual cash flow bind for his January estimated tax he met his needs after he received more than thirty-seven hundred dollars in Random House royalties. A steady stream of *New Yorker* payments produced more than seventeen hundred dollars in the first half of 1954, keeping him going until the royalties from his juveniles in July. The magazine also ran a grandfather story in January, describing the ginseng craze during which central New Yorkers harvested the root for export to the Chinese.

Adams returned to his New York City novel at the first of the year. By 10 March he was discouraged, telling Baumgarten that he had two or three chapters to go on the third draft of the novel. Conceding he was tired and bored, he said that he would attempt to rewrite the end before leaving Beaufort. In April, however, he told Brandt he had given up hope of finishing the novel before leaving. A hope, he told Holbrook, was that if he ignored the novel for a month, some difficulties might resolve themselves.[1]

An item that would not resolve itself was the juvenile on the Hatfield-McCoy feud. He remained convinced it could be nothing but a history of murder after murder, a study of gangsterism. Although he was sure it would be a bad book for the Landmark series, he was equally certain Cerf had his heart set on it.

Baumgarten, alarmed that Adams did not believe in the book and saying, "I trust your instinct," contacted children's book editor Bonino. Bonino shared their unhappiness and urged a new subject be proposed. But when Cerf returned from one month in California, the determined publisher wrote Adams that "though my desk was loaded with junk of various descriptions, did I find a single Hatfield or a single McCoy? The answer is a reverberating No. What the hell have you been doing with all these God given hours?" Adams told Baumgarten he had no suggestion for another subject. To Cerf he wrote he was working on his novel and would discuss the juvenile when he came north.[2] One week later he suggested to Baumgarten a new topic of Francis Marion, South Carolina's Swamp Fox of the Revolutionary War.

While the trio of Adams, Baumgarten, and Bonino plotted to divert Cerf, the author's salvation came from Brigham. On the same day he suggested Marion, Adams wrote him to ask for information on the Hatfields and McCoys. The director of the American Antiquarian Society replied that research would have to be extensively conducted in the field because various feuds of the time did not get into newspapers. After Adams relayed his findings to Baumgarten, she agreed Brigham's letter "washes it all up." Cerf surrendered.[3]

Cerf also lost a battle he may not have known about at the time. Adams had proposed his publisher for an honorary degree from Hamilton. At another time, Heckscher recalled, Cerf had a tough time when proposed as a member in a New York club because he was called a professional funnyman until Heckscher told of *The Pony Express* incident, after which he was elected. At Hamilton College, McEwen, under pressure from Adams, admitted that Cerf had been vetoed by the Executive Committee of the Trustees. Bitterly disappointed, Adams promised no action until he had talked with McEwen.[4]

One reason for his passiveness was his admiration for McEwen's stand on Edward R. Murrow. The broadcaster had been selected by the trustees in January to be the commencement speaker, but Murrow's attack on Senator Joseph R. McCarthy on his 9 March *See It Now* program had raised an issue about the invitation. Although Adams made no public comment on McCarthy, he applauded McEwen for backing Murrow. If the invitation had been withdrawn, Adams said, he would have moved to have his name taken off the alumni list.

Before he came north, *Wagons to the Wilderness* was published by Winston 25 April. The story of thirteen-year-old Esty Lang's adventures as a cook's helper on a wagon train from Missouri to Santa Fe was called a "satisfying tale" in the

*New York Times Book Review* by George A. Woods, who overall criticized the series of young boy stories as monotonous. Adams dedicated the book to Martha Elliott's son with: "To my young friend and—I hope—constant reader, William Waight Elliott, this book is inscribed." She recalled that when he showed the dedication page to her son, the boy asked, "Uncle Sam, do they all have this?" He smiled and replied: "Every goddamn one of them." Every one was about thirty-three hundred copies, producing slightly more than thirteen hundred dollars in advance and royalty payments until his death.[5]

Not only was his Winston juvenile far from a literary or financial success, Adams believed that the grandfather stories were about played out. Although he had told Cerf in December the *New Yorker* had renewed his contract and he planned a couple of grandfather tales before going back to his novel, the magazine rejected "Grandfather Makes a Deal in Gems." Brandt, feeling the story was too masculine for *Woman's Day*, tried *Esquire*. Brandt's prediction about other magazines' reactions came true as Frederic Birmingham reported "the whole world would recognize this as a *New Yorker* reject."[6]

Despite the rejection in February Adams told Brandt he thought he had enough grandfather stories for a book. Four years earlier, in 1950, after the publication of a grandfather story about the circus and the purchase of tales about baseball and George Eastman by the *New Yorker*, Baumgarten had said the only thing that would satisfy her was for him to collect them into a book. After his comment to Brandt, she urged him to do it before he got tied up with other commitments. In February 1954 Adams thought he was ready. By then he had eleven stories in the *New Yorker*, another on a fugitive slave purchased and the Harriet Tubman sketch that could be adapted, plus three bought by *Woman's Day* and the boyhood article from the *Lincoln-Mercury Times*. Baumgarten was excited because "it looks as if we really will get the book now."[7]

In New York his meeting with Cerf in May produced agreements for Random House to publish *Grandfather Stories* and for Adams to do another Landmark book, not on Francis Marion but on Sir Isaac Brock. With his eye still on the Canadian market, Cerf wanted the story of the general who was instrumental in saving Canada for the British Empire in the War of 1812. To gain United States appeal Cerf wrote Adams he should play up the role of Tecumseh and Niagara Falls, and "If we can successfully carry out my jacket idea of Samuel Hopkins Adams being carried over the crest of the Falls in a barrel, our joint fortunes will be made."[8]

On the same day Cerf wrote Baumgarten that Adams seemed pleased with the new subject and "I take it for granted that you know all about General

Brock." She replied: "Of course I know all about General Brock. He has a hotel in Niagara Falls which is owned by Franchot Tone. That makes a perfect subject for a Landmark book for Sam." Although Adams said his ignorance of Brock was abysmal, he signed the contract.[9]

After seeing Cerf, Adams went to the Carmers. While there he was hit by a fever of 104 degrees that put him in the hospital. Burned out by the fever and with no appetite or desire to work, Adams recuperated at Wide Waters during June with Betty Steele and her husband. He had recovered sufficiently by July to have twelve at his Fourth of July party, including Becker. She had married Abner Sideman, circulation director of *Look* magazine, and had been promoted by Cerf to managing editor to replace the departed Saxe Commins but was still Adams's editor on his nonjuvenile work.

Present also was Scherman, who had left *Life* to be promotion manager of a new magazine, *Sports Illustrated.* Buoyed by advance word from Cerf of a Random House royalty payment of $8,400 coming in July, Adams sent Scherman to investigate a piano tuner's offer of a secondhand baby grand to replace his 1897 Wegman upright. Scherman reported it was a bargain at $395. Adams told of the purchase in a 5 July letter to Cerf, noting the previous night's picnic party of forty stayed until 1:00 A.M. around the piano. He thanked Cerf for his letter and said he would drink a mint julep to him.[10]

He proposed no toasts to General Brock. Because the general had died early in the War of 1812, the material on him was sparse. He also was concerned the United States would look bad in its conduct during the war. When Adams received none of the promised material from Random's Canadian office, he turned to Hamilton librarian Walter Pilkington and Holbrook.

He finished Brock, except for the introduction, in late September, convinced that the book would not sell. While he wrote the Brock book, Becker and Baumgarten were trying to gather the various grandfather stories. Becker planned to put them in order for the book's table of contents, and Baumgarten took on the task of tracking them down, battling Adams's tendency to forget what he had written. His wish to use the Harriet Tubman sketch meant that the original intent to focus on grandfather Adams was enlarged to include grandfather Hopkins.

One stumbling block was *Woman's Day*, which had bought but not used "The Diary of a Canal Bride." On 9 July Mabel Souvaine had explained she wanted to cut the long story to get it in the magazine but that its board wanted the piece kept almost intact. Souvaine offered to release the story if Baumgarten could find another buyer. She was unsuccessful, and Adams wrote

Souvaine to explain his predicament. His friend answered that he could use the story before *Woman's Day* ran it, thereby killing use of the story by the magazine that did not carry reprints. Saying, "It's darn big of me, too," Souvaine, who had visited Wide Waters, added, "But then, you're sorta cute and I like you."[11]

Another complication arose when Becker said she would edit the manuscript after she got the stories in order. Adams ran up the distress flag to Baumgarten, saying that he wanted to do the editing, corrections, and introductory material before the copy was set in type. Noting it was not the first time Baumgarten had been cast in the role of the rescue squad, he said one had to handle Becker carefully and the last thing he wanted was to hurt her feelings. Baumgarten said she would get the material and arranged for a contract that, because the book was a collection of stories, had a low advance of $750. Adams agreed with the terms, saying Random House probably would lose money on the book.

He also continued his interest in the writing of his friends. He kept prodding Betty Carmer about her husband's Rivers of America book, *Susquehanna*, and when he received a copy of Conrad's *Gulf Stream North*, about the menhaden coast and its black fisherman in Florida, he wrote Conrad, calling it a classic. Conrad replied he had read nearly everything Adams had written and asked if he could quote him, a request that Adams granted. "You're a gem, a little shinier and a little brillianter for being a little older," Conrad said.[12]

Carl and Carol Brandt came to Wide Waters in October with John Marquand and Vicky Brandt, with whom Adams had a standing offer of a cribbage game. In a letter to Adams, Marquand thanked his host and expressed hopes that hurricane Hazel had not caused damage. The hurricane did take down a maple on his shoreline, but the loss of a tree was not a major concern for Adams.[13]

What was of concern was a heart attack. Although he did not mention the attack to those at Brandt & Brandt, he told Holbrook three weeks later the heart attack had slowed him but his doctor did not think it serious. When he got to New York in early December, he did not keep his heart attack secret. He was eager to get away from digitalis but was having trouble breathing at night and had a loss of appetite. In Beaufort his doctor kept him off heart medicine, and he recovered his appetite and was working four to five hours a day.[14]

As he started editing *Grandfather Stories* 1 October, he had estimated the work would take about one month, but he found it involved more rewriting than planned. The *New Yorker* removed a possible problem by publishing in

October and November three stories on an indentured servant, a hustler, and a skating horse thief. After his arrival in Beaufort, Adams told Brandt he would be taking his time with the book and was at peace.[15]

His financial matters were never at peace. After his heart attack in October, Adams, who received only about one thousand dollars in 1954 after his eighty-four hundred dollar July royalties, needed cash in October. A few weeks later, however, he sold some stock at a large profit and was set for the remainder of the year. From the beginning of 1954 through the end of his life his finances often caused short-lived anxiety as he and Baumgarten jockeyed his resources to satisfy his needs and those of the tax collectors. Some surprises occurred like the fifteen-dollar sale for the use of his "Your Right to be Wrong," about academic freedom, for a greeting card. But the biggest financial surprise came from *It Happened One Night.*

Over the years "Night Bus" and *It Happened One Night* had been in constant demand. Frank Vreeland had done a play adaptation, *Night Bus*, in 1941, and interest in the story had not waned with Brandt & Brandt selling foreign and anthology rights and answering queries on television rights. Recognizing that the copyright would revert to Columbia Pictures in 1961 and hearing rumors that the studio was considering a musical film based on the story, Brandt moved on what he called a "macabre" deal to get money for the rights before they went to the studio. A puzzled Adams, who admitted he had no brain for legal matters, told Brandt to go ahead, and the agent closed the deal for $11,500, of which Adams's daughters and granddaughter received $9,000 and he, $315, as more and more he was concerned with the future needs of his family. In 1956 Columbia released a Dick Powell produced and directed musical, *You Can't Run Away from It*, starring Jack Lemmon and June Allyson. The Technicolor film, at least the twentieth movie adapted from an Adams work, was judged unsuccessful.[16]

In late 1954 he forecast a leaner 1955 because Eisenhower was threatening his Social Security. On the brighter side, his heart was good. He worked to polish Brock, delayed in part by Katherine Messenger's battle with a fatal disease that would kill her the next year. He avoided writing the introduction to put off the $750 advance until 1955. He also edited *Grandfather Stories* and was cheered by a short sketch in Cerf's "Trade Winds" column in which the publisher, while noting Adams put to shame writers half his age with his work ethic, quoted an unnamed friend: "Everything that happens to Sam is important to him. His interest never flags. He not only listens to what other people have to say, but is prepared to abandon long-cherished prejudices if they are convincing enough." Adams thanked Cerf and said he was sorry they would miss Beaufort because Cerf was going to Hawaii. Cerf replied: "If only I could learn your philosophy of sitting lazily in the sun twiddling my thumbs, and not doing one stroke of work from one end of the month to another. (Don't bother writing any insulting answers to this jibe. I'll be gone!)"[17]

Adams's progress on *Grandfather Stories* picked up, and by the end of January he was nearly done, buoyed by a favorable report from Baumgarten that Becker said she had read them "for the umpteenth time and still find[s] them utterly delightful." Physically he was regaining his strength. Cursing his salt-free diet to Brandt, who admitted he backslid, he prepared for George Harlan's second wedding, urged the Carmers to stop on their way to Florida, and sent *Grandfather Stories* to New York.

Except for his nostalgia pieces, Adams's output of magazine stories was trailing off by 1955. The market was in trouble with *Collier's* in its death throes and his interest waning. "I find as I grow older the inventive processes wear out. Also the whole fiction field today seems to be dying of undernourishment. The fiction magazines are dead or dying, and what stories are published seem mostly to be poor stuff," he told reporter Valarie Nicholson late in the year.[18]

Nonetheless, the tenacious Adams did publish. He resurrected an often-rejected article in 1955. Ten years earlier he had discussed with Ross an idea for a story on the Juke family tradition of criminality. Ross liked the idea, but the article was put off until 1950. When the *New Yorker* apparently had no further interest, Brandt tried to sell it to no avail, and it went into the B-file until Adams retrieved it, at Holbrook's urging, in 1954. He tried "The Juke Myth" at the *Saturday Review*, which ran the article and used it in its treasury two years later, the first of at least five anthologies that included the sociological study.

The spotty magazine market did not mean there were not new opportunities. When preparing a potential series for television on the Pony Express, a former actor had read Adams's juvenile book and asked Brandt whether Adams would be interested in writing the three pilot films. Brandt told Adams he said it was unlikely that he would begin a new type of writing, television scripts. Adams, who had turned eighty-four, agreed.[19]

After the Harlan wedding in March, Adams sent off the finished Brock manuscript that Bonino had said would not be published until 1956. He was far from content with the book, telling Baumgarten it was poor and nobody would buy it. She replied that she did not believe a word he said.[20] While they discussed Brock, Adams and Baumgarten made little mention of *Grandfather Stories*.

Then on 1 April 1955 Brandt telephoned to deliver what Adams thought was an April Fool's joke, except that immediately afterward he received another call, from Cerf. The news from Brandt and Cerf was that the Book of the Month Club had chosen *Grandfather Stories* as its midsummer selection. After his call, Brandt wired Adams that his book was the sole choice for the period. The selection carried a payment of forty thousand dollars, half for Random House and half for Adams. He wrote Brandt of his joy, adding that this was the first time that anything of the sort had happened to him with the nearest thing being the Critics' Circle award on the Woollcott biography.[21]

To Marquand, on the Book of the Month Club board, Adams wrote immediately, thanking him. His fellow author answered he would like to take credit, but Amy Loveman and Clifford Fadiman were as enthusiastic about the book as he. "Not only do I think it remarkable as a piece of living history, but every page is entertaining."[22]

At Brandt & Brandt and Random House the reaction to the Book of the Month news was elation. Although Adams remained astonished and confided to Baumgarten that the book never looked that good to him, Baumgarten said she and Becker "are so full of joy you must feel the radiation down in Beaufort." Brandt said, "I am really dancing in the streets." Adams, noting he would have been pleased if the book had just made the recommended list, said one of the most heartwarming things about the selection was that people of whom he was fond were so enthusiastic over his good luck.[23]

So was his college. Adams was responsive to a plan by Pilkington to have Hamilton feature his *Grandfather Stories* at commencement, in part because he had dedicated the book to the college. Originally slated to be published in May, the collection was delayed by the Book of the Month Club, pushing the date into July. Becker, however, agreed to furnish the manuscript, page proofs, plate proofs, and finished Random House books before commencement, and he agreed to autograph copies.

While Hamilton honored Adams, Auburn was making its plans. The Daubers Club, a group affiliated with the Cayuga Museum of History and Art, scheduled a dinner for him in June. Adams was a reluctant honoree, telling Carmer that his feelings would not be hurt if he declined to attend. He was uncomfortable about the dinner as he prepared to go north in early May. The gaiety of Beaufort had taken its toll as he battled insomnia and was back on a daily dose of digitalis. Elliott, who had a busy winter as his almost constant companion, warned Kilborne: "Jeff, he is anything but well—he has gone down considerably since you have seen him. I give him most of my time for

I am afraid he won't be here very much longer. When you see him you will know what I mean." She asked that he buy a white carnation for Adams to wear at the dinner.[24]

Adams, too, was aware of his declining health. After he left Beaufort, he cut stops to conserve his energy for New York with its round of interviews and a Book of the Month party for his new book. He attended the Book of Month Club reception but turned down a Cerf invitation to go to *What's My Line?* so he could be at the annual meeting of the Players Club where he was given an honorary life membership.

He arrived back at Wide Waters on 31 May and began bracing himself for the party. After a bad night's sleep on 6 June, he went to the Owasco Country Club where 150 gathered in the candlelit, flower-festooned rooms. After dinner, all were in the main room, and a nervous Adams saw his life pass before his eyes.

The program was a mix of roast and testimonial. McEwen began with a tone of lightness. He called Adams a "disturbing influence," citing his introduction of football to the college and his unnamed choice for an honorary degree who was a good man but hard to sell to his board of trustees. Between speeches, toastmaster Robert Hole, a Hamilton graduate and a banker in Auburn, offered anecdotes. One mentioned Adams's forgetfulness concerning what he had written. His former caddie recalled playing in a charade game in which the Adams's team was acting out *The Unspeakable Perk* but was unable to guess the title. When the contestant conceded and gave the title, Hole quoted Adams as saying: "My God, I've never heard of it, what's that?"[25]

Louis Jones continued the gentle joshing, discussing Adams's martinis and then becoming serious to note his contributions to the Cooperstown seminars where an "innumerable group of young writers in the state have turned to him for help and counsel." He urged Adams to "get down to work" and write his autobiography to leave "the record of one of the most interesting and significant lives of our time."

The suggestion was seconded by *New Yorker* contributor Morris Bishop, who cited Adams's series on patent medicines, which "made a deep impression on me and was profoundly upsetting to the country." Noting his grandfather Adams represented to a large extent Adams himself and that he took his spirit from the countryside, the Cornell professor said he displayed the vigor and strength of the area tempered with a consciousness of its beauty. About an autobiography, he noted Adams had lived through the period of greatest change in all history, modern or ancient.

Lithgow Osborne spoke for his neighbors. A summer resident from across the lake, he noted Adams lived "obstinately and persistently on the wrong side of the lake." He lauded his loyalty to the community, his interest in succeeding generations as he sought "answers about mankind and the universe," and his "eager and zestful spirit" that overcame physical handicaps and personal sorrows such as the death of Jane Adams.

The main speaker was Carmer. Having been selected by the *New York Times* to review *Grandfather Stories*, to Adams's delight, Carmer said: "We're not here to honor a book. We're not here to honor anybody. We're just here to express love and affection for one who is very dear to us." Calling Adams the "ideal of the professional writer," Carmer said each year his work was better. He noted an emphasis on the dignity of the individual — grandfather Adams could not be regimented — "you and I know what would happen if we tried to regiment Sam."

In a short speech Adams thanked the attendees. Despite his misgivings he thought it was a grand affair although none of his family was there. He had discouraged the Adells from attending; Hester Adams was working in the bookstore; and Mildred Harlan was in a New York hospital with phlebitis. The dinner was tiring as he told Cerf that he was alive but not much more. The publisher replied in Cerf fashion: "Very nice — but someday I am going to tell the real truth about you and this whole beautiful myth will be dispelled!"[26]

The Cerfs came to Wide Waters later that summer. After their visit, Adams received a surprise. He wrote the Cerfs that when he came into the living room, he found himself being addressed from the corner by a woman with advice on how to cook brown bread. The voice came from a television set. Adams, who used a radio to get the news at breakfast, was enthusiastic about being able to see Phyllis Cerf on *Down You Go* and Cerf on *What's My Line?* He cautioned Cerf the chances were that he would now squander his hours watching television.[27]

Bogged down on his New York novel, he turned back to a revived attempt at light fiction. When he was in New York he had discussed a story with Bud Hart at *Redbook* magazine, the only outlet he felt was daring enough to publish the serial. Finding it difficult to work with the constant interruptions of his breathing apparatus, Adams struggled with "Blackout," which had as its principal character a young woman who became pregnant with no memory of how she got in the condition.

He was eager to have the manuscript in shape for Becker when she and thirteen others came for the Fourth of July party. He remained resistant to his doctor's pleas that he adopt a salt-free diet, telling Carol Brandt he would rather die well salted. He almost got his wish during the party at Wide Waters that began Friday, with the Fourth of July on Monday. "We thought we would lose Sam on Saturday night," Becker wrote Baumgarten. "Doctor coming to see him twice a day, etc. He is fading rapidly. Yet, on Monday, he was up sitting by the piano singing popular tunes." To Brandt he wrote nothing of his second heart attack. He did admit he was cutting his Cooperstown seminar on doctor's orders, saying being an invalid was a distasteful adjustment.[28]

The effects of the attack were not mentioned by Mary Margaret McBride in a column on her short stay with the author. He regaled her with stories such as meeting scientist Guglielmo Marconi, who was diffident and tongue-tied in strange company but went into the next room and played Chopin and Bach on the piano for hours. She peppered him with questions until he complained, "You're trying to make me talk like a philosopher and I am not one." He did tell her that he had little use for the leaners in the world. "You can't substitute your own strength for another's weakness, though the strong are always trying to do it," adding his vital essentials of life were work and to love and be loved.[29]

He did go to Cooperstown for one day, when the New York State Historical Association honored him in a terrace party attended by three hundred persons, including a panel for a tête-à-tête with Adams. At the home of the Baseball Hall of Fame Carmer could not resist noting that in *Grandfather Stories* Adams told of baseball being played in Rochester in 1827, twelve years before Abner Doubleday was credited with founding the game. Adams said: "I am perfectly willing to concede that Cooperstown is the home of the ice cream soda, the movies and the atomic bomb, and that General Doubleday wrote Shakespeare. But," and he read a newspaper account of the Rochester game.[30]

Robertson, whom Adams had urged to come to Cooperstown after a several year absence, also referred to his new book, complaining "these stories are perfect without any women in them." Then she praised Adams for including "The Diary of a Canal Bride" from the woman's point of view. Adams's overall response was, "If this book is as good as they say it is, I'd better raise the price." After the love-feast at Cooperstown, he told Cerf he had a good time without doing any perceptible damage. The doctor agreed and pronounced him improved although he was still battling insomnia, unhappy about his salt-free diet, and complaining about not getting a full blood supply to his brain, making work difficult.[31]

24. Samuel Hopkins Adams in 1955 at a Cooperstown, New York, meeting. Speaking at a testimonial were, from left, fellow authors Carl Carmer and Constance Robertson, New York State Historian Louis Jones, and Hamilton College Secretary Wallace Johnson. Courtesy of Hamilton College.

He needed the muses for his light fiction serial, "Blackout," that Becker thought was dreadful but told Adams, who she believed would not live to finish it, that it was a fine beginning. After Baumgarten read the story, she felt "very sad about it" but said Brandt saw it as a Fabian piece. Brandt reported Hart wanted the whole manuscript before giving it to his superior.[32]

The Book-of-the-Month Club (BOMC) edition of *Grandfather Stories* came out about 1 July, promoted by the *Book-of-the-Month Club News*. It contained the sketch of Adams by Peggy Wood and a report by Marquand, calling Adams "a master of the form that lies somewhere between the short story and the anecdote." He further said, "The unconquerable spirit of Sam Adams is inherent in his work, and his trained observation is always tempered by his irrepressible humor, his gentleness and his human understanding." The

BOMC edition was followed by the Random House edition on 24 July. He was excited as his publishers kept updating a growing list of good reviews.[33]

The news about his health was not so good. In a 15 July letter to Baumgarten that he asked not be shared with Brandt, he confided that although he had been pronounced out of danger after his latest attack and no evidence of thrombosis existed, he had overheard his doctor say he should limit his activities. He said he did not want any sympathy but he had altered his estimates of life expectancy. He asked if he could get all the BOMC payment, which earlier he had spread over two years. Ever to the rescue, Baumgarten suggested that he could give Random House an interest-free note on the remainder of the advance any time he felt pressed. He said the financial solution, also suggested by Cerf, was perfect although he never took advantage of it.[34]

On 24 July some forty people gathered at Wide Waters to toast grandfather Adams with French 75's and celebrate the publication of *Grandfather Stories*. Much of the talk revolved around the reviews. He had already seen an advanced copy of the Carmer review that Cerf said "I believe you wrote yourself." Noting the review was on page one of the *New York Times Book Review* with a Random House advertisement and an interview with Adams on inside pages, Cerf warned of a possible investigation by the Anti-Trust Division of the government.[35]

The Carmer review, illustrated by an old print that Adams said was stunning, praised the book's social history, its use of period vocabulary, and its subtle humor. Carmer had joked at the Daubers' dinner that when the *Times* had asked whether it would be a favorable review so it could go on page one at double the length and fee, he replied, "It will be a favorable review."[36]

"The reviews are marvelous, aren't they?" Baumgarten asked the day after the party. They kept coming, but it was fellow Rochesterian Lewis Gannett who, in the daily *Herald Tribune* review, best captured the spirit of the book. Similar to Bishop's observation at the Auburn dinner, he saw the book more revealing of Adams than of his grandfather: "If you have ever seen Samuel Hopkins Adams beaming among friends, telling stories, singing at the piano, or climbing down a ladder on crutches because he couldn't wait to go swimming, as I have, you will know what I mean. The man has inexhaustible curiosity, inexhaustible vitality, and inexhaustible affection for people."[37]

The publication of *Grandfather Stories* brought such a flood of telegrams and letters that Adams had to hire a secretary. He was especially pleased to hear from former colleague Ellery Sedgwick, Norman Thomas, and John Foster Dulles, who as President Eisenhower's secretary of state had been *Time*'s "Man of the Year" in January. He was less enthusiastic about a letter from Hollywood columnist Hedda Hopper, who thanked him for being kind to her when they were in New York. He said he only saw the woman once, he told his old *McClure* colleague Witter Bynner, who renewed a short correspondence with Adams.[38]

In her letter to Adams about the reviews Baumgarten offered the fervent wish "I hope we sell millions." It did not, but in September Random House sales were nearing 19,000, which Cerf called "a right good clip," and the next month sales were well over the 21,000 mark. The book broke onto the *Herald Tribune*'s "What America Reads" on 7 August and made the listing fourteen weeks. In the middle of the nonfiction list most weeks, the book eventually sold more than 27,000 Random House copies, besides the BOMC total that Adams estimated was 100,000 to 150,000.[39]

Although he did not receive the Book of the Month Club initial advance of $9,250 until August, Adams was ready to join the consumer culture of the 1950s. At the end of July, he was buying an electric chair elevator and a new station wagon and was collecting antiques again. Later he told Cerf that his doctor had ordered the chair elevator because he did not want Adams climbing stairs more than once a day. The doctor and Adams were also concerned about the author's almost constant state of nausea from his digitalis.[40]

His spending on material goods was joined by his lending his name again to a renewed appeal, this time to President Eisenhower, opposing a new round of Smith Act trials of alleged Communists. Joining with seventy-one others, he protested prosecution for mere membership in the party. It marked the end of the FBI's interest in Adams, according to the released documents.[41]

With no appetite and no ability to do any work, he agreed in August to go into Auburn Memorial Hospital for tests on his dosage of medicine. Before he left, he wrote Conrad an apology for not feeling up to seeing him when he called from Auburn and blamed the lack of sales success of *Gulf Stream North* on the reading public. He entered the hospital 16 August after telling Brandt, who had just made a special visit to Wide Waters, that it was just to balance the medicine that had lowered his weight to 150 pounds. Recalling Betty Richardson Steele had said she could not stand the mad pace of Adams, Brandt observed, "You are a ring-tailed wonder but I think a little quiet and calm will do you good." After he left the hospital, he wrote Van Doren the Labor Day party was still on despite his unavailing medical stay.[42]

Although Adams told Brandt his appetite was returning, a worried Mildred Harlan wrote the agent after taking Adams to Utica for three days: "He isn't working any more! He also is worried about himself." After Labor Day, however, she was more optimistic, noting he had slept eleven hours. "I am giving credit to Irita Van Doren who was here for the weekend."[43]

As he recovered, Adams watched sports on his new television set, regained his strength, and even ventured to Syracuse for an autographing session at a bookstore. By the end of the month he reported that his stair elevator was installed and that although he could not sit in it because of his stiff leg, he was able to ride it by standing on the footboard.

Uncertain about his friend's health, Brandt rallied the troops for the Columbus Day weekend. From Boston came John Marquand, after a Harvard Overseers meeting, and the young Carl Brandt, whom the family called Denny, from his Harvard studies. Carl and Carol Brandt drove from New York with their dog Beau, rendezvousing with the Boston car in Albany and going to Wide Waters caravan style. Vicky Brandt skipped school for a day and flew to Ithaca where she was met by her father. It was the final get-together of the full group.

While Adams was battling the effects of digitalis, Bonino wrote him that Cerf had read *General Brock and Niagara Falls* and wanted a few chapters to describe modern Niagara Falls, including the General Brock hotel and monument, as an introduction to the history. She asked whether he wanted to do it or have Random House hire a free-lance writer to tackle the job. Saying that he was not well enough to do it, Adams told her to get someone else and criticized Cerf's obsession with the book. The publisher, admitting that Adams's skepticism about "Cerf's Folly" was shared by everybody, welcomed his acceptance of the other writer but remained convinced of the success of the book, vowing "A Cerf never gives up—especially when he suspects he has made a blithering fool of himself!"[44]

Not only did Adams back away from further work on Brock, he also turned down a request by *Life* for a grandfather story. Before he left Wide Waters, he signed his will on 31 October. In it he left Wide Waters to Katherine Adell, a trust fund for Hester Adams consisting mostly of stock valued at more than $120,000, and three hundred feet of lake frontage to Mildred Harlan, who also received his Oldsmobile and the stock from Jane's estate. He left the Ford station wagon to Preston and Mae Huff. To Hamilton College he left his Currier and Ives prints, plus the Stevenson portrait. Other relatives and friends got special possessions. The estate would near one-quarter of a million dollars.[45]

On the road south Adams and Kilborne went to New York where Adams saw Frank Taylor, now with Western Printing & Lithography Company that dealt mostly with reprints and Bantam Books paperbacks. The hustling Taylor suggested he do a juvenile for Walt Disney and asked for an outline featuring a young boy. Adams gave him a précis of *Chingo Smith of the Erie Canal*.[46]

He and Kilborne stopped in North Carolina, seeing George Leonard at Southern Pines. Bud Leonard, who called Adams a "sort of godfather" from his teenage days at Wide Waters, showed him the local library where he and Nicholson discussed writing. He said he was disappointed when writers produced potboiler stories, trite in formula, weak in style.

The description fit "Blackout," which he finished soon after his arrival in Beaufort. Displeased with the manuscript, he asked Baumgarten and Brandt for help and put it aside until the summer, turning to the juvenile he had suggested to Taylor. December 1955 produced the news of an offer of a thousand dollar advance from Books Abridged to reprint *Grandfather Stories*, of a planned eighty-fifth birthday party, of Carol Brandt's decision to join Brandt & Brandt, and of a Charleston heart specialist's diagnosis of angina, about which Brandt said, "Once they really know they can do things."[47]

# 20

# STORYTELLER
## 1956–1958

ADAMS approached his eighty-fifth birthday with a new positivism tempered by a recognition, if not acceptance, that his health was placing increasing limitations on what he could do. The discovery that angina was affecting his heart meant that instead of the dreaded digitalis, he could use a tiny nitroglycerine pill to alleviate the cramping pains in the chest.

Any January money woes were alleviated when Random House paid some eleven thousand dollars, the yearly maximum of ten thousand dollars under the *Grandfather Stories* contract plus juvenile royalties. He told Bernice Baumgarten the money would be sufficient for the remainder of 1956. He was also cheered by the news that North American Library was bringing out a thirty-five cent paperback edition of *Grandfather Stories* with a four thousand dollar guarantee on publication. The edition was published in 1959.

The word from Baumgarten and Brandt about "Blackout" was also encouraging as they furnished him a detailed analysis of the story with their suggestions for improvements, including lessening the melodrama and making the heroine less of an automaton. Although he accepted their comments, he put aside the romantic serial so that he could concentrate on the juvenile that Frank Taylor wanted for Walt Disney.

About the only thing that concerned Adams in January was a Beaufort birthday party. It had begun as a small gathering at a plantation but, after one hundred invitations had been sent, grew until it was moved to the Ladies Island Country Club. The party featured Gay Nineties costumes with Adams in red suspenders. He stayed until 1:30 A.M., playing the piano for a sing-along and talking with friends such as Jo Pinckney, Paul Bonner, and former writer Elliott Springs, a cotton mill owner who had made Adams a vice president of the twenty-nine-mile short-line Lancaster & Chester Railway.[1]

Three days after Adams's birthday, H. L. Mencken died after several years as an invalid. When Adams had heard his friend was ill from a massive stroke in 1948, he had written Mencken that although nobody was indispensable, he came as close as anyone in America. In 1950 he tried again, telling Mencken about the derivation of *clapboard* but confessing he really wanted to find out how he was. Mencken's secretary replied he remained too ill to write. Now the iconoclast was gone.[2]

Gone, too, were Adams's contemporary muckrakers. Beginning with David Graham Phillips's murder two days before Adams's fortieth birthday in 1911, the toll had mounted with Thomas W. Lawson dying in 1925; Lincoln Steffens and Finley Peter Dunne in 1936; Charles Edward Russell in 1941; Ida Tarbell and William Allen White in 1944; Ray Stannard Baker in 1946; Will Irwin in 1948; George Kibbe Turner in 1952. With the exception of Upton Sinclair, whom some considered more a novelist than a muckraker, only Adams remained.[3]

Adams himself was becoming more susceptible to his chronic illnesses. After his party, he got a cold, which developed into the flu, incapacitating Adams for almost one month. Despite the fever from the flu sapping his strength he continued to entertain guests, including Brandt and Marquand, who came for two days from Pinehurst, and E. B. and Katharine White of the *New Yorker*, who paid a social call. The visit of the Whites possibly encouraged him to submit a new grandfather story to the magazine that bought "Grandfather and the Cold Year." It was his last appearance in the magazine, but his contract continued for the rest of his life.

The two days with Brandt at Beaufort were full of business, but it was another visitor who sparked Adams's interest in another magazine. While Serrell Hillman, on the *New York Times* Washington staff and a stringer for *Sports Illustrated*, was visiting Adams, they discussed Adams's football experiences and the Kid McCoy-James Corbett prizefight he had covered in 1900. Hillman relayed the ideas to the magazine's Andy Crichton, who ordered two articles at four hundred dollars each. Adams agreed to the order, and Brandt closed the deal with the proviso that they be done when Adams came north.

Brandt was also interested in Adams's already published stories, identifying them for Leo Margulies of King-Sized Publications, which already had bought "Inquest" and "The 7 Curses" for *The Saint Detective Magazine* for United States and English publication in 1955. *The Pony Express* was sold to

Goodson-Todman Productions for possible television scripts. And *Grandfather Stories* remained popular as Doubleday produced a condensed version in *Best in Books* in March, with three thousand dollars split between Adams and Random House.

Brandt's increased activity was, in part, because Carol Brandt was in the office. She handled motion picture and television rights and relayed a request by actor Charles Coburn to the firm's dramatic department. Coburn wanted to play grandfather Adams if someone would fashion a play. She also continued her practice of helping Marquand start his novels, going to Pinehurst with her son in March. Because of her short stay she did not visit Adams, instead inviting him to stay with them when in New York in May.[4]

As Adams began his trek north, he still had four chapters to go on his Chingo Smith juvenile. He said the steam was running low in the boiler, but he might be able to finish the book during his stops with friends and a visit with the Cecil Adells, who had settled in Red Bank, New Jersey. In New York he stayed with the Brandts, met with Peter Lyon for his biography of S. S. McClure, did research on the McCoy-Corbett fight, and discussed possible work for Sions. New York was too much, however, and he went to the Carmers with swollen legs and had Kilborne drive him to Cayuga County.

The New York visit had forced him to recognize his limits. At Owasco Lake he heard from Brandt that Sions was anxious for a nostalgic piece on the Albany night boat, which Brandt said "was a very convenient way to meet a lady you were not supposed to meet." Calling the idea swell, Adams wrote his agent that research was no longer physically possible for him. He urged Sions to find someone else, and Brandt reported he and Sions recognized Adams's common sense.[5]

Adams was not without work. He still had to do the two *Sports Illustrated* pieces after which he told Baumgarten he would finish the juvenile that she called "one of the nicest books you've written, and whenever you finish it, Random House should be delighted to publish it." She was right. When Cerf returned from Europe and heard reports about the new juvenile from his Random House colleagues after the Fourth of July party, he told the author: "A pox on Frank Taylor and his paper-back dynasty; *I* want to see this manuscript just as soon as you can get it down to me!"[6]

Before the Fourth of July party, he finished the *Sports Illustrated* story about his experiences on the Hamilton College football team. Rewriting the article several times, he was discouraged with the result, pleading for Brandt's help.

Brandt liked it as it was, however, and sent the article to the magazine, asking for a quick decision to "buck Sam up." The agent had assessed his friend's unhappy mood correctly because Adams said the magazine's rapid acceptance cheered him. He said he hoped the prizefight story would be easier.[7]

Concerning his juvenile, a more optimistic Adams explained to Cerf he had only offered the manuscript to Taylor because of the Disney connection, which never panned out, and not as a paperback book, assuring the publisher that he was as likely to quit Random House as to sell Wide Waters. He said he was allowing himself one month to finish the manuscript, explaining that his heart condition had cut back his work schedule.[8]

On 10 July he finished the story on the fixed fight between McCoy and Corbett except for a few facts he asked *Sports Illustrated* to check. He was critical of his capabilities, but Brandt called it "elegant." The magazine accepted it and asked Adams to sharpen the drama, which he did. After rejecting a suggestion for a story on horses from Sions, he also turned down Jerry Korn of *Collier's* for a piece on the Erie Canal for its "American Tradition" series, telling his agent he had no vitality left and he was working on the juvenile perhaps two hours a day. He said even that left him exhausted.[9]

Although his weight had dropped to 144 pounds on 1 August, he was cheered by a visit from Richard and Betty Steele and Buddy Richardson, his California "family." The news from the Cerfs was not so encouraging. The European trip had tightened Cerf's schedule, and he called off a planned August visit to Wide Waters but still expressed his interest in reading the new juvenile. Adams's 144 pounds represented a decrease of about forty from his former healthy physique. Arthritis had settled into his infirmed hip, and his teeth and hearing bothered him. With sparse white hair and a withered face, Adams now stooped as he walked. But his blue eyes still sparkled, his remaining fingers could play the piano, and his childish, high-pitched voice was firm.

He entertained Wallace Johnson and Irita Van Doren over Labor Day, but the planned Columbus Day visit by the Brandts was a loss. The cancellations of the Cerfs and the Brandts were offset, at least in part, by a black-tie stag party by his friends in November. Arranged by William Walling and Kilborne, who offered Boscobel that he had renamed Wrongside, the party drew more than forty. Brandt declined because "I am very short of breath and it is difficult for me to travel," but those who came included Scherman, Abner Sideman, Clune, Louis Jones, and Johnson, a fixture at Wide Waters that summer. Adams's worsening health was apparent to Clune, who described the author

25. Samuel Hopkins Adams reading on the porch of the little cottage. Courtesy of Hamilton College.

as a "small, frail man." His modesty was still present when Walling proposed a toast to "Mr. America," and Adams waved off further comments, urging the group to sing instead.[10]

After the party, Adams made plans for the trip south. After an attack of neuritis in his right wrist, however, a pessimistic Adams wrote Brandt a New York visit was off. Brandt sought to boost Adams's morale, writing him: "Look here, pal, once you get down into the warm country, you're going to have lots of energy. And you're going to be a helluva lot better; let's have no nonsense." Korn, having conceded the Erie Canal, suggested the Pony Express with Adams using his original research. Saying a condensation would be a snap but seeing the possibility of developing the story into another Landmark, Adams proposed an expanded topic, the importance of mail to the pioneers. Korn said he would hold a place in the magazine, but before Adams started the new piece, the Crowell-Collier Publishing Company folded *Collier's* and the *Woman's Home Companion.*[11]

In Beaufort in November 1956 Adams had yet to finish the Chingo Smith juvenile, which Taylor again was pushing because Disney had had success with "Johnny Tremaine." But Adams's exhaustion from the trip developed into illness, requiring daily visits by a doctor and a nurse. A concerned Baumgarten urged him to send her what he had, and she would decide whether it was ready for Disney.

Concerned also was Cerf, who sent him some new Random House books and gently scolded him for not corresponding. Although Adams had been told by his doctor not to write anything, even letters, he answered Cerf that he was not mad at him, just ill. He wrote the same day to Holbrook, discussing the "strange death" of Thomas Mott Osborne and offering him help with a planned book on patent medicines the next summer, adding he might not be around then.[12]

His comment seemed prophetic when he celebrated New Year's Day by having a heart attack. Kilborne and Elliott responded by getting a doctor and an oxygen tank in twenty minutes. Severe though the attack was, the doctors said no additional damage was done to his heart. The medication, however, brought a return of his skin affliction and insomnia, stopping work. Anxious, he asked Baumgarten to come to Beaufort to help him.

In New York the situation at Brandt & Brandt was also not good. Brandt was having such trouble breathing that he was undergoing radioactive treatments for emphysema. Baumgarten herself was battling a virus that forced her to suggest again that he send the manuscript. Urging her to take care of herself, he now battled the hives. Drugged each night, against his protests, he got sleep and promised an early return to Chingo Smith.

Baumgarten was heartened by reports that Adams had attended the wedding of Auburnian Mary Ann Wadsworth to Jerome Rich, but the author said the wedding came to him. Attired in a blue-and-white stripped dressing gown, he was in the bungalow's living room where the ceremony was performed. Although he could not work, he wrote letters, including one offering encouragement to Paul Bonner, who was struggling with a new novel.[13]

Adams's insomnia allowed him to read even more than usual. He found Rebecca West's novel *The Fountain Overflows* boring, Daphne du Maurier's *The Scapegoat* disappointing, and Grace Metalious's *Peyton Place*, which he expected to be artificial pornography, shocking but an honest study of small town characters. He was pleased by his Beaufort friend Ann Head's first novel based in South Carolina, *Fair With Rain*. Later she said he "was a wonderful friend and adviser for over 20 years. I knew him before I ever sold a piece of material. He criticized my work honestly and often."[14]

As his hives eased, Adams had a parade of relatives and friends who supplied tender loving care. His morale also improved, but his optimism about his own health was tempered by a growing concern over Brandt. After the agent finished his hospital treatment, his doctors sent him south to stay with Marquand. Neither man was able to drive, so they did not visit Adams, who was told by Marquand that Brandt would never work a full day again. Adams's anxiety was lessened by word from Brandt, back in New York, that Carol and Denny Brandt were running the office so well that he had little to do. Marquand also concerned Adams. When he read an interview in the *Charlotte Observer* in which Marquand said his current novel, *Women and Thomas Harlow*, would be his last, Adams told him he could not quit. He suggested a novel on the advertising business or a Southern story. Marquand replied the comment was a joke and vowed to visit Wide Waters in the summer or fall.[15]

In Beaufort he returned to Chingo Smith, working three or four hours a day until he finished on 22 March, just before Frank and Nan Taylor arrived with their son, Adams. Taylor still wanted the book for Disney, taking it with him to deliver to Baumgarten. Adams told her it was too long for Bonino, but she countered: "I don't believe for a moment that Random House won't be crazy about it." Having no delusions about Disney, he waited eagerly for her assessment. She said the book was wonderful as it stood and sent it to be typed.[16]

The apparent good fortune of the book was not matched by word of his friends. While Carol Brandt wrestled with having lawyers go over all of Adams's book contracts to include provisions for future television rights, Carl Brandt was back in hospital for another radiated iodine treatment and to learn how to make more constant use of oxygen. An Easter visit by William and Peggy Wood Walling was called off because she was busy with the last episodes of *I Remember Mama*. Holbrook, who had excited Adams with his plans to write about patent medicines, dropped the project because another book had been proposed.

As he readied himself for the trip north, he again sent a smoke-without-fire message to Baumgarten, asking about a payment for a film strip on *The Pony Express* and claiming he needed the money. After she said the $160 would be on his next accounting but she was sure she could get it ahead of time, he said to forget it. Concerning his health, he wrote Marquand that he felt better than he had in two or three years and Gannett that he hoped to do another book or two.[17]

Adams arranged to have Johnson drive him north, bypassing most of the usual stops and making the thousand-mile trip to Utica in two and one-half days. After he stayed with friends in Auburn, paying only a visit to Wide Waters to see the Huffs with their daughter, Jonnie Mae, and granddaughter, Salina, he and Kilborne went to New York. Prepared to visit Brandt in the hospital if need be, he was delighted to have dinner with the Brandts in their apartment. The high point was the decision by his agent to spend two weeks at Wide Waters during which they would be joined by the rest of the family, including Beau, over Labor Day. Adams immediately asked Marquand, who accepted.

While seeing Baumgarten, Adams signed a contract for Chingo Smith after Bonino liked the book so much she offered a one thousand dollar advance and wondered if the boy was a real person. Adams admitted he spun him out of his imagination. Adams and Cerf had hoped to go to the Dutch Treat Club together, but with the publisher called out of town Adams went without him. While there he was approached by Lowell Thomas with a young man who said he wanted to meet the author of *Grandfather Stories* that his wife had been reading to him. Calling Billy Graham "the most magnetic preacher I have ever heard," Adams told Clune: "I liked Graham very much. He is dead sincere. He is a much more literate man than I imagined." He also said he had heard him preach, and "He is not a ranter and he doesn't resort to any hammy theatrics. . . . You could have heard the buzz of a fly during his pauses."[18]

He could not reschedule with Cerf because Clune was driving him to Rochester for a 27 May awards dinner. Although he had sworn off speechmaking, he relented when the Friends of the Rochester Public Library proposed he receive its first annual Literary Award. As usual, Adams faced the event with trepidation. Described by a reporter at the dinner as seemingly fragile and thin, he listened in the library's main foyer as Louis Jones, in a speech entitled "Sam Adams and the New York State Renaissance," said: "From every point of view, from the beginning of this century, he has been a successful writer. More than that he has been a successful human being." The reporter, who had noted the frailty, said that when Adams spoke, "the charm, vitality and wit bubbled as always." He told the audience what it wanted to hear, that he wished he had been born in Rochester, which he called "something more than a mecca." He then discussed his grandfather Adams's second wife, who although unnamed in *Grandfather Stories*, was named Clematis, "which is probably why my grandfather always addressed her as Mrs. Adams." He concluded by expressing regret over the razing of his father's Plymouth Church for a new highway, "thanks to the juggernaut of a misguided progress."[19]

Although Adams expected a medal, he received a silver bowl fashioned by the School for American Craftsmen at Rochester Institute of Technology. With it was a citation that read, in part: "Devotion to country, pride in the achievements of America, love for and faith in people, contempt for the corrupt and false, and a warm suggestion of the human and the commonplace are strikingly and vigorously evident in the writing of Samuel Hopkins Adams."[20]

Back home he was kept busy as he arranged for an oxygen tank for Brandt's visit, learned of the death of his first wife, Elizabeth Remmel, on 1 June in California, attended the commencement of Hamilton College where only he and Tom Coventry remained of the Class of 1891, and entertained the Bill Wallings after Peggy Wood received an honorary degree from Hobart College. His biggest challenge was dealing with Brandt's salt-free diet. He had abandoned his own.

The Fourth of July party had grown by additional invitations to Random House's editor Albert Erskine, publicist Jean Ennis, and receptionist Janet Flagg, Adams's former granddaughter-in-law. Although his legs had swollen again, his doctor had given him a shot and said that his winter attack appeared to have improved the functioning of his heart. That prompted Adams not only to entertain a dozen out-of-towners but to schedule a picnic for forty.

Financially, a letter from Washington amazed him. Reporting to the government that he was due a ten-dollar pension raise and anticipating twenty dollars for two months in arrears, he told Baumgarten he had received a notification that his next check would be for $248.50. He asked why he should continue working when all he needed to do was write the government and get a check for any amount that came into its head.[21]

During the making of arrangements for the Brandt visit, the relationship between Adams and Carol Brandt deepened. He was unhappy she was combining business with pleasure by scheduling a visit with author Theresa Lewis in Watertown over Labor Day. She answered his protests by shortening her business trip and then said: "I must say I've had more pleasure—or, in fact, the only pleasure in terms of Carl's recent and ghastly illness—from creating a correspondence between us than I dreamed could happen."[22]

His working relationship with Random House also pleased Adams. He was eager that his fiction juvenile be historically accurate, so he asked Bonino to send *Chingo Smith* to a historian, David Ennis, an expert on the Erie Canal.

He met with Adams, and they corrected three or four historical errors. William J. Tyrrell also recalled doing a checking job for Adams, not on his manuscript but a friend's. After he was negative, Adams replied: "She's going to take a writing course. She's still young yet, she's only 60."[23]

After going to Cooperstown in mid-July, a reinvigorated Adams decided it was time to get to work. On 24 July, he wrote Baumgarten that he was ready for the final rewrite of the *Police Gazette* novel. True to his word, he told Baumgarten several days later he was at work on the novel. Adams was mellow when Brandt visited. The talk at Wide Waters between the two men focused on the novel. While Brandt got a good rest, Adams reported to Baumgarten he was re-making his novel because Carl had made so many valuable suggestions.

After the Brandts left, he and Carl Brandt exchanged letters about how much they had enjoyed the two weeks together, about Ayn Rand's *Atlas Shrugged* that Adams called phony—Brandt agreed—and about their respective states of health. Brandt urged Adams to do more about salt and even plotted with Mildred Harlan to get him to use a special type. Carol Brandt also thanked Adams for a wonderful time. None of the letters mentioned Marquand, who had missed the weekend.

Adams's health improved after late June when he had told Baumgarten that he was taking enough nitroglycerine to blow up. A heart flutter after the Brandt visit, however, prompted him to keep someone in the house with him. He was also bothered with deteriorated hearing, and Brandt got him a good price on an aid in New York. Health aside, Adams was buoyed in September by news that the Carnegie Foundation had chosen *Grandfather Stories* for two hundred and fifty libraries throughout the British Commonwealth to give a picture of early American life. Holbrook also pleased him by putting the patent medicine book back on, and he again pledged his aid.

He hoped to finish his novel before going south and welcomed Baumgarten's promise of whatever assistance she could give. Requests by the New York City Cancer Society and Random House for television appearances persuaded him to tackle New York again, hoping to stay with Van Doren. The only cloud in Adams's sky was concern about Jo Pinckney, from whom he had gotten a letter with optimism that did not sound genuine. He was right as his friend died in October 1957 about the time he hoped she would be at Wide Waters.

He wrote Brandt 2 October that he was using the special salt he had left and the Carnegie action was pleasant but that books on the period were probably scanty. Concerning his novel, he said he needed Brandt's sage counsel. Brandt replied 8 October that he would get him more salt, the Carnegie action was "very nice," and the novel would work out. He reminded, "Even if I'm not in the next room, I'm only a mail away, so shout if you need help."

Five days later Gertrude Case, who was running Wide Waters for Adams, received a telephone call and sent for Kilborne. They made a preluncheon cocktail and then told Adams that Carl Brandt was dead. Three days after he had written Adams, Brandt was operated on for just-discovered cancer of the bladder and died on 13 October from shock. Writing to Elliott of the shattering blow that Sunday, a dazed Adams confessed that nothing had hit him so hard since Jane's death. For the first time in his life, Adams said, he might never have the energy or desire to work again.[24]

Two days later, suffering further from an ulcerated tooth that had produced a setback with his heart, he told Johnson he felt lost. Marquand and Carol Brandt both wrote; he sharing the loss and telling of his regret that he had not come to Wide Waters on Labor Day, and she thanking him for his contribution to CARE and expressing pleasure that Frank Taylor would be in the area that weekend. Adams wrote her that he was glad for the two weeks with Brandt. He returned to his work and wrote Baumgarten the novel's end was in sight but he had concern about the office pressure on her. When Taylor came that weekend, Adams learned his blow had doubled. Baumgarten was leaving Brandt & Brandt.[25]

Although he told Holbrook he felt as if the earth were dissolving beneath him, he told Cerf he was writing and as long as he could work, he found life worthwhile. The Frank Taylors, Akin and Peggy French, and John Hersey came that fall. Paying a visit to Wide Waters also was Heckscher, who in 1956 had become the director of the Twentieth Century Fund, a philanthropic organization. "Sam kept connected with young people," Nan Abell remembered, adding: "What a smart thing to do." Although the New York "gang" was not conservative as Adams was, Peggy French explained: "Among us who knew him there was great affection that transcended business. I knew a lot of authors but none like Sam."[26]

Meanwhile, he was making his plans for the New York visit that he now felt was imperative. He was torn as to what to do about Brandt & Brandt. Although he did not wish to go into the office, he wanted to know young Carl Brandt better and was eager to see Baumgarten before she and Cozzens moved to Virginia. Assurances from her that she would continue to handle his writing because "it is a comfort to *me* that you cannot escape my autocratic rule" and from Carol Brandt that she wanted to see him put the office on his itinerary.[27]

He and Cerf made special arrangements so he would not have to climb stairs to the Random House offices, and they planned to go to the Dutch Treat Club together. In July Cerf had sent a copy of *General Brock and Niagara Falls*, which was scheduled for the fall, but they continued to joke about General Brock, with Cerf reporting: "Phyllis and I—not to mention General Brock—look forward to your imminent arrival with unrestrained enthusiasm," and Adams saying he still had work to do on his novel because he had to live up to the reputation established by his book on General Brock.[28]

Adams had better hopes for the novel, which he shipped off to Baumgarten in early November with the ending still open for her suggestions. He said cutting was needed as he went to a football game and entertained seventeen at dinner. It was a typical Adams mistake concerning his stamina, and he suffered a setback that delayed his trip south. With his plans in a jumble, Mildred Harlan drove up from New York and took him down to the city where he kept his appointments. Charles Schlesinger of Brandt & Brandt remembered he came in on the arm of Vicky Brandt "like a ghost of the literary past," and Cerf would later recall: "Toward the end of his life he had dreadful arthritis, and it was painful to watch him get in and out of an automobile, which sometimes would take him five minutes. But he was a gutsy old man, and when he came to the office, if people tried to help him, he'd get furious and brush them off. We all loved him."[29]

After visiting the Carmers, he arrived in Beaufort on Thanksgiving. Although his doctor found his most recent setback had not affected his heart, Adams was content with reading *Chingo Smith of the Erie Canal* proofs rather than making the changes Baumgarten had suggested in the novel. She had moved to Belle Haven, Virginia, and on 10 December urged him to wait on the novel until after the holidays when "I will by that time be so much closer to you geographically that all you will have to do is to give a loud yell for me to hear."

After his meeting in New York with the Brandts, the relationships strengthened. Afterward, he wrote Carol Brandt that all his loyalty was with them. Carol Brandt wrote Adams to urge him to stay away from salt, not to be too gay and festive, and to remember: "Carl Jr. and I know that we can count upon you for ever and ever. You know very well that I always have upon you and upon Jane. For my money, I'd like to race you to the pearly gates and not have to stay one hour later than you find this merry little world fun. My only anxiety is that I'm afraid I'll find myself not admitted to those pink clouds where you and Carl will be deservedly."[30]

In January 1958 the Beaufort Chamber of Commerce named him its honorary president. Commenting later on Adams and Beaufort, the *Charleston Courier* observed: "He became an intimate part of that charming community. Mr. Adams loved Beaufort and the people there warmly responded." His love was not blind. Although he enjoyed the plantation society and asked for social compromise by his Northern visitors on racial matters, he abhorred the Dixieslingers. In urging Marquand to do a Southern novel he targeted the noble-hearted Southern gentleman who could not detach himself from his old traditions. Yet Adams did not let the Southern attitude spoil his love for his friends, for the countryside, and for Southern events in the Lowcountry. One event that he especially enjoyed was the annual cattle sale at Bray's Island to which he invited Marquand, whom he was eager to see. Marquand declined the invitation but promised to come to Beaufort later in February. When Marquand again bowed out, Adams told Carol Brandt he did not want to press his friend, and she urged him to wait until fall when she would come up to Wide Waters with him.[31]

Adams also remained involved with central New York. He lent his support and advice to an attempt to save an old canal building in Syracuse, urging letters be sent to lawmakers. With characteristic optimism and his muckraker's belief in the power of public opinion, he said: "The life and death of the bill now before the Legislature will depend on the individual citizens of New York State. I am certainly for the preservation of the grand old Weighlock building." The building was saved and became the Erie Canal Museum in Syracuse.[32]

He continued his interest with his colleagues. After telling Holbrook of his struggles with the novel, he discussed patent medicines for Holbrook's book. He also sought to help another friend, state Senator George Metcalf, by urging young Carl Brandt to meet with him about a book he was writing on William H. Seward, part of which Adams said he had read and liked. A book he did not like was Allen Churchill's *Park Row*, which he reviewed. He told Carol Brandt the book on New York newspapering at the time when he was a reporter was a shoddy job. His review held few punches and was cited later by Lewis Gannett as "possibly the most vigorous book review of 1958."[33]

His own novel was still not going well. On 1 April, however, he sent the manuscript to a typist and told Brigham he was exhausted. He hoped the typing would be done by 1 May, allowing fall publication. His doctor assured him that if he took life easy, he would be all right. At the same time he asked Brigham for material on public health practices in the 1820s and 1830s.[34]

In April 1958 Adams wrote Cerf to thank him for a prominent display in a Madison Avenue window of *Chingo Smith of the Erie Canal*. Cerf and Adams must have been delighted by the *Chingo Smith* reviews. The story about a Huck Finn–type boy and his adventures on the Erie Canal and in the South told a rags-to-riches tale that took the boy from doing odd jobs to becoming captain of his own packet boat. The book came out at a time when the American Dream was much in the public's consciousness, and this was not lost on reviewers. His last juvenile was dedicated to Richard Hamilton Steele "with the affectionate regards of Uncle Sam." The book would sell more than eleven thousand copies by 1961 and send Adams out of juveniles a winner.[35]

Carol Brandt received the manuscript of the novel, called *The Fanatic*, in May and coordinated its editing between Random House and Baumgarten. After reading it, Brandt praised its "nostalgia and charm, excitement and pace" but confided to Baumgarten it was long. Baumgarten did tell him it was lengthy. She also had another ending for the book, retitled *Tenderloin*, about two newspapermen in New York during the 1890s.

A major difficulty he had had with the novel was the complexity of plot. His two heroes were the brash, musical Tommy Howatt of the *Police Gazette*, the intended hero of the novel, and the erudite Dan Adriance of the *Star*. Both had romances with different women. Added were muckraking looks at the police corruption and the crooked politics of Tammany Hall, the tragedy of a man who commits suicide because of soiled honor, and the ambiance of the Tenderloin district.

He had begun the book as a look at newspapering in the days of the *Police Gazette*. But to counter the sordidness of the Tenderloin, he brought in a self-appointed crusader against vice, the Reverend Brockholst Farr, modeled on the crusading Reverend Charles Parkhurst, and he took over the novel. The focus, however, was the Tenderloin, the atmosphere of which he sought to recapture. William McFee explained in the *Saturday Review*: "The curious thing about Adams as a writer . . . is that none of his contemporaries in our time influenced him. So far as 'Tenderloin' is concerned, Hemingway, Conrad, Faulkner, Fitzgerald, and O'Hara were nonexistent." The result, McFee said, was "not a novel in the ordinary sense, a narrative of actual people. It is the discursive libretto of a musical." Evidently readers agreed; buying about twenty-six thousand copies.[36]

A trip to the New York City area began at the Lewis Gannetts where he and James Thurber renewed their acquaintance. Thurber, who was writing a series of articles on Ross for the *Atlantic Monthly*, had earlier asked Adams for permission to use some of the material from his Woollcott biography. At the Gannetts the two *New Yorker* contributors went into a corner and reminisced about Ross. Adams was delighted to talk with Thurber again. Having his own deficiencies, Adams was especially appreciative of the help Thurber's wife provided the nearly blind author, adding a postscript to her in a thank-you letter after Thurber sent him two books. Later Gannett remembered, "Sam was not at all well, but he was so delighted by Jim's conversation that he refused to go to bed until long after midnight."[37]

Adams paid a price. Suffering another attack, he was told by a heart specialist to go home at once. Staying with Auburn friends, he had good and bad days, but his doctor sent him to Wide Waters on Declaration Day. On 20 May Adams had sent a letter to Carol Brandt at her home, saying he was no longer capable of any work on *Tenderloin*, but he did want the novel published. Having a profound distaste for self-pitiers, he said they were close enough friends so they could dispense with any hand wringing and tear shedding.

The matter-of-fact Carol Brandt, who told Baumgarten the letter made her weep, sent her a copy. She also showed the letter to Marquand, who suggested they drive to Auburn to see Adams. Spending an hour with him, she reported that he was indeed frail "and his ability to make a comeback is definitely less." Marquand pledged to his friend that, if needed, he would see the novel through to publication, and Carol Brandt said, "Sam was most, most happy about this." Baumgarten, who had said before getting the letter that she thought Adams was immortal, maintained, "Still I can't believe that he won't recover from this attack triumphantly, as always, and outlive us all."[38]

Random House had been contacted by Baumgarten on 14 May when she told Cerf: "Our Sam is a miracle. He no sooner mailed off the Police Gazette novel than he began to talk about his next!" Cerf said reports on *Tenderloin* were "simply great." Baumgarten, who admitted she had had her fingers crossed about the novel's acceptance, also asked Cerf if Becker, who had retired from Random House, was available to edit the manuscript, but he said that Albert Erskine, a top editor at Random House, wanted to do the editing. Told by Adams that the novel might have to be published posthumously, Cerf said he had a ten-dollar bet that he would outlive them all. Just in case, however, Marquand repeated his offer to read it after the changes and cuts were made, and Baumgarten also volunteered to help.[39]

Adams's restorative powers were still with him. When at end of May as his doctor tried to get his pulse below the 100-rate with an improved digitalis,

Adams asked about serializing *Tenderloin*, scheduled an appearance at commencement, and sought to get Elliott and the Carmers together in August. Under the eye of Fran Merriam he was told by his doctor to go to work, and he made revisions in the novel. When he wrote Carol Brandt on 3 June that he had been working all day and was dizzy, she quickly told him not to overwork.

Adams began to bombard both Carol Brandt and Baumgarten with letters as he made changes in *Tenderloin*, offered to do some antique prowling for Baumgarten, and sought to help Harold Freedman of the Brandt & Brandt drama department with the possibility of a musical play based on the novel. Not so cheerful were his missing commencement and the postponement by Random House of the novel until early in 1959. After he complained, Carol Brandt replied that a serious novel was better launched at the beginning of a new year rather than having to compete with novelty books at Christmas and repeated, "in the role of a nagging wife," that he not overdo.[40]

The Carmers pushed up their visit to mid-June so they could be at Wide Waters with the Wallings. During the visit Adams gave Carmer his opera cape for the opening of the *Tenderloin* musical, if it happened. "I'll accept it gladly, Sam," Carmer was reported as saying, "provided I can lend it to you for the opening of *Tenderloin*." Adams replied, "I'll never live to see the opening, but you wear the cape." Carmer did.[41]

Another visitor was George Harlan, who said of his grandfather: "He was formidable when someone crossed him, but I did not find him frightening. I had the feeling that I wanted to be liked by him. However, I never had a feeling of acceptance until the last summer when he would invite me up to his room. I was honored, and he told me wonderful stories about New York City."[42]

The Carmers and Wallings were followed by the Fourth of July group that included Erskine, who extended his visit three days to go over *Tenderloin*. Adams was still bothered about the ending and complained in a letter to Clune: "It is a discouraging, never ending, struggling life—this writing business! But do you know of a better one?" The strenuous work with Erskine was too much for Adams; he suffered another severe heart attack, which limited his work and brought a nurse. He notified Holbrook that "intimations of mortality come thicker. You had best stop on your way East, rather than when you are returning to Oregon."[43]

As contract talks continued on a musical, Adams became more excited and Carol Brandt more soothing. She assured him that play negotiations took time and she, Marquand, and Vicky Brandt were planning to visit him in October.

She sent him the play contracts 5 August and when she had not heard back from him on 25 August, she wrote his attorney to ask how he was.[44]

According to the Associated Press, he was dead. On 14 August the wire service filed:

> NEW YORK (AP)—Samuel Hopkins Adams, 87, novelist, historian and former newspaperman, died today in his home in Auburn, N.Y., Random House, his publisher, announced.
>
> Adams had been ill with a heart ailment. He recently completed a novel, "Tenderloin," a story of New York City in the 1890's, to be published in January.[45]

When the wire service report was received at the New York *Herald Tribune*, an alert editor phoned upstairs to Van Doren for verification. She immediately called Mildred Harlan, who said: "Sam is much alive and is expecting fourteen for dinner tonight." It was stated that a telephone message at the switchboard at Random House had been garbled and the false report resulted.

When Holbrook stopped his way to New York several days later, the two men reminisced about the report of his loss aboard the *Titanic* and that he was now one up on Mark Twain, who in 1897 had cabled the Associated Press from London: "The reports of my death are greatly exaggerated." For the bulk of the time, however, they discussed patent medicines. Adams had been eager to discuss Holbrook's book with him, but when he got *The Golden Age of Quackery*, he was flabbergasted. "Sam is the hero of this book," Holbrook told a Rochester newspaper later. At Wide Waters they discussed Adams's belief that nostrums were still being sold by so-called doctors in magazine ads and on television. Adams said they were now harmless rather than dangerous but labeled the advertising as "the same old Kickapoo pitch."[46]

The false report of his death apparently alerted the Associated Press and the *Citizen-Advertiser* that the time had come to interview Adams. Jessica Wellner, the vivacious wife of the newspaper's editor and a writer herself, was selected. When he was contacted by the Associated Press, Adams roared: "What is this—a concealed obituary? I don't intend to die yet." Later he confided to Wellner, "I didn't know they remembered me." She did her interview, and it became the only one ever published in an Auburn newspaper. The interview also ran in papers across the nation and, in it, he admitted, "There's nothing burning inside now." In looking over his career, he summed up his writing: "I think a storyteller ought to tell a story."[47]

Later Louis Jones commented, "He never pretended that he was a great literary artist but he was surely what he pretended to be, a master storyteller."

26. Samuel Hopkins Adams at Wide Waters on Owasco Lake. This photograph illustrated a 1958 interview with Adams, months before his death. Courtesy of Hamilton College.

Clune remembered Adams saying: "The novelist's first and greatest function is to tell a story. The greatest writing has always been story telling. Wasn't that what Homer, Shakespeare, the Greek dramatists, Tolstoy, Balzac—all the great ones—have done?"[48]

Although Adams did not like the Hillman profile that would appear later in the *Saturday Review*, the Wellner interview went without comment. Perhaps the reason was the answer Carol Brandt received to the 25 August letter from attorney H. Dutton Noble, saying Adams was failing slowly. Perhaps it was Adams's 31 August letter, stating that his mind was dim because of Demerol. Perhaps it came from Van Doren, who was scheduled to spend Labor Day at Wide Waters.[49]

Whatever, the word filtered down to New York and to Virginia, where Baumgarten with resignation on 1 September told Carol Brandt: "I can't believe this is the end of Sam. He has been part of my life always, as Carl was, and I firmly expected him to live forever." Carol Brandt did not give up, writing 2 September that the musical contracts were signed and closing, "I haven't written you because, in truth, I hadn't very much to say except to send our love and our concern." Three days later, Adams wrote in a barely decipherable hand to ask why he had not heard from her, also telling her that he was turning over all financial management to Noble.[50]

Concerned that Adams could not make corrections, she covered the novel by sending Marquand a set of galleys. Her suspicions were confirmed when she wrote 16 September, enclosing contracts on *Tenderloin* for his signature. Mildred Harlan replied that he wanted Brandt to sign them, using her literary power of attorney. Cecil and Katherine Adell arrived after Labor Day, and while Mary Melnick and another nurse tended Adams, his daughter took over correspondence. To Cerf, who wrote a note about *Tenderloin*, "I feel in my bones that this is going to be one of the most successful of all your books," she said her father was somewhat improved and even played a few hands of bridge.[51]

His day nurse, Melnick, who had come to Wide Waters on and off since his 1955 heart attack, recalled: "He did a lot of reading and told stories. Although his hip was giving him a pain, he was lucid and always did what he was told." Ever hospitable, he had urged her to bring her children to the lake. "He visited with the little ones and signed a copy of *The Erie Canal*." Although Melnick remembered the weather was good in September, "he was very anxious to go south." In late September Johnson, who had been at Wide Waters for Labor Day, returned. "I saw him three times during the day but about a minute after I went into his room he would drift into a sleep," he wrote a friend.[52]

The plan was to fly him down on an ambulance airplane, but when it was delayed for several days, Kilborne arranged with the Wade family in Moravia to take him in their ambulance. "Unlike the airplane, it was equipped with oxygen, although we did not need to use it," recalled Melnick, who accompanied Adams south. Rowland Wade, with a relief driver and the nurse, put Adams in the ambulance on 1 October.

Carol Brandt had remained anxious about her friend and the lack of communication from Auburn. She wrote Noble at the end of September to ask whether the Brandt family should drive up on 11 October, explaining she did not contact Adams directly because he would say come even if it would be too tiring. Noble replied Adams continued to fail gradually but was going to Beaufort.[53]

The ambulance took him up Wide Waters driveway, turned onto Whiskey Lane, which would be renamed Sam Adams Lane, passed the Champany home, and went onto Rockefeller Road heading south. "We drove straight down," Wade recalled. Knowing Adams from his visits to the movie theater in Moravia, Wade said: "I admired him immensely. He was on a cot in the ambulance and when I hit a bump, I'd look back at him in the rear view mirror and he would wink at me."[54]

In Beaufort they brought Adams to his bungalow on North Hermitage Road where Elliott and his Southern nurses took over. Adams was pleased to see visitors, who dropped in for a few minutes, but he was no longer interested in any letters being read, content just to know who had written. In late October Elliott reported to Carol Brandt that his specialist said the end could come at any time. Still hopeful, Carol Brandt, who was about to leave on a trip to California, replied that she would try to join Marquand in a visit after the first of the year. She also sent the Elliott letter to Baumgarten, who returned it with a note: "This seems to me hideously sad. It should end quickly."[55]

One letter that may have been read to Adams was a brief note on 7 November from Cerf, who later would say that Adams was a popular author and that his books had authentic historical interest. Cerf said advertising and publicity was beginning for *Tenderloin* and predicted, "This ought to be the biggest book you have had in a long, long time."[56]

"I think Sam battled death to the end," Elliott recalled. On 11 November Adams got pneumonia. "The last days he was too ill to really talk but always smiled at me," she said.[57] On Saturday, 15 November, in Clinton, Hamilton College finished its first undefeated football season with an 18–0 win over Union College, and that night, in Rochester, *It Happened One Night* was on a television Late Show. At five minutes past midnight Elliott received a phone call from the nurse next door. Samuel Hopkins Adams was dead.

# NOTES
# BIBLIOGRAPHY
# INDEX

# NOTES

## Abbreviations

| | |
|---|---|
| AAS | American Antiquarian Society |
| ARL | Arents Research Library, Syracuse University |
| BAC | Bennett A. Cerf |
| BB | Bernice Baumgarten |
| B-M | Bobbs-Merrill publishers |
| CB | Carl Brandt |
| FG | Ferris Greenslet |
| HBL | Horace B. Liveright |
| HM | Houghton Mifflin publishers |
| RLS | Roger L. Scaife |
| SHA | Samuel Hopkins Adams |
| SHH | Stewart Hall Holbrook |

## 1. Boyhood, 1871–1887

1. Samuel Hopkins Adams, *Grandfather Stories* (New York: Random House, 1955), 22. Hereafter, Adams is referred to as SHA. Full citations of his work are in the Adams bibliography. John Adams was a direct ancestor of SHA and the older brother of Henry Adams, direct ancestor of the presidents, John Adams and John Quincy Adams.

2. Samuel Miles Hopkins, *Memorial Book; Myron Adams* (Privately printed, n.d.), 8.

3. Charles D. Broadbent, "A Brief Pilgrimage; Plymouth Church of Rochester," *Rochester History* 40, no. 4 (Oct. 1978): 2–3.

4. *Rochester (N.Y.) Times-Union*, 17 Nov. 1958, 11. Hereafter, New York state newspapers are cited by city only.

5. Rudolph W. Chamberlain, *There Is No Truce; The Life of Thomas Mott Osborne* (New York: Macmillan, 1935), 28.

6. *Auburn Daily Advertiser*, 6 May 1903, 5; SHA, *Grandfather Stories*, 4.

7. *Auburn Daily Advertiser*, 29 Oct. 1901, 4; SHA, *Grandfather Stories*, 269.

8. SHA, *Grandfather Stories*, 5–6.

9. Ibid., 199.

10. Ibid., 4, 6.

11. Myron Adams signal book, Burke Library, Hamilton College, Clinton, N.Y.

12. Stanley J. Kunitz and Howard Haycraft, eds., *Twentieth Century Authors; A Biographical Dictionary of Modern Literature* (New York: H. W. Wilson, 1942), 7; *Boston (Mass.) Globe*, 31 July 1927, 40.

13. *New York Times Book Review*, 24 May 1955, 12; *Boston (Mass.) Globe*, 31 July 1927, 40.

14. Tape recording of dinner speech, 7 June 1955, Cayuga Museum of History and Art, Auburn, N.Y.

15. *Cleveland (Ohio) Press*, 11 Oct. 1920, 10; *New York Post*, 16 Nov. 1944, 33.

16. Katherine Adams Adell to author, 11 June 1990; File 37713, Record Unit 305, Smithsonian Institution Archives, Washington, D.C.

## 2. Collegian, 1887–1891

1. SHA, *Grandfather Stories*, 14.

2. SHA, "Minora Canamus," *Hamilton Alumni Review*, July 1941, 217.

3. Ibid., 213.

4. SHA, "Foreword," in *The Class of 1891 of Hamilton College*, 1.

5. SHA, "Minora Canamus," 213.

6. SHA, "Foreword," 2.

7. Hamilton College faculty minutes, 136, 139, 144, Burke Library.

8. SHA, "Foreword," 3; Hamilton College faculty minutes, 148.

9. *Cleveland (Ohio) Press*, 11 Oct. 1920, 10; SHA, "Minora Canamus," 213.

10. SHA, "How I Write," *The Writer*, Apr. 1936, 107.

11. SHA in Gelett Burgess, ed., *My Maiden Effort; The Personal Confessions of Well Known American Authors Collected by the Authors' League of America* (New York: Doubleday, Page, 1921), 1–3.

12. *New York Times Book Review*, 4 Dec. 1955, 6.

13. Interview with Katherine Adell, 12 June 1989; *New York Herald Tribune Book Review*, 26 June 1955, 2. All Adell interviews were in Eatontown, N.J.

14. SHA, "Sam Adams," *Collier's*, 30, quoted in Charles Crittenden Baldwin, *The Men Who Make Our Novels* (New York: Dodd, Mead, 1924), 12.

15. Ellen H. Fladger, archivist of Union College, Schenectady, N.Y., to author, 14 Mar. 1990; SHA, "Fifty Years of Football," *Hamilton Alumni Review*, Oct. 1940, 6.

16. "Samuel Hopkins Adams 1871–," *Wilson Bulletin for Librarians*, Apr. 1934, 500.

17. George Budd, "Hamilton's First Football Game," *Hamilton Literary Magazine*, Nov. 1902, 101.

18. Budd, "Hamilton's First Football Game," 100.

19. SHA to Samuel Miles Hopkins, 2 Nov. 1890, SHA Papers, Burke Library.

20. SHA to Charles B. Rogers, 30 Sept. 1936, Alexander Woollcott Papers, Houghton Library, Harvard Univ., Cambridge, Mass.

21. SHA, "Old Timers on Early Union Game," *Hamilton Life*, 7 Nov. 1925, 3.

22. Ibid., 3; Budd, "Hamilton's First Football Game," 101.

23. SHA, "Old Timers," 3, 5; George Daley, "Famous Sports Writer Relates Experiences as Union Star in Hamilton-Union Games," *Hamilton Life*, 8 Nov. 1932, 1.

24. *Hamilton Review*, Feb. 1891, 124.

25. *Auburn Citizen–Advertiser*, 2 Sept. 1958, 2; SHA, "Minora Canamus," 210.

26. *Hamilton Literary Monthly*, May 1891, 379.

## 3. Reporter, 1891–1899

1. *Rochester Democrat and Chronicle*, 27 Oct. 1935, 2B; Kunitz and Haycraft, *Twentieth Century Authors*, 7.

2. *Editor and Publisher*, 5 Feb. 1910, 6; SHA, *Tenderloin*, 10.

3. Chester S. Lord, "What to Print," *Saturday Evening Post*, 17 Sept. 1921, 10–11.

4. Will Irwin, *The Making of a Reporter* (New York: G. P. Putnam's Sons, 1942), 109.

5. *Syracuse Post-Standard*, 1 Dec. 1957, 13; SHA, *Success*, 304.

6. SHA, *Tenderloin*, 25. Dumbbell tenements were so named because of the configuration of the apartments.

7. James H. Wilson, *The Life of Charles A. Dana* (New York: Harper and Brothers, 1907), 510; Irwin, *Reporter*, 113; Walter Winchell, *Syracuse Herald-American*, 23 Nov. 1958, 33.

8. Interview with George Harlan, 15 Sept. 1990, Toronto, Canada.

9. Adams said days later he saw the man, clean-shaven, among some railroad officials at a station.

10. Jesse Lynch Williams, "'Sam' Adams as His Associates Know Him," *Book News Monthly*, Jan. 1915, 217; Irwin, *Reporter*, 110.

11. Frank M. O'Brien, *The Story of the Sun* (New York: George H. Doran Company, 1918), 359; Chester S. Lord, "Reporters and Reporting," *Saturday Evening Post*, 1 Oct. 1921, 12.

12. SHA, *Tenderloin*, 10.

13. *Auburn Citizen–Advertiser*, 30 July 1948, 4. Earlier Adams told John Farrar of *Bookman*, Mar. 1927, 110, stories of Roosevelt, "how he had once known him well and found him a very poor athlete and an indifferent horseman, although indefatigable and with real enthusiasm for sports."

14. Certificate presented to SHA, 27 May 1957, SHA file, Rochester Public Library, Rochester, N.Y.; Michael Schudson, *Discovering the News: A Social History of American Newspapers* (New York: Basic Books, 1978), 71; Jesse Lynch Williams, "'Sam' Adams," 217.

15. *New York Herald Tribune Book Review*, 26 June 1955, 2; Franklin Pierce Adams, *The Diary of Our Own Samuel Pepys* (New York: Simon and Schuster, 1935), vol. 2 (1926–34): 643; *Syracuse Post-Standard*, 1 Dec. 1957, 13.

16. "Samuel Hopkins Adams," in "Chronicle and Comment," *Bookman*, Aug. 1905, 562.

17. SHA to W. R. Burlingame, 20 June 1896, Charles Scribner's Sons Papers. Published with permission of the Manuscripts Division, Department of Rare Books and Special Collections, Princeton Univ. Libraries, Princeton, N.J.

18. *Auburn Citizen–Advertiser*, 2 Aug. 1948, 4.

19. SHA to David T. Wilder, 17 Jan. 1950, SHA Papers, Burke Library.

20. Elmira College catalog 1892–93, Elmira College archives, Elmira, N.Y., 47; interview with Katherine Adell, 1 Aug. 1989.

21. *Charleston (W.Va.) Daily Gazette*, 20 Oct. 1898, 6.

22. Lord, "Reporters and Reporting," 86.

23. SHA, "Bathed in the Aura of the Glory-Story," *New York Times Book Review*, 23 Mar. 1958, 10.

24. *Rochester Democrat and Chronicle*, 15 July 1952, 15; *New York Times Book Review*, 17 June 1945, 3.

## 4. Magazine Writer, 1900–1904

1. Harold S. Wilson, *McClure's Magazine and the Muckrakers* (Princeton, N.J.: Princeton Univ. Press, 1970) 192.

2. *New York World*, 31 Aug. 1900, 2.

3. Peter Lyon, *Success Story, The Life and Times of S. S. McClure* (New York: Charles Scribner's Sons, 1963), 186; Kunitz and Haycraft, *Twentieth Century Authors*, 7.

4. *New York Herald Tribune Book Review*, 26 June 1955, 2, 2; SHA to Henry W. Boynton, 18, 20, 24 Apr., 10 and 12 July 1901, Henry W. Boynton Papers, Box 3, Folder 7, Amherst College Archives, Amherst, Mass.

5. "Samuel Hopkins Adams" in "Chronicles and Comment," *Bookman*, Aug. 1905, 564–65.

6. John Farrar, "Gossip Shop," *Bookman*, Mar. 1927, 110.

7. Irwin, *Reporter*, 90–92.

8. *Trow's New York City Directory*, eds. from 1891 to 1916; *Sanborn Fire Insurance Maps*, 7:36; interview with Katherine Adell, 2 Aug. 1989.

9. George Madden Martin to SHA, 25 Aug. 1945, SHA Papers, Burke Library.

10. Wilson, *McClure's*, 158.

11. Lyon, *Success Story*, 247–48.

12. Walter Johnson, *William Allen White's America* (New York: Henry Holt, 1947), 142–43; Robert J. Collier to Theodore Roosevelt, 24 and [30] Oct. 1904; Roosevelt to Collier, 25, 27, and 31 Oct. 1904; Roosevelt to Albert Shaw, 25 and 27 Oct. 1904, Theodore Roosevelt Presidential Papers microfilm (Washington, D.C.: Library of Congress, 1967).

13. Robert J. Collier to Theodore Roosevelt, [30] Oct. 1904, Theodore Roosevelt Presidential Papers, Library of Congress.

14. *Auburn Citizen–Advertiser*, 2 Sept. 1958, 2.

15. Baldwin, *Men Who Make Our Novels*, 553; Will Irwin log, 10 and 21 Dec. 1906; Irwin to Inez Gillmore, 21 Dec. 1906, Irwin Papers, Beinecke Library, Yale Univ., New Haven, Conn.

16. Kunitz and Haycraft, *Twentieth Century Authors*, 7.

17. James Harvey Young, *The Toadstool Millionaires* (Princeton, N.J.: Princeton Univ. Press, 1961), 216–17.

18. Richard Hofstadter, *The Age of Reform* (New York: Alfred A. Knopf, 1955), 186.

19. Louis Filler, *Crusaders for American Liberalism* (New York: Harcourt, Brace, 1939), 144.

20. See David Livingston Dykstra, "Patent and Proprietary Medicines: Regulation Control Prior to 1906" (Ph.D. diss., University of Wisconsin, Madison, 1991), 4–8, for the best definitions of nostrums, patent medicines, and proprietary medicines. Generally, nostrums

were an all-inclusive title; patent medicines referred to the copyrighting of a trademark; and proprietary medicines indicated ownership of the formula. The distinctions were seldom made, however, so the terms were almost interchangeable.

21. David F. Musto, *The American Disease; Origins of Narcotic Control* (New Haven, Conn.: Yale Univ. Press, 1973), 3.

22. Norman Hapgood, "The Epidemic of Exposure," in "Editorial Talks," *Colliers,* 25 Mar. 1905, 23; idem, *The Changing Years; Reminiscences of Norman Hapgood* (New York: Farrar and Rinehart, 1930), 177–78.

23. "On the Making of McClure's Magazine," *McClure's,* Nov. 1904, 112.

24. *Cleveland (Ohio) Press,* 11 Oct. 1920, 10.

## 5. Muckraker, 1905–1906

1. When Robert Collier took over *Collier's Weekly,* he changed the title to *Collier's* on 4 Feb. 1905.

2. Hapgood, *Changing Years,* 178; Irwin, *Reporter,* 155.

3. SHA to Dr. Harvey Wiley, 29 May 1905, Wiley Papers, Box 58, Manuscript Division, Library of Congress, Washington, D.C.

4. SHA, "Medical Support for Nostrums," *Maryland Medical Journal,* 49 (Feb. 1906): 66.

5. *Auburn Citizen–Advertiser,* 31 July 1948, 4; Young, *Toadstool Millionaires,* 218. Young reported Adams told him that when he was blackmailed, he went west to the hometown of the nostrum maker and met with the mayor, who said the individual had been surprised with another man's wife and had jumped out a window, breaking his leg. After Adams got word to the man that he knew the story, the detectives were withdrawn.

6. SHA to A. P. Saunders, 31 May 1905, n.d.; Saunders to SHA, 5 June 1905, SHA Papers, Burke Library. Cologne was a commercial name for alcohol.

7. "Peculiar Economy," *Collier's,* 8 July 1905, 6–7. Some critics of reformers cite the limited reach of a magazine but fail to note that articles in one magazine were cited in others and often excerpted in newspapers.

8. The clause, printed in red ink, read, "It is mutually agreed that this contract is void, if any law is enacted by your state restricting or prohibiting the manufacture or sale of proprietary medicines."

9. *New York Times,* 19 Oct. 1905, 6.

10. Stewart Hall Holbrook (hereafter cited as SHH), *The Golden Age of Quackery* (New York: Macmillan, 1959), 16–17. Holbrook said Peruna drunks became a generic besides a specific term.

11. James Harvey Young, *Pure Food; Securing the Federal Food and Drugs Act of 1906* (Princeton, N.J.: Princeton Univ. Press, 1989), 202.

12. Montrose J. Moses, "Samuel Hopkins Adams: Newspaper Reformer," *Book News Monthly,* Jan. 1915, 214.

13. Irwin, *Reporter,* 155; Robert Miraldi, *Muckraking and Objectivity; Journalism's Colliding Traditions* (Westport, Conn.: Greenwood Press, 1990), 35; SHH, *Quackery,* 26; Justin Kaplan, *Lincoln Steffens: A Biography* (New York: Simon and Schuster, 1974), 124; Cor-

nelius Regier, *The Era of the Muckrakers* (Chapel Hill: Univ. of North Carolina Press, 1932), 181, 183, 211.

14. Young, *Toadstool Millionaires*, 235–36.

15. Robert M. Crunden, *Ministers of Reform; The Progressives' Achievement in American Civilization, 1889–1920* (New York: Basic Books, 1982), 188; Dykstra, "Patent Medicines," 215. Crunden said Adams's influence on Heyburn and Heyburn's on Roosevelt apparently led Roosevelt to commit himself.

16. Miraldi, *Objectivity*, 43, 46–47.

17. Young, *Toadstool Millionaires*, 224; "The Great American Fraud," *Journal of the American Medical Association* 48 (11 May 1907): 1616.

18. *New York Times*, 23 Feb. 1906, 8. As the Senate considered the bill, Heyburn read a letter from Charles Reed, chairman of the American Medical Association's legislative committee, claiming 135,000 physicians and 2,000 counties wanted passage. *Congressional Record*, 59th Congress, 1st sess. (1905–6) 40, bk. 3:2748.

19. Young, *Pure Food*, 219; David Cassedy, "Muckraking and Medicine: Samuel Hopkins Adams," *American Quarterly* 16 (spring 1964): 86.

20. Upton Sinclair, "What Life Means to Me," *Cosmopolitan*, Oct. 1906, 594.

21. For text of Roosevelt's speech see David Chalmers, *The Social and Political Ideas of the Muckrakers* (New York: Citadel Press, 1964), 3–8.

22. Will Irwin, "Samuel Hopkins Adams," on back jacket cover of *The World Goes Smash* (Boston: Houghton Mifflin, 1938).

23. A. H. Ohmann-Dumesnil, "Collier's Methods Exposed," *Saint Louis Medical and Surgical Journal* 90 (Apr. 1906): 186–207.

24. SHA, "Patent Medicines under the Pure Food Law," *Collier's*, 8 June 1907, 12; idem, "Medical Support," 67; SHH, *Quackery*, 286.

25. Theodore Roosevelt to Joseph Gurney Cannon, 27 May 1906, Theodore Roosevelt Papers microfilm.

26. *Congressional Record*, 59th Congress, 1st sess. (1905–6) 40, bk. 9, 8892, 8906–7, 8988, 8998, 9000; bk. 10, 9073–74, 9739–40.

27. Young, *Pure Food*, 275–76, 292–93.

28. *New York Times*, 3 May 1906, 3; SHA, "Public Health and Public Hysteria," *Journal of the Public Health Association* 1 (Nov. 1911): 774; *Auburn Citizen*, 20 July 1906, 5. The *Auburn Citizen* and *Auburn Advertiser Journal* were merged into the *Auburn Citizen–Advertiser* in 1931.

29. Young, *Toadstool Millionaires*, 173.

30. SHH, *Quackery*, 284–85.

31. Lyon, *Success Story*, 243; Wilson, *McClure's*, 175–76.

32. Will Irwin log, [Mar.], 1 and 10 May 1906; Irwin to Inez Haynes Gillmore, 3 May 1906, Irwin Papers, Beinecke Library.

33. *Collier's Magazine Memorandum Book*, 1–16, Manuscripts Division, Library of Congress. The account book begins on 6 Nov. 1905 and ends in Dec. 1910.

34. "In 14 Cities at Once," *Editor and Publisher*, 13 Oct. 1906, 1–2; *Ridgway's*, 27 Oct. 1906, 5.

35. *New York Times Book Review*, 24 July 1955, 12.

## 6. Writer, 1907–1909

1. For the best account of the killing and legal actions see Gerald Langford, *The Murder of Stanford White* (Indianapolis, Ind.: Bobbs-Merrill, 1962).

2. Will Irwin to Inez Gillmore, 12 Feb. 1907, Irwin Papers, Beinecke Library.

3. Interview with Katherine Adell, 1 Aug. 1989.

4. *Auburn Citizen*, 17 July 1906, 5; Will Irwin log, [3] and 24 Oct. 1906, Irwin Papers, Beinecke Library. Information on the divorce, usually granted only on the grounds of adultery, consists of the final decree in the archives of the New York City court system.

5. Will Irwin to Inez Gillmore, 24 Jan. 1914, Irwin Papers, Beinecke Library.

6. Will Irwin to Inez Gillmore, 1 Nov. 1907, Irwin Papers, Beinecke Library.

7. Interview with Katherine Adell, 1 Aug. 1989.

8. Will Irwin to Inez Gillmore, [15] Aug. 1909 and 12 Feb. 1912, Irwin Papers, Beinecke Library.

9. Will Irwin to Inez Gillmore, [Aug. 1909], Irwin Papers, Beinecke Library.

10. SHA to Booth Tarkington, 12 June 1943, Booth Tarkington Papers, Special Collections, Colby College Library, Waterville, Me.

11. *New York Post*, 16 Nov. 1944, 33; *New York Times*, 23 Dec. 1908, 3.

12. Peter Temin, *Taking Your Medicine; Drug Regulation in the United States* (Cambridge, Mass.: Harvard Univ. Press, 1980), 32. Temin noted that of the first 1,000 judgments obtained under the 1906 law only 135 dealt with drugs

13. SHA to Harvey Washington Wiley, 26 Mar. 1907; Wiley to SHA, 1 Apr. 1907; quoted in Temin, *Taking Your Medicine*, 32.

14. SHA to Harvey Wiley, 2 July 1907; confidential clerk to SHA, 8 July 1907, Wiley Papers, Manuscript Division, Library of Congress.

15. Charles Phelps Cushing, "Who Writes These Mystery Yarns? The Great Detective Solves Another Puzzle," *Independent*, 9 Apr. 1927, 383; Kunitz and Haycraft, *Twentieth Century Authors*, 7. Stanley J. Kunitz in his *Twentieth Century Authors, First Supplement* (New York: H. W. Wilson, 1955), 5, corrected the error.

16. *The $50,000 Verdict; An Account of the Action of Robert J. Collier vs. the Postum Cereal Co., Ltd. for Libel* (New York: P. F. Collier and Son, 1911), 4–5.

17. *The $50,000 Verdict*, 7. Collier said the *Post* ad ran in forty-four newspapers in New York State alone. The verdict was set aside on a technicality, and Collier, claiming vindication, dropped the suit.

18. SHA to D. L. Chambers, 16 Apr. 1911, B-M Papers, Lilly Library, Indiana University, Bloomington, Ind.

19. *Auburn Citizen–Advertiser*, 2 Sept. 1958, 2.

20. "Stories of Plot and Adventure," *Outlook*, 16 Feb. 1907, 377; Richard Hughes Remsen, "Messrs. White's and Adams's *The Mystery*," *Bookman*, Mar. 1907, 84; *New York Times Saturday Review of Books*, 19 Jan. 1907, 29; "Thalassa! Thalassa!" *Independent*, 25 Apr. 1907, 797; "More Author's Letters," *Bookman*, Sept. 1916, 34.

21. SHA to D. L. Chambers, 16 Apr. 1911, B-M papers, Lilly Library.

22. *New York Times Saturday Review of Books*, 8 Feb. 1908, 72; *New York Sun*, quoted in *Auburn Citizen*, 4 Feb. 1908, 7; "The Flying Death," *Bookman*, Mar. 1908, 27.

23. "The '91 Manuscript Prize," *Hamilton Literary Magazine*, Oct. 1905, 60–61; SHA, *A. Woollcott: His Life and His World*, 52–53.

24. *Secretary's Record of Phi Beta Kappa*, 203, Burke Library.

25. Will Irwin to Inez Gillmore, 29 June 1909, Irwin Papers, Beinecke Library.

26. Will Irwin to Inez Gillmore, 11 Aug. 1909, Irwin Papers, Beinecke Library.

27. *Collier's Magazine Memorandum Book*, 1–16. Of the full years reported in the book Adams received $3,018.51 in 1906 and $2,582.98 in 1907 for pay and expenses. The book shows no entries for Adams in 1910.

28. *Auburn Daily Advertiser*, 1 Sept. 1909, 4, 6; *Auburn Citizen*, 1 Sept. 1909, 5.

29. SHA to Thomas Mott Osborne, 16 Dec. 1909; Osborne to SHA, 21 Dec. 1909; Oswald Garrison Villard to Osborne, 31 Dec. 1909, Box 79, Osborne Papers, George Arents Research Library for Special Collections in Bird Library, Syracuse Univ., Syracuse, N.Y.

## 7. Detective, 1910–1912

1. Although Adams was friends with socialists and listed himself as a moderate socialist in *Who's Who in New York* (but as a Democrat in *Who's Who in America*), no evidence has been found of him supporting the doctrine.

2. *Auburn Daily Advertiser*, 4 Feb. 1909, 2.

3. In the Smithsonian Institution Archives, Record Unit 161, Division of Reptiles and Amphibians, 1873–1968, Folder 1, Box 1, are sixteen letters with a cover letter saying Adams wanted the correspondence on snake poison kept for possible future use.

4. "The Editor's Outlook," *Success*, May 1910, 301.

5. Stephen Birmingham, *The Late John Marquand* (Philadelphia: J. B. Lippincott, 1972), 65–66; interview with Carl Brandt, Jr., 6 Mar. 1990, New York City.

6. SHA financial records, Brandt & Brandt offices, New York City. The book also received in 1913 a British royalty of $106.76 from publisher Frank Palmer. Hereafter, all financial reports are from the Brandt & Brandt records unless otherwise stated.

7. Hugh Greene, *The American Rivals of Sherlock Holmes* (New York: Pantheon Books, 1976), 11; Ellery Queen [Frederic Dannay and Manfred Bennington Lee], pseud. ed., *101 Years Entertainment; The Great Detective Stories 1841–1941* (Boston: Little, Brown, 1941), 246; Howard Haycraft, *Murder for Pleasure; The Life and Times of the Detective Story* (New York: D. Appleton-Century, 1941), 100–101.

8. *New York Times Review of Books*, 6 Oct. 1912, 558; "The Secret of Lonesome Cove," *Nation*, 13 Oct. 1912, 309; "Far Horizons in Fiction," *Independent*, 7 Nov. 1912, 1074.

9. Adams also received $219.50 in Feb. 1913 from British publisher Frank Palmer.

10. "Chronicle and Comment," *Bookman*, Aug. 1912, 589; SHA to [blanked out], 10 July 1916, SHA Papers, Burke Library.

11. SHA, "Tuberculosis: The Real Race Suicide," *McClure's*, Jan. 1905, 235.

12. SHH, *Quackery*, 283.

13. Arthur J. Cramp, comp. and ed., *Nostrums and Quackery*, vol. 1 (Chicago: Press of the American Medical Association, 1911). Adams was often quoted.

14. Will Irwin to Inez Gillmore, 10 and 12 Feb. 1912, Beinecke Library. The four-part Irwin series, "The American Spenders" appeared in the *Saturday Evening Post* in June and July 1912. The first three articles were in a fictional eastern city of thirty thousand named Avalon.

15. Jesse Lynch Williams, "'Sam' Adams," 217.

16. Moses, "Samuel Hopkins Adams," 216.

17. *Minutes Book of Hamilton College Alumni Association of the City of New York*, Burke Library; Walter Pilkington, *Hamilton College; A History 1812–1962*, (Clinton, N.Y.: Hamilton College, 1962), 223.

18. Carl Carmer, 7 June 1955, recording of dinner speeches in Auburn, N.Y., Cayuga Museum of History and Art.

19. SHA, "The Genesis of 'The Long Tryst,'" *Hamiltonian*, 1914, 196–97.

20. Blanche Colton Williams, *Short Stories for College Classes* (New York: D. Appleton-Century, 1929).

21. Irwin, *Reporter*, 164; Clifford F. Weigle and David G. Clark, introduction to Will Irwin, *The American Newspaper* (Ames: Iowa State Univ. Press, 1969), x.

22. SHA, "Why I Wrote 'The Clarion'," *La Follette's Weekly*, Nov. 1914, 8.

23. Moses, "Samuel Hopkins Adams," 215.

24. *New York Times*, 17 Nov. 1958, 31; *Auburn Daily Advertiser*, 2 Feb. 1909, 6.

25. Arthur Bartlett Maurice, "History of Their Books," *Bookman*, Nov. 1929, 273.

26. SHA, *Clarion*, 69.

27. Ibid., 69–70.

28. Ibid., 199.

## 8. Romantic, 1913–1914

1. Inez Gillmore to Will Irwin, 5 and 11 May 1910, Irwin Papers, Beinecke Library.

2. Will Irwin to Inez Gillmore, 16 Jan. 1913, Irwin Papers, Beinecke Library.

3. "Venereal Quacks, the Law, and the Newspapers," *Survey*, 25 June 1914, 90–91.

4. Inscription is in a copy of book in SHA papers, Burke Library. White died in 1946 at the age of seventy-three.

5. "Crusading Chronicler," *MD*, Jan. 1971, 189; SHA author card, Houghton Library.

6. "To Teach People How to Keep Well," *McClure's*, Feb. 1913, 101.

7. "How Cancer Education of the Public Got Started," *Cancer News*, Fall 1958, 6; "Minutes of the House of Delegates," *Journal of the American Medical Association* 60 (28 June 1913): 2089.

8. An advertisement in *Editor and Publisher*, 6 Oct. 1917, 11, claimed twenty million Kewpie dolls and statuettes had been sold, dozens of articles of merchandise had Kewpie trademarks, and hundreds of thousands of Kewpie books had been bought.

9. Will Irwin to Inez Gillmore, 24 Mar. and 8 Apr. 1914, Irwin Papers, Beinecke Library.

10. Burns Mantle, *Best Plays of 1899–1909* (New York: Dodd, Mead, 1944), 368, 393; *New York Times*, 4 Sept. 1900, 7; 1 Sept. 1901, sec. 2, 12.

11. Arthur Cyril Gordon Weld entry in *Dictionary of American Biography*, 19: 625.

12. *Rochester Democrat and Chronicle*, 23 June 1959, 21.

13. *New York Times*, 18 Oct. 1906, 9; Will Irwin to Inez Gillmore, 4 Aug. 1914, Irwin Papers, Beinecke Library.

14. Marguerite Courtney, *Laurette* (New York: Rinehart, 1955), 80–82;

15. *New York Times*, 4 May 1909, 9; Laurette Taylor, "Jane Adams," *Canal Town* brochure for Peoples Book Club (Chicago: Sears, Roebuck, 1943), 13.

16. *New York Times*, 20 Sept. 1911, 13.

17. *New York Tribune*, 25 Dec. 1913, 7; Courtney, *Laurette*, 82.

18. Moses, "Samuel Hopkins Adams," 216.

19. *Cleveland (Ohio) Press*, 10; *New York Post*, 16 Nov. 1944, 33; Will Irwin to Inez Gillmore, 9 Dec. 1913, Irwin Papers, Beinecke Library.

20. Will Irwin to Inez Gillmore, 4 Aug. 1914; 26 Dec. 1913; 31 Dec. 1913, Irwin Papers, Beinecke Library.

21. Interview with George Harlan; Will Irwin to Inez Gillmore, 5 Mar. 1914, Irwin Papers, Beinecke Library.

22. Will Irwin to Inez Gillmore, 9 Jan. 1912 and 9 Feb. 1914, Irwin Papers, Beinecke Library.

23. SHA to Inez Gillmore, 9 Feb. 1914, Irwin Papers, Beinecke Library.

24. Will Irwin to Inez Gillmore, 11 Jan. and 8 July 1914, Irwin Papers, Beinecke Library.

25. SHA to Inez Gillmore, 10 May 1914, Irwin Papers, Beinecke Library,

26. *Auburn Citizen*, 27 Apr. 1914, 7; *Utica Observer*, 4 May 1914, 6.

27. Will Irwin to Inez Gillmore, 1 June 1914, Irwin Papers, Beinecke Library.

28. Will Irwin to Inez Gillmore, 8 Apr. and 14 July 1914, Irwin Papers, Beinecke Library.

29. Will Irwin to Inez Gillmore, 8 Sept. and 7 Oct. 1913, Irwin Papers, Beinecke Library.

30. Irwin, *Reporter*, 155–56; SHA, "How I Write," 108.

31. Will Irwin to Inez Gillmore, 16 July 1914, Irwin Papers, Beinecke Library.

32. Will Irwin to Inez Gillmore, 4 Aug. 1914, Irwin Papers, Beinecke Library.

33. Will Irwin to Inez Gillmore, 7 Apr. 1914, Irwin Papers, Beinecke Library.

34. Moses, "Samuel Hopkins Adams," 215–16.

35. FG to SHA, 6 Apr. 1914, HM Papers, Houghton Library.

36. Roger L. Scaife to SHA, 1 June 1914, HM Papers, Houghton Library.

37. FG to SHA, 11 Sept. 1914; RLS to SHA, 12 Sept. 1914; SHA to RLS, 21 Sept. 1914, HM Papers, Houghton Library.

38. Franklin Pierce Adams, "The Conning Tower," *New York Tribune*, 29 Sept. 1914, 8; *Standard Remedies*, Mar. 1915, 7–10, quoted in Young, *The Medical Messiahs: A Social History of Health Quackery in Twentieth Century America* (Princeton: Princeton Univ. Press, 1967), 52.

39. RLS to SHA, 3 Dec. 1914, HM Papers, Houghton Library.

40. Ward Macauley, "The Clarion," *Publisher's Weekly*, pt. 2, 17 Oct. 1914, 1286; "The 'Best Book' of the Year," *Publishers' Weekly*, 23 Jan. 1915, 245–46.

41. Moses, "Samuel Hopkins Adams," 216.

42. SHA to FG, 13 Dec. 1914; FG to SHA, 14 Dec. 1914, HM Papers, Houghton Library.

## 9. Columnist, 1915–1916

1. Richard Kluger, *The Paper; The Life and Death of the New York Herald Tribune* (New York: Alfred A. Knopf, 1986), 189; *New York Tribune*, 17 Nov. 1914, 8.

2. "New York's Vigorous Stand Against Fakes and Quackery," *Survey*, 17 June 1915, 68.

3. "A' Top O' the World," *Editor and Publisher*, 13 Feb. 1915, 707; *Tribune* ad, *Editor and Publisher*, 13 Mar. 1915, 793.

4. Filler, *Crusaders for American Liberalism*, 169–70; "Guaranteed Advertising," *Editor and Publisher*, 21 Nov. 1914, 452; Moses, "Samuel Hopkins Adams," 216.

5. *New York Tribune*, 9 Feb. 1915, 5; Baldwin, *Men Who Make Our Novels*, 13–14.

6. SHA to FG, 1 Feb. and 23 May 1915; FG to SHA, 17 Aug. 1915, HM Papers, Houghton Library.

7. SHA, "Tipperary Boosters Lie about Famed Spot," *New York Tribune*, 9 Feb. 1915, 8.

8. *New York Times*, 17 Feb. 1915, 11. The story from Chicago said she believed the decree had been entered on Aug. 8, thirteen days before her marriage to Post.

9. *New York Tribune*, 8 May 1915, 8; *Auburn Citizen*, 10 May 1910, 4.

10. FG to SHA, 3 May 1915; SHA to FG, 11 Apr. and 23 and 26 May 1915, HM Papers, Houghton Library.

11. Franklin Pierce Adams, "The Conning Tower," *New York Tribune*, 27 May 1915, 8.

12. Cayuga County *Book of Deeds*, 209, 80–81; 212, 213–14; 214, 294–95; 230, 487; interview with Katherine Adell, 26 June 1990. The third purchase, on 1 Apr. 1918, was for 67 plus acres and the fourth, on 23 Feb. 1923, for 177 acres.

13. SHA to FG, 29 May and 22 June 1915; FG to SHA, 5 June 1915, HM Papers, Houghton Library.

14. Baldwin, *Men Who Make Our Novels*, 14; "Adams and His Tomahawk," *Editor and Publisher*, 3 July 1915, 97.

15. *New York Tribune* promotion box, 6 July 1915, 1.

16. Baldwin, *Men Who Make Our Novels*, 13.

17. "Adams Hits Boston Papers," *Editor and Publisher*, 11 Dec. 1915, 730.

18. Will Irwin to Inez Gillmore, 23 Sept. 1915, Irwin Papers, Beinecke Library.

19. *New York Tribune*, 25 Sept. 1915, 8; *New York Times Review of Books*, 31 Oct. 1915, 421; "Recent Fiction," *Literary Digest*, 23 Oct. 1915, 913–14.

20. Inez Gillmore to Will Irwin, 27 Dec. 1915, Irwin Papers, Beinecke Library.

21. Inez Gillmore to Will Irwin, 16 Jan. 1916, Irwin Papers, Beinecke Library; interview with Katherine Adell, 9 Aug. 1992.

22. "Dishonest Ads Must Go," *Editor and Publisher*, 5 Feb. 1916, 1055; editorial, *Editor and Publisher*, 25 Mar. 1916, 1294.

23. *New York Tribune*, 8 Feb. 1915, 16; *Variety Film Reviews 1907–1970* (New York: Garland Publishing, 1988), 10 Mar. 1916, no page; SHA to RLS, 20 and 23 Mar. 1916, HM Papers, Houghton Library.

24. Interview with Katherine Adell, 1 Aug. 1989.

25. *New York Times Book Review*, 6 Aug. 1916, 309, 311; H. W. Boynton, "Some Stories of the Month," *Bookman*, Aug. 1916, 65. In addition to 9,914 regular copies the novel sold 4,950 cheap editions and 500 in Canada.

26. Maurice, "History of Their Books," 274.

27. Baldwin, *Men Who Make Our Novels*, 14; Will Irwin to Inez Gillmore, 21 Feb. 1907, Irwin Papers, Beinecke Library.

28. Alexander Woollcott to D. H. Silberman, 7 Sept. 1940, Joseph Hennessey and Beatrice Bakrow Kaufman, eds., *The Letters of Alexander Woollcott* (New York: Viking Press, 1944), 248–49.

29. Baldwin, *Men Who Make Our Novels*, 14.

30. Philip L. Gerber, *Theodore Dreiser* (New York: Twayne Publishers, 1964), 125.

31. *New York Times*, 3 Nov. 1916, 6; *New York Evening Post*, 31 Oct. 1916, 4.

32. FG to SHA, 17 and 22 Aug. 1916; SHA to FG, 19 Aug. 1916, HM Papers, Houghton Library; Moses, "Samuel Hopkins Adams," 216.

33. SHA to FG, 22 and 27 Sept. 1916; FG to SHA, 26 Sept. 1916, HM Papers, Houghton Library.

34. SHA to FG, 5 Nov. 1916; FG to SHA, 3 Nov. and 11 Dec. 1916, HM Papers, Houghton Library.

## 10. Propagandist, 1917–1919

1. SHA to RLS, 6 Mar. 1917; RLS to SHA, 7 Mar. 1917, HM Papers, Houghton Library.

2. The undated booklet was titled "Read What Samuel Hopkins Adams in the *New York Tribune* Has to Say about Dallas Publications and the *Dallas Dispatch*," and was issued by the Dallas newspaper.

3. *New York Herald Tribune*, 26 Oct. 1942, 11.

4. *The Vigilantes*, a pamphlet issued from 505 Fifth Avenue, New York, 2, 9, 13; *New York Tribune*, 10 Feb. 1918, sec. 3, 4. The group sent free proof sheets of articles, stories, poems, and cartoons to some fifteen hundred newspapers with a total circulation of more than fifty million.

5. Inez Gillmore to Will Irwin, 16 Jan. 1916, Irwin Papers, Beinecke Library; interview with Katherine Adell, 1 Aug. 1989.

6. *New York Times Book Review*, 11 Nov. 1917, 453.

7. The company estimated that 3,517 copies would break even. It sold 5,983 copies with 5,475 regular editions, 230 in Canada and 278 other copies. Adams earned $1,109.54 in advances and royalties.

8. *New York Times Book Review*, 17 June 1945, 3. The book was reprinted in 1970.

9. George Creel, *How We Advertised America* (New York: Harper and Row, 1920), 224–46; Stephen Vaughn, *Holding Fast the Inner Lines; Democracy, Nationalism, and the Committee on Public Information* (Chapel Hill: Univ. of North Carolina Press, 1980), 16–17; James R. Mock and Cederic Larson, *Words That Won the War: The Story of the Committee on Public Information, 1917–1919* (Princeton, N.J.: Princeton Univ. Press, 1939), 110–11; George Creel, *Report of the Chairman of the U.S. Committee on Public Information 1917–1919* (Washington, D.C.: Government Printing Office, 1920), 74.

10. David H. Bennett, *The Party of Fear; From Nativist Movements to the New Right in American History* (Chapel Hill: Univ. of North Carolina Press, 1988), 181, 184; SHA to FG, 5 Sept. 1917; FG to SHA, 5 Nov. 1917, HM Papers, Houghton Library.

11. Creel, *How We Advertised America*, 225.

12. Marie Louise Marrilet, an "importer" of American-made gloves and lingerie, sued over a May 1916 Adams column. She had sought fifty thousand dollars.

13. Woodrow Wilson to Albert Sidney Burlson, 4 Oct. 1917, Arthur S. Link, ed., *The Papers of Woodrow Wilson* (Princeton, N.J.: Princeton Univ. Press 1983), vol. 44, 21 Aug. to 10 Nov. 1917, 301–2.

14. Creel, *Report of the Chairman*, 24.

15. Mock and Larson, *Words that Won*, 115–16.

16. Creel, *How We Advertised America*, 85; Alfred E. Cornebise, *War as Advertised: The Four Minute Men and America's Crusade 1917–1918* (Philadelphia: American Philosophical Society, 1984), 33; William McCormick Blair, "William McCormick Blair Writes a Brief Historical Sketch for the Final Four Minute Men News," *Four Minute Men News*, ed. F, 24 Dec. 1918, 6.

17. "Notice" and "Foreword," *The Beggar's Purse* (Boston: Smith and Porter Press, 1918).

18. Herbert Hoover was food administrator 1917–19.

19. FG to SHA, 15 May 1918; SHA to FG, 17 May 1918, HM Papers, Houghton Library.

20. Baldwin, *Men Who Make Our Novels*, 14–15.

21. SHA to FG, 31 May [1918]; RLS to SHA, 1 June 1918, HM Papers, Houghton Library.

22. SHA to Gertrude Battles Lane, 22 May 1918 and 3 June 1918, Gertrude Battles Lane Papers, Manuscript Division, Library of Congress.

23. FG to SHA, 25 Nov. 1918; SHA to FG, 29 Nov. 1918, HM Papers, Houghton Library.

24. FG to SHA, 25 Jan. 1919, HM Papers, Houghton Library.

25. *Nation*, 22 Feb. 1919, 288; *New York Times Review of Books*, 26 Jan. 1919, sec. 8, 33–34; clipping from unnamed Wisconsin newspaper in HM Papers, Houghton Library; "A Selected List of Current Books," *Wisconsin Library Bulletin*, Mar. 1919, 79; SHA to RLS, 21 Apr. 1919; RLS to SHA, 24 Apr. 1919, HM Papers, Houghton Library.

26. The short stories in *Everybody's* were "I.I.I.: A Story of the New Washington," "Half a Million, Cold," "Silver Stripes among the Gold," and "Mister Hune."

27. The articles in *Red Cross Magazine* were "The Miracle of Reeducation" and "You and Our Maimed Soldiers."

28. Carl Sandburg to Henry Justin Smith, 31 May 1919, *The Letters of Carl Sandburg*, ed. Herbert Mitgang (New York: Harcourt, Brace and World, 1968), 163–65.

29. *Catalog of Copyright Entries, Motion Pictures, 1912–1939* (Washington, D.C.: Copyright Office, Library of Congress, 1953), 252.

30. *Variety Film Reviews*, vol. 1, 19 Dec. 1919, no page; SHA to Alma Levin Pritchard, 16 Feb. 1946, SHA Papers, ARL.

31. *Auburn Citizen*, 6 Sept. 1919, 2; *Auburn Citizen–Advertiser*, 2 Sept. 1958, 2.

32. SHA to FG, 29 Nov. and 7 Dec. 1919; FG to SHA, 3 Dec. 1919, HM Papers, Houghton Library.

## 11. Chronicler, 1920–1924

1. SHA to FG, 26 Jan. 1920, HM Papers, Houghton Library.

2. FG to SHA, 31 Jan. 1920; SHA to FG, 4 Feb. 1920, HM Papers, Houghton Library.

3. Marie M. Meloney to SHA, 20 Oct. 1920; SHA to Meloney, 2 and 16 Nov. 1920, Meloney Papers, Rare Book and Manuscript Library, Columbia Univ.

4. RLS to SHA, 25 Mar. 1920, HM Papers, Houghton Library. *Wanted: A Husband* sold 7,774 regular, 4,608 cheap, 484 Canadian, and 442 Australian copies with a break-even point of 3,957 copies.

5. RLS to SHA, 24 May 1920; SHA to RLS, 8 June 1920, HM Papers, Houghton Library.

6. Interview with Lydia Mead Engelbert, 31 July 1991, Cobleskill, N.Y.

7. FG to SHA, 2 Sept. 1920; SHA to FG, 5 Sept. 1920, HM Papers, Houghton Library.

8. SHA to Thomas Mott Osborne, 24 Nov. 1920, Osborne Papers, ARL.

9. FG to SHA, 21 May 1921. HM Papers. Houghton Library.

10. J. P. Gavit, *Literary Review,* 29 Oct. 1921, 115, in *Book Review Digest—1921,* 4; *New York Times Book Review and Magazine,* 6 Nov. 1921, 16.

11. RLS to SHA, 7 Nov. 1921; SHA to RLS, 10 Nov. 1921, HM Papers, Houghton Library.

12. Maurice, "History of Their Books," 272–73; *New York Times,* 25 Dec. 1921, sec. 6, 1.

13. James Stanford Bradshaw, "The Journalist as Pariah: Three Muckraking Newspaper Novels by Samuel Hopkins Adams," *Journalism History* 10:1–2 (spring–summer 1983): 10–13; interview with George R. Metcalf, 18 July 1990, Auburn, N.Y.

14. SHA to FG, 22 Jan. 1922; FG to SHA, 24 Jan. 1922, HM Papers, Houghton Library.

15. RLS to SHA, 30 Jan., 3 and 28 Feb., 29 Mar. 1922; SHA to RLS, 1 and 24 Feb. 27, Mar. 1922, HM Papers, Houghton Library.

16. *Auburn Citizen,* 24 Jan. 1922, 5.

17. SHA to FG, 17 Oct. 1921, HM Papers, Houghton Library.

18. Interview with Katherine Adell, 9 Aug. 1992; *Cleveland (Ohio) Press,* 11 Oct. 1920, 10.

19. SHA to Arthur Bartlett Maurice, 17 Apr. 1922, Maurice Papers, Princeton Univ. Libraries.

20. *New York Times Book Review,* 3 Dec. 1922, 24–25.

21. The 3,249 copies were more than the company-estimated 1,550 copies to cover publication costs.

22. *Auburn Advertiser-Journal,* 6 Nov. 1922.

23. Robert Hudson, *The Writing Game: A Biography of Will Irwin* (Ames: Iowa State Univ. Press, 1982), 143–44; SHA to Marie M. Meloney, 30 Sept. 1920, Meloney Papers, Rare Book and Manuscript Library, Columbia Univ.

24. *Rochester Times-Union,* 28 May 1957, 23.

25. Serrell Hillman, "Samuel Hopkins Adams: 1871–1958," *Saturday Review,* 20 Dec. 1958, 15.

26. Bennett A. Cerf, *At Random; The Reminiscences of Bennett Cerf* (New York: Random House, 1977), 33, 36, and 39.

27. Farrar, "Gossip Shop," *Bookman,* May 1923, 374; *New York Times Book Review,* 28 Jan. 1923, 24.

28. BAC, *At Random,* 39, 40; F. Scott Fitzgerald to Mr. X, n.d., Matthew J. Bruccoli and Margaret M. Duggin, eds., *Correspondence of F. Scott Fitzgerald* (New York: Random House, 1980), 131.

29. BAC, *At Random,* 40.

30. BAC, "Trade Winds," *Saturday Review of Literature,* 14 Oct. 1944, 39; Baldwin, *Men Who Make Our Novels,* 15.

31. *New York Times,* 26 Nov. 1923, 15.

32. "The Bookman's Guide to Fiction," *Bookman,* Apr. 1924, 207.

33. Maurice, "History of Their Books," 272.

34. RLS to SHA, 20 Mar. 1922; SHA to RLS, 3 Apr. and 2 Nov.[1922], HM Papers, Houghton Library.

35. *Syracuse Post-Standard,* 23 Mar. 1924, sec. 3, 4.

36. "The Live-Letter Office," *Collier's,* 9 June 1923, 20.

37. Review of *Siege, Nation,* 16 Apr. 1924, 456; "Fiction," *Outlook,* 9 Apr. 1924, 613–14; BAC, *At Random,* 40.

38. RLS to SHA, 10 Sept. and 14 Oct. 1924; SHA to RLS, 6 Oct. 1924, HM Papers, Houghton Library. The novel sold 10,000 cheap editions and 1,310 in Canada.

39. SHA to Mildred Woodruff, 15 Mar. 1924, SHA Papers, Seymour Library, Auburn, N.Y.

40. Interview with Katherine Adell, 9 Aug. 1992.

41. Inez Irwin diary, 17 July to 4 Aug. 1924, Irwin Papers, Beinecke Library; interview with Katherine Adell, 25 June 1990; telephone interview with Elizabeth Richardson Steele, 22 July 1992, Newport Beach, Calif. Cream of Wheat also used Buddy Richardson's portrait.

42. *New York World,* 30 Nov. 1924, 8e.

43. Other sales were 10,000 cheap editions and 2,203 in Canada; SHA to RLS, 6 Oct. 1924, HM Papers, Houghton Library.

44. *Cleveland (Ohio) Press,* 11 Oct. 1920, 10.

45. Baldwin, *Men Who Make Our Novels,* 10.

46. SHA to Julian Street, 12 Apr. and 2 May 1924, Street papers, Princeton Univ. Libraries.

## 12. Sensationalist, 1925–1929

1. Zelma Brandt to Horace B. Liveright, 27 Aug. 1925, SHA Papers, ARL.

2. "In Our Midst," *New Yorker,* 21 Feb. 1925, 18. The article that Adams wrote has never been identified although it was probably "Opera Hats."

3. Baldwin, *Men Who Make Our Novels,* 16.

4. SHA to [CB], 22 Sept. 1925; Zelma Brandt to HBL, 9 Dec. 1925, SHA Papers, ARL.

5. Gary Carey, *Lost Films* (New York: Museum of Modern Art, 1970), 60; *Variety Film Reviews 1921–1925,* vol. 2, 17 June 1925, no page; 16 Dec. 1925, no page.

6. Interview with George Harlan, 15 Sept. 1990, Toronto, Canada.

7. SHA, "Business Man Wants to Join Circus, Pretty Matron Would be Chorus Girl," *Philadelphia (Pa.) Bulletin,* 27 June 1925, E, 3.

8. Will and Inez Irwin diaries, 10–23 Jan. 1926, Irwin Papers, Beinecke Library.

9. SHA to Joseph Ibbotson, 22 Mar. 1926, SHA papers, Burke Library; interview with George Harlan, 15 Sept. 1990, Toronto, Canada.

10. Interview with Beatrice Champany, 19 Sept. 1992, Auburn, N.Y.

11. "Mr. Adams at 79," in "Keeping Posted," *Saturday Evening Post,* 7 Jan. 1950, 100.

12. Lithgow Osborne to Thomas Mott Osborne, 26 Jan. 1926; Lithgow Osborne to Dorothy Noble, 12 Feb. 1926, Osborne Papers, ARL.

13. *Auburn Citizen*, 11 June 1926, 6.

14. SHA to Joseph Ibbotson, 10, 22 Jan. 1926 and 15 Nov. [1927], SHA Papers, Burke Library.

15. *New York Times Book Review*, 14 Feb. 1926, 8; "The New Books—Fiction," *Saturday Review of Literature*, 17 Apr. 1926, 726.

16. Maurice, "History of Their Books," 174.

17. Zelma Brandt to HBL, 9 Mar. 1926; HBL to Zelma Brandt, 11 Mar. 1926; SHA to Carl Brandt, 16 March 1926, SHA Papers, ARL.

18. Baldwin, 16; SHA to Julian Street, 11 Mar. 1926, Street Papers, Princeton Univ. Libraries.

19. Julian Street to SHA, 13 Mar. 1926, Street papers, Princeton Univ. Libraries.

20. The subtitle is on a manuscript copy in Burke Library.

21. SHA, "How I Write," 125.

22. Marian Richardson to BB, [2] and [4] Aug. 1926, SHA Papers, ARL.

23. Interview with George Harlan, 15 Sept. 1990, Toronto, Canada; interview with Katherine Adell, 26 June 1990.

24. SHA to Leila [Marian Richardson], 6 Dec. 1926, SHA Papers, ARL. Leila Cavendish was an Adams pet name.

25. SHA to Joseph Ibbotson, 24 Aug. and 7 Sept. 1926, SHA Papers, Burke Library.

26. "Fiction," *Saturday Review of Literature*, 25 Sept. 1926, 140–41; *New York Herald Tribune Books*, 28 Nov. 1926, 14.

27. SHA to Zelma Brandt, 15 and 21 Oct. and 2 Nov. 1926, SHA Papers, ARL.

28. Robert Connelly, *The Motion Picture Guide* (Chicago: Cinebooks, 1986), 10:274.

29. Burton Kline to CB, 23 Nov. 1926, SHA Papers, ARL.

30. SHA, *Revelry*, 70.

31. Marian K. Richardson to SHA, 31 Nov. 1926, SHA Papers, ARL.

32. The ad was sent to every newspaper with a circulation of more than ten thousand.

33. *New York World*, 12 Nov. 1926, 2; SHA to Leila [Marian Richardson], 14 Nov. [1926], SHA Papers, ARL.

34. Farrar, "Gossip Shop," *Bookman*, Mar. 1927, 110–11.

35. *New York World*, 10 Nov. 1926, 15; *New York World*, 13 Nov. 1926, 13; SHA to CB, 19 Nov. 1926, SHA Papers, ARL; *New York World*, 25 Nov. 1926, 16.

36. *New York World*, 12 Nov. 1926, 13; 26 Nov. 1926, 9.

37. John Haynes Holmes to Boni and Liveright, [n.d.], SHA Papers, ARL.

38. *New York World*, 1 Dec. 1926, 17; Will Irwin diary, 12 Jan. 1927, Irwin Papers, Beinecke Library.

39. Farrar, "Gossip Shop," *Bookman*, Mar. 1927, 111; *New York World*, 9 Jan. 1927, 10M.

40. *New York Times Book Review*, 24 May 1955, 12.

41. *Auburn Citizen*, 8 Feb. 1927, 7; *Cleveland (Ohio) News*, quoted in *Auburn Citizen*, 8 Mar. 1927, 12.

42. Biographers, such as Kunitz and Haycraft in *Twentieth Century Authors*, 8, used the one hundred thousand figure, saying also that the book was suppressed in Washington and condemned in state legislatures.

43. "Chronicle and Comment," *Bookman*, Sept. 1916, 34; Upton Sinclair to SHA, 11 July 1927; SHA to Sinclair, 25 July 1927, Upton Sinclair Papers, Lilly Library.

44. "Games and Amusements," *Outlook*, 28 Sept. 1927, 122–23; *New York Herald Tribune Books*, 23 Oct. 1927, 23; Elizabeth Stead Taber, "Favorite Indoor Sports," *Bookman*, Dec. 1927, lv.

45. *New York Times*, 1 Aug. 1927, 25, and 7 Sept. 1927, 35; *New York World*, 7 Sept. 1927, 3.

46. SHA to Julian Street, 4 Sept. [1927], Street Papers, Princeton Univ. Libraries; *New York Times*, 13 Sept. 1927, 37; *New York World*, 13 Sept. 1927, 13; Mantle, *Best Plays of 1927–1928* (New York: Dodd, Mead, 1944), 3, 6, 401.

47. *Variety Film Reviews 1926–1929* (New York: Garland Publishing, 1983), vol. 3, 29 Feb. 1928, no page; *New York Times*, 28 Feb. 1928, 18.

48. Farrar, "Gossip Shop," *Bookman*, Mar. 1927, 110.

49. Interview with Katherine Adell, 2 Aug. 1989; interview with George Harlan, 15 Sept. 1990, Toronto, Canada.

50. Mark Sullivan, *Our Times* (New York: Scribner's, 1926), 6:398; "Fiction," *Saturday Review of Literature*, 8 Sept. 1928, 110; "Fiction Notes," *Bookman*, Aug. 1928, xxii–xxiii.

51. Hudson, *Writing Game*, 146, 149, 151–53.

52. SHA to HBL, 12 and 22 Feb. 1929; HBL to SHA, 10 Nov. 1928 and 14 Feb. 1929, HBL Papers, Van Pelt Library.

53. Jay Robert Nash and Stanley Ralph Ross, *The Motion Picture Guide* (Chicago: Cinebooks, 1987), 9:3859.

54. *New York World*, 1 May 1929, 16; HBL to BB, 14 June 1929, Adams Papers, ARL.

55. Will and Inez Irwin diaries, 23 to 31 May 1929, Irwin Papers, Beinecke Library; HBL to SHA, 14 May 1929, HBL Papers, Van Pelt Library.

56. SHA to HBL, 15 May 1922; HBL to SHA, 22 May 1929, HBL Papers, Van Pelt Library.

57. Interview with Katherine Adell, 8 Aug. 1992.

## 13. Historian, 1930–1934

1. *Auburn Citizen–Advertiser*, 19 Dec. 1953, 4. This probably was written by Agnes Osborne, daughter of the paper's reviewer. "Sniff" is a variant of dominoes.

2. "Samuel Hopkins Adams 1871–," *Wilson Bulletin for Librarians*, Apr. 1934, 500.

3. SHA to Clarence Brigham, 1 Feb. and 15 Mar. 1930, American Antiquarian Society Correspondence, American Antiquarian Society (hereafter cited as AAS), Worcester, Massachusetts.

4. HBL to BB and SHA, 9 Jan. 1930, HBL Papers, Van Pelt Library.

5. BB to SHA, 11 Jan. 1930, SHA Papers, ARL; BAC, *At Random*, 41–42, 70, 77–79, 81–85.

6. Tom Smith to BB, 8 May 1930; SHA to BB, [19 May 1930], SHA Papers, ARL.

7. *Syracuse Post-Standard*, 9 July 1930, 8.

8. Joseph Ibbotson to SHA, 20 and 28 Jan. 1930; SHA to Ibbotson, 25 Jan. 1930, SHA Papers, Burke Library.

9. FG to BB, 5 Sept. 1930. SHA papers. ARL.

10. BB to SHA, 8 Sept. 1930; SHA to BB, 1 Oct. 1930, SHA Papers, ARL.

11. *New York Times Book Review*, 26 Oct. 1930, 3; *New York Herald Tribune Books*, 2 Nov. 1930, 2; Charles Lee Snider, *North Carolina Historical Review*, 9 (Jan.–Oct. 1932): 98–103.

12. *New York World*, 30 Nov. 1930, 3E.

13. *Christian Science Monitor*, 22 Nov. 1930, 13; SHA to Clarence Brigham, 3 Oct. 1930, AAS Correspondence, AAS; "Samuel Hopkins Adams, 1871–," *Wilson Bulletin for Librarians*, 500.

14. SHA, "How I Write," 125.

15. Nash and Ross, *Motion Picture Guide*, 9:3788; BB to SHA, 20 Jan. 1931, SHA Papers, ARL.

16. Hudson, *Writing Game*, 156–58.

17. Will Irwin diary, 20 Aug. and 8 Dec. 1930, Irwin Papers, Beinecke Library.

18. *Variety's Film Reviews 1930–1933*, vol. 4, 1 Dec. 1931, no page.

19. Harry M. Daugherty, *The Inside Story of the Harding Tragedy* (New York: Churchill, 1932), 198, 233; *New York Evening Post*, quoted in the *Auburn Citizen–Advertiser*, 10 Feb. 1932, 6.

20. Interview with Marion Kennedy, 20 June 1990, Auburn, N.Y.; Lithgow Osborne to SHA, 26 Feb. 1932, Osborne Papers, ARL.

21. SHA to Lithgow Osborne, 1 and 28 Mar. 1932; Osborne to SHA, 7 Apr. 1932, Osborne Papers, ARL.

22. BB to SHA, 22 Mar. and 7 Apr. 1932; Tom R. Smith to BB, 5 Mar. 1932; SHA to BB, 9 Apr. 1932, SHA Papers, ARL.

23. BB to SHA, 4 Oct. and 13 Dec. 1932; SHA to BB, 9 Apr. 1932, SHA Papers, ARL.

24. *Auburn Citizen–Advertiser*, 17 Aug. 1933, 5.

25. *Rochester Times–Union*, 18 Dec. 1934, 17.

26. Interview with Alice Eyerman, 10 Aug. 1992, Wilkes Barre, Pa.

27. FG to SHA, 18 Jan. 1933; SHA to BB, 23 Jan. 1933, SHA Papers, ARL.

28. FG to SHA, 30 Jan. 1933; SHA to BB, 9 Feb. [1933]; BB to SHA, 15 Feb. 1933, SHA Papers, ARL.

29. Frank Capra, *The Name above the Title; An Autobiography* (New York: Macmillan, 1971), 160. Elizabeth Kendall, *The Runaway Bride; Hollywood Romantic Comedy of the 1930s* (New York: Alfred A. Knopf, 1990), 36–37, said Capra's inspiration came from Adams's "Last Trip" although the director cited "Night Bus."

30. Capra, *Name above the Title*, 160; Nash and Ross, *Motion Picture Guide*, 4: 1421; Kendall, *Runaway Bride*, 38.

31. William Kittedge and Steven M. Krauzer, *Stories into Film* (New York: Harper and Row, 1979), 32–34.

32. *Variety's Film Reviews 1934–1935*, vol. 5, 27 Feb. 1934, no page; *New York Times*, 23 Feb. 1934, 23; Nash and Ross, *Motion Picture Guide*, 4: 1422.

33. The maneuvering included legal correspondence, a brief by the Authors League, a breakaway from Liveright by Sherwood Anderson, and much discussion between May and Nov. 1933.

34. SHA to BB, [22 Oct. 1933]; BB to SHA, 25 Oct. 1933; FG to BB, 26 Oct. 1933, SHA Papers, ARL.

35. Interview with Frederik R-L. Osborne, 30 July 1990, Auburn, N.Y.

36. Hillman, "Samuel Hopkins Adams," 37.

37. Interview with Marion Kennedy, 20 June 1990, Auburn, N.Y.

38. Kunitz and Haycraft, *Twentieth Century Authors*, 7.

39. *New York Times*, 15 Apr. 1934, 22–23; *New York Herald Tribune Books*, 15 Apr. 1934, 14; R. B. M., "Fiction," *Saturday Review of Literature*, 5 May 1934, 680.

40. FG to BB, 25 July 1934, SHA Papers, ARL.

41. Interview with Michael Kowal, 7 July 1992, Niles, N.Y.

42. SHA to BB, [11 Feb. 1934], 11 and 14 July 1934, SHA Papers, ARL.

43. SHA to BB, 12 Sept. 1934; BB to SHA, 14 Sept. 1934, SHA Papers, ARL.

44. SHA to Joseph Ibbotson, 26 Sept. 1934, SHA Papers, Burke Library; Will Irwin diary, 22 Sept. 1934, Irwin Papers, Beinecke Library; SHA to Alexander Woollcott, 10 Nov. 1934, Woollcott Papers, Houghton Library.

45. Hamilton Class of 1891 newsletter, SHA Papers, Burke College.

## 14. Serialist, 1935–1939

1. SHA, "How I Write," 38–39.

2. CB to SHA, 7 and 25 Jan. 1935; SHA to CB, 8 and [13} Jan. 1935, SHA Papers, ARL.

3. *Auburn Citizen–Advertiser*, 1 Mar. 1935, 4.

4. SHA, "Old Age—I Spit in Its Eye!" *Saturday Evening Post*, 27 May 1950, 160.

5. SHA to CB, 12 Apr. and [17 Apr. 1935]; CB to SHA, 16 Apr. 1935, SHA Papers, ARL.

6. SHA to CB, [22 and 24 June 1935]; CB to SHA, 24 June 1935, SHA Papers, ARL.

7. SHA, "How I Write," 41.

8. SHA to CB, 12 and 22 July and [13 Aug. 1935], SHA Papers, ARL; Will Irwin diary, 24 to 27 Aug. 1935, Irwin Papers, Beinecke Library. The portrait was over the Adams fireplace and is now at Burke Library.

9. Lilla Worthington to SHA, 20 Sept. 1935; William Fadiman to Worthington, 19 Sept. 1935, SHA Papers, ARL.

10. FG to SHA, 18 Oct. 1935, HM Papers, Houghton Library; Tom Smith to SHA, n.d., SHA Papers, ARL.

11. BB to SHA, 15 July 1935, SHA Papers, ARL.

12. CB to SHA, 25 July 1935, SHA Papers, ARL.

13. *New York Times*, 19 Oct. 1936, 22; *Variety's Film Reviews 1934–1937*, vol. 5, 21 Oct. 1936, no page.

14. *Rochester Democrat and Chronicle*, 27 Oct. 1935, 2B.

15. Interview with George Harlan, 15 Sept. 1990, Toronto, Canada.

16. Lincoln Steffens to Frederic C. Howe, 21 Jan. 1936, Winter and Hicks, eds., *The Letters of Lincoln Steffens* (New York: Harcourt, Brace, 1938), 2:1014; SHA to Mildred Woodruff, 17 Dec. 1935, SHA Papers, Seymour Library; SHA to Lewis Stieg, 1 July 1937, SHA Papers, Burke Library.

17. SHA, "How I Write," 38.

18. Interview with Michael Kowal, 7 July 1992, Niles, N.Y.

19. *Auburn Citizen–Advertiser*, 15 Sept. 1936, 10.

20. Nash and Ross, *Motion Picture Guide*, 3:1077; SHA to BB, 22 Aug. 1936, SHA Papers, ARL.

21. BB to SHA, 19 Aug. 1936; SHA to CB, [21 Aug. 1936], SHA Papers, ARL; FG to SHA, 13 Aug. 1936; SHA to FG, 31 Aug. 1936, HM Papers, Houghton Library.

22. SHA to Alexander Woollcott, 26 May 1936, Woollcott Papers, Houghton Library; Woollcott to SHA, 28 May 1936, SHA Papers, Burke Library.

23. SHA to CB, 18 Oct. 1936; CB to SHA, 19 Oct. 1936; Oscar Graeve to CB, 11 Dec. 1936, SHA Papers, ARL.

24. SHA, "The Town I Like—Beaufort, South Carolina," *Lincoln-Mercury Times*, Nov.–Dec. 1950, 23.

25. SHA to CB, [11 Mar. 1937], SHA Papers, ARL.

26. CB to SHA, 22 Jan. 1937, SHA Papers, ARL.

27. CB to SHA, 3 Feb. 1937, SHA Papers, ARL.

28. Richard H. Waldo to SHA, 12 Aug. 1937, SHA Papers, ARL.

29. *Variety's Film Reviews 1934–1937*, vol. 5, 29 Sept. 1937, no page; *New York Times*, 29 Oct. 1937, 29; Nash and Ross, *Motion Picture Guide*, 6:2373–74.

30. Interview with George R. Metcalf, 18 July 1990, Auburn, N.Y.

31. Collier Young to SHA, 5 Mar. 1938; CB to SHA, 14 Mar. 1938, SHA Papers, ARL; Will Irwin diary, 5 Aug. 1938, Irwin Papers, Beinecke Library.

32. CB to Fulton Oursler, 5 Apr. 1938; Oursler to CB, 8 Apr. 1938, SHA Papers, ARL.

33. F. P., "The New Books," *Saturday Review of Literature*, 4 June 1938, 21; *New York Times Book Review*, 1 May 1938, 18.

34. Telephone interview with Legare Hole, 2 July 1992, Martha's Vineyard, Mass.

35. Harold F. Alderfer, "The Personality and Politics of Warren G. Harding" (Ph.D. diss., Syracuse Univ., 1928).

36. FG to SHA, 3 Nov. 1938; SHA to FG, 5 Nov. 1938, HM Papers, Houghton Library.

37. SHA to CB, 15 Nov. 1938, SHA Papers, ARL; William Allen White to SHA, 23 May 1939; Norman Thomas to SHA, 19 Jan. 1939, SHA Papers, Burke Library.

38. SHA to CB, 19 Jan. and 13 Feb. 1939; BB to SHA, 17 and 29 Feb. 1939, SHA Papers, ARL.

39. SHA to Arnold Gingrich, 2 Mar. 1939; Gingrich to CB, 13 Apr. 1939; CB to SHA, 17 Apr. 1939; SHA to CB, 22 Apr. 1939, SHA Papers, ARL.

40. CB to SHA, 10 Feb. and 27 Apr. 1939; SHA to CB, 5 May 1939, SHA Papers, ARL.

41. BB to SHA, 5 June 1939; SHA to CB, 6 June, 15 Aug., and 12 Sept. 1939, SHA Papers, ARL.

42. Harry M. Daugherty to HM, 12 Oct. 1939; FG to Daugherty, 18 Oct. 1939, Ray B. Harris Papers, (Microfilm ed., box 9, frames 560, 562), Ohio Historical Society, Columbus.

43. Will and Inez Irwin diaries, 24 to 29 Oct. 1939, Irwin Papers, Beinecke Library; SHA to BB, 18 Mar. 1939; BB to SHA, 21 Mar. 1939, SHA Papers, ARL.

44. *Rochester Democrat and Chronicle*, 4 Nov. 1939, 13; 1 Dec. 1939, 26.

45. *Rochester Democrat and Chronicle*, 4 Nov. 1939, 13; SHA to BB, 11 Nov. [1939]; BB to SHA, 14 Nov. 1939, SHA Papers, ARL.

46. *New York Times*, 24 Oct. 1939, 21; *New York Times Book Review*, 5 Nov. 1939, 3; *New*

*York Herald Tribune Books*, 29 Oct. 1939, 4; William Allen White, "The Ohio Gang," *Saturday Review of Literature*, 4 Nov. 1939, 6.

47. Interview with Beatrice Champany, 19 Sept. 1992, Auburn, N.Y.

48. SHA to CB, 7 Nov. 1939, SHA Papers, ARL.

49. BB to SHA, 9 Nov. 1939; SHA to BB, 11 Nov. [1939], SHA Papers, ARL.

50. "Hope for Poor Spellers," *Hamilton Alumni Review*, Oct. 1939, 70.

## 15. Ghostwriter, 1940–1942

1. Frank G. Slaughter, "When the Scalpel Sharpens the Pen," *Journal of The American Medical Association* 200 (3 Apr. 1967): 19; Slaughter to author, 21 Feb. 1990.

2. SHA to BB, 15 Jan. 1940, SHA Papers, ARL; SHA to Frank G. Slaughter, 15 Jan. 1940, HM Papers, Houghton Library.

3. CB to SHA, 15 and 24 Jan. 1940; BB to CB, 23 Jan. 1940, SHA Papers, ARL.

4. SHA to FG, 10 Feb. 1940; FG to SHA, 14 Feb. 1940, HM Papers, Houghton Library.

5. *New York Herald Tribune Books*, 18 Feb. 1940, 10; *New York Times Book Review*, 11 Feb. 1940, 23.

6. Telephone interview with Tom Belden, 14 May 1991, Rockville, Maryland.

7. Peggy Wood, "Samuel Hopkins Adams," *Book of the Month Club News*, July 1955, 4.

8. SHA to FG, 23 Mar. 1940, HM Papers, Houghton Library.

9. Frank G. Slaughter to BB, 17 Apr. and 13 May 1940; Tom B. Costain to BB, 21 May 1940, SHA Papers, ARL; Slaughter to author, 21 Feb. 1990.

10. Telephone interview with Elizabeth Richardson Steele, 22 July 1992, Newport Beach, Calif.

11. FG to SHA, 13 June 1940; SHA to FG, 8 July 1940, HM Papers, Houghton Library.

12. Edwin P. Hoyt, *Alexander Woollcott: The Man Who Came to Dinner* (London: Abelard-Schumn, 1968), 311.

13. Telephone interview with Elizabeth Richardson Steele, 22 July 1992, Newport Beach, Calif.

14. SHA to Paul Bonner, 11 Oct. 1940, Bonner Papers, Princeton Univ. Libraries; SHA to Allan Nevins, 29 Aug. and 8 Sept. 1940, Allan Nevins Papers, Rare Book and Manuscript Library, Columbia Univ.; SHA to Henry L. Mencken, 21 and 24 Apr. 1940; Mencken to SHA, 22 and 26 Apr. 1940, H. L. Mencken Papers, Rare Books and Manuscripts Division, New York Public Library, Astor, Lenox and Tilden Foundations, New York.

15. Interview with Ray S. Messenger, 18 June 1992, Clinton, N.Y.

16. SHA telegram to BB, 27 Nov. 1940; Frank G. Slaughter to BB, 30 Nov. 1940; Tom Costain to SHA, 2 Dec. 1940, SHA Papers, ARL.

17. SHA to CB, 16 Jan. 1940, SHA Papers, ARL; Will and Inez Irwin diaries, 17 Dec. 1940, Irwin Papers, Beinecke Library.

18. BAC, *At Random*, 149.

19. CB to Burt McBride, 4 Mar. 1941, SHA Papers, ARL.

20. Hillman, 37; interview with Ray S. Messenger, 18 June 1992, Clinton, N.Y.

21. Stuart Rose to CB, 18 and 21 Apr. 1941, SHA Papers, ARL.

22. Interview with George Harlan, 15 Sept. 1990, Toronto, Canada.

23. SHA to Alexander Woollcott, 10 Sept. 1941; Woollcott to SHA, 20 Sept. 1941, Woollcott Papers, Houghton Library.

24. Will and Inez Irwin diaries, 16 to 22 Sept. 1941, Irwin Papers, Beinecke Library.

25. Kunitz and Haycraft, *Twentieth Century Authors*, 7–8; Wayne S. Cole, *America First; The Battle Against Intervention 1940–1941* (Madison: Univ. of Wisconsin Press, 1953), 21, 172–73.

26. Author to Federal Bureau of Investigation (FBI), 7 Nov. 1989, 11 July 1990, and 22 Mar. 1991; FBI to author, 27 Nov. 1989, 18 July 1990, 31 Dec. 1990, 17 Apr. 1991, and 29 Aug. 1991. The bureau reviewed sixty-four pages and released forty-eight. The others were withheld mostly because the contents might invade other people's privacy, reveal confidential sources, or not be in the interests of national security, the FBI stated. Copies of the released materials are in the author's possession and, hereafter, all FBI references are based on these documents.

27. SHA to Henry Morton Robinson, 16 Mar. 1943, Henry Morton Robinson Papers, Rare Book and Manuscript Library, Columbia Univ.

28. SHA to BB, 11 Dec. 1941; BB to SHA, 12 Dec. 1941, SHA Papers, ARL.

29. BAC to Kenneth McKenna, 18 Dec. 1941, SHA Papers, ARL; BAC, *At Random*, 170.

30. Louis E. Swarts to CB, 7 and 10 Jan. 1942; CB to Swarts, 10 Jan. 1942, SHA Papers, ARL.

31. SHA to FG, 26 Jan. 1942; FG to SHA, 29 Jan. 1942, HM Papers, Houghton Library.

32. SHA to Alexander Woollcott, 16 Mar. 1942, Woollcott Papers, Houghton Library.

33. SHA to BB, 27 June and 9 July 1942; BB to SHA, 3, 7, and 9 July 1942; BB to Frank G. Slaughter, 13 July 1943, SHA Papers, ARL; Slaughter to author, 21 Feb. 1990.

34. SHA, "Why I Wrote Canal Town," *Canal Town* brochure.

35. Walter I. Bradbury to Carol Brandt, 19 Feb. 1959, SHA Papers, Burke Library.

36. SHA to Joseph Hennessey, 23 Mar. 1942, Woollcott Papers, Houghton Library; Woollcott to SHA, 7 June 1942, SHA Papers, Burke Library.

37. SHA to Alexander Woollcott, 17 July and 6 Aug. 1942, Woollcott Papers, Houghton Library; Woollcott to SHA, 21 July 1942, SHA Papers, Burke Library.

38. Interview with Elizabeth Richardson Steele, 22 July 1992, Newport Beach, Calif.

39. SHA to BB, 28 July 1942, SHA Papers, ARL; telephone interview with Walter Edmonds, 16 Aug. 1992, Concord, Mass.

40. *New York Herald Tribune Books*, 25 Oct. 1942, 28; *New York Times Book Review*, 1 Nov. 1942, 28.

41. *New York Times Book Review*, 25 Oct. 1942, 28; *New York Herald Tribune Books*, 25 Oct. 1942, 6; *New York Herald Tribune*, 26 Oct. 1942, 11. None of the four Adams books made the *Herald Tribune's* "What America Is Reading" lists during 1942.

42. BAC to SHA, 2 Nov. and 15 Dec. 1942; BB to SHA, 16 Nov. 1942, SHA Papers, ARL.

43. Telephone interview with Frank Taylor, 15 Mar. 1991, Key West, Fla.

44. *Collier's* to CB, 2 Oct. 1942; Julian Street, Jr., to CB, 14 Dec. 1942, SHA Papers, ARL.

45. DeWitt Wallace to SHA, 29 Dec. 1942; CB to SHA, 30 Jan. 1943; SHA to CB, 4 Jan. 1943, SHA Papers, ARL.

## 16. Biographer, 1943–1945

1. Alexander Woollcott to SHA, 4 Nov. 1942; SHA to Alexander Woollcott, 6 and 13 Nov. 1942, Woollcott Papers, Houghton Library.

2. SHA to BB, 4 Mar. 1943, SHA Papers, ARL.

3. Telephone interview with Frank Taylor, 15 Mar. 1991, Key West, Fla.

4. Alma Levin Pritchard to SHA, 8 Mar. 1943, SHA Papers, ARL.

5. Tom Costain to BB, 12 May 1943; Costain to SHA, 9 and 29 June 1943, SHA Papers, ARL.

6. SHA to BB, 5 July 1943; BB to SHA, 7 July 1943, SHA Papers, ARL.

7. BB to SHA, 13 Sept. 1943; Belle Becker to BB, 14 Sept. 1943, SHA Papers, ARL.

8. *Dies Committee Report*, 1200, 1240; *New York Times* ad, 18 May 1943, 17; FBI field report, 20 Jan. 1945; *Daily Worker*, 11 June 1945, 8, all are in the FBI file; *Auburn Citizen–Advertiser*, 19 Nov. 1958, 9.

9. Telephone interview with Frank Taylor, 15 Mar. 1991, Key West, Fla.

10. Ibid.; and interviews with Marion Kennedy, 20 June 1990, Auburn, N.Y., and George Harlan, 15 Sept. 1990, Toronto, Canada.

11. Joseph Hennessey to SHA, 19 Aug. 1943, SHA Papers, Burke Library.

12. Peggy Wood to SHA, 25 Oct. 1943, SHA Papers, Burke Library.

13. Charles A. Fecher, ed., *The Diary of H. L. Mencken* (New York: Alfred A. Knopf, 1989), 279–81; Edna Ferber to SHA, 4 Nov. 1943; John K. Winkler to SHA, 11 Oct. 1943, SHA Papers, Burke Library; SHA, *Woollcott*, 2; interview with Katherine Adell, 12 June 1989.

14. Danton Walker, *Danton's Inferno; The Story of a Columnist and How He Grew* (New York: Hastings House, 1955), 248; *New York Times Book Review*, 17 June 1945, 3.

15. Interview with Martha Elliott, 2 Mar. 1991, Beaufort, S.C.

16. Leda Bauer to Alma Pritchard, 4 Feb. 1944; SHA to Pritchard, 6 Feb. 1944; Pritchard to SHA, 9 Feb. 1944, SHA Papers, ARL.

17. SHA to BB, 17 Dec. 1943, SHA Papers, ARL.

18. SHA to Booth Tarkington, 22 Jan. 1944, Booth Tarkington Papers, Princeton Univ. Libraries.

19. SHA to BB, 1 and 5 Feb. 1944; BB to SHA, 8 Feb. 1944, SHA Papers, ARL.

20. SHA to BAC, 13 Feb. 1944; BAC to SHA, 18 Feb. 1944, SHA Papers, ARL.

21. SHA to BB, 11 Feb. 1944; BB to SHA, 14 Feb. 1944, SHA Papers, ARL.

22. BAC to SHA, 23 Mar. 1944, SHA Papers, ARL.

23. *New York Times Book Review*, 23 Apr. 1944, 6; Carl Carmer, "Good Historical Fiction," *Saturday Review of Literature*, 10 June 1944, 26; military letters, SHA Papers, Burke Library.

24. *Auburn Citizen–Advertiser*, 17 June 1944, 5.

25. William Scherman to author, 3 Oct. 1990; telephone interview with Joseph Merriam, 10 Jan. 1990, Wilton, Conn.

26. BB to Frank Taylor, 10 and 15 Aug. 1944, SHA Papers, ARL.

27. BAC to SHA, 21 and 24 July 1944; SHA to BAC, 23 July 1944, SHA Papers, ARL.

28. Robert Linscott, "Samuel Hopkins Adams," *Canal Town* brochure, 11.

29. BAC to BB, 15 Sept. 1944; BB to BAC, 19 Sept. 1944; BB to SHA, 19 and 20 Sept. 1944, SHA Papers, ARL.

30. SHA to BB, 22 July 1944, SHA Papers, ARL.

31. *Dallas (Texas) Times-Herald*, 10 June 1945.

32. *New York Post*, 16 Nov. 1944, 33.

33. George S. Kaufman to Frank Taylor, 27 Dec. 1944; SHA to BB, 30 Dec. 1944, SHA Papers, ARL.

34. BB to SHA, 7 Mar. 1945; SHA to BB, 8 Mar. 1945, SHA Papers, ARL.

35. Clifford Funkhouser and Lyman Anson to Random House, 21 July 1942; Stern and Rubin to Brandt and Brandt, 5 Aug. 1942, SHA Papers, ARL.

36. H. L. Mencken to SHA, 8 May 1945, Mencken Papers, New York Public Library; Mencken to SHA, 1 June 1945, SHA Papers, Burke Library.

37. Hillman, "Samuel Hopkins Adams," 15.

38. SHA to Clarence Brigham, 19 June 1945, AAS correspondence; SHA to Arthur Bartlett Maurice, 14 June 1945, Maurice Papers, Princeton Univ. Libraries.

39. *New York Herald Tribune Weekly Book Review*, 3 June 1945, 4; Richard Watts, Jr., "Impious Fraud," *New Republic*, 4 June 1945, 795; Dorothy Parker, "About the 'Town Crier' and His World," *Chicago Sun Book Week*, 10 June 1945, SHA scrapbook, Burke Library.

40. Edmund Wilson, "A Portrait of Alexander Woollcott," *New Yorker*, 9 June 1945, 73–74; SHA to BB, 22 June 1945, SHA Papers, ARL; Harold Ross to SHA, 14 June 1945, SHA Papers, Burke Library.

41. Maureen Daly, *My Favorite Suspense Stories* (New York: Dodd, Mead, 1968), 136.

42. *Syracuse Herald–American*, 22 July 1945, 20; *Syracuse Herald–Journal*, 24 July 1945, 12.

43. BB to SHA, 9 July and 19 Sept. 1945; SHA to BB, 25 July 1945, SHA Papers, ARL.

44. *Auburn Citizen–Advertiser*, 25 Aug. 1945, 6; *Congressional Record*, 79th Congress, 1st sess. (1945), vol. 91, pt. 13, app. 26 Nov. 1945, A5091–A5093, and 3 Dec. 1945, A5229–A5230.

45. SHA to CB, 9 and 13 Sept. 1945; CB to SHA, 12 Sept. 1945, SHA Papers, ARL.

46. SHA to CB, 1 and 5 Sept. 1945; CB to Carol Brandt, 19 Sept. 1945, SHA Papers, ARL.

47. Carol Brandt to SHA, 20 Sept. 1945; SHA to CB, 23 Sept., 8 and 24 Dec. 1945, SHA Papers, ARL.

48. Edith Osborne to Lithgow and Lillie Osborne, 24 Aug. 1945, Osborne Papers, ARL; interview with George Metcalf, 18 July 1990, Auburn, N.Y.

49. Edith Osborne to Lithgow and Lillie Osborne, 31 Oct. 1945, Osborne Papers, ARL.

50. SHA to BB, 26 Aug. 1945, SHA Papers, ARL.

51. SHA to BB, 28 Dec. 1942 and 20 and 27 Sept. 1945, SHA Papers, ARL; SHA to Lithgow Osborne, 13 Dec. 1945, Osborne Papers, ARL.

## 17. Regionalist, 1946–1949

1. D. O. Decker to CB, 29 Dec. 1941 and 7 Dec. 1945; William Rankin to SHA, 2 Aug. and 4 Dec. 1945, 23 Jan. 1946; SHA to CB, 8 Aug. 1945 and 2 Feb. 1946; CB to SHA, 10

Aug. 1945; CB to Rankin, 27 Aug. 1945; Rankin to CB, 24 Sept., 3 Nov. and 4 Dec. 1945; CB to Decker, 7 Dec. 1945, SHA Papers, ARL.

2. "First Guesses on the Pulitzer Awards," *Saturday Review of Literature*, 27 Apr. 1946, 14–15.

3. SHA to BAC, 13 June 1946; BAC to SHA, 19 June 1946; SHA to BB and to Belle Becker, 14 June 1946; Becker to SHA, 25 June 1946, SHA Papers, ARL.

4. SHA to William Scherman, 5 May 1946, William Scherman private papers, Hanover, N.H.; interview with Katherine Adell, 12 June 1989.

5. SHA to CB, 27 June 1946; Belle Becker to SHA, 27 June 1946, SHA Papers, ARL.

6. Belle Becker to SHA, 2 July 1946; BAC to SHA, 3 July 1946; SHA to CB, 5 July 1946, SHA Papers, ARL.

7. Belle Becker to SHA, 29 July 1946; BB to SHA, 31 July, 23 Aug., and 7 Oct. 1946; SHA to BB, 6 June, 1, 6, and 25 Aug. 1946, SHA Papers, ARL.

8. SHA to BB, 3, 4, 17, 20, and 30 Aug. 1946; BB to SHA, 6 Sept. 1946, SHA Papers, ARL.

9. Belle Becker to SHA, 4 Sept. 1946; SHA to Becker, 29 Aug. and 5 Sept. 1946, SHA Papers, ARL.

10. Will Irwin diary, 8 Sept. 1946, Irwin Papers, Beinecke Library.

11. *Auburn Citizen–Advertiser*, 9 Sept. 1946, 4.

12. Interview with George Harlan, 15 Sept. 1990, Toronto, Canada; Katherine Messenger to Frederik R-L. Osborne, 11 Sept. 1946, Osborne Papers, ARL.

13. Interview with Katherine Adell, 12 June 1989; SHA to BB, 26 Sept. 1946; BB to SHA, 2 Oct. 1946; SHA to Belle Becker, 7, [11] and 13 Oct. 1946, SHA Papers, ARL.

14. *Proceedings of the American Antiquarian Society* (Worcester, Mass.: AAS, 1946), 56: 157–58.

15. *New York Herald Tribune*, 17 Sept. 1943, 23; 23 Sept. 1943, 21; SHA to CB, 31 Aug. 1946; CB to SHA, 10 Sept. 1946, SHA Papers, ARL; *Auburn Citizen–Advertiser*, 15 Dec. 1947, 4.

16. SHA, "Introduction," in Courtney, *Laurette*, viii.

17. BAC to SHA, 6 and 14 Jan. 1947; SHA to BAC, 11 Jan. 1947, SHA Papers, ARL.

18. *New York Herald Tribune Weekly Book Review*, 16 Mar. 1947, 8; *New York Times Book Reviews*, 16 Mar. 1947, 10; Nathan L. Rothman, "Old New York," *Saturday Review of Literature*, 12 Apr. 1947, 57; Walter D. Edmonds, *New York History* 28 (July 1947): 357–58.

19. BAC to BB, 4 Apr. 1947, SHA Papers, ARL.

20. Katherine Messenger to Lillie Osborne, 9 Mar. 1946, Osborne Papers, ARL.

21. Interview with Lydia Mead Engelbert; BB to SHA, 18 June 1947, SHA Papers, ARL.

22. Clarence Brigham to SHA, 17 June 1947; SHA to Brigham, 20 June 1947, AAS correspondence.

23. *New York Herald Tribune Book Review*, 26 June 1955, 2.

24. SHA to CB, 20 Feb. 1947; CB to SHA, 25 Feb. 1947, SHA Papers, ARL.

25. BAC to SHA, 9 Apr. 1947, SHA Papers, ARL.

26. BAC to SHA, 24 June 1947; SHA to BAC, 27 Sept. 1947, SHA Papers, ARL; BAC, "Trade Winds," *Saturday Review of Literature*, 5 July 1947, 6; SHA to Betty Steele, 29 Sept. 1947, Elizabeth Richardson Steele private papers.

27. Belle Becker memorandum on *Plunder*, 8 Sept. 1947, SHA Papers, ARL.

28. SHA to Clarence Brigham, 7 Dec. 1947, AAS correspondence; SHA to BAC, 1 Jan. 1948, SHA Papers, ARL.

29. Saxe Commins to SHA, 5 Jan. 1948; SHA to BB, 10 Jan. 1948, SHA Papers, ARL.

30. SHA to Saxe Commins, 5, 15, and 22 Jan. 1948; Commins to SHA, 12 and 20 Jan. 1948, SHA Papers, ARL.

31. August Heckscher to author, 10 Nov. 1990.

32. SHA to SHH, 11 Jan. 1948, SHH Papers, Univ. of Washington Libraries, Seattle, Wash.; BB to SHA, 26 Feb. 1948; Belle Becker to SHA, 8 and 18 Mar. 1948, SHA Papers, ARL; *New York Herald Tribune Book Review*, 11 Apr. 1948, 8; Jonathan Daniels, "Atomic Age Antics," *Saturday Review of Literature*, 8 May 1948, 11–12; *New York Times Book Review*, 11 Apr. 1948, 7, 27.

33. SHA to BB, 1 Aug. 1948, SHA Papers, ARL; *Auburn Citizen–Advertiser*, 11 Sept. 1948, 6.

34. SHA to Betty Steele, 29 Sept. 1947, Elizabeth Richardson Steele private papers; SHA to BAC, 30 Nov. 1948, SHA Papers, ARL.

35. BB to SHA, 28 Dec. 1948; BAC to SHA, 31 Dec. 1948 and 11 Jan. 1949, SHA Papers, ARL.

36. SHA to Joseph Ibbotson, 30 Apr. 1949; SHA to Helen Seymour Weaver Hutchinson, 9 Apr. 1949, SHA Papers, Burke Library.

37. CB to Harry Sions, 13 May 1949; CB to SHA, 20 May 1949, SHA Papers, ARL. For further information on Letterio Calapai see *Illustrators of Children's Books, 1946–1956* (Boston: Horn Book, 1958), 86.

38. Belle Becker memorandum, 16 June 1949, SHA Papers, ARL.

39. BAC to SHA, 21 June 1949; SHA to BAC, 1 July 1949, SHA Papers, ARL.

40. SHA to CB, 24 June 1949, SHA Papers, ARL; SHA to Louis Jones, 8 Aug. 1947, Louis Jones Papers, courtesy of the New York State Historical Association Library, Cooperstown, N.Y. Hereafter the New York State Historical Association is cited as NYSHA Library. Louis Jones to author, 27 Feb. 1990.

41. Interview with George Harlan, 15 Sept. 1990, Toronto, Canada.

42. CB telegram to SHA, 26 Aug. 1949; SHA to CB, 26 Aug. 1949; CB to SHA, 29 Aug. 1949, SHA Papers, ARL.

43. CB to SHA, 18 Nov. 1949; SHA to CB, 20 Nov. and 19 Dec. 1949, SHA Papers, ARL.

44. Belle Becker to SHA, 11 and 14 Nov. 1949, SHA Papers, ARL.

45. SHA to Belle Becker, 17 Nov. 1949; BAC to SHA, 22 Nov. 1949; SHA to BAC, 2 Dec. 1949, SHA Papers, ARL.

## 18. Juvenilist, 1950–1953

1. CB to Tom Davis, 10 Jan. 1950, SHA Papers, ARL.

2. Harry Sions to SHA, 17 Jan. 1950, SHA Papers, ARL.

3. SHA to CB, 10 Jan. 1950; CB to SHA, 23 Jan. 1950, SHA Papers, ARL.

4. Belle Becker to SHA, 3 Jan. 1950; SHA to Becker, 6 Jan. 1950, SHA Papers, ARL.

5. CB to SHA, 30 Jan. and 3 Feb. 1950, SHA Papers, ARL.

6. SHA to CB, 5 Feb. 1950; SHA to Belle Becker, 10 Feb. 1950, SHA Papers, ARL.

7. SHA to Joseph Ibbotson, 8 Feb. 1950, SHA Papers, Burke Library; interview with Katherine Adell, 2 Aug. 1989; interview with Martha Elliott, 2 Mar. 1991, Beaufort, S.C.

8. SHA to CB, 12 Feb. 1950, SHA Papers, ARL; Hillman, "Samuel Hopkins Adams," 15, 37.

9. *Auburn Citizen–Advertiser*, 2 Sept. 1958, 2; interview with Nan Abell, 24 Nov. 1990, Riverside, Conn.

10. Interviews with Peggy French and Nan Abell, 24 Nov. 1990, Riverside, Conn.

11. SHA to Robert McEwen, 2 Mar. 1950, SHA Papers, Burke Library.

12. SHA to Ben Hibbs, 22 Apr. 1950; SHA to CB, 23 and 24 Apr., 18 May 1950; CB to SHA, 26 Apr. 1950, SHA Papers, ARL.

13. *Rochester Democrat and Chronicle*, 6 May 1950, 1.

14. *New York Times Book Review*, 28 May 1950, 5; *New York Herald Tribune Book Review*, 28 May 1950, 6; Roger Burlingame, "Rise of a Bobbin-doffer," *Saturday Review of Literature*, 10 June 1950, 14; Carmer to SHA, 4 Nov. 1949; SHA to Carmer, 25 May 1950, Carmer Papers, NYSHA Library.

15. *Daily Worker*, 26 June 1950, 11.

16. SHA to Belle Becker, 2 Mar. 1950; Allan Ullman to SHA, 7 Mar. 1950; BAC to SHA, 2 May 1950, SHA Papers, ARL; BAC, "Trade Winds," *Saturday Review of Literature*, 19 Aug. 1950, 4.

17. BAC to SHA, 7 June 1950; Belle Becker to SHA, 7 June 1950, SHA Papers, ARL.

18. SHA to BAC, 10 July 1950; BAC to SHA, 12 July 1950; BAC to BB, 14 July 1950, SHA Papers, ARL.

19. CB to SHA, 22 June, 1 and 19 July 1950; Harry Sions to CB, 29 June and 16 Aug. 1950, SHA Papers, ARL.

20. *New York Times Book Review for Children*, 12 Nov. 1950, 6; *New York Herald Tribune Book Review*, 12 Nov. 1950, 14.

21. SHA to BB, 28 Oct. 1950; BAC to SHA, 16 Nov. 1950, SHA Papers, ARL.

22. SHA to Clarence Brigham, 1 Dec. 1950, AAS correspondence; Cleveland Amory, "Trade Winds," *Saturday Review of Literature*, 11 Sept. 1954, 8; SHA to BAC, 30 Apr. 1951, SHA Papers, ARL.

23. "S. H. A. Hits 80," *Hamilton Alumni Review*, Mar. 1951, 135; SHA to BAC, 25 Apr. 1951, SHA Papers, ARL.

24. *Rochester Democrat and Chronicle*, 24 Feb. 1951, 3.

25. SHA to SHH, 5 Jan. 1951, SHH Papers, Univ. of Washington Libraries; BAC, "Trade Winds," *Saturday Review of Literature*, 3 Feb. 1951, 4; SHA to BAC, 11 Apr. 1951, SHA Papers, ARL.

26. BAC to SHA, 17 and 27 Apr. 1951; SHA to BAC, 30 Apr. 1951, SHA Papers, ARL; *Auburn Citizen–Advertiser*, 2 Sept. 1958, 2.

27. SHA to CB, 7 June 1951; CB to SHA, 11 June 1951, SHA Papers, ARL.

28. Interview with Marion Kennedy, 20 June 1990, Auburn, N.Y.

29. SHA to CB, 2 June 1951; CB to SHA, 4 June 1951, SHA Papers, ARL.

30. Robert Henderson to SHA, 30 June 1951; Kathryn Bourne to CB, 30 Aug. 1951, SHA Papers, ARL.

31. BAC to SHA, 19 Oct. 1951, SHA Papers, ARL.

32. BAC to SHA, 26 Nov. 1951, SHA Papers, ARL.

33. BAC to SHA, 26 Nov. and 21 Dec. 1951; SHA to BAC, 20 and 22 Nov. 1951, SHA Papers, ARL.

34. C. Funkhouser to SHA, 6 Dec. 1951; SHA to CB, 19 Dec. 1951; CB to SHA, 27 Dec. 1951, SHA Papers, ARL; Funkhouser v. Loew's Incorporated, 108 F. Supp. 476 (Western Division, 1952); 208 F. 2d 185 (Eighth, 1953), 348 U.S. 843 (Supreme Court, 1954).

35. Interview with Katherine Adell, 12 June 1989.

36. CB to Clara Savage Littledale, 31 Jan. 1952; Littledale to CB, 8 Feb. 1952, SHA Papers, ARL.

37. Harold J. Michel to CB, 7 Mar. 1952, SHA Papers, ARL.

38. SHA to BB, 23 Apr. 1952, SHA Papers, ARL.

39. SHA to BB, 25 and 28 May 1952; BB to SHA, 27 May and 7 July 1952; SHA to BAC, 12 June 1952; BAC to SHA, 16 June 1952, SHA Papers, ARL.

40. SHA to BB, 6 July 1952, SHA Papers, ARL; *Rochester Democrat and Chronicle*, 15 July 1952, 15.

41. SHA to BB, 6 July 1952; BB to SHA, 9 July 1952, SHA Papers, ARL; SHA financial records, *New Yorker*.

42. Clifford K. Shipton, "Samuel Hopkins Adams," *Proceedings of the American Antiquarian Society*, 69 (Apr. 1960): 7–8.

43. John Marquand to SHA, 28 Aug. 1952; SHA to Marquand, 6 Oct. 1952, Marquand Papers, Houghton Library.

44. *New York Herald Tribune Book Review*, 26 Feb. 1950, 3.

45. Interview with Ray Messenger, 18 June 1992, Clinton, N.Y.; SHA to BB, 22 Oct. 1952; BB to SHA, 27 Oct. 1952, SHA Papers, ARL.

46. *Rochester Democrat and Chronicle*, 27 Sept. 1952, 11.

47. FBI reports, 19 Oct. 1951 and 19 Jan. 1953, SHA file. The post office action was reported under the Freedom of Information request to the FBI. C. R. Clauson to author, 6 Sept. 1991.

48. SHA to BB, 1 Oct. 1952, SHA Papers, ARL.

49. SHA financial records, *New Yorker*.

50. SHA to Irita Van Doren, 12 Sept. 1953, Van Doren Papers, Manuscript Division, Library of Congress.

51. SHA to CB, 30 Dec. 1953, SHA Papers, ARL.

## 19. Grandfather, 1954–1955

1. SHA to SHH, 26 Apr. 1954, SHH Papers, Univ. of Washington Libraries.

2. BB to SHA, 24 Feb. 1954; Louise Bonino to SHA, 28 Feb. 1954; BAC to SHA, 11 Mar. 1954; SHA to BB, 14 Mar. 1954; SHA to BAC, 14 Mar. 1954, SHA Papers, ARL.

3. SHA to BB, 21 Mar. and 1 Apr. 1954; BAC to BB, 16 Apr. 1954, SHA Papers, ARL; SHA to Clarence Brigham, 21 Mar. 1954, AAS correspondence.

4. August Heckscher to author, 10 Nov. 1990; SHA to Robert McEwen, 25 Mar. and 12 Apr. 1954; McEwen to SHA, 31 Mar. and 7 Apr. 1954, SHA Papers, Burke Library.

5. *New York Times Book Review*, 22 Aug. 1954, 22; interview with Martha Elliott, 2 Mar. 1991, Beaufort, S.C.

6. SHA to BAC, 13 Dec. 1953; Frederic A. Birmingham to CB, [1 Feb. 1954], SHA Papers, ARL.

7. SHA to CB, 18 Feb. 1954; SHA to BB, 28 Oct. 1950 and 26 Feb. 1954; BB to SHA, 18, 26, and 30 Oct. 1950, SHA Papers, ARL.

8. BAC to SHA, 21 May 1954, SHA Papers, ARL.

9. BAC to BB, 21 May 1954; BB to BAC, 24 May 1954; SHA to BB, 11 June 1954, SHA Papers, ARL.

10. BAC to SHA, 29 [June] 1954, SHA Papers, ARL.

11. Mabel Souvaine to BB, 9 July 1954; Souvaine to SHA, 26 July 1954, SHA Papers, ARL.

12. SHA to Earl Conrad, 16 and 28 June 1954; Conrad to SHA, 26 June and n.d. 1954, Conrad Papers, Bourke Library, Cayuga Community College, Auburn, N.Y.

13. John Marquand to SHA, 20 Oct. 1954, Marquand Papers, Houghton Library.

14. SHA to SHH, 1 Nov. 1954, SHH Papers, Univ. of Washington Libraries.

15. SHA to CB, 20 Dec. 1954, SHA Papers, ARL.

16. CB to SHA, 25 Oct.1954; SHA to CB, 27 Oct. 1954, SHA Papers, ARL.; Nash and Ross, *Motion Picture Guide*, 9:3960.

17. BAC, "Trade Winds," *Saturday Review*, 15 Jan. 1955, 7–8; SHA to BAC, 9 Jan. 1955; BAC to SHA, 12 Jan. 1955, SHA Papers, ARL.

18. *Pinehurst (N.C.) Outlook*, 2 Dec. 1955.

19. Alan Dinehart to CB, 4 Mar. 1955; CB to SHA, 10 Mar. 1955, SHA Papers, ARL.

20. SHA to BB, 28 Mar. 1955; BB to SHA, 31 Mar. 1955, SHA Papers, ARL.

21. CB telegram to SHA and SHA to CB, 1 Apr. 1955, SHA Papers, ARL.

22. SHA to John Marquand, 1 Apr. 1955; Marquand to SHA, 5 Apr. 1955, Marquand Papers, Houghton Library.

23. BB to SHA, 6 Apr. 1955; CB to SHA, 12 Apr. 1955; SHA to BB, 8 Apr. 1955, SHA Papers, ARL.

24. SHA to Carl Carmer, 18 Apr. 1955; SHA to Charles Kilborne, 27 Apr. 1955; Martha Elliott to Kilborne, [1 May 1955], Carmer Papers, NYSHA Library.

25. Tape recording of dinner speeches, 7 June 1955, Cayuga Museum of History and Art, Auburn, N.Y.

26. SHA to BAC, 8 June 1955; BAC to SHA, 13 June 1955, SHA Papers, ARL.

27. SHA to Bennett and Phyllis Cerf, 26 June 1955, SHA Papers, ARL.

28. Belle Becker to BB, 5 July 1955, SHA Papers, ARL.

29. *Oakland (Calif.) Tribune Daily Magazine*, 9 Sept. 1955, D21.

30. *Oneonta Star*, 9 July 1955; *Rochester Times Union*, 24 July 1955, 13E.

31. SHA to BAC, 11 July 1955, SHA Papers, ARL.

32. Belle Becker to BB, 5 July 1955; BB to Becker, 13 July 1955; CB to SHA, 14 July 1955, SHA Papers, ARL.

33. John P. Marquand, "Grandfather Stories," *Book of the Month Club News*, July 1955, 3.

34. SHA to BB, 15 and 21 July 1955; BB to SHA, 18 July 1955, SHA Papers, ARL.

35. BAC to SHA, 19 July 1955, SHA Papers, ARL.

36. *New York Times Book Review*, 24 July 1955, 1.

37. BB to SHA, 25 July 1955, SHA Papers, ARL; *New York Herald Tribune*, 22 July 1955, 13.

38. SHA to Witter Bynner, 25 Oct. 1955, Bynner Papers, Houghton Library.

39. BB to SHA, 25 July 1955; BAC to SHA, 13 Sept. and 10 Oct. 1955, SHA Papers, ARL.

40. SHA to BAC, 11 Sept. 1955, SHA Papers, ARL.

41. *New York Times*, 8 Aug. 1955, 9.

42. SHA to Earl Conrad, 12 Aug. 1955, Conrad Papers, Bourke Library; SHA to CB, 14 Aug. 1955, SHA Papers, ARL; SHA to Irita Van Doren, 26 Aug. 1955, Van Doren Papers, Manuscript Division, Library of Congress.

43. Mildred Harlan to CB, 2 and 8 Sept. 1955, SHA Papers, ARL.

44. Louise Bonino to SHA, 22 Aug. 1955; BAC to SHA, 8 and 13 Sept. 1955, SHA Papers, ARL.

45. SHA will, 1374, Cayuga County Surrogate's Office, Auburn, N.Y.

46. SHA to BB, 23 Nov. 1955, SHA Papers, ARL.

47. CB to SHA, 27 Dec. 1955, SHA Papers, ARL.

## 20. Storyteller, 1956–1958

1. *Charleston (S.C.) News and Courier*, 29 Jan. 1956.

2. SHA to Henry L. Mencken, 18 Dec. 1948 and 4 Feb. 1950; unsigned carbon to SHA, 6 Feb. 1950, Mencken Papers, New York Public Library.

3. Chalmers, *Ideas of the Muckrakers*, 15–18, lists twelve men and one woman who wrote nearly one-third of the two thousand muckraking articles and professionalized this type of journalism. They were Adams, Baker, Christopher P. Connolly, Burton J. Hendrick, Irwin, Lawson, Alfred Henry Lewis, Phillips, Russell, Sinclair, Steffens, Tarbell, and Turner. The only survivors in 1958 were Adams and Sinclair.

4. Charles Coburn to SHA, 27 Feb. 1956; SHA to CB, 2 Mar. 1956; Carol Brandt to SHA, 7, 22, and 29 Mar. and 9 Apr. 1956, SHA Papers, ARL.

5. CB to SHA, 25 May and 5 June 1956; SHA to CB, 28 May 1956, SHA Papers, ARL.

6. BB to SHA, 28 May 1956; BAC to SHA, 6 July 1956, SHA Papers, ARL.

7. SHA to CB, 15 June and 3 July 1956; CB to SHA, 19 and 29 June 1956; CB to Andrew Crichton, 19 June 1956, SHA Papers, ARL.

8. SHA to BAC, 10 July 1956, SHA Papers, ARL.

9. CB to SHA, 24, 30 July and 27 Sept. 1956; SHA to CB, 1 Aug. and 28 Sept. 1956, SHA Papers, ARL.

10. CB to William H. Walling, 27 Sept. 1956, SHA Papers, ARL; *Rochester Democrat and Chronicle*, 6 Nov. 1956, 19.

11. SHA to CB, 4, 9, and 30 Nov. 1956; CB to SHA, 7, 14, 15, and 16 Nov. 1956, SHA Papers, ARL.

12. BAC to SHA, 20 Dec. 1956; SHA to BAC, 24 Dec. 1956, SHA Papers, ARL; SHA to SHH, 24 Dec. 1956, SHH Papers, Univ. of Washington Libraries.

13. SHA to Paul Bonner, 26 Jan. 1957, Bonner Papers, Princeton Univ. Libraries.

14. SHA to CB, 25 Feb. 1957, SHA Papers, ARL; *Charleston (S.C) News and Courier*, 17 Nov. 1958.

15. SHA to John Marquand, 24 Mar. 1957; Marquand to SHA, 27 Mar. 1957, Marquand Papers, Houghton Library.

16. SHA to BB, 30 Mar. 1957; BB to SHA, 10 Apr. 1957, SHA Papers, ARL.

17. SHA to John Marquand, 4 May 1957, Marquand Papers; SHA to Lewis Gannett, 3 May 1957, Mrs. Lewis Gannett Papers, Houghton Library.

18. *Rochester Democrat and Chronicle*, 9 June 1957, 1H.

19. *Rochester Times–Union*, 28 May 1957, 23; *Rochester Democrat and Chronicle*, 28 May 1957, 1.

20. Certificate given to SHA, 27 May 1957, SHA file, Rochester Public Library.

21. SHA to BB, 13 June 1957, SHA Papers, ARL.

22. SHA to Carol Brandt, 24 June 1957; Carol Brandt to SHA, 26 June and 2 July 1957, SHA Papers, ARL.

23. David Ennis to Nancy Larrick, 17 July 1957, SHA Papers, ARL; William J. Tyrrell to author, 18 Aug. 1990.

24. SHA to Martha Elliott, [13 Oct. 1957], Carmer Papers, NYSHA Library. Brandt was sixty-eight when he died.

25. Carol Brandt to SHA, 21 Oct. 1957; SHA to Carol Brandt, 28 Oct. 1957; SHA to BB, 23 Oct. 1957, SHA Papers, ARL; John Marquand to SHA, 21 Oct. 1957, Marquand Papers, Houghton Library.

26. SHA to SHH, 10 Nov. 1957, SHH Papers, Univ. of Washington Libraries; SHA to BAC, 23 Oct. 1957, SHA Papers, ARL; interviews with Nan Abell and Peggy French, 24 Nov. 1990, Riverside, Conn.

27. BB to SHA, 1 and 6 Nov. 1957, SHA Papers, ARL.

28. BAC to SHA, 23 July, 25 Oct. and 6 Nov. 1957; SHA to BAC, 28 Oct. and 7 Nov. 1957; *New York Times Book Review for Children*, 17 Nov. 1957, 28; *New York Herald Tribune Book Review*, 17 Nov. 1957, 30.

29. Interview with Charles Schlesinger, 6 Mar. 1990, New York City; BAC, *At Random*, 171.

30. SHA to Carol Brandt, 2 Dec. 1957; Carol Brandt to SHA, 5 Dec. 1957, SHA Papers, ARL.

31. *Charleston (S.C) News and Courier*, 18 Nov. 1958, 8–A; SHA to John Marquand, 17 Jan. 1958; Marquand to SHA, 27 Jan. 1958, Marquand Papers, Houghton Library; SHA to Carol Brandt, 8 Mar. 1958; Brandt to SHA, 10 Mar. 1958, SHA Papers, ARL.

32. *Syracuse Post-Standard*, 17 Nov. 1958, 2.

33. SHA to SHH, 1 Feb. 1958, SHH Papers, Univ. of Washington Libraries; SHA to Carl Brandt, Jr., 22 Jan. 1958; SHA to Carol Brandt, 28 Feb. 1958, SHA Papers, ARL; Lewis Gannett, "Samuel Hopkins Adams, Working Writer," *Authors Guild Bulletin*, Dec. 1958, 4.

34. SHA to Clarence Brigham, 1 Apr. 1958, AAS correspondence.

35. SHA to BAC, 7 Apr. 1958; BAC to SHA, 14 Apr. 1958, SHA Papers, ARL; *New York Times Book Review for Children*, 13 Apr. 1958, 42; *New York Herald Tribune Book Review*, 11 May 1958, 4; R. H. V. "Books for Young People," *Saturday Review*, 28 June 1958, 28.

36. *New York Herald Tribune Book Review*, 18 Jan. 1959, 6; William McFee, "A Forgotten Gotham," *Saturday Review*, 17 Jan. 1959, 62–63; *New York Times Book Review*, 18 Jan. 1959, 30.

37. *Syracuse Herald–Journal*, 24 June 1959, 26.

38. Carol Brandt to BB, 26 May 1958; BB to Brandt, 28 May 1958, SHA Papers, ARL.

39. BB to BAC, 14 and 26 May 1958; SHA to BAC, 21 May 1958; BAC to SHA, 23 May 1958, SHA Papers, ARL; BAC, *At Random*, 235.

40. Carol Brandt to SHA, 9 June 1958, SHA Papers, Burke Library.

41. "Hill Talk," *Hamilton Alumni Review*, Mar. 1961, 134.

42. Interview with George Harlan, 15 Sept. 1990, Toronto, Canada.

43. *Rochester Democrat and Chronicle*, 18 Nov. 1958, 23; SHH, *Quackery*, 283–84.

44. Carol Brandt to H. Dutton Noble, 25 Aug. 1958, SHA Papers, ARL. The musical, which starred Maurice Evans as the crusading clergyman and was directed by George Abbott, opened 17 Oct. 1960 and ran 216 performances.

45. *Auburn Citizen–Advertiser* files.

46. *Rochester Times–Union*, 1 Aug. 1958, 12; SHH, *Quackery*, 283, 285–86; *Portland Oregonian*, 8 Dec. 1958, 16.

47. *Auburn Citizen–Advertiser*, 2 Sept. 1958, 2.

48. Louis Jones, "Samuel Hopkins Adams," *New York History*, 40 (Jan. 1959): 66; *Rochester Democrat and Chronicle*, 18 Nov. 1958, 23.

49. H. Dutton Noble to Carol Brandt, 15 Sept. 1958; SHA to Brandt, 31 Aug. 1958, SHA Papers, ARL; SHA to Irita Van Doren, 11 July 1958, Van Doren Papers, Manuscript Division, Library of Congress.

50. BB to Carol Brandt, 1 Sept. 1958; SHA to Brandt, 5 Sept. 1958, SHA Papers, Burke Library; Brandt to SHA, 2 Sept. 1958, SHA Papers, ARL.

51. BAC to SHA, 17 Sept. 1958; Katherine Adell to BAC, 20 Sept. 1958, SHA Papers, ARL.

52. Interview with Mary Melnick, 5 Aug. 1990, Fleming, N.Y.; Wallace Johnson to J. Robert Williams, 19 Nov. 1958, SHA Papers, Burke Library.

53. Carol Brandt to H. Dutton Noble, 29 Sept. 1958; Noble to Brandt, 30 Sept. 1958, SHA Papers, ARL.

54. Telephone interview with Rowland Wade, 2 Feb. 1991, Moravia, N.Y.

55. Martha Elliott to Carol Brandt, c. 26 Oct. 1958; Brandt to Elliott, 28 Oct. 1958; BB to Brandt, 13 Nov. 1958, SHA Papers, ARL.

56. BAC to SHA, 7 Nov. 1958, SHA Papers, ARL.

57. Interview with Martha Elliott, 2 Mar. 1991, Beaufort, S.C.

# BIBLIOGRAPHY

## Books

*The Great American Fraud*. New York: P. F. Collier and Son, 1905, 1906, 1907; Chicago: American Medical Association, 1907, 1912; Denver: Nostalgic American Research Foundation, 1978.

With Stewart Edward White. *The Mystery*. New York: McClure, Phillips, 1907; New York: Grosset and Dunlap, 1907; London: Hodder and Stoughton, 1907; New York: Doubleday, Page, 1920, 1924; Canada: Musson Book, 1907; New York: Arno Press, 1975.

*The Flying Death*. New York: McClure's, 1908; New York: Doubleday, Doran, 1908; Canada: Musson Book, 1908.

*Average Jones*. Indianapolis: Bobbs-Merrill, 1911; New York: Grosset and Dunlap, 1911; London: Frank Palmer, 1913; New York: Arno Press, 1976.

*The Secret of Lonesome Cove*. Indianapolis: Bobbs-Merrill, 1912; New York: Grosset and Dunlap, 1912; London: Hodder and Stoughton, 1913.

*The Health Master*. Boston: Houghton Mifflin, 1913.

*The Clarion*. Boston: Houghton Mifflin, 1914; New York: Grosset and Dunlap, 1917.

*Little Miss Grouch; A Narrative Based upon the Private Log of Alexander Forsyth Smith's Maiden Transatlantic Voyage*. Boston: Houghton Mifflin, 1915; London: John Murray, 1916.

*The Adams Articles*. New York: Trow Press, 1915; also published as *Samuel Hopkins Adams on Fraudulent and Deceptive Advertising*, New York: Tribune Association, 1916.

*The Unspeakable Perk*. Boston: Houghton Mifflin, 1916; New York: A. L. Burt, 1916; London: Hodder and Stoughton, 1916.

*Our Square and the People in It*. Boston: Houghton Mifflin, 1917; Freeport, N.Y.: Books for Libraries Press, 1970.

*Common Cause; A Novel of War in America*. Boston: Houghton Mifflin, 1919.

*Wanted: A Husband*. Boston: Houghton Mifflin, 1920; New York: Grosset and Dunlap, 1920.

*Success.* Boston: Houghton Mifflin, 1921; New York: Grosset and Dunlap, 1921; London: Constable, 1921.

*From a Bench in Our Square.* Boston: Houghton Mifflin, 1922; Freeport, N.Y.: Books for Libraries Press, 1969.

*Flaming Youth* [Warner Fabian]. New York: Boni and Liveright, 1923; London: Stanley Paul, 1923; New York: Macaulay, 1924; microfilm, New Haven, Conn.: Yale Univ., 1978.

*Sailors' Wives* [Warner Fabian]. New York: Boni and Liveright, 1924; New York: Macaulay, 1924; London: Stanley Paul, 1924.

*Siege.* New York: Boni and Liveright, 1924; New York: Grosset and Dunlap, 1924; London: Brentano, 1927.

*The Piper's Fee.* New York: Boni and Liveright, 1926. Appeared also as part of series, *Romane der Welt,* edited by Thomas Mann and H. G. Scheffauer.

*Revelry.* New York: Boni and Liveright, 1926; London: Brentano, 1927; Spele and Kring Vita Huset, Stockholm: P. A. Norstedt and Forlang, 1927.

*Summer Bachelors* [Warner Fabian]. New York: Boni and Liveright, 1926; London: Stanley Paul, 1926; photoplay ed., New York: Macaulay, 1927.

Ed. *Who and What; A Book for the Clever.* New York: Boni and Liveright, 1927.

*Unforbidden Fruit* [Warner Fabian]. New York: Boni and Liveright, 1928; London: Stanley Paul, 1928; Cleveland International Fiction Library, 1928. Appeared also in a German translation by Hans Reisinger as *College Girls,* Berlin: Ullstein, 1930, and excerpts in the French magazine *Vu.*

*The Flagrant Years, A Novel of the Beauty Market.* New York: H. Liveright, 1929; London: John Hamilton, 1930; also published in Netherlands ed. as *Brandende Jaren, Roman var Jeugd,* Amsterdam: A. J. G. Strengholt, 1930.

*The Godlike Daniel.* New York: Sears Publishing, 1930.

*The Men in Her Life* [Warner Fabian]. New York: Sears Publishing, 1930; London: Stanley Paul, 1930. Published also in Netherlands ed. as *Broadway,* Amsterdam: A. deLange, 1931.

*Week-End Girl* [Warner Fabian]. New York: Macaulay, 1932; London: Stanley Paul, 1932.

*The Gorgeous Hussy.* Boston: Houghton Mifflin, 1934; New York: Grosset and Dunlap, 1936.

*It Happened One Night.* Akron, Ohio: Saalfield Publishing, 1935. Published also under original title, *Night Bus,* New York: Dell Publishing, 1950.

*Widow's Oats* [Warner Fabian]. New York: Macaulay, 1935; London: Stanley Paul, 1935.

*Perfect Specimen.* New York: Liveright Publishing, 1936.

*Maiden Effort.* New York: Liveright, 1937.

*The World Goes Smash.* Boston: Houghton Mifflin, 1938.

*Both Over Twenty-One.* New York: Liveright, 1939.

*The Incredible Era: The Life and Times of Warren Gamaliel Harding.* Boston:

Houghton Mifflin, 1939; New York: Capricorn Books, 1964; New York: Octagon Books, 1973.

*Whispers.* New York: Liveright, 1940.

*The Book of Ariel* [Anonymous]. Garden City, N.Y.: Doubleday, Doran, 1942.

*The Harvey Girls.* New York: Random House, 1942; Racine, Wis.: Western Printing and Lithography, 1943; Cleveland, Ohio: World Publishing, 1944; London: John Long, 1944; New York: Dell Publishing, 1946, 1956.

*Tambay Gold.* New York: J. Messner, 1942.

*Canal Town.* New York: Random House, 1944; Peoples Book Club ed., Chicago: Consolidated Book Publishing, 1944; Cleveland, Ohio: World Book Company, 1944, London: John Long, 1945; condensed version published by Armed Services, 1944; Syracuse, N.Y.: Syracuse Univ. Press, 1988.

*A. Woollcott; His Life and His World.* New York: Reynal and Hitchcock, 1945; Cleveland: World Publishing, 1945; condensed version, New York: Omnibook, 1945; Toronto: McClelland and Stewart, 1945; *Alexander Woollcott, His Life and His World,* London: Hamish Hamilton, 1946; German translation, Infantry Journal, 1947; Freeport, N.Y.: Books for Libraries Press, 1976.

*Banner by the Wayside.* New York: Random House, 1947.

*Plunder.* New York: Random House, 1948.

*Safe Money; The Record of One Hundred Years of Mutual Savings Banking at the Auburn Savings Bank* Auburn, N.Y.: Auburn Savings Bank, 1949.

*The Pony Express.* New York: Random House, 1950, 1978; Landmark ed., Eau Claire, Wis.: E. M. Hale, 1950; Chicago: Spencer Press, 1950; New York: Bantam Books, 1953; London: G. Bell and Sons, 1961; also appears in an Austrian ed. as *Der Pony Express,* Wien: Bergland Verlag, 1952, and a Mexican ed. as *El Expres Pony,* translated by Nurian Pares, Mexico: Editorial Inter Continental, 1957; Hindi and Arabic eds. also published. Filmstrip, New York: David J. Goodman, 1957.

*Sunrise to Sunset.* New York: Random House, 1950; London: John Long, 1951; New York: Bantam Books, 1953.

*The Santa Fe Trail.* New York: Random House, 1951; Landmark ed., Eau Claire, Wis.: E. M. Hale, 1951; Chicago: Spencer Press, 1951.

*The Erie Canal.* New York: Random House, 1953; Landmark ed., Eau Claire, Wis.: E. M. Hale, 1953.

*Wagons to the Wilderness.* Philadelphia: John C. Winston, 1954.

*Grandfather Stories.* New York: Random House, 1955; condensed versions in *Books Abridged,* New York: Books Abridged, 1955; and in *Best in Books,* New York: Nelson Doubleday, 1956; New York: New American Library (Signet), 1959; Syracuse, N.Y.: Syracuse University Press, 1989.

*General Brock and Niagara Falls.* New York: Random House, 1957; Landmark ed., Eau Claire, Wis.: E. M. Hale, 1957.

*Chingo Smith of the Erie Canal.* New York: Random House, 1958. An abridged version appears as "Portrait of a Hoggie," 300–6, with Erie Canal lyrics in "Songs of the Canal," 296–300, in *New York Portrait; A Literary Look at the Empire State,* edited by Jack Ishmole and Sally Ronshein. New York: Holt, Rinehart and Winston, 1965.

*Tenderloin.* New York: Random House, 1959; New York: New American Library (Signet), 1960.

## Parts of Books

"The Genesis of 'The Long Tryst.'" In *Hamiltonian, 1914.* Clinton, N.Y.: Hamilton College, 1914.

"Higher than a Sour Apple Tree." In *America in the War,* by Louis Raemaekers, 106–7. New York: Century, 1918.

"My Maiden Effort." In *My Maiden Effort; The Personal Confessions of Well Known American Authors Collected by the Authors' League of America,* edited by Gelett Burgess, 1–3. New York: Doubleday, Page, 1921.

"The Indissoluble Bond." In *Marriage; Short Stories of Married Life by American Writers,* 173–88. New York: Doubleday, Page, 1923.

With Rupert Hughes, Anthony Abbot (Fulton Oursler), Rita Weiman, S. S. Van Dine, and John Erskine. *The President's Mystery Story,* propounded by Franklin D. Roosevelt. New York: Farrar and Rinehart, 1935.

"The Timely Death of President Harding." In *Aspirin Age,* edited by Isabel Leighton, 81–104. New York: Simon and Schuster, 1949.

"Introduction." In *Laurette,* by Marguerite Courtney, vii–ix. New York: Rinehart, 1955.

## Collaborative Books

*That None Should Die,* by Frank Slaughter. New York: Doubleday, Doran, 1941; London: Jarrold's, 1942.

*Spencer Brade, M.D.,* by Frank Slaughter. New York: Doubleday, Doran, 1942; London: Jarrold's, 1943.

## Booklets and Pamphlets

"Blinky." The Department of Hygiene of New York published for the Association for Improving the Condition of the Poor, Nov. 1897.

*"Keeping the Faith"; Gimbel Brothers and the New York Tribune.* New York: Tribune Association, 1916.

"The Beggar's Purse." Boston: Smith and Porter Press, 1918.

"Testimonials." Chicago: American Medical Association, 1940, based on an Adams *New York Tribune* column, 2 Feb. 1915.

"Foreword." In *The Class of 1891 of Hamilton College*, 1–7. Clinton, N.Y.: Hamilton College, 1941.

"Why I Wrote *Canal Town*." Published in Peoples Book Club pamphlet for the promotion of *Canal Town*. Chicago: Sears, Roebuck, 1943.

"As It Looks to—Samuel Hopkins Adams '91." Published as a four-page promotion flyer by the Hamilton College Alumni Fund, 1950.

## Periodical Writings

"The Wager." *Hamilton Literary Monthly*, Jan. 1889, 202.

"The Pool in the Grounds." *Hamilton Literary Monthly*, Mar. 1889, 261–67.

"Daniel Defoe and Robert Louis Stevenson." *Hamilton Literary Monthly*, Dec. 1989, 133–42.

"The Conception of Human Progress in Tennyson." *Hamilton Literary Monthly*, Feb. 1892, 215–19.

"Department Store." *Scribner's*, Jan. 1897, 4–27.

"Training of Lions, Tigers, and Other Great Cats." *McClure's*, Sept. 1900, 386–98.

"Spotters." *Ainslee's*, Feb. 1901, 66–72.

"Little Black Satchel." *Munsey's*, Sept. 1901, 912–14.

"Such as Walk in Darkness." *McClure's*, Aug. 1902, 300–6. In *Short Story Classics American*, edited by William Patten, 4:1199–1210. New York: P. F. Collier and Son, 1905; in *Dawgs*, edited by Charles Wright Gray. Garden City, N.Y.: Garden City Publishing, 1925, 1927, 1928, 1932; New York: H. Holt and Company, 1925; in *Best Loved Stories about Dogs*. Garden City: Sun Dial Press, 1925, 1939; in *Hamiltonian*, 1929, 172–77; in *American Short Story Classics*, edited by Althia Berry and Cecilia Stuart. New York: Macmillan, 1945; in *Masterpiece Library of Short Stories*, vol. 16; in *Great Dog Stories*. New York: Ballantine Books, 1955; in *Best Book of Family Fun*. New York: M. Evans, 1958; in *Best Book of Dog Stories*, edited by Pauline Rush Evans. New York: Doubleday, 1964.

"The Flying Death." *McClure's*, Jan. 1903, 280–86; Feb. 1903, 424–28. In *Ellery Queen's Mystery Magazine*, Jan. 1944.

"State of Kentucky vs. Caleb Powers." *McClure's*, Mar. 1904, 465–75.

"Little Fat Fiddler." *McClure's*, Apr. 1904, 652–58.

"Dan Cunningham." *McClure's*, June 1904, 215–20.

"Despotism versus Anarchy in Colorado." *Collier's Weekly*, 25 June 1904, 10–12.

"Meat: A Problem for the Public." *Collier's Weekly*, 30 July 1904, 8–10.

"King Coal." *McClure's*, Aug. 1904, 409–16.

"Realm of Enchantment." *McClure's*, Sept. 1904, 520–32.

"Doubtful States and the Silent Vote." Seven-part series, *Collier's Weekly*, 24 Sept. 1904–29 Oct. 1904.

"I. Indiana: Politics by the Square Inch." *Collier's Weekly*, 24 Sept. 1904, 10–11, 26.

"II. Illinois: A Study in Splits." *Collier's Weekly*, 1 Oct. 1904, 10, 12.

"III. Wisconsin: A Reconstruction of Partisanship." *Collier's Weekly*, 8 Oct. 1904, 12–13.

"IV. Missouri: The War Against Boodle." *Collier's Weekly*, 15 Oct. 1904, 14–15, 18.

"V. West Virginia: Corruption Rampant." *Collier's Weekly*, 22 Oct. 1904, 13–14, 25.

"VI. Delaware: A State Bought and Paid For" and "VII. Maryland and Kentucky: Where Tradition Rules." *Collier's Weekly*, 29 Oct. 1904, 23–26.

"Notes from a Trainer's Book." *McClure's*, Dec. 1904, 188–97.

"Tuberculosis: The Real Race Suicide." *McClure's*, Jan. 1905, 243–49.

"A Man and a Brother." *McClure's*, Feb. 1905, 359–65.

"Modern Surgery." *McClure's*, Mar. 1905, 482–92.

"Studies of a Strike." *Collier's*, 1 Apr. 1905, 17–18, 25.

"William Rockefeller: Maker of Wilderness." *Collier's*, 22 Apr. 1905, 15, 18.

"Typhoid: An Unnecessary Evil." *McClure's*, June 1905, 145–56.

"Last Resort." *Harper's Weekly*, 2 Sept. 1905, 1276–77, 1280–81.

"The Great American Fraud." *Collier's*, 7 Oct. 1905, 14–15, 29.

"Peruna and the 'Bracers'." *Collier's*, 28 Oct. 1905, 17–19. In *The Muckrakers*, edited by Arthur and Lila Weinberg. New York: Capricorn Books, 1964.

"Substitute." *McClure's*, Nov. 1905, 60–66.

"Liquozone." *Collier's*, 18 Nov. 1905, 20–21.

"Editorial Bulletin." *Collier's*, 25 Nov. 1905, 30.

"The Subtle Poisons." *Collier's*, 2 Dec. 1905, 16–18.

"Preying on the Incurables." *Collier's*, 13 Jan. 1906, 18–20.

"Medical Support for Nostrums." *Maryland Medical Journal* 49 (Feb. 1906): 60–68.

"The Fundamental Fakes." *Collier's*, 17 Feb. 1906, 22–24, 26, 28.

"A Matter of Principle." *McClure's*, Mar. 1906, 485–95.

"Food or Fraud? A Question for Congress." *Collier's*, 17 Mar. 1906, 13, 15.

"Warranted Harmless." *Collier's*, 28 Apr. 1906, 16–18, 30.

"The Mystery." With Stewart Edward White. *American Illustrated Magazine*, May 1906, 12–23; *American Magazine*, June 1906, 129–43; July 1906, 310–22; Aug. 1906, 388–98; Sept. 1906, 498–510; Oct. 1906, 661–70; Nov. 1906, 97–105; Dec. 1906, 164–71; Jan. 1907, 324–33.

"Yellow Fever: A Problem Solved." *McClure's*, June 1906, 178–96.

"The Sure-Cure School." *Collier's*, 14 July 1906, 12–14, 22, 24.

"Curbing the Great American Fraud." *Collier's*, 21 July 1906, 16–17.

"The Miracle Workers." *Collier's*, 4 Aug. 1906, 14–16.

"The Specialist Humbug." *Collier's*, 1 Sept. 1906, 16–18.

"The Scavengers." *Collier's*, 22 Sept. 1906, 16–18, 24, 26.

"B. Jones, Butcher." *McClure's*, Sept. 1906, 510–20.

"Dynamite: The Power Untameable." *American Magazine*, Oct. 1906, 626–33.

"Editorials." *Ridgway's*, 6, 13, 20, 25 Oct.; 3, 10, 17 Nov. 1906, 5–8; 24 Nov.; 1 Dec. 1906, 9–12; 8, 15, 22, 29 Dec. 1906; 5 Jan. 1907, 9–11.

"'Strictly Confidential.'" *Collier's*, 17 Nov. 1906, 7.

"Forsaken Mountain." *Collier's*, 8 Dec. 1906, 24–26, 28.

"Aftermath." *Collier's*, 5 Jan. 1907, 11–12.

"The Poisoning of the City of Scranton: The Price in Death and Illness which Has Been Paid to Provide Dividends for the Owner of a Water Supply." *Ridgway's*, 2 Feb. 1907, 33–35.

"Sherlock Holmes Understudy: Letter to S. E. White." *Bookman*, Mar. 1907, 5–7.

"Typhoid: What Are We Going to Do about It?" *New York State Journal of Medicine* 7 (Mar. 1907): 102–4.

"The New York Police Force." *Collier's*, 30 Mar. 1907, 15–17.

"Rochester's Pure Milk Campaign." *McClure's*, June 1907, 142–49.

"Patent Medicines under the Pure Food Law." *Collier's*, 8 June 1907, 11–12, 24, 26.

"Futility." *Collier's*, editorial, 27 July 1907, 9.

"Religious Journalism and the Great American Fraud." *Collier's*, 3 Aug. 1907, 9–11. Reprinted in part by the *Journal of the American Medical Association*, 49 (10 Aug. 1907): 510–12.

"Religious Journalism and the Great American Fraud." *Collier's*, 12 Oct. 1907, 17–18. Reprinted in part by the *Journal of the American Medical Association* 49 (23 Nov. 1907): 1790–91.

"Balanced Account." *Everybody's*, Jan. 1908, 38–46.

"The Holy War of To-Day." *Collier's*, 21 Mar. 1908, 12–13.

"Indigenous Poetry." *Collier's*, 27 June 1908, 18–19.

"Guardians of the Public Health." *McClure's*, July 1908, 241–52. In *Years of Conscience*, edited by Harvey Swados. Cleveland, Ohio: World Publishing, 1962.

"The Discovery of Paris." *Collier's*, 14 Nov. 1908, 18–19.

"The Real Venezuelan Peril." *Collier's*, 14 Nov. 1908, 11–12.

"The Solving of the Milk Problem." *McClure's*, Dec. 1908, 200–207.

"Paris Through a Prism." *Collier's*, 19 Dec. 1908, 12–13.

"Burnt Money." *Everybody's*, Jan. 1909, 23–34.

"Medico-Strategist." *Collier's*, 2 Jan. 1909, 22–23, 26–27.

"Paris Through a Prism." *Collier's*, 9 Jan. 1909, 10–11.

"What Will Gomez Do?" *Collier's*, 9 Jan. 1909, 9.

"Pittsburgh's Foregone Asset, the Public Health." *Charities and the Commons*, 6 Feb. 1909, 940–50.

"Adventures of a Somnambulist." *American Magazine*, Mar. 1909, 428–36.

"In the Revolution Belt." *Collier's*, 3 Apr. 1909, 14–15, 27, 28.

"Grimsden House." *Everybody's*, May 1909, 694–702.

"The Indecent Stage." *American Magazine*, May 1909, 41–47.

"Art of Advertising." *Collier's*, 22 May 1909, 13–15.

"Fair Trade and Foul." *Collier's*, 19 June 1909, 19–22, 26.

"Three Men." *American Magazine*, Oct. 1909, 643–46.

"Chosen Instrument." *Everybody's*, Feb. 1910, 158–67.

"What Has Become of Pure Food Law." *Hampton's*, Feb. 1910, 234–42.

"The B-Flat Trombone." *Success*, Apr. 1910, 231–33, 265–67.

"The Joke's on You." *American Magazine*, May 1910, 51–59.

"Red Dot." *Success*, May 1910, 305–7, 346–48.

"Romance of the Right-Of-Way." *Saturday Evening Post*, 19 May 1910, 28–32.

"Pin Pricks." *Success*, June 1910, 402–4, 431–33.

"The Mercy Sign." *Success*, July 1910, 462–65, 492–94.

"Tenderfooting for Mountain Sheep." *Sunset*, July 1910, 25–34.

"Warring on Injurious Insects." *American Magazine*, July 1910, 291–303.

"The Real Reason for High Prices." *Cosmopolitan*, Sept. 1910, 460–65.

"Poison Bugaboo." *Everybody's*, Oct. 1910, 518–25.

"Open Trail." *Success*, Nov. 1910, 722–24, 771–75.

"The Fire-Blue Necklace." *Success*, Dec. 1910, 814–16, 851–53.

"Tomfoolery with Public Health." *Survey*, 17 Dec. 1910, 453–57.

"The Man Who Spoke Latin." *Success*, Jan. 1911, 14–15, 48–49, 67. In *The Boys' Book of Great Detective Stories*, edited by Howard Haycraft, 237–58, New York: Harper and Row, 1938; in *101 Nights Entertainment*; in *The Great Detective Stories*, pseud. edited by Ellery Queen, 243–61, Boston: Little, Brown, 1941; in *The American Rivals of Sherlock Holmes*, edited by Hugh Greene, 182–201. New York: Panthenon Books, 1976.

"Lemon in the Tariff." *McClure's*, Jan. 1911, 353–60.

"Big Print." *Success*, Feb. 1911, 22–28, 46.

"The Million-Dollar Dog." *Red Book Magazine*, Mar. 1911, 899–911.

"Flash-Light." *Success*, Apr. 1911, 22–23, 58–60. Retitled "The One Best Bet" and included in *Fourteen Great Detective Stories*, edited by Vincent Starrett, 334–53. New York: Modern Library, 1928; in *World's Best One Hundred Detective Stories*, vol. 1, edited by Eugene Twing, 11–29. New York and London: Funk and Wagnalls, 1929; in *Classic Stories of Crime and Detection*, edited by Jacques Barzun and Wendell Hertig Taylor, 1–29. New York: Garland Publishing, 1976.

"The Health Master." *Delineator*, May 1911, 361–62; June 1911, 461–62; July 1911, 9–10; Sept. 1911, 151–52.

"The Long Tryst." *American Magazine*, July 1911, 274–85. In *Hamilton Literary Magazine*, May 1916, 373–88; in *Hamiltonian*, 1933, 154–63; and in *Compact*, Mar. 1953, 40, 42, 88, 89, 91, 92, 94–100; in *Short Stories for College Classics*, edited by Blanche Colton Williams. New York: Appleton-Century, 1929.

"Leland O. Howard." *American Magazine*, Oct. 1911, 721–23.

"Public Health and Public Hysteria." *Journal of the American Public Health Association* 1 (Nov. 1911): 771–74.

"The Message." *Sunday Magazine of the New York Tribune*, 19 Nov. 1911, 6–7, 17–18.

"The Great Game." *Sunday Magazine of the New York Tribune*, 3 Dec. 1911, 3–4, 12–16; 10 Dec. 1911, 6–7, 18–19; 17 Dec. 1911, 12–13; 18–19; 24 Dec. 1911, 12–14, 17; 7 Jan. 1912, 8–9, 18–19; 14 Jan. 1912, 11–16.

"The Fraud Medicines Own Up." *Collier's*, 20 Jan. 1912, 11–12, 26–27.

"Tricks of the Trade." *Collier's*, 17 Feb. 1912, 17–18, 24, 26.

"Re-made Lady." *Delineator,* Mar. 1912, 183–84.

"Chester Kent Cures a Headache." *Sunday Magazine of the New York Tribune,* 10 Mar. 1912, 3–4, 14; 17 Mar. 1912, 7–8.

"Law, the Label and the Liars." *Collier's,* 13 Apr. 1912, 10–11, 36, 38–39.

"Votes (Whang!) for (Biff!!) Women (Smash!!!)." *Collier's,* 20 Apr. 1912, 11–12.

"Magic Lens, with Several Sequels." *Delineator,* May 1912, 385–86.

"The Fraud above the Law." *Collier's,* 11 May 1912, 13–15, 26, 28. Reprinted with additions in *Journal of the American Medical Association* 58 (25 May 1912): 1616–20.

"Red Placard." *Delineator,* June 1912, 483–84.

"North America vs. South." *Collier's,* 22 June 1912, 18–20, 26.

"Ingenuous Impressions." *Collier's,* 20 July 1912, 16–17, 29.

"Nostrums and the Medical Profession—A Criticism from a Layman." *Journal of the American Medical Association* 59 (2 Nov. 1912): 1640–41.

"The Case of John Smith." *Sunday Magazine of the New York Tribune.* 1 Dec. 1912, 10–11, 18.

"The Dishonest Paris Label." *Ladies' Home Journal,* Mar. 1913, 7–8, 81.

"Health; Public and Private." *McClure's,* Mar. 1913, 166, 168, 171–72, 175–76, 179; Apr. 1913, 209, 211–12, 215, 216; May 1913, 198, 201–2, 205–6, 208, 210.

"Grandma Sharpless Drives a Quack Out of Town." *Delineator,* Mar. 1913, 173–74, 220–24.

"Milady in Motley." *Collier's,* 15 Mar. 1913, 8–9, 26.

"Saving Hope in Cancer." *Collier's,* 26 Apr. 1913, 10, 25–26.

"What Can We Do about Cancer?" *Ladies' Home Journal,* May 1913, 21–22.

"My Business Partner—'Gym.'" *Collier's,* 31 May 1913; 19, 28.

"Omitted from Publication." *McClure's,* June 1913, 92–102.

"Great Adventurer." *Everybody's,* Aug. 1913, 166–80.

"Human Carpentry." *Collier's,* 6 Sept. 1913, 27.

"U.S. Inspected and Passed." *Survey,* 6 Sept. 1913, 95–98.

"House That Caught Cold." *Delineator,* Oct. 1913, 10, 77.

"What Is the Matter with Your Stomach?" *Ladies' Home Journal,* Oct. 1913, 19, 96, 98–99.

"President and Passenger." *Collier's,* 11 Oct. 1913, 5–6, 26–28.

"Blue Mondays." *Ladies' Home Journal,* Nov. 1913, 20, 78–79.

"Oxyfakery: The Tin-Can Sure-Fire School." *Collier's,* 8 Nov. 1913, 19, 32.

"When the Star Killed an Epidemic." *Delineator,* Nov. 1913, 16, 60–61, 66–67, 73.

"Publicity and Ethics." *Journal of the American Medical Association* 61 (8 Dec. 1913): 2098–99.

"The Genesis of 'The Long Tryst,'" *Hamiltonian,* 1914, 196–97.

"Why I Wrote 'The Clarion.'" *La Follette's Magazine,* Nov. 1914, 8–9.

"Do Patent Medicines Control the Press? An Example." *Journal of the American Medical Association* 63 (3 Dec. 1914): 2062.

"Little Miss Grouch." *Delineator,* Jan. 1915, 4–5, 23–24; Feb. 1915, 7–8, 32–34; Mar. 1915, 11–12, 38–42, 44–45; Apr. 1915, 9–10, 38–41; May 1915, 18–19, 42, 44–45, 50–51.

"'Only a Cold.'" *Ladies' Home Journal*, Feb. 1915, 4.

"Would You Believe It of These Girls?" *Ladies' Home Journal*, Mar. 1915, 5–6, 65.

"Fairy Princess." *Everybody's*, Aug. 1915, 141–55.

"Jitney Partners for the Dance." *Everybody's*, Dec. 1915, 675–81.

"What Hamilton Means to Me." *Hamilton Literary Magazine*, Jan. 1916, 193–94, and 1916 *Hamiltonian*, 46–48.

"Our Square." *Everybody's*, Mar. 1916, 328–53.

"The Unspeakable Perk." *Ainslee's*, May 1916, 32–75; June 1916, 53–70; July 1916, 71–94.

"Triumph." *Collier's*, 29 July 1916, 9–11, 26.

"The Chair That Whispered." *Collier's*, 26 Aug. 1916, 5–7, 30, 32.

"MacLachan of Our Square." *Collier's*, 2 Sept. 1916, 10–11, 23.

"The Great Peacemaker." *Collier's*, 30 Sept. 1916, 10–11, 31.

"Orpheus." *Collier's*, 11 Nov. 1916, 14–16, 34, 37–38.

"'Tazmun.'" *Collier's*, 16 Dec. 1916, 16–17, 20–21, 23.

"Wamble, His Day Out." *Collier's*, 13 Jan. 1917, 16–18, 22–23, 25.

"Enter Darcy." *Collier's*, 17 Feb. 1917, 14–15, 33, 35, 37; 24 Feb. 1917, 16–17, 41–42, 44–46; 3 Mar. 1917, 18–19, 28–32, 35; 10 Mar. 1917, 21, 46–48, 51–52.

"A Letter to Nowhere." *Associated Sunday Magazine* supplement, 21 Feb. 1917.

"The Meanest Man in Our Square." *Collier's*, 24 Mar. 1917, 19–21, 23, 26.

"Paula of the Housetop." *Collier's*, 7 July 1917, 16–20, 23.

"The Little Red Doctor of Our Square." *Collier's*, 25 Aug. 1917, 14–16, 28, 31, 34, 36.

"Room 12 A." *Everybody's*, Nov. 1917, 19–23, 112, 114, 116.

"Invaded America." *Everybody's*, Dec. 1917, 9–16, 86; Jan. 1918, 28–33, 82, 84; Feb. 1918, 30–32, 74–76, 78, 80–83; Mar. 1918 55–56, 58, 60, 62, 64. Published also as a twenty-page booklet, New York: National Americanization Committee, 1918.

"'Excess Baggage.'" *Collier's*, 5 Jan. 1918, 18–19, 48, 50; 12 Jan. 1918, 16–17, 27–30.

"A Little Privacy." *Collier's*, 9 Mar. 1918, 18–20.

"The Beggar's Purse; A Fairy Tale of Familiar Finance," *Saturday Evening Post*, 23 Mar. 1918, 3–4, 34, 37. Published also as a thirty-eight-page booklet, Boston: Smith and Porter Press, 1918.

Article on speechmaking. *Four Minute Men News*. Edition C (Apr. 1918).

"Front-Page Frankie." *Everybody's*, Apr. 1918, 34–40, 85–87.

"Orator of the Day." *Collier's*, 25 May 1918, 8–9, 39–40.

"Three Days Leave." *Metropolitan*, July 1918, 15–18, 62, 64–66.

"Fighting-Fit." *Collier's*, 20 July 1918, 9, 24–27.

"The Briber." *Collier's*, 27 July 1918, 8–9, 25–26.

"Common Cause." *Saturday Evening Post*, 27 July 1918, 5–8, 34, 37, 40, 44.

"Private Smith Is Cordially Invited." *World's Work*, Sept. 1918, 528–37.

"Uncle Sam, M.D." *Collier's*, 21 Sept. 1918, 5–6, 19, 26, 28.

"Whisperings." *Woman's Home Companion*, Oct. 1918, 25–26, 85.

"The Dodger Trail." *Collier's*, 5 Oct. 1918, 8–9, 24, 26; 12 Oct. 1918, 13, 27–30.

"Sam Adams." *Collier's*, 12 Oct. 1918, 30.

"Washington, Nous Voilà!" *Collier's*, 22 Feb. 1919, 11.

"Famine—The New Threat Against the World." *Delineator*, Mar. 1919, 7, 50.

"I. I. I.: A Story of the New Washington." *Everybody's*, Mar. 1919, 22–26, 90–95.

"Loose Leaves of Diplomacy; I—Food Wins Switzerland." *Collier's*, 8 Mar. 1919, 9, 36–37.

"Loose Leaves of Diplomacy; II—Skaal to the Norsemen!" *Collier's*, 22 Mar. 1919, 10, 48–49.

"The Record of a Rescue." *Carry On*; a publication of the Medical Department of the United States Army. In *Auburn Citizen*, 25 Mar. 1919, 3.

"Loose Leaves of Diplomacy; III—Holland and Her Ships." *Collier's*, 29 Mar. 1919, 9, 49, 51.

"Half a Million, Cold." *Everybody's*, Apr. 1919, 31–38.

"U.S. Adv.—An Experiment in Idealism." *Collier's*, 26 Apr. 1919, 18, 31, 34.

"Loose Leaves of Diplomacy. IV—The Friendly Scandinavians." *Collier's*, 3 May 1919, 22, 37, 38.

"The Miracle of Reeducation." *Red Cross Magazine*, May 1919, 45–51.

"Silver Stripes among the Gold." *Everybody's*, May 1919, 17–22, 92, 94–95.

"Mister Hune." *Everybody's*, June 1919, 38–44, 101–4.

"A Stand-Off." *Red Book Magazine*, June 1919, 25–27, 29, 169–70, 172, 174.

"To Keep Europe Alive—Milk." *Delineator*, June 1919, 2, 50, 52.

"You and Our Maimed Soldiers." *Red Cross Magazine*, June 1919, 61–66.

"The Color Scheme of War." *Collier's*, 7 June 1919, 11, 20, 36–37.

"'Blinks'." *Collier's*, 14 June 1919, 13, 26, 42, 44, 46.

"The One Big Union." *Collier's*, 19 July 1919, 14, 22, 28, 30–31.

"Rx—American or German." *Collier's*, 16 Aug. 1919, 9–10, 24, 26.

"Cab, Sir?" *Everybody's*, Sept. 1919, 50–56, 109–12. In *Stories Editors Buy and Why*, comp. Jean Wick, 141–67. Boston: Small, Maynard, 1921.

"The Anxious Class." *Pictorial Review*, Nov. 1919, 16, 96, 105–6.

"Hand-Made Americans." *Red Cross Magazine*, Nov. 1919, 35–36, 70–72.

"A. B. Frost: An Unartistic Criticism." *Collier's*, 13 Dec. 1919, 13, 30.

"The Fighting Spirit." *Saturday Evening Post*, 31 Jan. 1920, 10–11, 152, 154, 157–58.

"The House of Silvery Voices." *Collier's*, 20 Mar. 1920, 18–20, 52.

"Pink Roses and the Wallop." *Saturday Evening Post*, 27 Mar. 1920, 12–13, 120, 123, 126.

"The Home Seekers." *Collier's*, 10 Apr. 1920, 13–14, 35, 38, 42, 48.

"The Guardian of God's Acre." *Collier's*, 12 June 1920, 18–20, 50, 52, 54, 56–57.

"A Patroness of Art." *Collier's*, 17 July 1920, 5–6, 19, 21, 24, 28, 31.

"Doom River Red." *Red Book Magazine*, Oct. 1920, 32–34, 36, 148–58, 161.

"Is This a Solution of the Strike Problem?" *Pictorial Review*, Oct. 1920, 14, 130, 132.

"Barbran." *Collier's*, 25 Dec. 1920, 8–9, 16, 18, 28, 30.

"Coal and—Grasshoppers." *Delineator*, Jan. 1921, 14.

"Why Boys Leave Home." *Delineator*, Mar. 1921, 4–5.

"For Mayme, Read Mary." *Collier's*, 19 Mar. 1921, 5–6.

"Andy Dunne and the Barker." *Saturday Evening Post*, 7 May 1921, 5–7, 93–94.

"Amateurs and Others." *Red Book Magazine*, June 1921, 66–70, 136–42.

"Enchantment." *Pictorial Review*, June 1921, 7–9, 55; July 1921, 26, 28, 76–78; Aug. 1921, 12–13, 38–41; Sept. 1921, 24–25, 39, 43, 48–49.

"H. C. G. Brandt; Random Memories." *Hamilton Literary Magazine*, June 1921, 269–70.

"Salvage." *Delineator*, June 1921, 8–9.

"On Sale Everywhere." *Collier's*, 16 July 1921, 7–8, 22–25.

"Silverwing." *Ladies' Home Journal*, Aug. 1921, 10–11, 112, 115–16, 118–20.

"Shoal Waters." *Saturday Evening Post*, 27 Aug. 1921, 14–15, 48, 53.

"My Bootlegger." *Collier's*, 17 Sept. 1921, 9–10, 22–24. In *A Cavalcade of Collier's*, edited by Kenneth McArdle, 228–37. New York: A. S. Barnes, 1959.

"Plooie of Our Square." *Collier's*, 29 Oct. 1921, 7–8, 22, 24–26.

"The Town That Wasn't." *Red Book Magazine*, Dec. 1921, 81–85, pp. 146–51.

"Apollyon vs. Pollyanna." *New Republic*, 12 Apr. 1922, supplement entitled "The Novel of Tomorrow," 2–3. In *The Novel of Tomorrow and the Scope of Fiction*, 3–7. Indianapolis: Bobbs-Merrill, 1922.

"Prohibition, as Our Readers See It." *Leslie's Illustrated Weekly*, 15 Apr. 1922, 495–97, 516–17; a clipped article appears in *Prohibition in the United States, 1889–1926*, bound by Harvard University Library, n.d.

"The Isle o' Dreams." *Red Book Magazine*, Aug. 1922, 46–51, 114, 116, 118, 120.

"No Trespassing." *Elks*. Aug. 1922, 28–31, 62–64.

"Poor Tessie." *Saturday Evening Post*, 4 Nov. 1922, 12–13, 108–10, 112–13.

"Vandorn's Hired Help." *Saturday Evening Post*, 13 Jan. 1923, 7–9, 33–34, 36, 38 40.

"Another Car Gone!" *Collier's*, 20 Jan. 1923, 11–12, 27–28. In *Literary Digest*, 3 Mar. 1923, 64, 66–69.

"The Eye of the Beholder." *Red Book Magazine*, Mar. 1923, 68–73, 148–56.

"First Up Best Dressed." *Collier's*, 3 Mar. 1923, 3–4, 20, 22–25.

"Science Has Its Say about Alcohol." *Collier's*, 7 Apr. 1923, 5–6, 25.

"Doubling the Guards on Health." *World's Work*, May 1923, 97–103.

"Fade-Outs of History." *Collier's*, 12 May 1923, 14, 27.

"Riches Have Wings." *Chicago Sunday Tribune Magazine*, 23 Sept. 1923, 9–11, 14.

"The Vanishing Country Doctor." *Ladies' Home Journal*, Oct. 1923, 23, 178, 180.

"Why the Doctor Left." *Ladies' Home Journal*, Nov. 1923, 26, 218–20.

"Wandering Fires." *Snappy Stories*, 20 Dec. 1923, 19–25.

"Siege." *Collier's*, 24 Nov. 1923, 5–6, 28–32; 1 Dec. 1923, 14–15, 25–28; 8 Dec. 1923, 17–18, 31–33; 15 Dec. 1923, 15–16, 24, 26, 28; 22 Dec. 1923, 15–16, 24–26; 29 Dec. 1923, 12–13, 21–22, 24; 5 Jan. 1924, 14–15, 30–32; 12 Jan. 1924, 16–17, 24, 26–27; 19 Jan. 1924, 17–18, 35–37; 26 Jan. 1924, 16–17, 34–36; 2 Feb. 1924, 15–16, 23–24, 26; 9 Feb. 1924, 17–18, 24, 30–32.

"Medically Helpless." *Ladies' Home Journal*, Feb. 1924, 31, 149–50.

"The Cruel Tragedy of 'Dope'." *Collier's*, 23 Feb. 1924, 7–8, 32.

"How People Become Drug Addicts." *Collier's*, 1 Mar. 1924, 9.

"How to Stop the 'Dope' Peddler." *Collier's*, 8 Mar. 1924, 13, 31.

"Sailors' Wives." *Telling Tales*, 25 May 1924, 137–58; 10 June 1924, 38–49, 25 June 1924, 196–216; 10 July 1924, 86–99; 25 July 1924; 10 Aug. 1924, 74–83, 25 Aug. 1924, 203–13; 10 Sept. 1924, 92–97.

"The Ostrich." *Chicago Sunday Tribune Magazine*, 12 Oct. 1924, 2–3, 6.

"It Did Happen." *Liberty*, 1 Nov. 1924, 14–20.

"Old Timers on Early Union Game." *Hamilton Life*, 7 Nov. 1925, 3.

"Smithy." *Liberty*, 21 Nov. 1925, 45–49.

"Our Own Lysistrata." *New Yorker*, 23 Jan. 1926, 44.

"Trimmed with Feathers." *Country Gentleman*, Feb. 1926, 17, 69.

"Gigolo." *Red Book Magazine*, Mar. 1926, 31–36, 134–37.

"My Attention Has Been Called." *Lincoln Magazine*, Mar. 1926.

"The Masque-Ball." *Liberty*, 6 Mar. 1926, 23–24, 27, 29–30.

"A Touch of Green." *Collier's*, 17 Apr. 1926, 10–11, 50–53.

"Two Weeks Off." *Shrine*, July 1926, 36–37, 69.

"Emperor Learns a Tune." *Pictorial Review*, Aug. 1926, 19–21, 66.

"A Man of Courage." *Liberty*, 13 Nov. 1926, 7–12.

"A Sabbatical Year for Marriage." *Harper's Monthly Magazine*, Dec. 1927, 94–100. In *Reader's Digest*, Nov. 1941, 26–28; in the *Reader's Digest Reader*, 87–89. New York: Doubleday, Doran, 1940.

"A Long Yell for Nero." *Collier's*, 21 Jan. 1928, 5–7, 39–41.

"Fifi and the Helping Hand." *Pictorial Review*, Apr. 1928, 36, 39.

"Swim, Roman, Swim." *Chicago Sunday Tribune*, 16 Sept. 1928, sec. 6, 9, 13.

"The Flagrant Years." *Hearst's International* combined with *Cosmopolitan*, Jan. 1929, 18–25, 150–56; Feb. 1929, 42 46, 117–18, 120–22; Mar. 1929, 62–65, 168–70, 172–74, 176–80; Apr. 1929, 70–73, 162, 164, 166, 168, 171–72, 174, 176; May 1929, 92–95, 206–14.

"Tourists Accommodated." *Cosmopolitan*, Sept. 1929, 96–98, 101–2, 104.

"The Fairy Princess." *Love Magazine*, Feb. 1931.

"Behind the Doctor's Sign." *Tower Magazine*, Mar. 1931.

"Terror Beach." *Detective*, May 1931.

"Ninth Love Letter." *Love Story*, June 1931.

"The 7 Curses." The *Illustrated Detective Magazine*, Nov. 1931, 55–59, 117–20. In *Best American Mystery Stories*, vol. 2, edited by Carolyn Wells, 203–23, New York: John Day, 1932; in the *Saint Detective Magazine* (U.S.), Apr. 1955; and the *Saint Detective Magazine* (British), July 1955.

"Bells at Night." *Detective*, Feb., Mar., Apr., May, June 1933.

"The Gorgeous Hussy." *Illustrated Love Magazine*, Mar., Apr., May, June, July, Aug. 1933.

"Last Trip." *Collier's*, 25 Mar. 1933, 22.

"Night Bus." *Cosmopolitan*, Aug. 1933, 42–47, 138–49. In *Box Office; A Collection of Famous Short Stories from which Outstanding Motion Pictures Have Been Made*, edited by Marjorie Barrows and George Eaton. New York: Ziff-Davis, 1943; in *Au-*

thors' Gold, edited by Marjorie Barrows. Chicago: Consolidated Book Publishing, 1948; in *The Quintessence of Beauty and Romance*, edited by Marjorie Barrows, Chicago: Spencer Press, 1955; in *Authors' Gold*, ed. George Eaton, Chicago: Peoples Book Club, 1957.

"Far Away Voice." *Liberty*, 21 Oct. 1933, 66–67.

"Fire." *Liberty*, 19 May 1934, 54.

"In Person." *Motion Picture*, Apr. 1935, May 1935, 36–38, 64–66, June 1935, July 1935, and Aug. 1935.

"Catlin, First Portrayer of Indian Life." *American Collector*, 4 Apr. 1935, 3, 7.

"Inquest." *Liberty*, 19 Oct. 1935, 16, 22.

"They Have to be Rough." *Cosmopolitan*, Nov. 1935, 48–49, 144.

"The President's Mystery Story." *Liberty*, 23 Nov. 1935, 18–25.

"Perfect Specimen." *Cosmopolitan*, Dec. 1935, 70–80, 82, 84, 86, 88, 90, 92, 94, 96, 98, 101–2, 104, 106, 108–16.

"On the Nose." *Collier's*, 28 Dec. 1935, 7–9, 42–43.

"How I Write." *The Writer*, Apr. 1936, 107–8, 125. In *The Writer's Handbook*, edited by Samuel G. Houghton, 38–43. Cambridge, Mass.: Hampshire Press, 1936.

"Bachelor's Quarters." *This Week*, 14 June 1936, 3, 9.

"West to East." *College Humor*, Sept. 1936, 6–9, 61. In *Toronto Star Weekly*, 1938.

"Maiden Effort." *Maclean's Magazine*, 1 Mar. 1937, 7–10, 26, 28, 32, 34, 36; 15 Mar. 1937, 20–22, 30, 32, 41–42; 1 Apr. 1937, 20–22, 38, 40, 41–42; 15 Apr. 1937, 20–22, 34, 36, 38, 40, 45; 1 May 1937, 20–22, 53–54, 56.

"The Lady Who Blighted His Life." *Liberty*, 3 July 1937, 54–55.

"Compound Interest." *American Cavalcade*, Aug. 1937.

"Kolinsky Calling." *Liberty*, 21 Aug. 1937, 37.

"The World Goes to Smash." *Liberty*, 18 Sept. 1937, 5–10; 25 Sept. 1937, 26–28, 30–32; 2 Oct. 1937, 24–26, 28–29; 9 Oct. 1937, 38–43; 16 Oct. 1937, 32–37; 23 Oct. 1937, 34–40; 30 Oct. 1937, 32–37; 6 Nov. 1937, 38–44; 13 Nov. 1937, 44–50; 20 Nov. 1937, 52–58.

"Wireless for Mr. Lander." *This Week*, 26 Sept. 1937, 4–5, 11.

"Here Comes a Lady." *Pictorial Review*, Mar. 1938, 22–24, 53, 56. In *The Peoples Reader*, compiled by Marjorie Barrows, 28–39, Chicago: Peoples Book Club, 1949.

"The Unreckonable Factor." *Liberty*, 25 June 1938, 41. In *Ellery Queen's Mystery Magazine*, Sept. 1942; in *Reader's Digest*, Dec. 1942, 95–96; in *Matilda Ziegler Magazine for the Blind*, 1974; and in *Scholastic Scope*, Aug. 1975.

"Both Over Twenty-One." *Star Weekly* of Toronto, 26 Nov. 1938.

"Miracle in Stone." *New Yorker*, 10 Dec. 1938, 84–86.

"How to Talk about Antiques." *Coronet*, Jan. 1939, 23–26.

"All Bets as Usual." *Maclean's Magazine*, 1 June 1939, 12–13, 42–45.

"Sing a Song of Colleges." *Coronet*, Aug. 1939, 37–39, 113.

"Unlawful Entry." *Canadian Home Journal*, Oct. 1939, 14–15, 59–61, 70, 72.

"A Case of Bibliocide." *New Yorker*, 21 Oct. 1939, 39–42.

"The Money Fighter." *Bluebook*, Jan. 1940, 32–43.

"A Shining Candle." *Liberty*, 18 May 1940, 42–44.

"Art of Johnnie Hell." *New Yorker*, 22 June 1940, 32, 34–35; in *Reader's Digest*, 9 Sept. 1940, 97–99.

"Fifty Years of Football." *Hamilton Alumni Review*, Oct. 1940, 6–7.

"Sack of Snakes." *New Yorker*, 1 Mar. 1941, 30–34.

"College without Walls." *Saturday Evening Post*, 14 June 1941, 39–40.

"Minora Canamus." *Hamilton Alumni Review*, July 1941, 210–18.

"Diagnosis." *Liberty*, 16 Aug. 1941, 39.

"The Office Butterfly." *Esquire*, Nov. 1941 37, 115–17.

"Tambay Gold." Newspaper Enterprise Alliance, thirty-one installments from 5 Jan. to 9 Feb. 1942.

"Home Town of a Prophet." *New Yorker*, 23 May 1942, 38, 40, 42, 44–46, 49–51.

"The Corpse at the Table." *Saturday Review of Literature*, 5 Sept. 1942, 13–15. In *Reader's Digest*, Oct. 1942, 81–84; in *Alfred Hitchcock Presents: Bar the Door*, New York: Dell Publishing, 1946, 1962. Presented also by Radio Reader Digest on 22 Aug. 1943.

"Notes on an Unpleasant Female." *New Yorker*, 12 Sept. 1942, 40, 42–50. In *New College Omnibus*, edited by Franklin P. Rolfe, William L. Davenport, and Paul Bowerman. New York: Harcourt, Brace, 1946; in *Design for Reading*, New York: American Book; in *Curiosities of Medicine*, edited by Berton Roueche. Boston: Little, Brown, 1958 and 1963; in *Rhetorical Book 6*. Boston: Ginn, 1974.

"Presidential Campaign Slanders." *Life*, 2 Oct. 1944, 53–56, 58, 60.

"Aisle Seats for Mr. Woollcott." *Harper's*, Jan. 1945, 154–59.

"Alexander Woollcott, Town Crier." *Harper's*, Feb. 1945, 269–79.

"Alexander Woollcott: His Life and His World." *Liberty*, 15 Sept. 1945, 43–57.

"Aunt Minnie and the Accessory after the Fact." *Liberty*, 6 Oct. 1945, 26–27. In *Ellery Queen's Mystery Magazine*, Oct. 1949; in *Murder for the Millions; A Harvest of Horror and Homicide*, edited by Frank Owen, 213–19. New York: Fell, 1946; in *My Favorite Suspense Stories*, edited by Maureen Daly, 136–43. New York: Dodd, Mead, 1968; in *Stories of Crime and Detection*, edited by Joan Berbrich. New York: McGraw-Hill Books, 1974. *Read*, 15 Nov. 1978, 12–17.

"Slaves of the Devil's Capsule," *American Weekly*, Nov. and Dec. 1945. The first and second of four articles were in the *Congressional Record*, 79th Congress, 1st sess. (1945) vol. 91, pt. 13, app. A5091–3 and A5229–30.

"Reviewords," *Saturday Review of Literature*, 9 Mar. 1946, 19.

"Poolville Postmaster." *Woman's Day*, July 1946, 26, 64–65.

"Words to Live By from Samuel Hopkins Adams." *This Week*, 23 Feb. 1947, 2; published as "The Brotherhood of Man" in *Words to Live By*, edited by William Nichols, 88–89. New York: Simon and Schuster, 1948.

"Our Forefathers Tackle an Epidemy—The Cholera of 1832." *New York Folklore Quarterly*, 3 (summer 1947): 93–101.

"My Grandfather and the Plague." *New Yorker*, 18 Oct. 1947, 88, 90, 92–96.

"Slave in the Family." *New Yorker*, 6 Dec. 1947, 32–36. In *New York Portrait; A Literary Look at the Empire State*, edited by Jack Ishmole and Sally Ronshein, 362–73. New York: Holt, Rinehart and Winston, 1965.

"It's an American Idea—Let's Not Give It Up." *Good Housekeeping*, Mar. 1949, 33, 233–35.

"Dr. Bug, Dr. Buzzard and the USA." *True*, July 1949, 32–33, 69–71.

"Grandfather's Parlous Trip." *New Yorker*, 19 Nov. 1949, 69–70, 72, 74, 76, 79–80.

"There's More to Crabbing than You Think." *Saturday Evening Post*, 7 Jan. 1950, 26–27, 87–88, 90.

"Grandfather and the Montague Collar." *New Yorker*, 18 Mar. 1950, 85–86, 88–93.

"The Criminal and the Genius." *This Week*, 16 Apr. 1950, 19–20.

"Old Age—I Spit in Its Eye!" *Saturday Evening Post*, 27 May 1950, 31, 160, 162.

"I'd Rather Go Crabbing." *Ford Times*, Aug. 1950, 26–29. In *Ford Treasury of the Outdoors*, 155–57, New York: Simon and Schuster, 1952.

"The Mail Goes Through." *Blue Book*, pt. 1, Aug. 1950; pt. 2, Sept. 1950.

"Grandfather's Circus Days." *New Yorker*, 30 Sept. 1950, 62, 65–71.

"The Town I Like—Beaufort, South Carolina." *Lincoln-Mercury Times*, Nov.–Dec. 1950, 23–27. In *Port Royal under Six Flags*, edited by Katherine M. Jones, 356–60. Indianapolis: Bobbs-Merrill, 1960.

"Grandfather and the Chimera." *New Yorker*, 25 Nov. 1950, 68, 71–78.

"Grandfather and a Winter's Tale." *New Yorker*, 20 Jan. 1951, 64, 66–70. In *The Tavern Lights Are Burning; Literary Journeys Through Six Regions and Four Centuries of New York State*, edited by Carl Carmer, 343–49. New York: David McKay, 1964.

"Grandfather Goes to a Ballgame." *New Yorker*, 19 May 1951 96, 98–106. In *Scholastic*, 7 May 1952, 51–52.

"Unsung Eden." *Holiday*, June 1951, 114–21, 150–58.

"A Finger Lakes Boyhood." *Lincoln-Mercury Times*, July–Aug. 1951, 1–5. In *The Tavern Lights Are Burning*, edited by Carl Carmer, 354–59. An abridged version appears in *Cayuga County: An Anthology of People Places and Events*, edited by Shiela Edmonds, 53–56. Scipio, N.Y.: Pica Press, 1978.

"Scandal that Killed a Sport." *Holiday*, Aug. 1951, 66, 68–69, 108.

"Grandfather Meets a Celebrity." *Woman's Day*, Sept. 1951, 56, 134–36, 138.

"Santa Fe Trail." *Blue Book*, Nov. 1951.

"Grandfather Attends a Spectacle." *New Yorker*, 8 Dec. 1951, 78, 81–82, 84–88.

"That Was Rochester." *New Yorker*, 23 Aug. 1952, 27–30, 32–41.

"Department of Amplification." *New Yorker*, 18 Oct. 1952, 93–96, 98–100.

"Grandfather Judges a Sporting Event." *Woman's Day*, Dec. 1952, 64, 133–36.

"Isle of Blight." *Fantastic Stories*, Jan.–Feb. 1953, 67–84.

"Grandfather and the Big Breach." *New Yorker*, 26 Sept. 1953, 89–90, 92, 94–99.

"Carolina Cruise." *Holiday*, Nov. 1953, 80, 82–85, 87–91, 116.

"Edisto, the Tranquil Isle." *Ford Times*, Nov. 1953, 42–48.

"Treasure Hunt." *New Yorker*, 16 Jan. 1954, 61–67.

"Your Right to Be Wrong." *This Week,* 14 Feb. 1954, 2.

"Grandfather's Criminal Career." *New Yorker,* 27 Mar. 1954, 90, 92–97.

"Grandfather Goes to a Preview." *New Yorker,* 2 Oct. 1954, 88, 90–99.

"Grandfather Attends a Vendu." *New Yorker,* 6 Nov. 1954, 91–92, 94, 96–97, 100–101, 104, 106.

"Grandfather Encounters a Nonpareil." *New Yorker,* 27 Nov. 1954, 93–94, 96, 98, 100, 103–5.

"Memoirs of a Forgotten Club." *Esquire,* Dec. 1954, 133, 216–20.

"The Juke Myth." *Saturday Review,* 2 Apr. 1955, 13, 48–49. In *The Saturday Review Treasury,* edited by John Haverstick, 515–20, New York: Simon and Schuster, 1957; in *Readings in Sociology.* New York: T. Y. Crowell Publishing, 1960, 1973; in *Speed and Comprehension.* New York: T. Y. Crowell Publishing, 1961; in *The Art of Prose,* edited by Paul A. Jorgensen and Frederick B. Shroyer. New York: Charles Scribner's Sons, 1962; in *Studying Man in Society,* edited by Thomas W. LaVerne and James H. North. Glenville, Ill.: Scott, Foresman, 1971.

"Grandfather and the Turnout." *New Yorker,* 14 May 1955, 137–44, 147.

"Grandfather and the Cold Year." *New Yorker,* 19 May 1956, 88, 90, 92, 94, 97–103.

"There's No Fraud Like an Old Fraud." *Sports Illustrated,* 12 May 1958, E5–E8.

"Even Football Was Gay in the '90s." *Sports Illustrated,* 22 Sept. 1958, M5–M8.

"New Year's Day in the '80's." *Reader's Digest,* Jan. 1959, 150–54. In *America Remembers; Our Best-loved Customs and Traditions,* edited by Samuel Rapport and Patricia Schartle. Garden City, N.Y.: Hanover House, 1956.

## Reviews

"The Confessions of Harry Orchard." Review of *The Confessions and Autobiography of Harry Orchard,* by Albert E. Horsley. In *Bookman,* Mar. 1908, 57–59.

"The Civic Theatre." Review of *The Civic Theatre,* by Percy Mackaye. In *Survey,* 29 Mar. 1913, 904–5.

"Carl Carmer Hears a Drum." Review of *Listen for a Lonesome Drum,* by Carl Carmer. In *Hamilton Alumni Review,* Oct. 1936, 15–16.

*Muller Hill,* by Harriet McDougal Daniels. In *Hamilton Alumni Review,* Jan. 1944, 102.

"Ray Stannard Baker Continues His Story." Review of *American Chronicle,* by Ray Stannard Baker. In *New York Times Book Review,* 4 Mar. 1945, 4, 28.

"A Happy Marriage." Review of *All Our Lives: Alice Duer Miller,* by Henry Wise Miller. In *New York Times Book Review,* 24 June 1945, 6.

"Provocative Thinking." Review of *A Pattern of Politics,* by August Heckscher. In *Auburn Citizen–Advertiser,* 15 Sept. 1947, 4.

"Mr. Creel Breaks Some Lances." Review of *Rebel at Large.* In *New York Times Book Review,* 23 Nov. 1947, 6.

*Meem,* by Lee H. Bristol, Jr. In *Hamilton Alumni Review,* Jan. 1949.

*Pageant of American Humor*, edited by Edward Seaver. In *New York History*, July 1949, 340–42.
"York State Folks: Nobody Quite Like 'Em." Review of *Dark Trees to the Wind*, by Carl Carmer. In *New York Herald Tribune Book Review*, 6 Nov. 1949, 4.
"With a Nostalgic Flavor." Review of *Youth's Companion*, edited by Lovell Thompson. In *New York Herald Tribune Book Review*, 31 Oct. 1954, 4.
"Bathed in the Aura of the Glory-Story." Review of *Park Row*, by Allen Churchill. In *New York Times Book Review*, 23 Mar. 1958, 10.

## Films Adapted from Adams's Work

*The Clarion*. Equitable (World) Motion Pictures, 1916.
*Triumph*. Universal Film Manufacturing, 1917; copyright, Bluebird Photoplays, 1917.
*Fighting Mad*. Los Angeles: Universal Film Manufacturing, 1919.
*Wanted: A Husband*. Los Angeles: Famous Players–Lasky, 1919.
*Flaming Youth* [Warner Fabian]. Los Angeles: Associated First National Pictures, 1923.
*Siege*. Universal Pictures, 1925.
*Wandering Fires* [Warner Fabian]. Maurice Campbell Production, Arrow, 1925.
*Summer Bachelors* [Warner Fabian]. Los Angeles: Fox Film, 1926.
*Sailors' Wives* [Warner Fabian]. Los Angeles: Associated First National Pictures, 1928.
*The Wild Party* [based on *Unforbidden Fruit* by Warner Fabian]. Los Angeles: Paramount Famous Players–Lasky, 1929.
*What Men Want* [Warner Fabian]. Los Angeles: Universal Pictures, 1930.
*Men in Her Life* [Warner Fabian]. Los Angeles: Columbia Pictures, 1931.
*Week-Ends Only* [Warner Fabian]. Los Angeles: Fox Film, 1932.
*It Happened One Night*. Los Angeles: Columbia Pictures, 1934.
*In Person*. Los Angeles: RKO Radio Pictures, 1935.
*The Gorgeous Hussy*. Los Angeles: Metro-Goldwyn-Mayer, 1936.
*The President's Mystery*. Los Angeles: Republic Pictures, 1936.
*Perfect Specimen*. Los Angeles: Warner Bros. Pictures, 1937.
*Harvey Girls*. Los Angeles: Loew's, 1945.
*You Can't Run Away from It*. Los Angeles: Columbia Pictures, 1956.

## Plays Adapted from Adams's Work

Watkins, Maurine. *Revelry*, produced by Robert Milton at Masque Theatre, New York, beginning 12 Sept. 1927 for 48 performances.
Vreeland, Frank. *Night Bus*. New York: Longman's, Green, 1941.
Weidman, Jerome, and George Abbott, book; Jerry Bock, music; Sheldon Harnick, lyrics, *Tenderloin*. New York: Random House, 1960, 1961.

## Records Based on Adams's Work

*Riding the Pony Express.* Dramatized and produced by Howard Tooley from *The Pony Express,* Enrichment Records, 1952, 1954, 1964.
*The Erie Canal.* Dramatized by Elise Bell from *Erie Canal,* Enrichment Records, 1957, 1964.

# INDEX